CATERPILLARS of
EASTERN NORTH AMERICA

A GUIDE TO IDENTIFICATION
AND NATURAL HISTORY

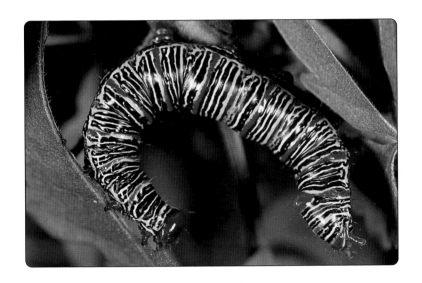

DAVID L. WAGNER

WITH SPECIAL ACKNOWLEDGMENT FOR SUPPORT RECEIVED FROM THE
UNITED STATES FOREST SERVICE FHTET PROGRAM AND DISCOVER LIFE IN AMERICA

Princeton University Press
Princeton and Oxford

Published by Princeton University Press
41 William Street
Princeton, New Jersey 08540

In the United Kingdom:
Princeton University Press
3 Market Place
Woodstock, Oxfordshire OX20 1SY

Library of Congress Cataloging-in-Publication

Wagner, David L., 1956–
    Caterpillars of Eastern North America: A Guide to identification and natural history/
David L. Wagner.
        p. cm.—(Princeton field guides)
    "With special acknowledgment for support received from the United States Forest
Service FHTET Program and Discover Life in America."
    Includes bibliographical references (p.).
    ISBN: 0-691-12143-5 (cl. : alk. paper)—ISBN 0-691-12144-3 (pb. : alk. paper)
        1. Caterpillars—North America. I. Title. II. Series.

QL548.W34 2005
595.78'139'097—dc22   2004062834

British Library Cataloging-in-Publication Data is available

This book has been composed in Univers, Univers Condensed and Frutiger

Dedication
To my children Virginia and Ryan, wellsprings of pint-sized adventures, good times, and fond memories, I dedicate this work

Printed on acid-free paper.

pup.princeton.edu

Edited and designed by D & N Publishing, Hungerford, Berkshire, UK

Printed in Singapore

10 9 8 7 6 5 4 3

CONTENTS

PREFACE

I recently attended a seminar at Harvard University to hear Stefan Cover speak. He started off simply enough. "Everyone needs an obsession. Mine is ants." Everyone chuckled ... more than a few heads nodded in agreement. For the past ten years mine has been caterpillars. They have provided a bounty of trip memories, abundant photographic opportunities, led to dozens of collaborations and friendships, some of which will be lifelong, and introduced me to a world full of beauty, change, carnage, and discovery. Stefan was right.

My goal in writing this guide is twofold. First, to provide larval images and biological summaries for the larger, commonly encountered caterpillars found east of the 100th meridian. Sounds simple, yet the problems associated with compiling such information are legion: literature is scattered, lacking, or, worse, especially in the case of some early accounts, wrong. For many common moths the species taxonomy is still under study, life histories are incompletely known, and distributional data have yet to be assembled. In this guide I offer a synopsis for each species that includes information on its distribution, phenology, and life history. Taxonomy has been updated, (Eastern) distributions adjusted, and information on the number of annual broods added for many of the species treated in Covell (1984), the "go to" book for Eastern moths. In addition, numerous caterpillars are illustrated here for the first time, dozens of new foodplant records are presented, and considerable previously unpublished life history information has been provided. But I caution that each species treatment is only a first step and that many accounts will require revision as our fauna becomes better known. Behaviors and phenomena previously believed to be exceptional or uncommon are shown to be otherwise: e.g., both Batesian and Müllerian mimicry appear to be more prevalent in caterpillars than previously recognized. Pronounced developmental changes (in form, coloration, and behavior), bordering on hypermetamorphosis, were seen in several families—striking examples occur among the daggers and slug caterpillars. Inducible color forms, e.g., darker morphs in high density inchworm and hornworm populations, are more common and taxonomically widespread than has been generally recognized.

My second goal for this work is to showcase some of the insect life that is right outside one's door or in nearby parks. Our National Forests and Parks are rife with biological riches. While it is almost a universal dream of biologists and weekend naturalists to someday explore a tropical rain forest, it is not necessary to be transported to a jungle to find beauty, view mysterious phenomena, or make new biological discoveries ... all exist as close as the nearest woodlot. All that it takes is to walk more slowly, watch more closely, and develop a greater appreciation for what E. O. Wilson calls "the little things that run the world."

This book was written so as to be understandable to a student in middle school but also detailed enough to provide new information to a seasoned museum curator, accomplished lepidopterist, applied entomologist, conservation biologist, or land manager. Admittedly the text bounces between these audiences, and awkwardly so at times ... my apologies. Because the audience will be mixed, I usually list both common and scientific names even when it is disruptive to do so. Space limitations dictate that I adopt a mostly telegraphic style except in the Remarks section where full text is provided. The more I had to relate about a species, the more telegraphic the text.

I am not sure what brings me more pleasure: the hunt, rearing, or photography. I enjoy reading about a species, researching its foodplants and habits, planning a trip, and then searching for its caterpillar. There is great satisfaction in caterpillar rearing and wrangling: watching them eat, grow, and ultimately metamorphose into something often completely unexpected and strikingly beautiful. Caterpillars that appear drab and mundane at arm's length often prove exquisite creatures when viewed through my camera's macro lens. Taking images that justly render their beauty or capture aspects of their behavior is very rewarding. It is my wish that this guide will enable others to share in all of this sport and facilitate the efforts of those wishing to contribute to our knowledge of Eastern moths, because so much remains to be discovered and told.

ACKNOWLEDGMENTS

Much of the knowledge that sits behind this guide resides in the reviewers who read the species accounts and in the dozens who shared observations and contributed in other ways. In this regard a special debt of gratitude is owed to Dale Schweitzer who, above all others, served as my mentor and advisor. My colleagues and friends, Richard Heitzman, Steve Roble, Jadranka Rota, Fred Stehr, and Bo Sullivan read drafts of nearly every chapter. Others who reviewed chapters, roughly in order of number of species accounts read, include Dale Schweitzer, Richard Peigler, James Adams, David Wright, George Balogh, Ben Williams, Charles Covell, Noel McFarland, Eric Hossler, John Peacock, Jim Tuttle, Marc Epstein, John Lill, Paul Opler, Brian Branciforte, Jessica Lowrey, John Foltz, and Paul Schaefer. Michael Thomas and Kevin Fitzpatrick reviewed the section on photography; Judy Dulin that on school projects. James Adams, Jeff Boettner, Bonnie Drexler, Richard Heitzman, Eric Hossler, Jeff Lougee, Jane O'Donnell, Dale Schweitzer, Fred Stehr, Bo Sullivan, Jessica Watson, Ron Wielgus, and Ben Williams provided helpful suggestions on the book's introductory sections.

Those who collected foliage daily, serviced the rearing lots, preserved vouchers, labeled specimens, kept records, and maintained the database played a quintessential part in this effort: Valerie Giles, Eric Hossler, Monty Volovski, Julia Joseph, Julie Henry, Susan Herrick, Jennifer Jacobs, and Brian Branciforte. Keith Hartan and Jadranka Rota pitched in on numerous occasions. The first three contributed hundreds, and perhaps thousands of hours beyond what I could afford to pay them—their commitment, enthusiasm, and friendship enabled all of this happen. I owe much to my friend Ben Williams who reared many egg lots to maturity and transported the fully grown caterpillars to the lab to be photographed.

Many colleagues sent gravid females, eggs, or caterpillars. First among these was Dale Schweitzer who has contributed livestock over the past decade. Numerous collections, roughly in order of the numbers of caterpillars that appear in this work, were made by Eric Hossler, Monty Volovksi, Ryan Wagner, Valerie Giles, Ben Williams, Mike Thomas, Doug Ferguson, Andy Brand, Jeff Fengler, and Bo Sullivan. Monty was especially enthusiastic and helpful, and on two occasions took vacation time to collect for this work. Smaller numbers of caterpillars were received from Laura Miller, Tom Allen, Paul Goldstein, Warren Kiel, Scott Smedley, James Adams, Michael Nelson, Julia Joseph, Teddy Lamb, Jenny Jacobs, Tim McCabe, Keith Hartan, Don Lafontaine, William Forrest, Paxton Mallard, John Peacock, Jadranka Rota, Paulette Haywood, Tom Hupf, Kate Kubarek, Jessica Lowrey, Jane O'Donnell, Virginia Wagner, George (Jeff) Boettner, Bryan Connolly, Fred Hohn, Chris Lamb, George Leslie, Nancy Lowe, William Oehlke, Kristian Omland, Ric Peigler, Dave Simser, Bob Wilson, George Balogh, Bill Conner, Jim Duquesnel, Donna Ellis, Julie Henry, Charlene Houle, Carol Lemmon, John Lill, Nam Nguyen, Carl Rettenmeyer, Linda Ruth, Brent Salazar, Juan Sanchez, Brian Scholtens, Justin Smith, Carolyn Bursey, Michael Canfield, Liz Day, Dave Doussard, Marc Epstein, Roy Kendall, Steve Talley, Gaines Taylor, and David Silsbee. Many others, too numerous to mention, passed along the occasional egg batch or caterpillar or two. This guide is built upon their efforts. Many of the above accompanied me on the innumerable trips that yielded the caterpillars that appear on these pages—I thank all for their companionship, enthusiasm, assistance, and memories now shared.

Several individuals contributed phenological and distributional data, foodplant records, personal observations, and other information: James Adams, George Balogh, Vernon Brou, Douglas Ferguson, Howard Grisham, Edward Knudson, Hanna Roland, and Bo Sullivan. Special thanks are due to Richard Heitzman who checked the range, phenology, annual broods, and foodplant records for all Missouri species that appear in this guide, and to Dale Schweitzer who generously offered his encyclopedic knowledge of moths and butterflies from start to finish. Identifications of parasites and pathogens were provided by Michael McAloon, Barry O'Connor, Ian Gauld, Scott Shaw, and David Wahl. Kathleen Tebo input many editorial changes and mailed chapters to and fro. Literature was sent by Larry Davenport, Dave Doussard, Richard Peigler, and Martha Weiss. Bryan Connolly, James Duquesnel, Les

6

Mehrhoff, and Ken Metzler helped out with botanical matters: providing identifications, collecting foliage, and/or sending directions to the nearest patch of this or that plant. Clint Morse supplied cuttings from the research plant collections at the University of Connecticut for several foodplants that could not be found near campus.

Principal financial support for this guide came from the U.S. Department of Agriculture, Forest Services, Forest Health Technology Enterprise Team, cooperative agreement number 01–CA–11244225–215. Richard C. Reardon has been especially supportive of efforts that led to this publication—his enthusiasm, persistence, and sense of humor are all greatly appreciated. Monetary support, lodging, logistical help, and volunteer assistance came from Discover Life In America's "All Taxa Biodiversity Inventory" in Great Smoky Mountains National Park. My numerous visits to the Park over the past five years have been among the most enjoyable of my career—and where else in North America could one see over 800 species of Lepidoptera in a single 24-hour period? Keith Langdon, Jeanie Hilten, and Becky Nichols were especially helpful. Numerous contracts from the Connecticut Department of Environmental Protection, and especially their State Income Tax Check-off Fund, and the Connecticut Chapter of The Nature Conservancy added dozens of species that otherwise would have been missed. Several tropical species were photographed with support from National Science Foundation grant DEB-0072702. The Edward C. Childs Family provided both financial support and summer lodging for our work in Great Mountain Forest, Norfolk, CT, from 1997 to 1999. Lastly, I want to thank my parents and Alexander Barrett Klots for opening the door to entomology and Jerry Powell, Fred Stehr, Douglas Ferguson, and others of their ilk for hauling me through it. I extend my sincere gratitude to Jane O'Donnell, Michael Nelson, Eric Quinter, Jadranka Rota, and Carl Schaefer for their help reviewing the galley proofs. David Price-Goodfellow and his designers at D & N Publishing made enormous contributions toward the book's appearance as well as content. Thank you. My editors, Robert Kirk and Ellen Foos, provided much support, sound advice, and guidance with the Queen's English.

PHOTOGRAPHIC AND ARTWORK CREDITS

Rene Twarkins took all the adult images and scanned the 1,200 larval images. More importantly, he dedicated hundreds of hours (and more than a dozen sleepless nights) to the image manipulations and management necessary for this book. His dedication to this effort, his expertise, and attention to detail are deeply appreciated. In the final weeks, Shawn Kennedy logged dozens of hours making necessary adjustments to all of the larval images. Valerie Giles contributed most of the line art. Shawn Kennedy prepared the wing coupling and arctiid crochets drawings. The majority of the images used in this guide were taken by me or those working in my lab. More than 75,000 images, not reproduced here, sit behind this work and are part of a photographic reference collection at the University of Connecticut. Over the four summers that Valerie Giles worked in the lab, she added thousands of images to this collection and kept the slides curated. Eric Hossler also contributed substantially to the collection of reference images. Don Lafontaine arranged the loan of many of the Canadian National Collection images. Those contributing the images that appear in this guide are listed below—their willingness to share these is gratefully acknowledged.

GEORGE BALOGH: *Proserpinus gaurae*; BOB BARBER: *Erynnis juvenalis* (insets); ANDY BRAND: *Composia fidelissima*; SARA BRIGHT: *Cyllopsis gemma, Neonympha areolata*; WILLIAM CONNER: *Cosmosoma myrodora*; DAVE DOUSSARD: *Trichoplusia ni*; JEFF FENGLER: *Anatrytone logan, Datana perspicua, Heterocampa umbrata, Libytheana carinenta, Parrhasius m-album, Protambulyx strigilis, Roddia vaualbum, Selenisa sueroides*; DOUG FERGUSON: *Acronicta oblinita, Cisthene packardii, Cisthene plumbea, Costaconvexa centrostrigaria, Crambidia pallida, Dasychira tephra, Datana contracta, Euchlaena obtusaria, Helicoverpa zea, Iridopsis pergracilis, Lycia ypsilon, Metanema determinata, Spodoptera frugiperda, Zale perculta*; WILLIAM FORREST: *Euxoa messoria, Haploa confusa, Haploa contigua, Hap-*

loa reversa, Hyles euphorbiae, Peridroma saucia, Pyrrhia exprimens (3), *Xestia badicollis* (3); VALERIE GILES: *Achalarus lyciades, Acronicta afflicta, Acronicta dactylina, Acronicta increta, Agrotis ipsilon, Alsophila pometaria* (inset), *Amphion floridensis, Anisota virginiensis, Anthocharis midea, Autographa precationis, Besma quercivoraria* (2), *Bombyx mori* (2), *Cabera erythemaria, Cabera variolaria, Callophrys gryneus, Callopistria mollissima, Callosamia promethea, Callosamia securifera, Calophasia lunula* (2), *Campaea perlata, Catocala antinympha, Catocala epione, Catocala insolabilis, Catocala muliercula, Catocala obscura, Catocala relicta* (2), *Catocala ultronia, Ceratomia amyntor, Clostera inclusa, Coryphista meadii, Crocigrapha normani, Cucullia convexipennis* (2), *Cucullia intermedia, Cyclophora pendulinaria, Cycnia tenera, Darapsa myron, Dasychira obliquata, Deidamia inscripta, Drepana arcuata, Epimecis hortaria, Eubaphe mendica, Euclea delphinii, Eupathenos nubilis, Euphydryas phaeton, Eutrapela clemataria, Feniseca tarquinius, Glaucopsyche lygdamus, Gluphisia septentrionis, Hemaris diffinis* (2), *Hemileuca grotei, Heterocampa guttivitta, Himella intractata, Horisme intestinata, Hydriomena transfigurata?, Hyles lineata, Hypercompe scribonia* (2), *Idia aemula, Idia lubricalis, Iridopsis larvaria, Lacosoma chiridota, Lochmaeus manteo, Lytrosis unitaria, Macrurocampa marthesia, Meteorus* sp., *Nymphalis antiopa, Ochropleura implecta, Odontosia elegans, Orthosia hibisci, Palthis asopialis, Papilio troilus* (3), *Parasa indetermina, Patalene olyzonaria, Plusia putnami, Probole alienaria, Prochoerodes lineola, Psaphida styracis, Pyrrharctia isabella, Raphia frater, Schinia rivulosa, Scopula limboundata, Sphecodina abbottii* (2), *Spilosoma congrua, Spilosoma virginica* (4), *Symmerista canicosta, Synchlora aerata* (2), *Zale lunata*; PAUL GOLDSTEIN: *Eacles imperialis*; STUART GREEN: *Imbrasia belina*; ERIC HOSSLER: *Acronicta interrupta, Acronicta ovata, Acronicta spinigera, Acronicta superans, Allotria elonympha* (2), *Baileya ophthalmica, Cisseps fulvicollis, Citheronia sepulcralis* (2), *Clemensia albata, Crocigrapha normani, Cyclophora pendulinaria, Egira alternans, Elaphria versicolor, Ennomos subsignaria* (2), *Erannis tiliaria, Eulithis diversilineata, Glena plumosaria, Hemileuca lucina, Heteropacha rileyana, Hydrelia inornata, Hyperaeschra georgica* (inset), *Hypoprepia miniata, Itame pustularia* (2), *Lapara coniferarum, Megalopyge crispata, Misogada unicolor, Morrisonia confusa, Nadata gibbosa, Nephelodes minians, Nepytia* nr. *pellucidaria, Panthea acronyctoides, Phosphila miselioides, Protitame virginalis, Rheumaptera prunivorata, Selenia kentaria, Simyra henrici, Smerinthus jamaicensis, Spodoptera ornithogalli, Timandra amaturaria, Tortricidia testacea, Zale helata* (2); CHARLENE HOULE: *Datana intergerrima*; JENNIFER JACOBS: *Dasylophia thyatiroides, Morrisonia latex*; DAN JANZEN: *Cocytius antaeus, Macrosoma conifera, Xylophanes pluto*; JULIA JOSEPH: *Paleacrita vernata, Panthea furcilla, Pleuroprucha insularia, Pseudothyatira cymatophoroides*; JEAN-FRANCOIS LANDRY: *Itame sulphurea*; MARC MINNO: *Atlides halesus, Fixsenia favonius*; RIC PEIGLER: *Sphingicampa bisecta*; NOBLE PROCTOR: *Melanchra picta*; JADRANKA ROTA: *Brenthia monolychna, Erynnis juvenalis, Lithophane patefacta* (inset); JANE RUFFIN: *Parasa indetermina*; PAUL SCHAEFER: *Leucoma salicis*; LEROY SIMON: *Acronicta rubricoma, Battus polydamas, Calpodes ethlius, Danaus gilippus, Erinnyis alope, Eumorpha fasciata* (2), *Manduca rustica, Rothschildia lebeau forbesi, Siproeta stelenes, Xylophanes tersa* (2); JEREMY TATUM: *Malcosoma californicum*; MIKE THOMAS: *Peridea angulosa*; JAMES TUTTLE: *Hemaris gracilis*; RENE TWARKINS: *Comadia redtenbacheri*; MARTHA WEISS: shelter forming in *Epargyreus clarus* (insets); DAVID WRIGHT: *Satyrium edwardsii*.

INTRODUCTION

Caterpillars, the larvae of butterflies and moths (order Lepidoptera), are the last group of large, common, backyard creatures for which there are no comprehensive field guides. Every week of the growing season I am asked to identify caterpillars and answer questions about them: What is this? What does it eat? Is it a pest? Is it harming my house or garden? What will it turn into? How might I raise it? This guide will help you answer these questions for near-ly all of the caterpillars likely to be encountered east of the Mississippi. Full species accounts with an image of the adult insect are given for 383 butterflies and moths; an additional 210 species are illustrated, but only briefly discussed (no adult images are provided); and 100 species are diagnosed, but not figured either as a caterpillar or adult. Included among these are forest pests, common garden guests, economically important species, especially hand-some caterpillars, and others known to draw public interest. Of course, the Mescal Worm and Mexican Jumping Bean caterpillars are here. Of the 593 species for which a photograph has been provided, 114 are butterflies, far more than their relative diversity or frequency of encounter would justify, but because of their popularity with gardeners, children, and other naturalists, their numbers are well represented here. The species accounts are salted with additional images that illustrate earlier instars, closely related species, common parasitoids, interesting behaviors, and other aspects of caterpillar biology. While the area of emphasis is the East, this guide should be useful across the whole of southern Canada, portions of the Pacific Northwest, and at the generic level for most of the United States.

The North American diversity of Lepidoptera is immense. Close to 13,000 moth and butter-fly species have been reported north of the Mexican border (Hodges *et al.* 1983, Poole 1996). Some 5,000 of these occur east of the Mississippi. Approximately 55% are "microlepidopter-ans," i.e., smaller moths, many of which are concealed feeders, fashioning and feeding with-in leaf shelters or boring into stems, fruits, and seeds. It is their counterparts, the "macrolepi-dopterans," that are the focus of this work. Most macrolepidopterans are exposed or "external" feeders that have distinctive forms, coloration, and patterning that readily allow for their identification. In some ways it is remarkable that a comprehensive field guide to such organisms has not appeared before now.

Caterpillars are enormously important in terrestrial food webs. They are the preferred grub, so to speak, for the nestlings of most of our songbirds. One piggish American Robin is reported to have devoured twice its own body mass in larvae over a 24-hour period. Spring would be silent

in a forest without caterpillars. Caterpillars yield moths, which are important prey items in the diets of bats, martins, flycatchers, goatsuckers, and other ver-tebrates. Many caterpillars are important macrode-composers, shredding fallen leaves, tunneling into dead wood, and consuming fallen fruits, thereby accelerating nutrient cycling processes. The silk in our sheets, parachutes, ties, lingerie, scarves, and other clothing comes from the Silkworm (*Bombyx mori*) and related moths. Adult moths and butterflies are important pollinators. Many of our most fragrant flowers, e.g., gardenia, narcissus, and jasmine, are moth-pollinated species. Hornworms or hawk moths are thought to be primary pollinators for about 10% of the tree species in tropical forests. Deserts also have many moth-pollinated plants. Indigenous peo-ples from every continent include caterpillars in their

Mopane worm (Imbrasia belina) harvest in Botswana.

diets. Mopane caterpillars (*Imbrasia belina*, Family Saturniidae) are harvested and eaten by the millions in Botswana, Zimbabwe, and elsewhere in southern Africa (inset). Silkworm (*Bombyx mori*) pupae are regarded as a delicacy in China.

Caterpillars play a major, although indirect, role in all of our lives by exerting a chronic force on plants to evolve mechanisms to discourage herbivores. Plants are immobile. Caterpillars are omnipresent. If a plant is to survive through evolutionary time, it must have defenses, many of which are chemical: latexes, alkaloids, terpenes, tannins, and myriad others. Many of these compounds have medicinal (opium, salicylic acid = aspirin, digitalis, and taxol), culinary (tea, coffee, pepper, cinnamon, paprika, cumin, and other spices), and commercial (rubber and turpentine) values. And should you have an appreciation for fine red wines, be assured that the tannins that give the wine its body and character are there for an entirely different reason. Tannins are digestibility reducers manufactured by many woody plants that cross-link proteins and make them chemically unavailable to the organisms that ingest them. Thus, if only in a roundabout way, life would be considerably less rich and less interesting (and much less flavorful) without caterpillars.

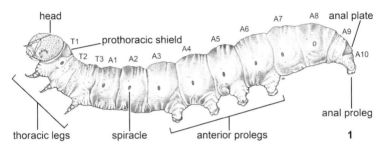

FIG. 1 *Lateral view caterpillar. T1 is the first thoracic segment, T2 the second thoracic segment, A1 the first abdominal segment, and so on.*

MORPHOLOGY

An insect's body is divided into three parts: head, thorax, and abdomen (Fig. 1). A diagnostic feature shared by all true caterpillars is an inverted Y-shaped line that extends down from the top of the head (Fig. 2). The lower arms delimit the **frontal triangle** or **frons**. Below the frons is a narrow plate, the **clypeus**, which runs between the two short **antennae**. The **labrum** or upper lip is positioned below the clypeus—its medial notch engages the leaf edge while the caterpillar is feeding. The caterpillar's six **lateral eyes** or **stemmata** are arranged, more or less, in a semicircle, with the fifth stemma usually offset toward the antenna. Located centrally on the lower side of the head is the labial

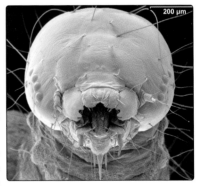

Frontal view of Brenthia monolychna *(Family Choreutidae). The spinneret of this microlepidopteran is especially well developed.*

spinneret (inset), the elongate spigot through which a caterpillar's silk is discharged. (Silk issues from the body as a liquid but turns to a solid fiber upon exposure to air.)

The caterpillar's three thoracic segments bear true **legs**, each of which terminates in a simple claw. Extending across the top of the first thoracic segment (T1) is a variously developed

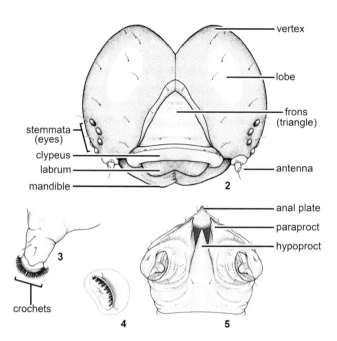

FIG. 2 *Head, frontal view.* FIG. 3 *Proleg, lateral view.*
FIG. 4 *Proleg with crochets, ventral view.*
FIG. 5 *Last abdominal segments of looper (Family Geometridae), ventral view.*

dorsal plate called the **prothoracic shield** (Fig. 1). Most of a caterpillar's mass is in its ten abdominal segments (A1–A10). **Prolegs**, the familiar, soft, hook-bearing legs of the abdomen, arise from the underside of abdominal segments three to six (A3–A6) and ten (A10) (Fig. 1). The number and relative sizes of the prolegs are often a clue to a caterpillar's identity. The prolegs bear a series of minute hooklets, called **crochets** (Figs 3, 4), that are used by the caterpillar to hold on to the substrate. Crochets, both their number and arrangement, are routinely used in keys by lepidopterists, although their use in this guide has been downplayed because they are difficult to view in living caterpillars. Structures of the last abdominal segment (A10) are often helpful in identification. The top of the segment bears a gumdrop-shaped **anal plate** (Fig. 1), which is sometimes pointed or otherwise modified. In inchworms the anus on A10 is flanked by the **paraprocts** and subtended by the **hypoproct** (Fig. 5).

Useful landmarks for orientation on the caterpillar's body include the spiracles and prolegs. **Spiracles**, the respiratory pores on the side of the caterpillar's body, are located on the first thoracic segment (T1) and the first eight abdominal segments (A1–A8) (Fig. 1). The spiracles on T1 and A8 are often twice the size of those that intervene. The midabdominal prolegs, as noted above, usually start on A3 and run to A6. In those moths with a reduced complement of prolegs, it is usually the anterior pairs that are reduced in size or absent.

For consistency, I use the term **stripe** for those markings that run parallel to the body axis and extend along a number of segments. An approximate terminology has been adopted to convey where the stripes are located: moving from the top of the body (dorsum) to the bottom (venter) are the **middorsal, addorsal, subdorsal, supraspiracular, spiracular, subspiracular,**

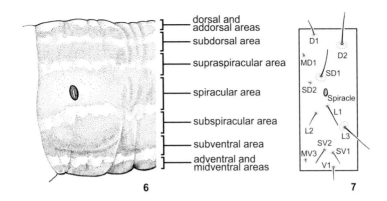

FIG. 6 *Abdominal segment, lateral view.*

FIG. 7 *Diagram of (primary) setal positions on idealized abdominal segment (head to left): D = dorsal, MD = microdorsal, SD = subdorsal, L = lateral, SV = subventral, and V = ventral. Hence there are two dorsal setae, 1 and 2, with D1 being more dorsal and more anterior than D2. Microdorsal setae are minute and require microscopic examination.*

subventral, **adventral**, and **midventral** stripes (Fig. 6). I use these terms to define relative position on a hypothetical cylinder (and ignore for the purposes of this guide technical arguments of homology that might be based, for example, on studies of larval development). Markings that wrap around the caterpillar's body are called **bands** or **rings**. The generic term **line** is used for shorter markings regardless of their orientation.

The size, arrangement, and number of setae on the head and body, or "**chaetotaxy**," have considerable significance in lepidopteran classification and identification. In this work I have largely avoided using chaetotaxy because most setae are difficult to see without the aid of a dissecting microscope. Nevertheless, there are several situations in the guide where specific setae are mentioned to assure a definitive identification. Setal nomenclature is easily learned—all the names are derived from a seta's position on the body (Fig. 7).

A glossary with numerous biological, morphological, and other specialized terms is provided at the end of this guide.

TELLING MACROS FROM MICROS

This book, with the exception of the slug caterpillars, smoky moths, flannel moths, and a few others, is focused on macrolepidopteran caterpillars. Macrolepidopterans are believed to represent a monophyletic group of "higher" Lepidoptera, most which feed exposed or externally on plants. Exceptions abound: some bore, a few form shelters, others are subterranean, etc. Many macrolepidopteran families have the crochets arranged in a line that runs parallel to the body axis. The majority of species of Lepidoptera and the overwhelming majority of individuals that you will encounter in nature are microlepidopterans (micros). Microlepidopterans are so diverse and heterogeneous as to defy ready characterization—most lepidopterists learn to recognize micros family by family until they garner a gestalt for their great variety. The lion's share of micros feed internally in leaf shelters, mines, galls, or tunnel into tissues. They tend to be rather simplified; warts, knobs, abundant secondary setae, spines, and other ornamentation are only occasionally evident. A significant portion of the common families has a well-differentiated prothoracic shield and rather plain thoracic and abdominal coloration. Microlepidopteran prolegs are often proportionately more slender and elongated. Their crochets are often arranged in a circle. One way to distinguish the two is to poke the caterpillar in question—if it wriggles backward with great rapidity it is certainly a micro (although if it does not wriggle backward, it can still be a micro since there are many micro families that do not respond in this way). This trick is especially helpful when you run across young macros that are too small to examine without a microscope.

NOT QUITE CATERPILLARS

The immature stages of wasps (especially sawflies) and some flies resemble caterpillars. Sawfly larvae are easily recognized by examining their heads or proleg complement. They have a single lateral eye (not six as in most Lepidoptera) and they lack a prominent protuberant labial **spinneret**. Most true caterpillars have four pairs of midabdominal prolegs (on A3–A6) or fewer; sawflies have five or more pairs (these usually beginning on A2). The prolegs of butterflies and moths bear numerous crochets; crochets are absent in sawflies, fly maggots, beetle larvae, and other caterpillarlike insects with fleshy abdominal legs. Some flower fly (family Syrphidae) larvae resemble caterpillars, but they lack a head capsule and always bear a pair of closely set spiracles at the rear of the body. Beetle larvae have from zero to six lateral eyes and lack a labial spinneret but are not likely to be confused with any of the caterpillars in this guide.

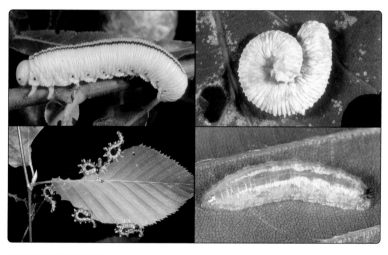

CATERPILLAR LOOK-ALIKES.
UPPER LEFT: Elm Sawfly (Cimbex americana) *on willow;*
UPPER RIGHT: Macremphytus *sawfly on dogwood;*
LOWER LEFT: Croesus latitarsis *sawfly on birch;*
LOWER RIGHT: syrphid or flower fly larva on beech (head to left).

CATERPILLAR LIFE CYCLE

All Lepidoptera have complete metamorphosis with four distinct life forms: the egg, **larva** or caterpillar, **pupa** or **chrysalis**, and adult. The egg stage typically lasts around 6–14 days, but it can be considerably longer in those species that pass the winter in this stage or for eggs laid in early spring when the temperatures may remain cool for weeks. The larval stage is the growth phase—some Lepidoptera increase their mass by more than 1,000 times as a caterpillar. To accommodate this growth, a caterpillar must molt, shedding its **cuticle** (integument or skin). The larva between molts is called an **instar**. Thus the first instar **ecloses** from the egg, the last or **ultimate** instar fashions the cocoon or cell in which pupation will take place, or, in the case of butterflies and some moths, spins the button of silk to which the chrysalis will attach. The majority of Lepidoptera have five or six instars. In some, like the Gypsy Moth (*Lymantria dispar*), the female caterpillar passes through an additional instar. Slug caterpillars (Limacodidae) go through as many as eight or nine instars. First instars may be dispersive, "ballooning" with the wind on strands of silk as do some of our inchworms and tussock moths or simply wandering great distances as do many catocaline noctuids (e.g., underwings). Prior to each molt the larva ceases feeding and becomes inactive—the next instar's head capsule may be observed within the prothorax of the quiescent, pre-molt larva. After the caterpillar sheds its old integument, it may take several hours before its new cuticle is hardened and it is again ready to feed. When the exact number of an instar is not known, it is often convenient to refer to these with terms such as middle, antepenultimate (second to last), penultimate (next to last), and/or ultimate instars.

The pupa, though sedentary, is a stage of great internal turmoil and transformation. Nearly all the larval tissues and organs—the eyes, mouthparts, legs, silk glands, muscles, etc.—will be digested and reorganized into the body of the adult insect. Prior to pupation the larva loses much of its patterning and its length decreases. In addition, the gut is evacuated. To the unaware, these caterpillars may appear diseased and close to death. Most moths pupate in a cocoon or cell fashioned in litter or soil. The naked pupa of true butterflies and a few moths is called a chrysalis; it tends to be sculptured, patterned, and may have a girdle of silk about the body near the juncture of the thorax and abdomen. In many species, the pupal stage lasts only 7–14 days while in others it may last many months, or in rare cases, two or more years. In those species that have facultative (partial) or staggered emergence, it is usually the pupal stage that holds in a state of suspended animation from one season to the next. But the record-holders here are the prepupal larvae of Bogus Yucca Moths (*Prodoxus*) of the American Southwest, which may remain viable and emerge as adults more than 30 years after they have ceased feeding!

Some species cycle through an entire generation in as few as four to five weeks—the Monarch being a familiar example. The longest life cycle belongs to the Arctic Woolly-bear (*Gynaephora groenlandica*), which routinely takes 14 years to complete its development. In Connecticut I would guess that our fauna is more or less divided between those species that have only one generation per year and those that have two; a small fraction have more than two broods and a handful take two full years to mature. Second, third, and additional broods are often facultative, meaning that some individuals in the population continue to emerge and reproduce while others enter **diapause** after a generation or two. (Diapause is a state of suspended development that normally coincides with a environmentally stressful period such as winter or the hot, dry portions of summer.) Members of facultative generations either continue to cycle through until the autumn brood(s) enter diapause or perish in inclement weather. Southward, most species add generations or broods. In southern Florida and Texas many moths and butterflies cycle through generations year-round.

Adults emerge from the pupa with short wings that must be expanded with **hemolymph**. Newly emerged adults, especially those with large, heavy wings, must be able to hang from a twig or other object to successfully enlarge their wings. The transformation from a hardly recognizable creature to a flight-ready adult is rapid, occurring, in some cases, over a span of only 20–60 minutes. It is one of nature's most captivating and awe-inspiring phenomena. At the age of six, I stumbled across a Buckeye Butterfly (*Junonia coenia*) emerging from its chrysalis. I did not know what I had found and was at the same time horrified and intrigued. Backing away, I watched from a safe distance. Within a span of five minutes, the Buckeye's hindwing spots were recognizable and, perhaps too, my path to become an entomologist had been largely fated. If you are rearing caterpillars, make sure you add to each container a twig or surface that your nascent adults may ascend and from which they can hang while pumping up their wings. Forewarning: wings with deformities and wrinkles after about 30 minutes are going to stay that way.

FINDING CATERPILLARS

There is no substitute for walking slowly and searching leaves, branches, and flowers individually. Only in this way will you learn about the insect's normal resting position, feeding behavior, threat displays, and other behaviors. Occasionally you might even observe interactions between a caterpillar and one of its natural enemies or see what stimuli evoke defensive or escape behaviors. The great majority will be found perched on leaf undersides, usually over a vein. Inspect leaf shelters. Leaves near the shoot apex are the most productive. I especially enjoy going out at night and searching by flashlight—most caterpillars feed principally at night. (In fact, one way to accelerate larval development times is to rear caterpillars in total darkness.) Nighttime searches are especially productive for those species that hide in crevices, perch along the trunk, or descend into ground vegetation at the base of their foodplant by day.

The most efficient way to secure caterpillars is with a beating sheet, which is just entomological for "drop cloth." The collapsible beating sheets sold by entomological supply houses are excellent, easily disassembled, durable, and dry quickly. White bedsheets also can be used to good measure—use them as drop cloths below vegetation that looks promising. Sheets are especially easy and efficient to employ when you are working with others (e.g., students).

Position a beating tray, sheet, umbrella, etc., under a limb of a shrub or tree and swiftly rap a branch, with the intent of knocking caterpillars from their perch, or grab a stem near its base, position the foliage over your sheet, and then strike the stem at any point above your hand. Usually a single swift rap or two is all that is necessary to dislodge the caterpillars. Do not jar the branch prior to striking it; the idea is to catch the caterpillars unaware. Many caterpillars have the ability to hang onto foliage tenaciously should they perceive the need to, e.g., during periods of high  winds. After striking a few branches inspect the sheet for caterpillars. After a preliminary search, tip the beating sheet and gently pour away loose leaves and twigs. Then look to see if any caterpillars remain attached to the beating sheet fabric. The clearing of loose debris is especially helpful when looking for early instars that would otherwise be missed. For this reason, you may want to seek out a smooth white fabric for your beating sheet. Return unwanted caterpillars to appropriate foliage. While beating is effective anytime of day, early evening is especially good as many caterpillars come out of hiding to feed at dusk.

When using a beating sheet, sample only a single plant species; otherwise, your foodplant records will be in doubt, and you will be in a quandary about what to feed your caterpillars. Accordingly, make sure to completely clear your beating sheets between plant species so you can be sure that your foodplant association records are correct. (Note: caterpillars often crawl onto or come to rest on non-host foliage, especially larvae that are diseased, parasitized, or prepupal. Confirm feeding damage and/or the production of excreta before recording a species as a foodplant.)

Caterpillars that feed on grasses, forbs, or other low vegetation may be sampled by sweeping. Pass your net swiftly across target vegetation (a dozen times or so) and then check its contents for caterpillars. If there is considerable debris in the net, it often helps to dump the contents out over a beating sheet. Again, dusk and early evening efforts are generally more productive, and this is often the only way to find those species that shelter beneath, on, or near the ground by day. Wear a headlamp so that both hands will be free. Biological supply companies sell specially designed sweeping nets—these have a stout rim and a muslin net bag. Sweep only one plant species at a time and return unwanted caterpillars to their proper foodplant.

Burlap bands fastened around a tree trunk are a useful way to survey for caterpillars that leave the foliage and descend along the stem during the day to seek shelter. Burlap banding is one of the principal methods employed by forest managers to census Gypsy Moth caterpillar populations. Wrap a strip of burlap 15–20cm in width around a trunk at chest height, then use a staple gun to attach the band along its top edge. Cut three or four incisions upwards into the burlap, stopping a couple centimeters short of the upper edge so that flaps of the burlap can be lifted up while you search for caterpillars.

WHERE TO SEARCH

I enjoy the hunt, especially after I have been reading up on a species' biology and have planned a trip. As often as not, I fail to find what I am looking for, but invariably stumble upon other caterpillars just as interesting. To find caterpillars, watch for one of the many telltale signs that signal a caterpillar is present. Inspect leaf edges where you suspect recent feeding. If there is any hint of browning, the damage is old and likely you are too late for the quarry. The type of feeding damage may immediately reveal the identity of a caterpillar—larentiine geometrids and young hornworms chew characteristic holes in the middle of the leaf blade rather than starting from a leaf edge. Hornworms and underwing caterpillars often sever the petiole of leaves upon which they have fed. Fresh feculae (droppings) provide another sign that can narrow the search. The large feculae of hornworms and giant silkworms are especially obvious. If you are feeling especially motivated, throw a drop sheet down below a foodplant of interest—within hours, telltale feculae will be present to guide your search. Caterpillars that bore into plant tissues typically push frass out the entrance of their tunnel; such debris is a quick giveaway once you learn what to look for. My assistant, Eric Hossler, once found a Slender Sphinx (*Hemaris gracilis*) caterpillar by watching a parasitic wasp that seemed to be especially interested in a particular patch of lowbush blueberry. Some species use silk to form shelters, or crawl into those fashioned previously by other caterpillars. At first your efforts will be trial and error, but usually after two or three caterpillars are located, you will start to understand the biology of the species, finding caterpillars only on leaves of a certain age, perched in a characteristic position, sitting over the midrib on the underside of the blade, positioned in a cavity hollowed out along one leaf edge, etc.

Woodland and forest edges can be productive, particularly relative to forest interiors. While some species prefer saplings or shoots with new foliage, others shun such and restrict their feeding to mature foliage. Slug caterpillars are common on branches and leaves near the ground, whereas other species occur at chest height or in the canopy. I always check somewhat isolated plants, in preference to searching in large stands, where hundreds of leaves might be examined before a caterpillar is found. Gardens, plantings, and other plants in your own yard will yield gems. Vacant lots and highly disturbed habitats are home to species rarely encountered elsewhere.

WARNING

If you are collecting caterpillars with children it is a good idea to use caution when handling both hairy and spiny caterpillars. Even the Woolly Bear and the Hickory Tussock are allergenic to some people, or prove problematic if dislodged setae come into contact with the eyes, mucosal membranes, or other sensitive skin. While these and other noxious species (*see* pages 35, 53, and 238) may be picked up with the fingertips if handled gently and with respect, it is not recommended, especially around children.

WHEN TO SEARCH

The annual peak in caterpillar diversity is late spring, when there is an abundance of new foliage that often is not yet fully protected, chemically or physically. Some caterpillars feed only on older summer foliage. Flower and seed specialists tend to come along later in the season. Those that feed on fallen leaves or tunnel in wood seem to be equally common year-round. For many of the larger species it is hard to beat late August and September, especially if you like searching for my three favorite groups, the daggers, prominents, and slug caterpillars. Flashlight searches at night are invariably productive at this time of year.

Timing is everything. The peak of activity for a species may be brief, spanning only two to three weeks. A species that seems impossibly scarce one week might be common the following, then just as quickly disappear for the remainder of the year. Of course, you can broaden the window of opportunity for your efforts by developing a search image for earlier instars (smaller larvae) or even eggs. Species with two or more generations provide second and third chances. Mountainous regions such as the Appalachians provide a special opportunity—a general rule of thumb is that every 300m (1,000ft) of altitude corresponds to a week or so in seasonal phenology. Thus a species that is mostly pupal at 150m (500ft), may be present as mature larvae at 450m (1,500ft), and as penultimate instars at 750m (2,500ft).

REARING CATERPILLARS

I would venture that a fair fraction of professional entomologists and especially moth enthusiasts were drawn into entomology in part by the rearing of giant silkworms and other interesting caterpillars. Caterpillars are little mysteries, much of the time you are not sure how they will turn out. I always enjoy checking my rearing room for the recent emergences so that I might associate an adult with what, up until that instant, had been an unidentified caterpillar.

While some will want to rear caterpillars simply because they enjoy watching metamorphosis or find it is an activity that they can share with their children or students, there are a number reasons why the serious student of entomology will want to delve into the business of rearing immature stages. It is one of the most efficient methods for obtaining series of some species, especially leafminers, gall makers, and other microlepidopterans. Immaculate individuals may be obtained for photography and released or vouchered and donated to a museum—reared specimens with full foodplant data are valuable study specimens, particularly if they prove to be part of a taxonomically difficult species complex. Carefully observed rearing lots will yield a wealth of information on feeding habits, periods of activity, development times, and other life history information. As noted elsewhere, rearing of wild-collected caterpillars is the principal means to document a species' parasitoid and pathogen fauna.

There is nothing magical about rearing: if one supplies fresh foliage, keeps the rearing containers free of mold, and provides benign temperature and moisture regimes, the successes will be many. I rear most of my singleton caterpillars in 15 dram and 40 dram plastic vials.

Larger collections are held in pint or quart take-out containers. I employ large plastic pretzel jars and one-gallon ice cream cartons on occasion. Into the latter, I cut windows and cover these with fine netting fabric. Several colleagues recommend sandwich boxes, in part, because they are very easy to clean. An especially attractive aspect of the take-out containers noted above is that the basket-type disposable coffee filters sit perfectly within and function like napkins, allowing the rearing containers to be cleaned quickly and with little fuss.

While closed containers are acceptable to many species, others require ventilation— Luna Moths (*Actias luna*), Cecropias (*Hyalophora cecropia*), and Buck Moths (*Hemileuca maia*) succumb to a wilting disease when reared in saturated atmospheres. It is often helpful to punch small holes into the lids of your rearing containers. For special collections, use water picks or other measures to insure that the foliage stays fresh. Keep larval densities low as overcrowding will result in smaller adults, unnatural larval color morphs, and promote the outbreak and spread of disease.

Coffee filters or paper toweling placed over the bottom of the rearing containers will absorb excess moisture and allow the feculae (excreta or droppings) to be quickly removed. In the last instar, a 3–5cm layer of very lightly moistened peat is often a better option than toweling. In the wild many caterpillars tunnel into soil to fashion their pupal cell. A few of the spring-active owlets may tunnel as deep as 10cm or more to pupate. Peat has other advantages: it soaks up excess moisture, releases moisture over a period of weeks, and serves as a mold retardant. Some caterpillars (e.g., daggers, brothers, and forester moths) fashion pupal chambers in soft wood and will die if they cannot find a suitable pupation medium. Chunks of styrofoam or pith may also be employed.

Provide appropriate foodplant material—some caterpillars will eat only new leaves, while others are obligate old-leaf specialists. Flower moths (*Schinia*), cucullias, and many blues prefer flowers. Others consume only seeds and fruit. This book will help you sort through the possibilities, but you can make reasonable guesses. For example, spring-active species with a single generation are almost certainly new-leaf specialists; fall-active caterpillars with bright colors are good candidates for flower-feeders; ground-foraging caterpillars will often accept a variety of forbs. When in doubt, provide a salad of choices, and then watch for the production of feculae and check for feeding damage. Oak is eaten by more species than any other plant in this guide. Other foodplants that are suitable to large numbers of forest caterpillars include alder, apple, birch, cherry, poplar, and willow. Some caterpillars will accept substitutions; it is often convenient to offer common foodplants from your yard or choose a plant species whose foliage stays fresh over longer periods. Forbs acceptable to a number of moth caterpillars that forage on low-growing plants include clover, dandelion, dock, fleabane, and lettuce. The latter can be purchased year-round. Because of its high water content, it is best to use the greenest portions of the outer leaves or purchase Romaine and other leafy varieties. Many boring (tunneling) moths, e.g., Goat Moths (Cossidae), Ghost Moths (Hepialidae), *Papaipema* (Noctuidae), may be reared on carrots. If you have a coring tool, carve out an initial tunnel, scarcely wider than the caterpillar's own diameter, into which you can introduce your larva (Richard Henderson pers. comm.).

Caterpillars should be minimally disturbed prior to molting and pupation. Pre-molt larvae can be recognized by their quiescent behavior and proportionately small head. Feculae production drops off prior to each molt. Many species spin a light sheet of silk into which they engage their crochets, thus anchoring the caterpillar so that it may, literally, crawl out of its old skin. The head of the ensuing instar is usually visible as a swollen lump within the first thoracic segment and the black lateral eyes of the next instar can be seen through the integument of the soon-to-be-shed skin (*see* page 407, Shivering Pinion, *Lithophane querquera*). Pre-molt larvae are vulnerable and have limited mobility; care should be taken not to dislodge them from their purchase. Prepupal larvae often enter an extended wandering

phase, appear somewhat shorter and plumper, show no interest in food, are dull in coloration, or lose their patterning.

For large rearing efforts, consider sleeving your caterpillars (inset). Your principal concerns will be to ensure that there is sufficient foliage of the appropriate age for the caterpillars in the sleeve and to remove prepupal caterpillars that might tunnel through the sides of the netting in their search for a suitable pupation site. In addition to being comparatively low maintenance, sleeving has the advantages of yielding full-sized adults whose development is synchronized with that of wild caterpillars. Additionally, disease outbreaks are exceedingly unlikely. The one- and five-gallon paint filter bags sold at larger hardware stores are fine-meshed and make excellent and economical sleeves. Insect net bags may be used as well, but they are expensive. Pillow cases will serve as sleeves and are very economical, especially if purchased used or on sale. Entomological supply houses sell sleeves that tie off at both ends and have a side zipper for easy access and servicing. We make our larger sleeves out of tenting fabrics (available over the Internet). Double-sleeve especially valuable caterpillar cohorts to provide greater distance between your livestock and potential predators. On numerous occasions I have observed predaceous stink bugs sitting on the outside of my sleeves, taking a meal from within. Birds may peck holes through the fabric to get at the occupants. Large sphinx and silkworm caterpillars are particularly apt to draw the attentions of birds. Always shake the branch vigorously before adding your caterpillars to the sleeve as spiders, assassin bugs, predaceous stink bugs, and other predators would like nothing better than to be sealed up with a clutch of caterpillars. Caterpillars placed on sunny branches generally do better. For species that feed on grass, forbs, and other small plants, transplant some foodplant into a pot and then sleeve an appropriate number of caterpillars within.

Insects are "cold-blooded," and thus their rate of development may be controlled by rearing them at different temperatures. Rearing indoors accelerates the development of spring-active species. Conversely, most caterpillars tolerate short stints of a week or more in a refrigerator if the temperatures are kept above freezing. As most caterpillars are principally nocturnal, it is often possible to accelerate the rate of development by rearing your caterpillars in complete darkness.

While it is laudable to release livestock into the wild, be steadfast in making certain that your releases are biologically and genetically appropriate. Never release insects from one province, state, or region into another. The potential for calamity is great: one could transfer pathogens and disease from one population to another or introduce inappropriate genes. At the very least, you will be scrambling the genetic history of two populations, corrupting any signal that might be studied by scientists in the future. Be circumspect about your decision to take a moth from that lighted gas station wall on your way through Alabama on your way back to Massachusetts—none of its progeny should be released in the Northeast. Additional suggestions for collecting and rearing caterpillars can be found in Covell (1984), Friedrich (1986), Dunn (1993), Winter (2000), Leverton (2001), and Wagner *et al.* (2002).

OVERWINTERING LARVAE AND PUPAE
The greatest rearing challenge is getting your livestock through the winter. It is not simply a matter of keeping everything alive—for most species you must break the obligatory diapause. In temperate insects, diapause is broken by a prolonged exposure to cold temperatures.

But how cold and how long? I generally hold my collections for 12–16 weeks at temperatures just above freezing. The key variables over this period are moisture and temperature, with the former being hardest to control. Many batches will desiccate and others will mold if you are not vigilant. A stairway leading out of a basement with a protected bulkhead or hatchway makes for an ideal location. The lots will be exposed to natural humidities and should stay above freezing. Keep a thermometer or plastic container of water next to your collections so that you can periodically check that they are not exposed to freezing temperatures. Another option is to winter your collections in a shallow hole dug in the ground that is then covered with sticks or wood and buried under 10–25cm of leaves. The tops of the containers should be open so the livestock is exposed to fluctuating humidities. I cover my containers with squares of nylon netting (or even squares of fabric), invert them so they will not fill with water, and place them on plastic garden flats. The latter also serves to exclude mice that might feed on the collections through the winter. Old wood sheds, garages, and back porches are also good overwintering sites, but depending on conditions (and the geographic regions from which you have made your collections) you will need to shield them from subfreezing temperatures and/or may have to lightly moisten your lots occasionally, etc. Collections from the South may be freeze-intolerant, while those from Maine may endure long periods of subfreezing temperatures. Advice from Dale Schweitzer, with whom I often consult about all things lepidopterological, "A good general rule is that underground pupae should not be exposed to temperatures below 20–25° F. Unless your climate frequently has nights below about 10° F the easiest approach might be keeping above-ground pupae outside in a shaded sheltered place." Carter and Hargreaves (1986) recommend keeping pupae in a cold but frost-free site.

STARTING WITH EGGS

When your searches are focused on single species, it is often possible to sleuth out the eggs, the most numerically abundant life stage for any insect. Those moths that lay their eggs in masses, such as buck moths and tent caterpillars, present little challenge to see other than the fact that their egg masses may be widely spaced and infrequently encountered. The eggs of giant silkworms, hornworms, swallowtails, and prominents are large, spherical, usually smooth, and quite visible to the unaided eye. Smaller species present special, but far from impossible, challenges. The famous American entomologist Harrison Dyar urged those interested in finding slug caterpillars to look for the flat, glassy eggs, which he claimed are both numerous and easily located once one develops a search image for the shiny spots on leaf undersides (Dyar 1899: 241). Eggs laid in the summer may hatch within 4–10 days, although exceptions abound. Those moths and butterflies that hibernate as eggs may spend the better part of their lives in this stage. For example, tent caterpillars (*Malacosoma*) spend five times as long in the egg stage as all the other stages combined. Leverton's book *Enjoying Moths* (2001) has additional tips for finding eggs.

Another means of obtaining eggs is to confine a mated female for a night or two. Corrugated or scratched cardboard, a twisted piece of toweling or paper, or other roughened surfaces, may stimulate egg-laying. While most females lay in virtually any situation, others have specific requirements and will refuse to lay unless a sprig of the foodplant, a piece of bark, bud or flower, etc. is supplied. Conversely, female prominents, daggers, and slug caterpillars seem to prefer smooth-walled containers. Styrofoam coolers may be used for large moths—many times the wings will be unblemished even after a night or two of confinement. Sleeving females on an appropriate foodplant nearly always works. Some species must feed for a night or two before they will lay. Other species seem to yield eggs more freely if held in completely clean, smooth vials for a night without any food and water: I often do this on the first night that I hold a female or after two or three nights of feeding without obtaining eggs. Some degree of ventilation is sometimes needed.

Gravid females of most moths come to light, but the preponderance of individuals arriving at lights will be males. According to Richard Heitzman, just after dark can be especially productive for females. I have found foggy, wet nights good for females, at least relative to the total number of moths that arrive at light. Females of some giant silkworms (e.g., the Cecropia, *Hyalophora cecropia*) and others fly mostly after midnight, so it may be necessary to run your lights throughout the night. More balanced sex ratios can be expected at baits and flowers.

Incubate your eggs under natural humidities, and in dry weather mist them occasionally. Eggs are susceptible to mold so it is a good idea to check them at least once a day. Eggs held with foliage from the foodplant in closed vials will nearly always mold before hatching. Viable eggs are often pale cream when laid, add color over the first day, then darken, clear, or in some other way change color again a day or so before the first instars issue. Eggs that stay cream-colored and/or collapse are typically infertile. If your eggs take more than ten days to two weeks to hatch they are likely dead or destined to overwinter. Newly hatched first instars are vulnerable creatures that soon starve or desiccate if they do not have ready access to appropriate foliage. A fair number of newborn caterpillars consume part or all of their eggshell for their first meal. I often mist newly hatched larvae, especially if they have been wandering without foliage for any period of time. I take greatest care with first instars of slug caterpillars; I transfer these individually to the underside of an oak-leaf sprig held in a small water pick, mist them thoroughly, and then let the leaves air-dry for a half hour or so while the minute caterpillars establish.

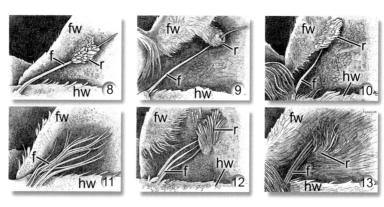

WING COUPLING MECHANISMS IN MOTHS: MALES ABOVE AND FEMALES BELOW.
FIG. 8 *male of* Metarranthis obfirmaria *(Family Geometridae);*
FIG. 9 *male of* Haploa lecontei *(Family Arctiidae);*
FIG. 10 *male of* Lymantria dispar *(Family Lymantriidae);*
FIG. 11 *female of* Metarannthis obfirmaria;
FIG. 12 *female of* Haploa lecontei;
FIG. 13 *female of* Lymantria dispar.
fw = forewing, f = frenulum, hw = hindwing, r = retinaculum.

SEXING ADULTS
A reliable means to determine the sex of most moths is to examine the frenulum, the coupling spine(s) that extends up from the base of the hindwing and engages specialized scales on the underside of the forewing (Figs 8–13). It is single and thickened in males; it is double-, triple-, or multispined in females. It is helpful to hold the wings together, preferably with a pair of spade-tipped forceps or stamp tongs, over the moth's "back" to view the frenulum. If done carefully,

Male Sallow (Sunira bicolorago). *When sexing adults, look for a line or gap between the male's claspers.*

Male Sallow (Sunira bicolorago) *with valves partially spread as they might appear immediately before coupling (with female).*

this does not harm the moth. The male antennae are generally more plumose or set with more sensory setae (males use their sensory setae to detect female sex pheromones). Sexual differences in the antennae are abundantly obvious in giant silkworm moths and tussock moths; examination of the antennae, with or without the aid of a lens, will usually reveal sexual differences in other moths. Many male Lepidoptera have specialized scent scales on their legs, wings, or abdomen that immediately reveal their sex, but knowing where to look usually requires prior knowledge as these scales are often concealed. Females tend to be larger and their abdomens fuller and more rounded, especially rearward. In many owlets the male spermatophore can be felt within the female's abdomen by gently pressing the abdomen between thumb and forefinger. Male Lepidoptera have side to side claspers (or valves) that hold the female during mating—look for a slit along the venter where the valves come together (insets). Females have a circular pore, often with associated extrusible pads, which they use to taste the foodplant or deposit egg(s). By gently pushing on the end of the abdomen it is often possible to expose enough of the genitalia to know what sex you are holding, but this will take practice. Remember: when searching about lights, the great preponderance will be males.

FEEDING FEMALES

Some females need to be fed before they will lay eggs. A feeding solution of one part sugar, maple syrup, or honey to two parts' water, offered in a tiny ball of cotton, will suffice. Sometimes it will be necessary to uncoil the female's tongue with a pin and place its tip in contact with the solution. I usually leave a small (4–5mm) feeding ball with the female, changing it every day or two. Another option is to offer females a small chunk of a grape, soaked raisin, or apple slice. I use raisin slices, perhaps 1/5th of a raisin, that stick fast to the side or the top of a vial, especially when traveling. This will prevent the female from getting stuck on her back, which often results when food is placed on the bottom of the vial. Change the fruit after 3–4 days, before it begins to mold. Females held in sleeves can be fed by misting a part of the sleeve and foliage with a sugar-water solution (Tom Allen, pers. comm.) or leaving a cotton plug soaked with food on the outside of the sleeve in a position where the female(s) can get to it. Although the water in this solution soon evaporates, nighttime moisture may dissolve enough of the sugar for the females to feed; alternatively, the sleeve can be lightly moistened with water once or twice a day. Confine females during the appropriate season, e.g., female fritillaries (*Speyeria*) rarely lay before the latter half of August or even September. Moths that emerge in the fall often pass the winter unmated, and do not pair and lay until the following spring.

NATURAL ENEMIES

The number of enemies a caterpillar faces is legion. Every major group of terrestrial vertebrates has species that prey on caterpillars. Visual predators surely have shaped the varied coloration and texture of caterpillars, and even their feeding and resting behaviors. Birds in particular have been a major selective force in the evolution of caterpillar appearance and behavior. Stated differently, caterpillars are visually and behaviorally fascinating creatures largely because of avian predation. A distant second in importance are the insect-feeding vertebrates such as frogs, lizards, snakes, shrews, and mice. Even bears, foxes, and other large mammals hunt for and consume caterpillars.

Many groups of invertebrates are predators of caterpillars. Their importance in controlling caterpillar populations is best appreciated in agricultural systems where birds and other vertebrate animals are relatively scarce. Without predaceous beetles, mites, spiders, earwigs, stink bugs, lacewings, ants, wasps, and myriad other insects, caterpillar populations would quickly consume the world's croplands, orchards, and forests. In the tropics and some temperate communities ants are major predators. Hornets and wasps harvest large numbers of caterpillars—some farmers even provide nesting boxes for wasps as part of an integrated pest management regimen to lower their dependence on pesticides. Robert Muller, whose hobby of late has been the mass rearing and release of giant silkworm moths (Saturniidae), has observed the introduced paper wasp (*Polistes dominulus*) consuming many of the caterpillars that he set out in his yard in Milford, Connecticut to augment local populations of silkworms.

Parasitoids have an enormous influence on caterpillar populations. Parasitoids are specialized predators, smaller than their prey, that feed like a parasite on or within the body of their victim. They are distinguished from true parasites because they nearly always kill their host—they just do it slowly, over a period of days, weeks, or even months, and usually from within. A common parasitoid life history strategy is to develop slowly and feed on non-essential tissues and organs, but then vanquish the host caterpillar in a final burst of growth. In this way their food (the caterpillar host) does not spoil and is able to behave normally, e.g., avoid the attentions of a bird that might consume both the caterpillar and developing parasitoid in a single act of predation. Many parasitoids are specialized, attacking a single caterpillar species or group of related species. Several of the largest and most diverse evolutionary lineages on this planet include caterpillar parasitoids: tachinid flies (>20,000 spp.), braconid

COMMON CATERPILLAR PARASITOIDS.

TOP ROW LEFT: Several Euplectrus *(Family Eulophidae) wasp larvae issuing from cadaver of noctuid.*

TOP ROW RIGHT: Microgaster scopelosomae *(Family Braconidae) wasp cocoon beneath third instar Sallow* (Eupsilia) *larva.*

SECOND ROW LEFT: Cotesia congregata *(Family Braconidae) wasp cocoons on Pawpaw Sphinx* (Dolba hyloeus).

SECOND ROW RIGHT: Meteorus *(Family Braconidae) wasp cocoon suspended from silken thread.*

THIRD ROW LEFT: Hyposoter *(Family Ichneumonidae) wasp cocoon beneath corpse of White-marked Tussock Moth* (Orygia leucostigma).

THIRD ROW RIGHT: Speckled Green Fruitworm (Orthosia hibisci) *with single tachinid fly maggot within its body. The black spot is necrotic tissue associated with the maggot's breathing tube, which it has pushed through the wall of the caterpillar's body.*

BOTTOM ROW LEFT: Same caterpillar with maggot freshly emerged from the Speckled Green Fruitworm caterpillar.

BOTTOM ROW RIGHT: Tachinid fly puparium above recently vanquished cadaver of Yellow-shouldered Slug (Lithacodes fasciola). *Tachind fly maggots pupate in their last larval skin, forming a hardened puparium.*

wasps (>40,000 spp.), ichneumonid wasps (>60,000 spp.), chalcidoid wasps (>400,000 spp.), and numerous smaller superfamilies and families (numbers are estimated species diversity). By comparison, true parasites are few in number. They include a number of mites (*see* page 165) and minute ceratopogonid flies, both of which feed on host hemolymph or "blood" but seldom harm their host.

At first you may find it both frustrating and disappointing if your hard-sought caterpillars prove to be parasitized. But parasite records are of great value, especially if the host (caterpillar) is known with certainty. There is much concern about the effects of parasitoids that have been introduced into North America to control pest species. One egregious example is *Compsilura concinnata*, a tachinid fly that was introduced to control the Gypsy Moth (*see* pages 245 and 296). Its host range, which includes more than 200 native butterflies and moths, is incompletely known; little quantitative data exist for its rates of parasitism of our native butterfly and moth species.

Like other multicellular organisms, caterpillars are attacked by viruses, bacteria, fungi, and other pathogens. Pathogens are important in regulating population numbers, especially under outbreak conditions when populations are dense and disease can pass easily from one individual to the next. Gypsy Moth populations east of the Appalachians are often regulated by the fungal pathogen *Entomophaga maimaiga* and a nuclear polyhedroris virus. The bacterium *Bacillus thuringiensis* is used widely to control caterpillar numbers in turf, gardens, orchards, and forests. Various formulations of "Bt" may be purchased from nearly any greenhouse, nursery, or agricultural supply store. Maybe it goes without saying that if you see a caterpillar that appears diseased, it should be immediately isolated from others that you are rearing. Caterpillars that blacken and ooze unpleasant odors are often victims of bacterial infections.

Caterpillar populations are kept in check by the collective impacts of the natural enemy complex. The exact mix and relative importance of the predators, parasitoids, parasites, and pathogens in the enemy complex varies from year to year and site to site. Outbreak species are those that occasionally escape their enemies and build to numbers where they defoliate acres of forest. But even these, within days, weeks, or generations, are inevitably found and their numbers driven down, sometimes to the point of scarcity! It is a race for survival—a race that most caterpillars will lose. From the beginning the odds are against the caterpillar. Each week the ranks are thinned in large measure. To compensate for these losses, insects may be very fecund—one Australian moth produces upwards of 50,000 eggs per female. Considering these numbers, it becomes obvious why it is so advantageous for the serious enthusiast to search for earlier life stages, the most numerous of which are the eggs (*see* page 19).

SURVIVAL STRATEGIES

Caterpillars employ a fascinating battery of stratagems to escape the attentions of their enemies or to thwart the attacks that follow once they have been discovered. Prior to discovery the principal tactic is crypsis—blending into the background so as to avoid detection. Caterpillars are exceptionally adept at matching the leaves or needles upon which they perch and feed. A wonderful example is the Double-toothed Prominent (*Nerice bidentata*) (*see* page 289) whose coloration and outline approaches that of the elm leaves upon which it feeds. Many leaf-feeders exhibit "countershading," whereby the lower portion of the body becomes progressively lighter green so that the insect's own shadow scarcely changes the overall impact of the caterpillar's coloration when viewed from a distance. Caterpillars may resemble petioles, twigs, bark, buds, flowers, fruits, or tendrils. The inchworms are consummate background-matchers—while beating foliage I am forever having to squeeze this and that to make sure that a plant fragment is not, in fact, a caterpillar. Several emeralds, e.g., the Camouflaged Looper (*Synchlora aerata*) (*see* page 200), go so far as to attach flower bits and other pieces of vegetation over their bodies to better blend into their background. Among the most striking bark and stick mimics are those that have markings that resemble foliose lichens, e.g., the Ilia Underwing (*Catocala ilia*) (*see* page 363) and Kent's Geometer (*see* page 179). Some caterpillars look like the dead leaves of their foodplants—the majority of these, interestingly, also quaver back and forth if disturbed, much like a dried leaf might do in the wind. Among those that rest on bark, a large fraction possesses a prominent subventral line of hairs or setae. While generally termed "shadow elimination hairs," they seem to function principally in another capacity, i.e., to disguise the outline of the caterpillar and make it difficult to distinguish bark from caterpillar (*see also* page 365, White Underwing). A few are highly polymorphic with forms so different that a predator would need to learn many search images to recognize all the individuals present in a single shrub or tree (e.g., The Little Wife, *Catocala muliercula*, *see* page 364). Others employ disruptive coloration, whereby bold bands and other prominent markings break up the caterpillar's otherwise recognizable appearance, and diminish the probability that it will be recognized (e.g., Abbott's Sphinx, *Sphecodina abbottii*, *see* page 270). Many resemble bird droppings. Interestingly, these typically have shiny integuments and thus appear as fresh wet droppings, considerably more so than if their integument were not so rendered. A few of our caterpillars mimic other protected animals: among the models are snakes, the cast skins of tarantulas (*see* page 44), sawfly larvae, and unpalatable caterpillars.

Some blues and hairstreaks enlist the help of ants to guard them from predators and parasitoids. Not only have lycaenids evolved special appeasement and nectar organs to moderate these interactions, but many also have stridulatory (sound-producing) structures that are used to "call" ants into service. The caterpillars' calls are substrate-borne, carried through the foodplants and other surfaces, so that ants walking nearby can detect the vibrations with their feet.

Silk may be used to build shelters or nests that serve to conceal the caterpillar as well as exclude enemies. Numerous groups spin a belay line upon which they rapidly descend if disturbed; once danger has passed, some will ascend their silken tether and return to their foodplant. This behavior is taken one step further in some ennomine geometrids: in advance of any disturbance, they spin down on a short belay 2–5cm in length to pass the hours of darkness.

A common strategy is to drop from the foodplant. A mere wisp of air (or breath) may be sufficient to make a cutworm release its grip. Among the Geometridae and Noctuidae there are caterpillars that are more animated in their response, literally hurling themselves from their perch if startled or molested. Some have strongly muscular wriggling responses that may go on for seconds. The wriggling may be so violent as to cast the caterpillar to and fro, a behavior that often buries the insect in loose surface litter.

Many species attempt to bite or feign like they are going to do so. Although none of our species inflicts a bite of any consequence to a human, I must admit to being startled occasionally, especially if the action is rapid as in many underwing (*Catocala*) caterpillars. While far from universal, I have almost come to expect that roughly handled caterpillars will regurgitate—the fluids are sometimes quite sticky and unappealing and, no doubt, in some cases noxious. False heads and eyespots have evolved in many moth and butterfly lineages, typically at the rear of the body such as in the Gray-patched Prominent (*Dasylophia thyatiroides*) (*see* page 316) and Turbulent Phosphila (*Phosphila turbulenta*) (*see* page 427). In swallowtails false heads occur over the thorax. Regardless of where they are situated, the caterpillars that bear them have an associated behavioral defense: they bite, regurgitate, or deliver a defensive substance at the time the false head is pecked or probed. Two of our sphingids make audible noises when perturbed: Walnut Sphinx (*Amorpha juglandis*) (*see* page 264) caterpillars hiss by forcing air out their spiracles, while those of the Abbott's Sphinx (*Sphecodina abbottii*) (*see* page 270) much like a mouse when provoked.

Caterpillars may defend themselves physically and/or chemically. Many warn of their unpalatability with aposematic (warning) coloration: the usual is some combination of red, orange, and yellow with intercalated black and white markings for accent, although just the latter two also work for many. Warningly colored caterpillars often feed gregariously, which serves to reinforce the message that they are unpalatable. Hairs and spines provide physical protection. The former, which are frequently deciduous and not infrequently microscopically barbed (tiger moths and others), provide protection from many birds and other enemies. (Curiously, cuckoos have a predilection for hairy caterpillars and have exaggerated whiskers about the base of the beak presumably to protect the eyes from thrashing caterpillars.) Brushfoots are well known for their armor of many-branched, stout spines. Caterpillars from three families, the giant silkworm moths, flannel moths, and slug caterpillars have hollow, poison-filled spines that deliver potent stings, with some tropical relatives reported to cause human deaths! Some tussock moth caterpillars release a potpourri of noxious compounds from the reddened glands atop abdominal segments six and seven that can be quite irritating to humans, and especially to those that are hypersensitive. An especially well-protected species is the Brown-tail Moth (*Euproctis chrysorrhoea*), another tussock, which bears hundreds of deciduous spicules (modified setae) along the dorsum that cause severe dermatological reactions in humans, and on rare occasions, even death (*see* page 453).

Some caterpillars sequester toxic compounds or manufacture them from precursors obtained from their foodplants. Toxin concentrations in the caterpillar's hemolymph ("blood") may be many times those found in the leaves of their foodplant. Tiger moths are among the most well protected, sequestering or manufacturing biogenic amines (e.g., histamine), pyrrolizidine alkaloids, cardiac glycosides, and other noxious substances. Smoky moths manufacture cyanide-containing compounds. As a general rule, expect that brightly colored caterpillars are protected or that they are mimics of unpalatable species.

For every stratagem enumerated above there are many that are not mentioned—the literature on defensive strategies is both enormous and engaging. Behavioral adaptations that aid in survival are especially numerous and varied. Natural enemies not only influence when some caterpillars eat, but also how they eat, or even what they eat (because survivorship will be higher on some foodplants than others), or how they defecate. And while it is easy to associate a given butterfly or moth caterpillar with one of the above defenses, in fact, most species stack strategy upon strategy, ruse upon ruse, in order to win the battle between predator and prey. My favorite case in point is the Spicebush Swallowtail (*Papilio troilus*). For the first three instars it mimics a bird dropping, then it molts into a snake mimic that resides within the confines of a leaf shelter. As a last line of defense, it will deploy and flail about its osmeterium, an eversible tentaclelike structure that is laden with butyric acid, a substance that to me smells like fresh vomit. Jeff Boettner (pers. comm.) has twice observed a Spicebush ward off vespid wasp attacks with its osmeterium—not only were the attacks terminated but the wasps seemed to have been temporarily felled to the ground as a result of their exposure to the osmeterial secretions.

PRESERVING LARVAE

The serious student may want to preserve eggs, larvae of various instars, and pupae for later study. Such specimens become the basis for future taxonomic and ultrastructural studies. The easiest way to preserve larvae is to drop them into gently boiling water and then remove both water and caterpillars from the heat source. As soon as the caterpillars are fully distended, usually within seconds of having been placed in the boiling water, they can be transferred to 70% ethanol. Caterpillars killed simply by immersion in ethanol often discolor, sometimes turning black within minutes. A superior larval specimen may be obtained by injecting the body cavity with fixative using a fine needle (#30 for very small caterpillars and #27 for larger specimens). Slowly fill the body with fixative until the caterpillar and its prolegs are fully distended. A simple fixative that yields excellent specimens is made by combining nine parts 70% ethanol with one part acetic acid. Recipes for other cold preservation fluids, based on various combinations of alcohol, formaldehyde, and glacial acetic acid, such as KAAD and Kahle's Fluid, are discussed in Stehr (1987) and Winter (2000).

Because many caterpillars continue to leak particulate matter from both ends of the gut after they have been preserved, it is best to transfer the specimens into fresh 70% ethanol after a week or two, before any material sets up on the specimen. Keep in mind that while higher concentrations of ethanol are preferred for DNA preservation, these can dehydrate tissues and cause the caterpillar to collapse and lose its form.

Specimens need to be fully labeled with locality, date of collection, collector, foodplant (hostplant or host), and cross-referenced to any photographs, parasitoids, reared adults, or field notes. I assign a unique rearing lot number (including my initials) to each egg or larval collection and associate this number with all my specimens, notes, and photographs. Pencils and indelible inks, such as those found in Pigma Pens, must be used. Heavy-weight archival papers are best; by contrast, notebook paper abrades easily in ethanol.

Unfortunately, caterpillar colors are prone to loss in fluid preservatives—greens fade within minutes of preservation. If a record of the larval coloration is important, then a photograph or an electronic image should be taken.

PHOTOGRAPHY

Even the best vouchers and most detailed notes are no substitute for a living creature—colors and behaviors are best captured with cameras. There are numerous books geared towards insect macrophotography (*see* Shaw 1984, 1987, West and Ridl 1994, Martin 2003, among others). Rather than repeat what you could find elsewhere and in more detail, I will only make a few general comments relative to my experiences with caterpillar photography, having taken most of the images for this guide.

I use a 60mm macro lens with two side flashes that are mounted on a bracketing system. The ability to swing the flashes in close to the lens is especially useful for very high magnification shots of eggs and early instars. For many shots, you may want to scale back the output from one of the flashes to enhance the perceived dimensionality of the subject. A selection of extension tubes (12mm, 20mm, 25mm, and 36mm) are kept at hand, so that I can fill the frame even with tiny caterpillars. The majority of my early images were taken with Kodachrome 25 and 64, but I have since moved to Provia 100 as it does much better with greens. I do not recommend Fujichrome Velvia®—the yellows and oranges are too warm and unreal—an animal in real life should never run second to a film image. Many of my images now are digital.

Caterpillars can be scarce and their lives ephemeral—a gorgeous caterpillar on Sunday could be a drab prepupa or parasitoid victim by Monday morning. Acquire your images as soon as you can and bracket; if appropriate, change the background composition to accentuate the caterpillar's coloration and posture. Slightly underexposed images are easily corrected with imaging software; the details lost in an overexposed image cannot be regained.

Caterpillars are usually very cooperative subjects for learning macrophotography, but some can be annoyingly active. Those that abhor daylight, like cutworms, or that are in their prepupal wandering phase can be maddeningly difficult. Many of these pause briefly if you blow a puff of air over their body. I am not a fan of chilling, but I employ a cooldown period in the refrigerator on occasion. Better substitutes are dark containers and patience. Most caterpillars settle quickly if offered a place to hide or just given a few minutes to find a perch. If I have restless subjects, I put these aside (e.g., in one-pint soup containers or on their own bouquets) and work with others, cycling back and forth until each caterpillar is in a position that would make for a good photograph.

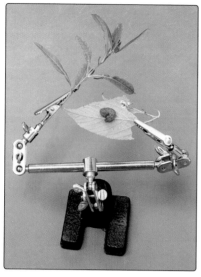

Black backgrounds are dramatic but unnatural and have another drawback: black tentacles, tufts, lashes, and other dark structures blend into the background, or worse, disappear in the image. I prefer natural-light photographs or, when using flashes, to bring backgrounds into close proximity with the caterpillar. Many of the images in this guide were taken with one or two small clamps (left): in the latter case, one to hold the substrate with the caterpillar and a second to position background foliage/matter. For better definition of hairs, especially those that are pale, direct or bounce some light from behind the subject.

Getting a caterpillar completely in focus can be challenging. While setting up for a shot, I often peer over the top of my camera to make sure my lens is in the same plane as the caterpillar (i.e., before looking into the viewfinder). This is also a good opportunity to check the position of your flash(es). Once the image has been composed, rock back and forth several times on your elbows, through the plane of focus, until you know precisely, by feel, when to depress the shutter. Typically you will take the image when the camera's plane of focus is ⅓ of the way through the subject's body. If you do a lot of macro work, you should purchase a macrophotography focusing screen. Cameras that allow you to preview the full depth of field are desirable but not essential. Nearly all of the images in this book were taken with the lens set at f/16, f/22 (with extension tubes the functional f may be much higher). A superior alternative to my handheld technique is to employ a tripod with a focusing rail, which allows longer exposure times, precise focusing, and frequently obviates the need for flashes. Caterpillars, being rather sedentary creatures, certainly lend themselves to the tripod option.

Because I try to maximize depth of field and do most of my photography under low light conditions, it is usually necessary to employ flashes. Images taken with natural light are more time consuming, but completely superior. Reflector discs can add much light to your subject—silver reflectors are recommended as they do not bias the colors in your image. (An alternative is to simply cover a piece of cardboard with somewhat crumpled aluminum foil.) Position reflectors at different angles to bring out the texture of your subject. Collapsible varieties fold up and fit into a pouch for easy carrying. Digital cameras, which require less light, should make natural-light photography more routine.

What kinds of images are needed? This and most other caterpillar guides illustrate only one or a few color forms of last instar larvae. For many species, such as the inchworms and tiger moths, a collection of images would be necessary for a taxonomist to sort out which features are of most value in making definitive identifications. Photographic collections of earlier instars are sorely needed, especially for those species where the appearance changes from instar to instar. Egg and pupal images are particularly scarce. While most of the images shown here are dorsolateral views, the serious student is encouraged to acquire dorsal, ventral, and frontal (head) shots for each caterpillar, all of which may prove helpful in identification. Such images can be simple reference shots and need not be natural or aesthetically pleasing images. For example, by confining a caterpillar in a clear CD case, it is possible to get useful images of the insect's venter.

I confess. Most of the images in this guide were taken in my lab using a set of more than 30 props: boxes of sand, trays of leaves, collections of sticks, and an ever-changing bouquet of appropriate background foliage. Natural resting postures and appropriate contexts, especially if associated with careful notes, are far superior. Do not compose false or misleading images—if you find a caterpillar on one plant species, make sure you photograph it on the same. If you encounter your subject wandering on the ground do not put it on a plant to image it, unless you know the plant to be an appropriate foodplant. Lastly, have fun, be creative, and do your best to capture interesting behaviors and other images likely to tell a story or spark an interest in caterpillars.

COLLECTING, VOUCHERING, AND CONSERVATION

Much remains to be learned about the life histories of Eastern moths and butterflies. Even the weekend biologist or student can make worthwhile contributions to our knowledge. As you read through this book, taxonomic problems and uncertainties about the foodplants and life cycles will surface by the dozens: *Acronicta lobeliae*, *Bomolocha*, *Colocasia*, *Cucullia*, *Hyperstrotia*, *Paectes*, *Pyreferra*, and *Spilosoma congrua* are but a handful of those in need of study. Pick a group and start rearing. Take notes, photograph, save voucher specimens as appropriate, and most importantly, share your findings.

The value of saving larval, pupal, and adult vouchers cannot be overemphasized. Well-labeled vouchers are the ultimate reference for a collection or observation. Specimen vouchers can later be examined and reexamined, dissected, or their DNA sequenced. Such is not possible with photographs. An obvious case for the importance of vouchers is seen when a species' taxonomy is still in doubt. The familiar Spring Azure (*Celastrina ladon* complex) is a case in point. What was previously thought to represent a single species is now thought to be a complex of six or more biologically distinct entities. Much published biological or distributional information on the "Spring Azure" now must be reconsidered or, worse, discarded.

Vouchers that are well preserved, labeled, and deposited in a public institution become a scientific legacy. As my colleague Jane O'Donnell often reminds me, "If a picture is worth a thousand words, a specimen is worth a million." Specimen vouchers are of quintessential importance in morphological and taxonomic studies. If one wanted to study microscopic features or examine internal structures, a specimen would be required. Each is its own microcosm of pollen, bacteria, viruses, and other microbes that might be studied in the future. There can be little doubt that long into the future biological specimens will be "mined" for their DNA, each having the importance of a well-preserved fossil. The possibilities are almost beyond our comprehension, e.g., trace amounts of plant material in the gut could be sequenced to determine a caterpillar's diet at the time it was preserved. Toxicological residues in a specimen could be used to study the extent of environmental contamination at some fixed point in the past. Future possibilities will be limited only by the lack of preserved specimens. My vouchers will be my longest legacy. If properly cared for they will be available for centuries—I doubt that any of my books, photographs, or articles will find appreciable use beyond this century's end.

I am an advocate of collecting and rearing and careful observation. These activities are at the same time rewarding and scientifically justifiable, but, just as important, for many children, students, and amateurs, they provide an entry point into the world of entomology, systematics, and invertebrate conservation. Collecting must always be carried out in an ethical and responsible fashion. The collecting policy of The Lepidopterists' Society (http://alpha.furman.edu/~snyder/snyder/lep/) should be read and followed, regardless of whether or not the intent is to release or voucher the reared individuals. While intentions are good, something can always go wrong; never remove more than a fraction (circa 5–10%) of the number of individuals you believe to be present in a population. In those species with very conspicuous caterpillars—for example, some flower-feeding hairstreaks or tent-making nymphalids—it is easy to impact a population through overzealous collecting.

Paradoxically, undercollecting is a greater peril to most Lepidoptera than overcollecting. This is because we still need to know a great deal about most of the species in this guide before we can recognize which might be declining, understand their biological requirements, or develop management practices for their preservation. Outside of the Northeast and Upper Midwest comparatively few moths receive legal protection or are used in conservation planning, simply because we know too little about them. More specimens in collections, more records in databases, and more long-term demographic studies would allow us to identify an appreciably larger set of imperiled species. My State of Connecticut has already lost some 30 species of Lepidoptera. Many of these losses would have been preventable had we known more. Numerous aspects of the life history may be learned by collecting, rearing, and observing caterpillars, e.g., the number of annual broods, cocooning behaviors, and the overwintering stage. We desperately need observations and studies evaluating the impacts of introduced biological control agents on native caterpillars. To my way of thinking, the U.S. Department of Agriculture is far too lenient with what it will allow to be introduced. To permit the mass release in present times of an Asian wasp such as *Pimpla disparis*, whose known host range includes many of our giant silkworms, swallowtails, tiger moths, and members of more than a dozen other families of native Lepidoptera (Schaefer et al. 1989), is unconscionable. Should you become engaged in rearing, an exercise which I find deeply rewarding, remember that an important part of this process is careful observation and good record keeping, so save and label any parasitoids, and share your findings.

CATERPILLAR PROJECTS FOR SCHOOLS, NATURE CENTERS, AND UNIVERSITIES

Caterpillars are ideal for school projects because they are at the same time enormously popular, accessible, attractive, harmless, tolerant of handling, and offer abundant opportunity for real discovery. The metaphors suggested by their developmental changes are powerful and important. Metamorphosis is about change and second opportunities—the ugly duckling story: anything (or anyone) may transform; good things come in little and uncelebrated packages; or conversely, sometimes elegant creatures become average and completely plebian with time. For some, simply watching the pupal transformations will be an epiphany. I am biased, of course, but I regard metamorphosis to be one of the most glorious phenomena in nature. Either the Monarch (*Danaus plexippus*) or Painted Lady (*Vanessa cardui*) make good subjects, because their beautiful adults develop over a period of just a few weeks (and there is no diapause). The former has the advantage of being common and widespread and has considerable associated biology around which to build lesson plans. Its migration biology is marvelous. The Monarch provides a good entry into the phenomenon of mimicry (one of nature's most compelling and obvious examples of organic evolution). Additionally, the massive winter die-offs in its overwintering site will allow the class to discuss conservation issues (e.g., climate change, sustainable use of forests, or the tensions that arise among people with limited resources and immediate needs). Also, children and their parents could be sent out to look for Monarch caterpillars, an activity that by itself is fun and rewarding, even if the caterpillars prove scarce. Painted Lady caterpillars are another option; they are commercially available year-round and can be raised on artificial diet.

Below I suggest some activities and projects that will provide a chance for students to see or work with caterpillars and/or their adults. The initial ones are fine for students of all ages and especially children; the latter five are more suitable for high school and university students.

1) Plant a butterfly garden and include a section for larval foodplants. Milkweeds are a must. Pearly everlasting is a magnet for American Painted Ladies. Bush clover is used by Gray Hairstreaks, Eastern Tailed-blues, and several skippers. Nettles (including stingless varieties) will draw Red Admirals, Eastern Commas, and myriad others. Support native landscaping businesses to the extent possible.

2) Visit a butterfly house or insect zoo. Few facilities allow rearing, but these insectaries provide ample opportunity to talk about metamorphosis, food chains, pollination, and the sustainable use of tropical rain forests.

3) If you have a student who is good with a digital camera that allows close-up imaging, simply collect, rear, and photodocument the life histories of a few species each marking period. Print out (enlarged) color images and post them in the classroom.

4) Raise monarchs and get involved with Orley Taylor's Monarch Watch (http://www.monarchwatch.org/). His Web site has classroom curricula for K-6, instructions for tagging migrating monarchs, life history information, lots of images, and other resources sure to please.

5) Go out with a bed sheet and baseball bat and have the students "beat" tree foliage. Beating invariably provides abundant opportunities to talk about background matching and natural selection, warning coloration, and a laundry list of defensive strategies. Give each participant a clear plastic vial (or yogurt container with clear lid) that can be used to hold the living insect while it is passed around and examined by the students, before it is returned to its foodplant. No need to limit the discussion to caterpillars—trees and shrubs are replete with beetles, stink bugs, spiders, and other interesting animals.

6) Pick a large nearby tree and study its caterpillar fauna intensively: keep a species list of caterpillars that you encounter, record density of caterpillars per leaf or shoot and extrapolate numbers to the entire tree, and estimate seasonal changes in caterpillar biomass. Employ burlap bands around the trunk. If you can borrow a pole pruner with extensions, try comparing canopy versus subcanopy caterpillar densities. Collect feculae samples with funnels to estimate how many caterpillars might be overhead, when they are seasonally most numerous, when they do most of their feeding, etc.

7) Build clay caterpillars of various types (e.g., artificial monarchs and inchworms), tie them out in appropriate habitats, record the frequency and nature of attacks as measured by bill beaks in your clay models. Or build caterpillars with eyespots or snake mimics and see if this affects "predation." Results will vary depending on the size of your models. Experiment.

8) Nest- and shelter-forming caterpillars are environmental engineers that model and shape their environment. Try building artificial leaf shelters and see if your constructions increase caterpillar density and/or diversity and, if so, in what ways.

9) Rear wild caterpillars individually in separate containers and assess the local parasitoid fauna. What percentage of caterpillars is parasitized? Work with a taxonomist to get your parasitoids identified. Are a substantial number of your parasitoids introduced biological control agents? What are the parasitism rates of brightly or warningly colored species relative to cryptic ones?

10) If your town is using pesticides, e.g., spraying for mosquitoes, try rearing families of caterpillars (e.g., from a single clutch of eggs) on sprayed leaves versus those you believe to be free of pesticide and compare survival. Alternatively, get some foliage from a genetically engineered crop and assess its impact on a range of pest and non-pest species.

Family order follows Kristensen (1998). Within families, I follow Hodges *et al.* (1983) or use an alphabetical listing. Species within a genus are usually presented alphabetically, with some exceptions to keep similar appearing species together. Families (and some subfamilies) are introduced with information about their diversity, diagnostic features, and life history, and then conclude with collecting and rearing tips. Short summaries are sometimes used to introduce more important tribes and large genera. Because of space limitations, much information that is rightfully introductory in nature is sprinkled into the species accounts—the reader is urged to cast about the Remarks section of the species accounts to locate information with relevance across a given family.

Italics are used in the Recognition section to emphasize reliable and readily observable characters. Keep in mind that coloration and patterning can be highly variable (e.g., in the inchworms and tiger moths). It is always advisable to back up and read the family account to make sure your caterpillar agrees with characters given there. The diagnosis is intended only for last instars (e.g., it is next to useless for many penultimate dagger moths). Use coloration with caution, especially if the feature is not in italics. In many cases, I have "over-diagnosed" a species, simply because I have not yet seen the extent of variation common to a species. Body lengths are approximate—sometimes they have been estimated from the adult forewing measurements given in Covell (1984) and the relative body proportions of a given species of caterpillar. Following the length measurement, earlier instars or similar and related species are introduced.

The Occurrence section provides information on habitat, distribution, and number of annual generations. This information is poorly known for many of the moths in this guide and should be used cautiously—e.g., as one moves southward, the number of annual generations gets especially confusing and inexact. As a matter of convention, I generally circumscribe the range beginning with the northwestern portion then move in a clockwise direction. The emphasis is entirely on the eastern portion of a species' range; only occasionally do I make mention of its presence farther west or south.

The plant on which a caterpillar is found often provides a singularly valuable clue to its identity. But be cautious in assuming that the plant on which a caterpillar is discovered is, *de facto*, the foodplant. Prepupal, diseased, and parasitized caterpillars wander; caterpillars drop from their perch if alarmed; many shrub- and tree-feeding species descend into proximate vegetation during the day. In the list of Common Foodplants, I have not attempted to list all known foodplants, especially for species I regard to be polyphagous. My reviewers and I made a special effort to ferret out erroneous foodplant records and offer new or corrected information. An especially important resource with regard to foodplant records is Robinson *et al.*'s worldwide compendium of lepidopteran foodplants (http://www.nhm.ac.uk/entomology/hostplants/).

Be advised that foodplant use varies considerably across a species' range. A strict lupine specialist in New England may only eat vetch elsewhere. Magnolia is favored by the Eastern Tiger Swallowtail (*Papilio glaucus*) in North Carolina, while cherry receives more eggs in Connecticut. Blues and hairstreaks are well known for their tendency to be locally specialized but regionally generalized in diet. Another point to keep in mind, which is especially relevant to rearing caterpillars, is that many captive-bred species may consume and grow rapidly on foodplants that are seldom, if ever, used in nature. In your notes, e-mail posts, and especially published reports, differentiate between natural foodplants and those on which a captive larva was lab-reared.

The Remarks section is a hodgepodge of taxonomy, biology, economic entomology, and anything else that seemed interesting or relevant. The only consistent component is that I comment on the overwintering stage near the end of each species account, unless this information is uniform for an entire family, tribe, genus, etc., and has been mentioned previously.

Remember that information relevant to a species may often be found in the accounts of related species. For a few butterflies and moths the overwintering stage was a best guess, based on the specimen data and conversations with other workers.

Larval and adult voucher specimens for this work have been deposited at the University of Connecticut. The specimens used for the adult images in this guide bear a label denoting such. Data for adults (State only) and larvae (locality, date of collection, foodplant, collector, and photographer) are posted on my website at the University of Connecticut and digital copies are available upon request.

If you cannot find your caterpillar in this guide you might also search Old World literature. The lepidopteran fauna of Europe and Asia is more thoroughly studied and there are several books that illustrate hundreds of caterpillars in color: e.g., Sugi (1987), Porter (1997), and Beck (1999). While the caterpillars figured in these volumes will be specifically distinct from those in our fauna, in many cases, they can narrow your search to a genus or set of related species.

CLASSIFICATION AND NOMENCLATURE

The scientific name of all organisms includes two parts: the generic and specific name. The genus is always capitalized and the species name is given in lower case letters; in printed materials the scientific name is placed in italics, underscored, or in some other way distinguished from surrounding text. When a scientific name is repeated in the body of a single page or paragraph, the genus name may be abbreviated by using the first letter only, e.g., *Alsophila pometaria* may appear as *A. pometaria*. Rarely only the specific name is used. Every organism has a unique scientific name but may have multiple common (vernacular) names. For example, adult and larval stages often have different monikers. The Corn Earworm is also known as the Cotton Bollworm, Soybean Podworm, and Tomato Fruitworm. The species in this guide that are found in Quebec have a French common name. I generally tried to provide a common (English) name and a recently accepted scientific name, except where to do so proved awkward. Common names were drawn largely from Covell (1984); a few were created for this guide.

In the Linnaean system, all animals are classified in seven categories: kingdom, phylum, class, order, family, genus, and species. Butterflies and moths comprise the order Lepidoptera within the class Insecta. Representatives of 24 families are illustrated in this guide. Additional categories, beyond the seven obligatory ranks (e.g., superfamilies and subfamilies, and tribes), are frequently interpolated in classifications, especially in large or heterogeneous taxonomic groups.

CATEGORY	LATIN NAME SUFFIX	EXAMPLE	COMMON NAME SUFFIX	EXAMPLE
Superfamily	-oidea	Noctuoidea	-oids	noctuoids
Family	-idae	Noctuidae	-ids	noctuids
Subfamily	-inae	Hadeninae	-ines	hadenines
Tribe	-ini	Xylenini	-ines	xylenines
Genus	variable	*Lithophane*	not applicable	pinions

HELPFUL WEBSITES

BioQuip: (This biological supply house specializes in entomology gear and supplies.)
http://www.bioquip.com/

The Caterpillars of Guanacaste:
http://janzen.sas.upenn.edu/caterpillars/database.lasso/

HOSTS—a database of the hostplants of the World's Lepidoptera:
http://www.nhm.ac.uk/entomology/hostplants/

The Lepidopterists' Society:
http://alpha.furman.edu/~snyder/snyder/lep/

Monarch Watch:
http://www.monarchwatch.org/

North American Butterfly Association:
http://www.naba.org/

The Xerces Society:
http://www.xerces.org/

SLUG CATERPILLARS – LIMACODIDAE

Relative to other Lepidoptera, slug caterpillars seem more fantasy than reality. They are rivaled only by the prominents in the diversity of their form, color, and armament. While some are rather ordinary, rounded and sluglike, others are peculiarly angulate, lobed, or spined. One of our more striking slug caterpillars is

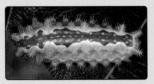

Euclea obliqua.

flattened and ringed by batteries of stinging hairs. And what may be North America's strangest caterpillar, the Monkey Slug or Hag Moth caterpillar, looks far more like the cast skin of a tarantula than it does a caterpillar. There are about 30 species in our region. Slugs are especially diverse in the tropics—more than 120 species occur in Costa Rica.

RECOGNITION

Easily recognized by an examination of their venter: instead of paired abdominal pro-legs, all have medial suckers on the first seven abdominal segments. Rather than crawl, the larvae glide. The head may be deeply retracted into the thorax. Even while feeding, the head is covered by a fleshy extension of the first thoracic segment (Epstein 1996).

LIFE HISTORY NOTES

The minute, flat, shiny, transparent eggs are laid singly or shingled in clusters on the undersides of older foliage. The egg is so thin that larval development is easily observed within. The early instars skeletonize patches of leaf tissue from either leaf surface. Larger caterpillars feed from a leaf margin, nearly always from the leaf underside. Slug caterpillars pass through several instars: usually seven but as many as nine in some species. The caterpillar passes the winter as a prepupa in a dense spherical cocoon of brown silk, impregnated with crystals of calcium oxalate that are released during the formation of the cocoon. The cocoon has a circular escape hatch (operculum) at one end that is popped open at emergence. The larvae are catholic in diet, but show a decided preference for smooth-leaved trees and shrubs: basswood, beech, cherry, maple, and oak are frequent foodplants. The fecal pellets are unique in that they have a distinctive cavity pushed into one end. Several genera possess stinging hairs whose punch is not unlike that of stinging nettle both in intensity and duration. Perhaps because of its greater size, the sting of the Saddleback Caterpillar (*Acharia stimulea*) is the most painful. The serious student of the family will want to obtain Dyar's (1896–1914) and Dyar and Morton's (1895–1896) set of papers on the New York State limacodid fauna and Epstein's (1996) monograph, which is rich in life history observations and illustrated with stunning scanning electron micrographs, photographs, and line drawings.

COLLECTING AND REARING TIPS

Limacodids come well to light—especially mercury vapor lights. Females should be held in smooth-walled containers: plastic bags, film canisters, or glass jars. Many collecting and rearing tips are scattered through the species accounts in this chapter, especially the Red-eyed Button Slug (*Heterogenea shurtleffi*) (*see* page 38).

RED-CROSSED BUTTON SLUG
Tortricidia pallida

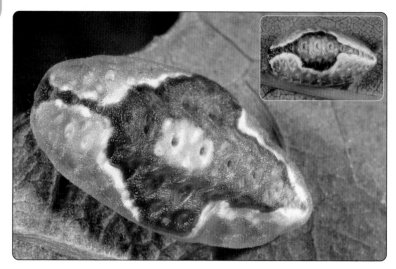

RECOGNITION Broadly oval, yellow-green, with red "coat-of-arms" mark, edged with bright red and/or brown line, embossed over dorsum. Forward-extending arm of mark flaring outward along front edge of thorax; *side arms reaching to edges of body, broad, often extending over two segments, smoothly angular; posterior extension of cross somewhat triangular, often narrowing abruptly over last segment or two.* No stinging spines. Larva to about 1cm. Early Button Slug (*Tortricidia testacea*) with more narrowed posterior arm (*see* opposite). In Abbreviated Button Slug (*T. flexuosa*) lateral arms of red dorsal mark shortened, extending only halfway to sides of body (Dyar 1899) (inset).

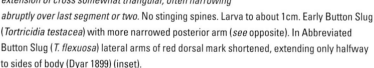

OCCURRENCE Woodlands and forests from Missouri to Connecticut south to Mississippi. Likely more widespread, especially westward, but records confused with those of Abbreviated Button Slug (*see* below). One generation northward with mature caterpillars in August and September; evidently two broods from Maryland and Missouri southward.

COMMON FOODPLANTS Beech, cherry, oak, willow, and many other woody plants.

REMARKS The development of the red buttons in *Tortricidia* is variable to the extent that some individuals cannot be reliably determined based on the characters given above. Moreover, there are no adult characters (including genitalia) that can be used to reliably separate the adults of the Red-crossed Button Slug from those of the Abbreviated Button Slug. Marc Epstein (pers. comm.) is not convinced that the two are distinct. In his support, I once had a female of what I thought was the Red-crossed Button Slug yield larvae that would key here to the Abbreviated Button Slug.

RECOGNITION Similar to previous species, broadly oval with red "coat-of-arms" mark, edged with bright red and/or brown line, over dorsum. *Posterior arm of cross often narrowed, and thus both anterior and posterior arms roughly similar in development.* Lateral arms usually reaching sides of body; typically spanning 2–3 segments (*see* inset), but sometimes narrowed to a single segment (above). Larva to about 1cm.

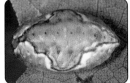

OCCURRENCE Woodlands and forests from Pacific Coast to Maine south to Georgia (in mountains) and Mississippi. One generation with mature caterpillars in July and August over much of East; Richard Heitzman (pers. comm.) records a partial second generation in Missouri.

COMMON FOODPLANTS Basswood, beech, birch, cherry, chestnut, hickory, oak, sour gum, witch hazel, and many other woody plants.

REMARKS Adults fly in May and June, nearly a month before our other button slugs. *Tortricidia* and other slug caterpillars are best found by searching the undersides of smooth-leaved, woody plants. Low branches and saplings are the most productive. Basswood, cherry, maple, and oak are good foodplants to begin your search. Cocoons may be overwintered in a cool garage; mesh-covered containers allow for easy misting or wetting once a month or so. To keep an eye on development, try what Marc Epstein does—he slices off a section of the cocoon and glues a microscope slide cover slip over the opening.

RED-EYED BUTTON SLUG
Heterogenea shurtleffi

RECOGNITION Broadly oval, smooth, *pale green caterpillar often with purple to red dorsal spot surrounded by diffuse yellow patch.* Dorsal red spot, when present, often infused with blue. Subdorsal stripes best developed rearward. *Anterior end with yellow ridge that is edged below with red.* Frequently with vague red middorsal spots over anterior segments. Rear projects to form stubby tail. Becoming translucent along sides. Larva to 1cm. Most similar in appearance to Early Button Slug (*Tortricidia testacea*) but reliably distinguished from it by yellow yoke at anterior end of body and more reduced dorsal markings.

OCCURRENCE Woodlands and forests from New York and New Hampshire (rarely) south to Florida and Texas. One generation in North; three or more southward, with mature caterpillars from May onward.

COMMON FOODPLANTS Beech, chestnut, ironwood, oak, and presumably other woody plants.

REMARKS This is a small species with rapid development, sometimes passing through its six larval instars in only a few weeks. It is unusual among our slugs in seeking out a crevice along the bark of its foodplant in which to spin its cocoon and pass the winter (Dyar 1898). To obtain eggs of slug caterpillars, hold females in smooth-walled containers: glass jars, film canisters, and self-sealing plastic bags all work. Add a small moistened plug of cotton. I incubate my eggs in open containers exposed to normal humidities, misting them lightly once every few days until they hatch. Upon emergence, I transfer each caterpillar with a pin onto the underside of a fresh oak leaf that is held in a water pick, then lightly mist the foliage so that each caterpillar will have an opportunity to drink some water.

Packardia elegans

RECOGNITION Elongate-oval, *yellow-green* slug with *pronounced tail. Dorsum dappled with darker greens and wavy (crenulate) yellow subdorsal stripes.* Pointed tail may be marked with a red line above. No stinging spines in last instar. Larva less than 1.5cm. Jeweled Tailed Slug (*Packardia geminata*) larger, blue-green, tending to be more densely pigmented with a whiter and straighter subdorsal line (inset). It co-occurs with the Elegant Tailed Slug over much of the East, and shares many of its same foodplants.

OCCURRENCE Woodlands and forests from northeastern Missouri to Quebec and Maine south to northeast Georgia. One generation with mature caterpillars from July to September.

COMMON FOODPLANTS Beech, cherry, oak, and other woody plants.

REMARKS The Elegant Tailed Slug shows a decided preference for low-growing vegetation. Caterpillars are commonly found on leaves growing within centimeters of the ground. Thin leaves on plants growing in shade are favored. The taxonomic status of a third member of the genus, *Packardia albipunctata*, is still under study, but it appears to be no more than a dark form of the Jeweled Tailed Slug. Occasionally the tail is broken off in *Packardia* larvae. For an unusual look into the world of slugs, place your caterpillar in a clear glass jar or on a glass slide and examine its transparent underside with a lens or microscope.

YELLOW-SHOULDERED SLUG
Lithacodes fasciola

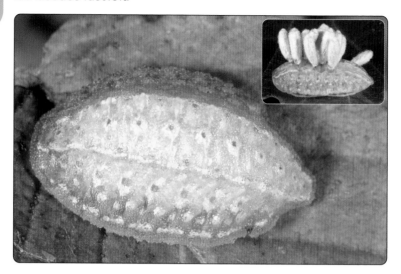

RECOGNITION Broadly *trapezoidal in cross section,* nearly two times wider than high. *Bright yellow-green with pocked and granulated surface.* Yellow subdorsal stripes connected by transverse yellow line behind head. Subspiracular stripe broken into yellow dots. Body pocked with yellow-edged depressions. Rear projects as short, squared-off tail. No stinging spines in last instar. Larva to 1.5cm. *Apoda* caterpillars are similar, but may be distinguished by the presence of dark edging along the inner side of their subdorsal stripes.

OCCURRENCE Woodlands and forests from southern Canada to Florida and Texas. One generation in North and two or more in South with mature caterpillars from May to November.

COMMON FOODPLANTS American hornbeam, apple, beech, birch, blueberry, cherry, chestnut, hickory, honey locust, hop hornbeam, linden, maple, oak, willow, and many other woody plants.

REMARKS Perhaps two-thirds of the Yellow-shouldered Slug caterpillars that I have collected have been parasitized by a tachinid fly. Parasitized caterpillars hosting a fly larva may be recognized by examining the body for a small black spot. Under a lens or microscope the blemish can be seen to be the breathing siphon of a fly maggot that is growing within the caterpillar. The slug's demise is inevitable—these attacks are always fatal and excruciatingly prolonged, with death coming only after the maggot has reached maturity and consumed much of the caterpillar's internal tissues. The caterpillar in the inset faces a similar fate having been parasitized by a braconid wasp whose 11 larvae have exited the host caterpillar and spun cocoons over its dorsum. In Connecticut the Yellow-shouldered is the most commonly encountered slug, especially on non-oak foodplants.

Apoda biguttata

RECOGNITION   *Pale blue-green* with creamy subdorsal stripe that is darkened along its inner edge. Integument granular, somewhat sparkling under hand lens. Body more or less trapezoidal in cross section. *Yellow subdorsal stripes are not connected by short transverse bar over prothorax.* Rear with *short, squared-off tail*. No stinging spines. Larva less than 2cm. Body not noticeably pocked as in the Yellow-shouldered Slug (*Lithacodes fasciola*). Yellow-collared Slug (*Apoda y-inversum*) with yellow rim along front edge of thorax, more pronounced subdorsal lines, and small blue-black spot over each segment along inner edge of subdorsal stripe; in my images body relatively higher and more trapezoidal as well (inset).

OCCURRENCE   Woodlands and forests from Missouri to Nova Scotia south to Florida and Texas. One generation in North and two or more in South with mature caterpillars from May onward.

COMMON FOODPLANTS   Especially beech and oak, but also reported from American hornbeam and hickory.

REMARKS   White oak is a preferred foodplant—searches are best focused on low branches. First instars of *Apoda* do not feed. Early instars carve distinctive tracks in the leaf as they feed, which are roughly the width of the caterpillar and 3–8 body lengths in reach.

SKIFF MOTH
Prolimacodes badia

RECOGNITION Coloration highly variable but *shape unmistakable*. Smooth, spindle-shaped caterpillar with flat dorsum and steeply angled sides. Abdomen cresting over A4 with small subdorsal flange to either side that is often brown. Posterior end produced into short, sharp tail. Rounded white spot above spiracles on A7 and A8. No stinging spines. Larva to 1.5cm.

OCCURRENCE Barrens, woodlands, and forests from Illinois to southern Maine south to Florida and Texas. One generation in North, evidently two or more southward with mature caterpillars from June onward.

COMMON FOODPLANTS Birch, blueberry, cherry, chestnut, gale, hawthorn, hop hornbeam, maple, rose, oak, poplar, willow, and many other woody plants.

REMARKS The Skiff Moth caterpillar's pattern often includes markings that resemble necrotic patches of leaf tissue. Occasionally caterpillars are found with an *unpaired*, white, oval spot on the body surface—this is the egg of a parasitic fly. Although these eggs may be removed with a pin, it is almost always too late as the fly maggot hatches quickly and is soon within the caterpillar's body. Curiously, many Skiff Moth caterpillars have a white spot on each side of the body that, at least to my eyes, resembles a tachinid fly egg. What a marvelous evolutionary ploy if this spot affords them some degree of protection (e.g., if there were a tachinid fly that ignored caterpillars assessed as having been previously parasitized by another female). Unlike many of its kin, this slug is sometimes encountered on leaf uppersides. If poked, the larva may exude clear droplets of fluid from ducts along the subdorsal flange. Males fly early and are among the first moths to arrive at lights.

Isochaetes beutenmuelleri

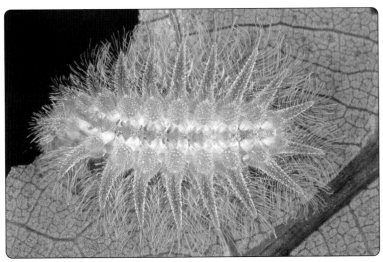

RECOGNITION *Flattened.* Late instars *pale green with crown of 18 hairy lobes that radiate from sides of body.* Largely transparent with heart and gut visible as dark green middorsal "stripe," flanked by upright translucent knobs bearing dozens of stinging spines. Last instar (inset) covered by densely setose fleshy lobes (*see* Remarks). Larva to 1cm.

OCCURRENCE Woodlands and forests from Missouri to southeastern New York south to Florida and Texas. One generation in northern part of range, evidently two or more generations in Gulf States with mature caterpillars from July onward.

COMMON FOODPLANTS Beech and oak.

REMARKS As they glide over a leaf, slug caterpillars deposit a shiny silken "runway." That of the Spun Glass Slug is easily tracked by tilting the leaf and following its shiny trail. Look for caterpillars by turning leaves or examining limbs from below—branches at chest height often yield caterpillars. The caterpillar figured here is typical for the middle through penultimate instars. The eighth and final instar is a strange insect, so enshrouded in hairs that the caterpillar's body is scarcely visible (inset). During the course of the last instar, the fleshy lobes elongate, giving the caterpillar greater height. One old account described the caterpillar as "one mass of delicate floss of finely spun glass." Prior to cocoon construction the "glass" lobes are shed.

MONKEY SLUG (HAG MOTH)
Phobetron pithecium

RECOGNITION Unique, sporting *three pairs of long "arms" and three additional pairs about half as long.* (In case you are looking for the head, two of the three shorter pairs arise from anterior end of body.) Arms deciduous—caterpillars often with missing or shortened lobes. Each arm densely packed with hairlike setae. Larva to 2.5cm.

OCCURRENCE Shrubby fields, woodlands, and forests from Quebec to Maine south to Florida and Arkansas. One generation in North and two or more in South, with mature caterpillars from June to November.

COMMON FOODPLANTS Apple, ash, birch, cherry, chestnut, dogwood, hickory, oak, persimmon, walnut, and willow, as well as many other woody shrubs and trees.

REMARKS Contrary to Forbes (1923) and popular belief, this caterpillar does not sting (or at least I failed to get a response from the single individual that I pressed into my arm). It is claimed that the Monkey Slug mimics the cast skin of a tarantula. At first I regarded the notion as fanciful, since over much of its range in the United States there are no tarantulas. Yet, credence is lent to the supposition when one considers that *Phobetron* is principally a tropical genus and that many of our eastern insectivorous birds winter in the Neotropics. My colleague Richard Heitzman has suggested that the adult female Monkey Slug mimics a bee, even to the point of having her legs appearing to be well provisioned with pollen (via her enlarged mesotibial scale tufts). Her largely diurnal mate (shown here), on the other hand, is clearly a wasp mimic. If ever there was a moth with reason for an identity crisis it is the Monkey Slug—should the above prove correct, then the same insect mimics three different organisms depending on its age and sex.

RECOGNITION *Stocky, trapezoidal in cross section.* Green with two rows of stinging spines down each side. Dorsal spines borne from red-orange warts connected by yellow stripe that extends rearward from T2. Faint beaded pattern running down dorsum. Larva to 2cm.

OCCURRENCE Woodlands and forests from Missouri to Long Island south to Florida and Mississippi. One generation through much of its eastern range, but with additional broods from Missouri southward where mature caterpillars occur from July onward.

COMMON FOODPLANTS American hornbeam, beech, chestnut, hickory, hop hornbeam, oak, and other woody plants.

REMARKS Upon completing a molt, slugs have the curious habit of consuming their old skin—it is unclear if the skin provides nutrients or this is done to "sanitize" the leaf where the caterpillar soon will be taking meals. The stinging spines of Nason's Slug are retractile: normally only their tips are exposed, but spines may be quickly everted and splayed in the presence of danger. Although regarded as generally scarce, this species is among the most common slugs in foothills of the southern Appalachians. *Natada* is an enormous worldwide genus—seven species fly sympatrically at La Selva Biological Station, a lowland tropical rainforest in northeastern Costa Rica, where I work.

CROWNED SLUG
Isa textula

RECOGNITION *Pale green, flattened, with lobes bearing numerous stinging spines radiating out from perimeter of body.* Additional stinging hairs arise from paired lobes running down dorsum. Middorsum often marked with red or yellow, especially in latter instars and over segments towards rear of body. Anterior end of body produced forward and edged with orange or red. Larva to 1.5cm.

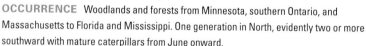

OCCURRENCE Woodlands and forests from Minnesota, southern Ontario, and Massachusetts to Florida and Mississippi. One generation in North, evidently two or more southward with mature caterpillars from June onward.

COMMON FOODPLANTS Commonly oak, also basswood, beech, elm, hickory, maple, and other woody plants.

REMARKS Upon encountering the Crowned Slug, one's first impression might be that this creature has somehow lost its way out of an Amazonian jungle. In fact, other *Isa* and related slugs are primarily tropical in distribution. So in a sense, with this slug we enjoy a bit of the jungle here in eastern North America. Grazing early-instar *Isa* caterpillars leave telltale zigzagging tracks, scarcely wider than the caterpillar, in the lower side of the leaf. The caterpillars may be active very late in the season, sometimes dropping down with autumn rains and winds. The first instars of our stinging slugs (e.g., *Acharia*, *Adoneta*, *Euclea*, *Isa*, *Monoleuca*, *Natada*, and *Parasa*) do not feed—perhaps, not surprisingly, this instar lasts but a day or two (Dyar 1896–1914).

Adoneta spinuloides

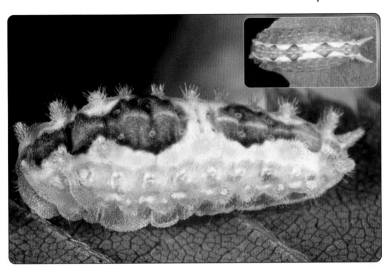

RECOGNITION Small with *undulating red- to purple-brown dorsal markings bounded with lemon yellow*. Body flattened above, sloping downward at rear of body. Sides blue-green. Anterior end with three pairs of reddish spine-tipped knobs; posterior end with one, larger, gumdrop-shaped pair. Lateral row of green stinging spines. Larva to about 1cm. A second member of the genus, *Adoneta bicaudata*, occurs locally in the East. The purple is more restricted in extent, limited mostly to two, rounded, diamond-shaped spots over the abdomen which are connected by a narrow middorsal line (inset). The posterior knobs are hornlike, being more narrowed, inwardly curved, and 2–3 times longer than those of *A. spinuloides*.

OCCURRENCE Woodlands and forests from Missouri to southern Quebec south to Florida and Mississippi. One generation in North, evidently two or more southward with mature caterpillars from June onward.

COMMON FOODPLANTS American hornbeam, basswood, bayberry, beech, birch, black gum, cherry, chestnut, oak, willow, and other woody plants.

REMARKS August and September are good months for "slug searches" in the Northeast. Early successional and open woodlands or woodland edges seem to be the most productive. Turn branches and inspect leaf undersides. Low-growing limbs and leaves on saplings are best. The sting of the Purple-crested Slug is mild, scarcely noticeable after just a few minutes. Like so many of our slugs, it is susceptible to attack by a tachinid fly, whose presence can be detected by carefully inspecting the integument for the fly maggot's black anal breathing tube, which the maggot pushes out through one wall of the caterpillar's body.

PIN-STRIPED VERMILION SLUG
Monoleuca semifascia

RECOGNITION *Salmon, pink, or most commonly bright red with dorsal and lateral areas each with set of three thin blue-black stripes.* Fascicles of 20 or more short, whitish, stinging spines grouped in four lines that run length of body. *Anterior end bears four dark (gumdrop-like) conical projections of equal size*; posterior end with only two proportionately longer projections. Two prominent patches of dark deciduous spines at posterior end of body. Larva less than 2cm.

OCCURRENCE Barrens northward, dry woodlands and forests in the South; Missouri to Long Island south to Florida and Texas. One generation northward with mature caterpillars in August and September; present throughout much of year in Florida.

COMMON FOODPLANTS Cherry, oak, pecan, persimmon, and presumably many other woody plants.

REMARKS This is a species of barrens and xeric woodlands. The three other *Monoleuca* that are listed by Kimball (1965) from Florida appear to represent nothing more than forms of the Pin-striped Vermilion Slug. The eggs, laid in clusters of 20 or more, are quite unlike those of other slugs: rather than being flattened, they are somewhat raised and covered with hairlike scales from the female's abdomen.

Euclea delphinii

RECOGNITION Exceptionally variable in color but *recognizable by its overall shape and the two or four patches of black deciduous spines at rear of body* (in last two instars). Ground color pink, orange, red, yellow, green, or tan. Anterior end possessing three pairs of elongate, subdorsal lobes each bearing numerous stinging spines; posterior end with two pairs of elongated subdorsal lobes. Sides with shallow depressions ringed with black or white situated between subdorsal and subspiracular lobes. Larva to 2cm. Stinging Rose Caterpillar (*Parasa indetermina*) has longer lobes, no detachable spine patches, and distinctive pinstriping over dorsum and sides.

OCCURRENCE Barrens, woodlands, and forests from Missouri to southern Quebec and Maine south to Florida and Texas. A single generation over much of East with caterpillars from late June to October; two generations in Missouri and presumably more in Deep South.

COMMON FOODPLANTS Apple, ash, basswood, beech, birch, blueberry, cherry, chestnut, hackberry, hickory, maple, oak, poplar, sycamore, willow, and many other woody plants.

REMARKS Eggs are laid singly or in small clusters. Dyar (1896) regarded Spiny Oak Slug caterpillars to be somewhat secretive and noted that they sometimes hide between leaves by day. Although exceeding other slugs in number of spines, the sting is mild, considerably less severe than that of the Saddleback Caterpillar (*Acharia stimulea*). The dark spine clusters, which are added in the last two instars to the rear of the body, are curiously variable in their expression—they may be essentially absent, occur as a single pair, or, as is most often the case, be represented by two pairs of four dark gumdrop-shaped patches. A tachinid fly has deposited two eggs (the white spots) on the larva in the lower right image.

SMALLER PARASA
Parasa chloris

RECOGNITION *Strongly humpbacked pink, tan, or orange caterpillar with white and red-edged venter and elongate "tail."* Abdomen marked with vague wavy lines. Anterior end with three fascicles of whitish stinging spines: largest group arising from top of hump. Posterior end with two prominent clusters of whitish stinging spines. Smaller spine clusters, which follow along a black subdorsal line, connect the two groups. Larva less than 2cm. Earlier instars less angulate with rosettes of exposed spines (inset)—while resembling a *Euclea*, the young caterpillars are distinctly humpbacked with enlarged anterior segments.

OCCURRENCE Barrens, woodlands, and forests from Missouri to southern New England south to Florida and Texas. One principal generation with mature caterpillars from July to October; at least a partial second generation from Missouri southward.

COMMON FOODPLANTS Apple, beech, birch, cherry, dogwood, elm, oak, and many other woody plants.

REMARKS Look for caterpillars on the leaf undersides of shaded branches. The stinging spines are retractible, with only the tips protruding when the caterpillar is feeding or resting. Once alarmed, the fleshy warts, bearing batteries of stinging spines, are everted.

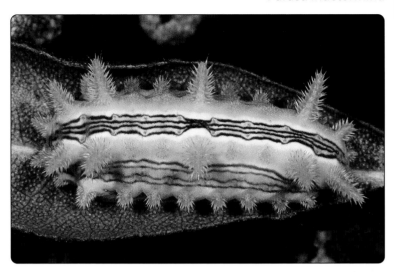

RECOGNITION Yellow, orange, or red caterpillar with *long, subdorsal lobes bearing numerous stinging spines on T2, T3, A1, A4, A7, and A8*. No patches of dark deciduous stinging spines at posterior end of body. Dorsum marked with four dark and three pale pinstripes; *sides of body also with four black pinstripes*. Larva to 2cm.

OCCURRENCE Coastal scrub, barrens, woodlands, and forests from Illinois to Long Island south to Florida and Texas. Evidently at least a partial second generation from Missouri southward with mature caterpillars from late June onward.

COMMON FOODPLANTS Apple, cherry, dogwood, gale, hickory, maple, oak, poplar, rose, and many other woody plants.

REMARKS Slugs soon become a favorite of most caterpillar hunters, largely because of their interesting forms and beautiful colors. They have even more to offer to those who have access to a dissecting microscope. The flat, transparent eggs allow one to watch the entire development of the caterpillar—a fascinating exercise to be sure.

SADDLEBACK CATERPILLAR
Acharia stimulea

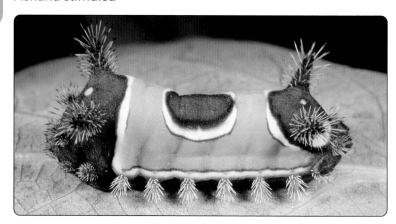

RECOGNITION A striking and aptly named caterpillar sporting beautiful *greenish saddle over the abdomen*. Saddle edged with white inwardly and outwardly. *Lobes at either end of body fiercely armed with stinging spines*. Larva to 3cm. In younger caterpillars body color more rusty and sting-bearing lobes at either end proportionately longer.

OCCURRENCE Fields, gardens, edges of wetlands, and woodlands, from Missouri to Massachusetts south to Florida and Texas. One generation over much of range with mature caterpillars from August through October.

COMMON FOODPLANTS Generalist on many plants including apple, aster, blueberry, buttonbush, cabbage, citrus, corn, grass, maple, oak; commonly reported from a variety of garden and ornamental species.

REMARKS Egg are laid in clutches. Initially Saddleback Caterpillars are gregarious, feeding in groups of 30–50 individuals. Older larvae are solitary (although some of its tropical relatives remain clustered). The sting of the Saddleback Caterpillar may be the most potent of any North American caterpillar. In part this is due to the caterpillar's size. The length and diameter of the stinging spines are considerably greater than those of the other slugs in our region. In addition, it has an enormous number of stinging spines, especially about the two ends of the body. When prodded the caterpillar arches its body in such a way as to bring more spines to bear on its attacker. Because the larval spines may accumulate about the cocoon, even this must be handled carefully if stings are to be avoided. The adult is uncommon at light, even in places where the caterpillars are frequently encountered.

Although they appear soft and harmless, flannel moth larvae are among our most well-defended insects. Beneath the soft outer hair are warts fortified with hollow, poison-filled stinging spines that are capable of delivering painful stings. Only four species of this largely Neotropical family extend into our region. The biological station where I work in Costa Rica is home to 15 species; the country has in excess of 40. Caterpillars of one particularly large Amazonian species reach more than 8cm; stings from this behemoth, "el raton" (the rat), have purportedly resulted in human deaths.

RECOGNITION
Accessory prolegs on abdominal segments A2 and A7 (in addition to normal complement on A3–A6) immediately distinguish our flannel moths. Neither pair of the accessory prolegs bears crochets in our North American species. Three rows of setal tufts (subdorsal, supraspiracular, and subspiracular) bear mixtures of stinging and longer hairlike setae. Look for a fleshy lobe positioned behind each of the spiracles (these are visible in White Flannel Moth image, *see* page 56).

LIFE HISTORY NOTES
The eggs are covered with hairlike scales from the female abdomen. Our megalopygids appear to be broadly polyphagous on woody plants. Like slug caterpillars, the head is enveloped by the thorax when the caterpillar is feeding (*see* image of White Flannel Moth). They overwinter in a dense, grayish, spindle-shaped cocoon often spun along the lower trunk of the food-plant. Adults emerge through a circular operculum at one end of the cocoon.

Reaction to the stings may be severe. Even hairs from the body may be problematic for some. Do not leave caterpillars where others, and especially children, might unknowingly handle these seemingly harmless creatures. Until potential symptoms and dangers are better understood, I recommend leaving these caterpillars where you find them. What few collecting and rearing tips I can add for flannel moths appear in the species accounts.

Larval development in Black-waved Flannel Caterpillar (Megalopyge crispata)

BLACK-WAVED FLANNEL CATERPILLAR
Megalopyge crispata (= *Lagoa crispata*)

RECOGNITION Orange to gray, densely hairy caterpillar with variously developed middorsal crest of darker setae. *Body tapering rearward to wispy tail that scarcely extends beyond body.* Larva less than 3cm. Earlier instars bear a wild flurry of long white setae (*see* top image on page 53). Caterpillars of Yellow Flannel Moth (*Megalopyge pyxidifera*) indistinguishable to my eye; Pennsylvania south to Florida and Mississippi.

OCCURRENCE Fields with woody growth, woodlands, and forests, from Missouri to New Hampshire (especially along coast in New England) south to Florida and Louisiana. One generation northward; presumably two or more southward with mature caterpillars from June onward.

COMMON FOODPLANTS Alder, apple, birch, blackberry, cherry, hackberry, oak, persimmon, poplar, sassafras, wax myrtle, willow, witch hazel, and many other woody plants.

REMARKS A good way to find caterpillars is to go into fields with widely scattered cherry saplings. Examine the underside of leaves on branches growing within a meter or so of the ground. Coastal meadows and fields are productive in southern New England. Once, while servicing my caterpillar collections, I managed to inhale what I suspect were setae from a *Megalopyge* caterpillar (or its cast skin). This precipitated a severe reaction: my nose started dripping, then running, but soon thereafter clogged completely. Pressure started to build in my sinus (just on one side), enough to put considerable internal pressure on my eye. About this time I decided to check myself into the nearest emergency room, where I did what most do in emergency rooms—sit and wait. Fortunately, the reaction subsided within an hour, so I discharged myself, and returned home to finish servicing my caterpillar collections. Thereafter, I have been reluctant to reproduce this experience by "reinoculating" myself.

RECOGNITION   Densely hairy, gray to tan caterpillar with middorsal crest of rusty to smoky setae. *Body tapering rearward to thick tail that extends well beyond body* (greater than two body segments). Larva less than 3cm. Middle instar disheveled, with long, often curly hairs extending in all directions and a tangle of rusty and smoky setae over dorsum; pelt considerably sparser— stinging spines visible along sides of body; "tail" setae long but not gathered into bundle (inset below).

OCCURRENCE   Woodlands and forests from Missouri (historic?) to Maryland south to Florida and Texas. In Deep South it has multiple generations with mature caterpillars from spring onward.

COMMON FOODPLANTS   Widely polyphagous on woody plants. Covell (1984) lists almond, apple, birch, hackberry, oak, orange, pecan, persimmon, and rose.

REMARKS   This caterpillar is known locally in Texas and elsewhere as the Asp. Reports of stings are common, especially from the Gulf States. People are occasionally stung while doing yard work or walking off-trail through woodlands, when the caterpillars are inadvertently brushed. The sting described below by Joe Culin (for the White Flannel Moth) is probably a typical reaction for our Megalopygids. Sensitive individuals who begin to develop systemic symptoms should seek immediate medical attention. Gravid females lay readily if held in a container for a night or two.

WHITE FLANNEL MOTH
Norape ovina

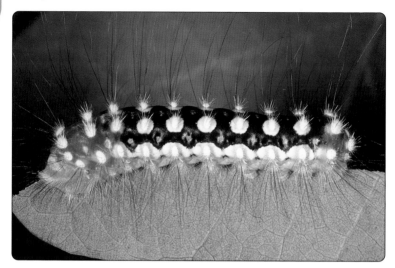

RECOGNITION *Distinctively patterned yellow, orange, and black caterpillar.* Stinging spines and postspiracular lobes clearly visible. Some lateral hairs more than two times body width. *Dark quadrangular patch over dorsum of A1–A7.* Thoracic segments smoky orange above. Larva less than 3cm.

OCCURRENCE Fields and woodlands from Missouri to Washington DC south to Florida and Texas. Two generations over most of range with mature caterpillars from late May onward; presumably with additional broods in Deep South.

COMMON FOODPLANTS Black locust, greenbrier, elm, hackberry, redbud, and presumably other woody plants. This caterpillar was reared on shade leaves of white oak.

REMARKS My colleague Joe Culin had this to stay about the White Flannel Moth: "…the guy who collected it said that it stung him but I picked it up with my fingertips and did not get stung. So, perhaps fool that I am, I gently rubbed the inside of my wrist over it. It took probably a minute and a half or two minutes, but it started with an itchy burning that within five minutes turned to a red spot the size of a quarter. After about 15 minutes, three white blisters appeared that lasted about two hours, burning the whole time, but gradually diminishing in intensity (the blisters also shrank to nothing in that time). After the blisters disappeared, the itching lasted another several hours, and the redness until the next morning." This caterpillar (shown above) took eight weeks to mature in the lab.

This heterogeneous family of about 1,000 species is most diverse in the Neotropics and Old World. Only four of the 22 species that occur north of Mexico are found in the East; most of the others are Southwestern. The caterpillars are stout and often flattened. As in related families, the head is partially covered by a fleshy extension of the prothorax. In our species the crochets, all of one size, are in a single band. At least two of the Eastern species feed on grape as do many Western smoky moths. Oddly, caterpillars of the Orange-patched Smoky Moth (*Pyromorpha dimidiata*) feed on dead leaves.

GRAPELEAF SKELETONIZER
Harrisina americana

RECOGNITION Boldly set with *ten bright yellow and 11 black bands*. Black bands include tufts of short, shiny black setae. *Gregarious*. Black subdorsal stripe with spur reaching subventer on T3 and A1. Sides waxy white. Four long white setae extend from either end of body. Larva to 1.5cm.

OCCURRENCE Fields and woodland edges from Missouri to New Hampshire south to Florida and Texas. One generation northward; up to three broods in Missouri with mature caterpillars from late May onward; breeding nearly year-round in parts of Florida and Texas.

COMMON FOODPLANTS Grape and Virginia creeper.

REMARKS Gregarious in early instars but then striking out in small groups; solitary by last instar. The larval aggregations, always on leaf undersides, are impressive with dozens of the bright, warningly colored caterpillars lined up side by side. Contact with the larvae (hairs) may result in a rash for 1–3 days. The life cycle takes about 65 days with 40 of these spent as a caterpillar. The pupa overwinters in a cocoon spun among fallen leaves at the base of the foodplant.

SKIPPERS – HESPERIIDAE

More than 280 skippers have been recorded north of Mexico, although a great many of these occur only along our southern border and especially in Texas. Skippers are very diverse in the tropics, particularly across ecotones where early successional areas and forest intermix. Although skippers are our most numerous lepidopteran garden visitors, few people are familiar with their distinctive caterpillars: they are a furtive lot, feeding at night and retiring to silken leaf shelters by day. The majority of our grass-feeding species are seldom seen. Because only a few skipper caterpillars are apt to be encountered by users of this guide, I have given them short shrift, especially the grass skippers (*Hesperiinae*). Readers are encouraged to consult Allen (1997), Allen *et al.* (2005), and Minno *et al.* (2005), which do more to give skipper caterpillars their due.

RECOGNITION

The narrow neck and enlarged head will distinguish nearly all of our skippers. The body is somewhat spindle-shaped, usually thickest in the midabdominal segments, and densely vested in short, fine setae (a hand lens may be needed to appreciate their number). Skippers possess an anal comb (a toothed, fan-shaped plate above the anus) that facilitates the ejection of their excreta. The crochets of two or three different lengths are arranged in a circle.

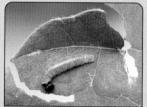

LIFE HISTORY NOTES

The relatively large hemispherical eggs are laid singly or, rarely, in small clusters. All instars construct shelters. Early instars either roll a leaf (grass-feeders) or cut two transverse channels into a blade, draw the free section upward, fold it over, and tie down the flap with silk (insets). Many grass skippers incorporate wax from glands on their abdominal venter into the walls of the shelter and cocoon. Nearly all overwinter as partly to fully-fed larvae.

COLLECTING AND REARING TIPS

The best way to secure livestock may be to follow an ovipositing female and gather a few eggs. Finding caterpillars of those species that feed on dicotyledonous foodplants is practically routine—the characteristic leaf-flap shelters are recognizable at a distance. By contrast, I have had little success searching for grass skippers. Watch for rolled leaves (young instars) or tubular shelters incorporating a few leaves (middle and late instars). In bunch grass-feeders it is often possible to find accumulations of pale brown frass in the vicinity of the larva. Patience or doses of luck are required—grass skippers rarely occur in high density. Often it is possible to switch grass- and sedge-feeders from their original foodplant to yard grasses such as bluegrass and orchard grass. I often supply potted grasses and sleeve the container, so that I do not have to worry about the daily maintenance of the caterpillars.

Temperate representatives have rather modest patterning and tend to be heavily salted with minute white spots. Many feed on broad-leaved plants, especially members of the pigweed (*Chenopodiaceae*), legume (*Fabaceae*), mallow (*Malvaceae*), and oak (*Fagaceae*) families. Foodplant identifications are helpful in establishing larval identities. The large eggs are ribbed or have reticulations.

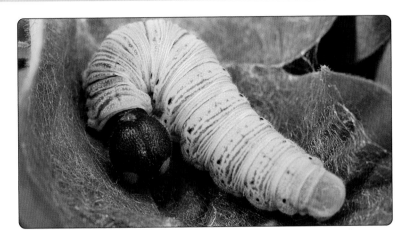

SILVER-SPOTTED SKIPPER
Epargyreus clarus

RECOGNITION Readily recognized by its *yellow color, somewhat wrinkled appearance, and bold orange head spots*. Each body segment ringed with alternating yellow and green bands. Often with elongate dark spot above spiracle on A1–A7. Larva to 3.5cm. Zestos Skipper (*Epargyreus zestos*) similar, but yellow rings subdued and averaging more green; it feeds on *Galactia* in southern Florida.

OCCURRENCE Woodland and forest clearings, fields, gardens, and empty lots from lower Canada south in East to Florida and Texas. Two or three generations over most of range with mature caterpillars from June onward; throughout growing season in Deep South.

COMMON FOODPLANTS Cassia, false indigo, groundnut, locust, rose acacia, wisteria, and other legumes.

REMARKS Skippers employ their anal comb to forcibly propel their excreta from the feeding shelter. The comb works as a mechanical latch that engages tissue about the anus. After a frass pellet has been pushed to the ready position, blood pressure in the hind end is increased to as much as 60 millibars before the comb finally releases and sends the pellet sailing—up to 153cm or 38 body lengths in this species (Weiss 2003). As both predatory and parasitic wasps are known to use the volatiles in feculae to locate their prey, there are clear survival advantages to caterpillars that have evolved mechanisms to "ballistically" eject their droppings.

BEAN LEAF ROLLER (LONG-TAILED SKIPPER)
Urbanus proteus

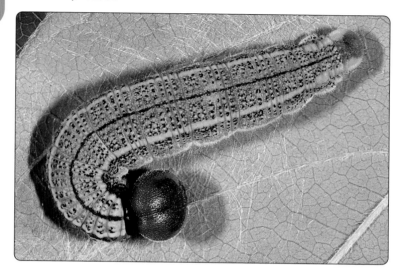

RECOGNITION Yellow-green caterpillar with fine black middorsal, broader yellow subdorsal, and creamy subspiracular stripes. *Adjacent to eyes, orange spots separated by large, black medial spot.* T1 with shiny black thoracic shield. *Subdorsal stripe gives way to diffuse orange patch over A8 that continues to anal plate.* Midabdominal prolegs marked with orange. Larva to 3.5cm. Dorantes Longtail (*Urbanus dorantes*) more subdued in coloration: head more uniformly brown, body tending towards brown, and subdorsal stripes wanting; beggar's ticks and other legumes. Several other Longtails (*Urbanus*) species occur sporadically in the Rio Grande Valley of Texas.

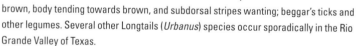

OCCURRENCE Forest edges, pinelands, fields, gardens, and other open habitats. Resident in Florida and Texas and perhaps along Gulf north to coastal South Carolina, straying northward to coastal New England, Illinois, and Kansas; at least three generations in Deep South with mature caterpillars throughout growing season.

COMMON FOODPLANTS Beans, beggar's ticks, butterfly pea, and others; especially viney legumes.

REMARKS The larva feeds concealed within a leaf shelter. The caterpillar makes its "nest" by drawing up the edges of a single leaflet or silking together two or more overlapping leaves. Through the course of its development, each larva will make several shelters, typically in the vicinity of one another. Opler (1992) notes that Longtails are freeze-intolerant and overwinter as reproductively arrested adults in tropical and subtropical areas of mild climate.

RECOGNITION Green to pinkish with smoky middorsal and orange subdorsal stripe running length of abdomen. Nearly black head and prothoracic shield. *Setae on head erect. Upper half of body densely salted with orange to white spots* that are especially conspicuous over dorsum. Spiracles relatively large, blackened. Larva to 3.5cm. Cloudywings (*Thorybes*) have similar caterpillars, but are less hairy, and the setae on head are shorter, down-curved, and mostly directed forward.

OCCURRENCE Woodland and forest trails and edges in North; oak and pine woodlands in South. Wisconsin to central New Hampshire, south to northern Florida and eastern Texas. In Northeast, one generation with caterpillars maturing late July to September; two broods over much of East with mature caterpillars from May onward.

COMMON FOODPLANTS Beggar's ticks and less frequently bush clover and wild indigo.

REMARKS Throughout its range the Hoary Edge has a long flight period, and often small facultative broods—expect to find the occasional caterpillar out of season. In the fall, mature larvae crawl down into leaf litter to form cocoons in which they will spend the winter. Pupation follows with the return of warmer springtime temperatures. Given that adults of the Hoary Edge are more apt to frequent wooded and partially shaded areas, I expect that the caterpillars also occur on plants found in more shaded areas than those routinely utilized by our cloudywings.

NORTHERN CLOUDYWING
Thorybes pylades

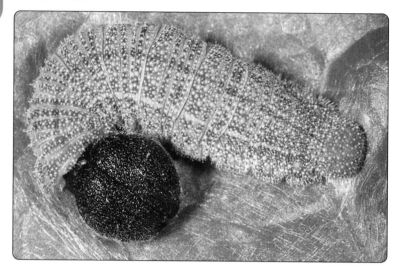

RECOGNITION *Pale green to brown body vested in short hairs, many of which arise from creamy spots.* Vague or blurry smoky middorsal stripe and a creamy to yellow subdorsal stripe that typically begins on T3 and runs to A8. Spiracles pale. Larva to 3cm. I am unaware of characters that can be used to separate caterpillars of the Northern Cloudywing from those of Southern Cloudywing (*Thorybes bathyllus*) and Confusing Cloudywing (*T. confusis*).
Also similar to Hoary Edge (*Achalarus lyciades, see* page 61) but not as hairy and the hairs on head directed forward in cloudywings.

OCCURRENCE Forest and woodland clearings, powerline right of ways, brushy fields, grasslands, and meadows, from central Canada south in East through Florida and much of Texas. A single generation in Northeast with caterpillars maturing in July and August; two or more broods in Missouri; present throughout the growing season in parts of Florida, along Gulf, and southern Texas.

COMMON FOODPLANTS Many legumes including beggar's ticks and bush clover.

REMARKS The aforementioned legume-feeding skippers (*Achalarus* and *Thorybes*) are conspicuous in their egg-laying behavior. A sporting way to secure livestock of known identity is to follow females as they move about patches of their foodplants. Ovipositing females have a distinctive fluttering flight, with frequent touchdowns to "taste" foliage of possible foodplants with their feet and genitalia. Presumably the caterpillars leave the plant and seek a cocooning site in leaf litter. Pupation presumably occurs in the spring. Careful study of our cloudywings will surely reveal differences in the larval characters and habits of our three Eastern species.

Erynnis icelus

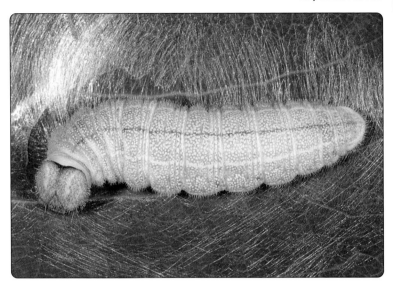

RECOGNITION Most readily distinguished by its diet, being our *only willow- and poplar-feeding skipper.* Pale green ground color abundantly dappled with white dots. Heart visible as darkened green middorsal stripe; creamy subdorsal stripe most evident on A1–A8. Head brown to orange-brown without prominent orange spots of many of our other duskywings. Larva to 2.5cm.

OCCURRENCE Forest clearings and roads, wet meadows, fields, and other open areas near rivers, lakes, and other bodies of water from central Canada south in East to northern Georgia and Alabama (mountains) and Ozarks. One generation with mature (overwintering) caterpillars from August to May.

COMMON FOODPLANTS Aspen, poplar and willow, but also locust (*see* below), as well as birch.

REMARKS Once one develops a search image for the larval shelters, caterpillars can be reliably found from June until leaf fall, especially by searching aspen. I have found caterpillars feeding on locust on two occasions. In many parts of the Appalachians bristly locust appears to be the principal foodplant of this skipper. While I initially suspected these individuals represented a cryptic species, I now am leaning toward the notion that duskywings may be more polyphagous than previously thought (cf. Juvenal's Duskywing). Opler (1992) also lists birch as a foodplant. The fully-fed larva overwinters in its shelter, dropping to the ground with leaf fall. In all our duskywings pupation occurs in late winter or early spring, often in a newly made leaf shelter.

JUVENAL'S DUSKYWING
Erynnis juvenalis

RECOGNITION Ground color ranges from pale waxy to yellow-green. Markings over body like those of other duskywings: there is a *green heart line and pale subdorsal stripe*, either or both of which may be indistinct. *Three orange spots on each side of light to deep orange-brown head*, occasionally upper two spots may fuse. Larva to 3cm. Two other oak-feeding duskywings

are widespread in East. Caterpillar of Horace's Duskywing (*Erynnis horatius*) tends to be a lighter, waxy blue-green, but there is significant overlap in appearance; unlike the Juvenal's Duskywing it is multiple-brooded. The head of the Sleepy Duskywing (*E. brizo*) often has only the lowermost orange spot (Scott 1986), although Allen (1997) figures a larva with all three sets. Additional oak-feeding *Erynnis* occur in south and west Texas. Until reliable characters are discovered, the identification of oak-feeding duskywings should be confirmed through rearing.

OCCURRENCE Forest clearings and roads, woodlands, balds, and oak barrens, straying into many habitats from southern Canada south in East to Florida and eastern Texas. One brood with mature (over-wintering) caterpillars from August to April.

COMMON FOODPLANTS Oaks; hickory frequently used in New Jersey (Bob Barber pers. comm.).

REMARKS The caterpillars are slow-growing, taking the whole summer to mature. The fully-fed caterpillar holes up in its leaf shelter and falls to the ground with other leaves. Bob Barber sent this series of three images in which a late season caterpillar's coloration mirrors that of the leaf upon which it has fashioned its shelter.

October 7

October 13

October 27

Pyrgus communis

RECOGNITION One of many skippers with a waxy green to pinkish body, ill-defined markings, and numerous whitish speckles. Gray-green heart line and creamy subdorsal stripes. *Body hairs, although short, proportionately longer than those of many other open-winged skippers, particularly, those setae arising from the reddish brown prothoracic "collar."* Larva to 2.5cm. Identification over most of range routine because it is the only skipper on Malvaceae, but in South (and especially Texas and Arizona) identifications should be confirmed through rearing. I am unfamiliar with characters that distinguish its caterpillars from those of other checkered-skippers (e.g., *Pyrgus oileus* and *P. albescens*), the Common Streaky-skipper (*Celotes nessus*), and other mallow-feeding skippers in the South and West. White-skippers (*Heliopetes*) have longer, pale brown hairs over head and the prothoracic collar bears more numerous and proportionately smaller setae. Two common species occur in south Texas, the most common one on mallows is the Laviana White-skipper (*H. laviana*).

OCCURRENCE Dry open habitats with exposed ground, such as beaches, streambeds, roadsides, waste lots, and farmyards. Resident from South Dakota to Virginia and southward, but straying to southern Canada and New England most summers. Two generations northward with a partial third as far north as West Virginia, where mature caterpillars occur from June onward (Allen 1997); continuously brooded in Deep South.

COMMON FOODPLANTS Mallow, hollyhock, and other members of the mallow family.

REMARKS A good species to search for when you are trapped at the mall or the car breaks down. Seriously, the Common Checkered-skipper is apt to turn up anywhere with dry open ground with mallows.

COMMON SOOTYWING
Pholisora catullus

RECOGNITION Body waxy green with multitude of white or yellow spots. Heart and subdorsal stripes thin and inconspicuous or absent. Adjacent segments often separated by yellowish ring. Head nearly black and without spots. *Black prothoracic collar broken over midline.* Larva to 2.5cm. Caterpillar of Hayhurst's

Scallopwing (S*taphylus hayhurstii*), which feeds alongside the Common Sootywing on pigweeds (Chenopodiaceae) and amaranths (Amaranthaceae), may be distinguished by its brown prothoracic shield and faint white subdorsal stripe. Some individuals have a reddish cast, especially posteriorly. A third species, the Mazans Scallopwing (S*taphylus mazans*), occurs from eastern and central Texas southward.

OCCURRENCE Farms, waste lots, and other disturbed habitats. North Dakota to central New England south to northern Florida and Texas in our area. Two full generations in Connecticut with mature (overwintering) caterpillars from fall through early spring, then again in July and August; three broods in Missouri and southern New Jersey; presumably occurring nearly year-round in parts of Deep South.

COMMON FOODPLANTS Pigweeds or lamb's quarters and amaranths, occasionally cockscomb.

REMARKS The pink-red eggs are laid singly on the upper side of a leaf. Like related species, the larva makes a shelter by severing the leaf along two parallel channels and then pulling the leaf edge up and over itself. The larva ventures out at night to consume leaf tissues adjacent to its shelter. In the fall, the mature larva falls to the ground and overwinters in a leaf shelter. Pupation occurs within the shelter in the spring. The Common Sootywing is one of our most easily located skippers—usually a five-minute search in a patch of pigweed is all that is necessary to find this insect from late July onward. Allen (1997) gives a nice account of its life history.

SICKLE-WINGED SKIPPER *Eantis tamenund*

Resident in south Texas, straying northward. Mature caterpillars year-round. Prickly ash and citrus.

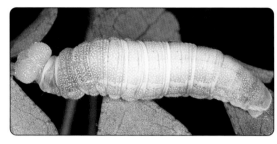

FLORIDA DUSKYWING *Ephyriades brunneus*

Southern third of Florida. Mature caterpillars year-round. Key byrsonima (or locustberry) and Barbados cherry.

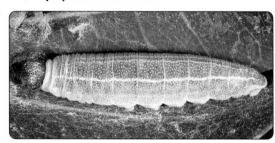

MANGROVE SKIPPER *Phocides pigmalion*

Coastal Florida. Mature caterpillars year-round. Red mangrove. Early and middle instars bright red with yellow bars over dorsum.

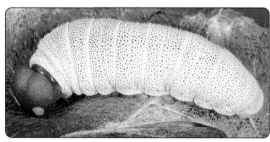

HAMMOCK SKIPPER *Polygonus leo*

Southern Florida. Mature caterpillars year-round. Jamaican dogwood and karum tree.

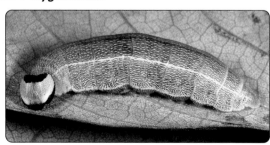

Grass Skippers – Subfamily Hesperiinae

A confusingly similar group of green to brown caterpillars with abundant short secondary setae. The head capsule patterns are often diagnostic. The eggs are hemispherical and without conspicuous ribbing. Although typically associated with just a few grass or sedge species in the wild, most are catholic in diet, especially in captivity. Caterpillars make a cylindrical shelter by rolling up a single leaf or by silking together adjacent blades. Most overwinter as larvae and pupate in the early spring. Diagnoses that appear below are based on my limited slide collection and the works of Scott (1986) and Allen (1997); definitive identifications are best based on reared adults.

LEAST SKIPPER
Ancyloxypha numitor

RECOGNITION Slender, elongate diminutive skipper. *Distinguished by its four pairs of white wax glands along the subventer of A4–A7.* Gland on A7 consisting only of anterior portion. White portion of prothoracic collar about twice the width of black portion. Head pattern diagnostic. Larva less than 2cm.

OCCURRENCE Wet meadows, swamps, and edges of watercourses from Saskatchewan to central Maine south through Florida and central Texas. Two or three generations over much of range; four or more generations in Deep South where mature caterpillars may be expected year-round.

COMMON FOODPLANTS Grasses, including bluegrass and rice cutgrass.

REMARKS The whitish subventral wax glands present in many of our grass skippers play an important role in their pupal ecology. As the prepupal larvae begin spinning their cocoons, the wax comes free from the body and is incorporated into the walls of the cocoon; some of the wax will later collect over the surface of the pupa. The extent to which the wax waterproofs the cocoon, excludes pathogens and other natural enemies, or in other ways enhances survival is poorly understood.

Thymelicus lineola

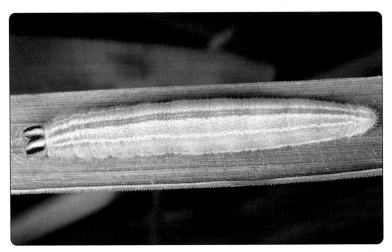

RECOGNITION *Distinguished from other grass skippers by whitish lines on head that run from vertex to mandibles and the absence of a constricted "neck."* White, paired wax glands on underside of A7 and A8. Rusty hairs contrast with green ground color. White lines on head sometimes bounded outwardly with black. Greenish middorsal stripe edged with pale addorsal stripe that in turn is flanked by cream subdorsal stripe that runs from T2 back over abdomen. Subspiracular stripe runs from A1–A8. Anal plate extends well beyond proleg. Ground color of head pale green. Larva to 2.5cm.

OCCURRENCE Many grassy habitats including fields, cool season grasslands, wet meadows, watercourses, and woodland and forest clearings. Central Canada south to North Carolina (mountains), Great Lakes States, and northeastern Missouri, spreading westward and southward. One generation with mature caterpillars in early spring.

COMMON FOODPLANTS Grasses, including bent grass, orchard grass, velvet grass, and timothy.

REMARKS Our most abundant skipper in many parts of the Northeast. Larvae are at home in yards, unmowed fields, and orchards. Look for fascicles of tied leaves anywhere where the grass goes uncut. Unlike most of our grass skippers, the European Skipper overwinters as an egg.

PECK'S SKIPPER
Polites peckius

RECOGNITION Dirty brown caterpillar with vague sprinkling of pale spots and dark middorsal stripe. Head very dark; collar black with whitish anterior margin. *On head look for indistinct white line to either side of midline and short white bar between eyes and mandibles.* Eighth spiracle conspicuously enlarged and blackened. Ventral wax glands absent. Larva to about 2cm. Three of its common congeners, the Crossline Skipper

(*Polites origenes*), Long Dash (*P. mystic*), and Tawny-edged Skipper (*P. themistocles*) lack the white bars over the head. Length of body hairs differs across genus. Among group considered here, hairs longest in Peck's Skipper, intermediate in Long Dash, and quite short in the other two. Hairs so sparse and short in Tawny-edged that integument may appear somewhat glossy. Caterpillar of Whirlabout (*P. vibex*) with green and white markings on head more pronounced (inset). Other *Polites*, as well as members of related skipper genera, are similar in appearance. Identifications are best confirmed through rearing.

OCCURRENCE Fields, wet meadows, pastures, lawns, and other open grassy habitats from central Canada south in East to Georgia (mountains) and northern Arkansas. Over much of range, two generations; southward with small third generation in fall; mature larvae occur nearly year-round.

COMMON FOODPLANTS Grasses, including bluegrass and rice cutgrass.

REMARKS Scott (1986) reports that both larvae and pupae overwinter. He also made the observation that because some skippers form shelters close to or even partially below ground and are human-tolerant, they can eke out an existence even in lawns.

Poanes hobomok

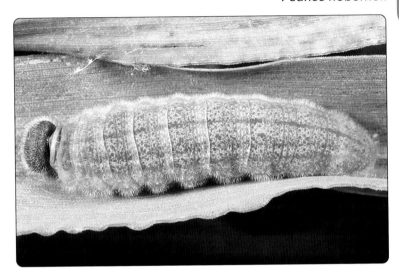

RECOGNITION Body tan to orange-brown with blurry dark spots and velvety vesture of short hairs. *Hairs pale, dense, longer than those of most grass skippers*—hairs approximately as long as width of shallow annulations that encircle each abdominal segment. A2–A8 often with very subtle brown subdorsal spot, which is about the size of one of the larger spiracles, located toward front end of each segment. Vague middorsal and even more poorly defined supraspiracular stripes, scarcely darker than ground color. *Head uniformly rusty brown* without patterning; hairs or setae erect. Thoracic collar light brown with thin, dark-brown ring. Larva to 2.5cm. Caterpillars of the double-brooded Zabulon Skipper (*Poanes zabulon*) are closely similar, and likely to be found in the same habitats. There are other *Poanes* in the eastern United States, but these are considerably less common and most are associated with marshes and other open wetlands.

OCCURRENCE Woodland and forest clearings and edges, parks, and stream courses, preferring sites with mixture of shade and sunlit patches. Nectaring individuals wander into nearby fields and gardens. Central Saskatchewan to Cape Breton south in East to northern Georgia and northeastern Oklahoma. One generation with overwintering caterpillars maturing from March to May.

COMMON FOODPLANTS Allen (1997) lists panic grass, love grass, and purple-top.

REMARKS A plain caterpillar even among skippers. The young larva forms a tubular shelter by rolling a single grass blade, usually near a joint. Comparatively little silk is used. Later it ties adjacent blades together to make an elongate shelter. Feeding occurs mostly at night.

GRASS SKIPPERS

DELAWARE SKIPPER *Anatrytone logan*
Southeastern Saskatchewan to southern Maine to Florida and Texas. One generation in North with mature caterpillars in early summer; two generations in Missouri. Bluestem and other grasses.

SACHEM *Atalopedes campestris*
Resident in Gulf States north to Delmarva Peninsula, but straying northward to Upper Midwest and New England. Three or more generations in Deep South with mature caterpillars nearly year-round. Grasses.

BLACK DASH *Euphyes conspicua*
Eastern Nebraska through Great Lakes States and southern Ontario; outlying Eastern populations from southern New England to Virginia. One generation with overwintering caterpillars maturing in spring. Sedges.

INDIAN SKIPPER *Hesperia sassacus*
Central Manitoba through lower Quebec and Maine south to North Carolina (mountains). One generation with mature caterpillars overwintering. Grasses.

FIERY SKIPPER *Hylephila phyleus*
Resident along Gulf, straying northward to Wisconsin, southern Ontario, and southern New England in some years. Multiple generations in Deep South with mature caterpillars almost year-round. Grasses, even breeding in lawns.

TAWNY-EDGED SKIPPER *Polites themistocles*
Central Canada to Cape Breton south in East to central Florida and east Texas. Two generations in New England with mature caterpillars in spring, then again in midsummer; active all year in Deep South. Grasses.

LITTLE GLASSYWING *Pompeius verna*
Minnesota to southern New Hampshire to northern Florida and Arkansas with outlying populations in Texas. One generation northward with mature caterpillars in spring; at least two generations in South. Grasses, especially purple-top.

NORTHERN BROKEN-DASH *Wallengrenia egeremet*
Eastern North Dakota to central Maine south to central Florida and east Texas. One generation northward with mature caterpillars in spring; at least two generations in South. Grasses, especially panic grass.

Delaware Skipper

Sachem

Black Dash

Indian Skipper

Fiery Skipper

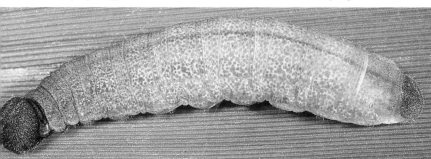

Tawny-edged Skipper

Little Glassywing

Northern Broken-dash

DUN SKIPPER
Euphyes vestris

RECOGNITION Handsome, elongate, pale green caterpillar with *distinctive black spot over top of burnt sienna head*. Head spot bounded by a white horseshoe-shaped mark; two other sets of white lines run from vertex to eyes. Thoracic collar white and black. Weakly defined, smoky or dirty green middorsal line. Posterior half of A1–A8 with seven shallow annulations. Pale streaking, sometimes  forming pinstripes over dorsum and sides. Larva to 2.5cm. This description applies more or less to the entirety of the nine Eastern *Euphyes*. *Euphyes* caterpillars are similar enough that identifications should be confirmed through rearing, especially if one's caterpillar happens to be from a wetland in the Southeast where many of our species fly. The Dun is by far the most widespread and abundant species of the genus in the East and our only *Euphyes* likely to breed in yards and wooded wetlands.

OCCURRENCE Woodland and forest clearings and edges, fields adjacent to woodlands, swamps, wetlands along powerline right of ways, and other semi-open, mesic to wet habitats. Central Saskatchewan to Prince Edward Island south in East to Florida and Texas. One generation in Northeast with mature larvae in late summer (through following spring); two or more broods southward; nearly year-round along Gulf.

COMMON FOODPLANTS Sedges such as chufa or yellow nutgrass.

REMARKS Although the adults of the Dun Skipper wander widely to seek nectar in fields, gardens, and other open habitats, look for its caterpillars in wetlands or along watercourses. The larva constructs an elongate shelter by binding together several leaves. The inside of the shelter is generously lined with silk. The upper end of the nest is plugged with silk and a white frothy substance prior to pupation (Heitzman 1964, Tveten and Tveten 1996).

COMMON ROADSIDE-SKIPPER *Amblyscirtes vialis*

Saskatchewan to Nova Scotia south to Georgia and northeastern Texas with outlying populations in northern Florida. One generation northward with mature caterpillars in spring; two generations from Ohio southward. Grasses.

DUSTED SKIPPER *Atrytonopsis hianna*

Southeastern Saskatchewan to New Hampshire south to Gulf States and northern Texas. One generation with mature caterpillars from late summer to early spring. Bluestem.

BRAZILIAN SKIPPER
Calpodes ethlius

Common in Florida but breeding north to at least North Carolina; frequently straying north to Missouri and New Jersey. In Carolinas mature caterpillars from June onward; year-round in parts of Florida and Texas. Canna.

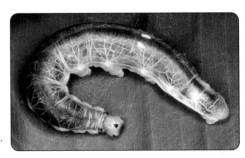

OCOLA SKIPPER *Panoquina ocola*

Resident in Gulf States north through coastal South Carolina, straying northward to Great Lakes States and southern New England. Multiple generations in Deep South with mature caterpillars year-round. Grasses.

SWALLOWTAILS – PAPILIONIDAE

Swallowtails are among the most familiar and photographed insects; there are few who do not appreciate the beauty of these butterflies. Several species are common in and around rural and urban areas—both the Tiger and Spicebush breed in Central Park. Caterpillars of Black Swallowtails are frequent guests in vegetable gardens and the Eastern Tiger Swallowtail larva feeds on many ornamental trees. The caterpillars too are favorites among children, perhaps because they are large, attractive, and predictable, the latter being a euphemism for lethargic. Seven common Eastern species are figured, another four are diagnosed. The family is best represented in the tropics and includes the world's largest butterfly, Queen Alexandra's Birdwing of Papua New Guinea, whose wing spread may exceed 30cm.

RECOGNITION

The stocky caterpillars are broadest near the juncture of the thorax and abdomen. All have an eversible forked structure called an osmeterium that issues from a slit on the dorsum of the first thoracic segment immediately behind the head (*see* pages 78 and 80). Although smooth to the touch, the body is set with minute fine hairs, especially below the spiracles. In all but the Pipevine Swallowtail, the head is held beneath the swollen thorax. The larval crochets, of three (rarely two) lengths, are arranged in a row paralleling the body axis; there may be a second smaller set of reduced crochets closer to the midline.

LIFE HISTORY NOTES

The eggs are large and spherical. The early instars rest on upper leaf surfaces, often mimicking bird droppings. Snake mimicry is common among the later instars. When roughly handled, attacked by ants, or approached by a wasp, the tentacles of the osmeterium can be everted and flailed about. Swallowtails overwinter as a chrysalis under an overhang, in leaf litter, under bark, or in other protected sites near the ground.

All of our swallowtails with the exception of *Battus*, which raft their eggs, lay single eggs on new foliage. I have had fair success finding eggs. The young caterpillars (*Papilio* only) are conspicuous, sitting directly over the midrib on upper leaf surfaces. Look for larvae on saplings and young trees growing along woodland or forest edges or on stand-alone plants in unmowed fields or under powerline right of ways. Prepupal larvae may wander several meters before choosing their pupation sites—on occasion I find them crossing roads, driveways, and sidewalks.

POLYDAMAS SWALLOWTAIL
Bathus polydamus

Peninsular Florida and lower Texas but straying northwards. Multiple generations with mature caterpillars throughout the growing season. Pipevine.

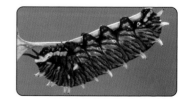

Battus philenor

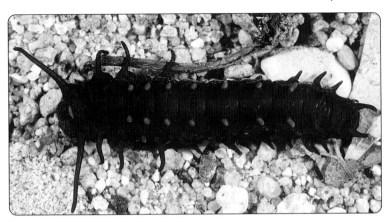

RECOGNITION Instantly recognizable by fleshy projections that extend from body. Usually dull or dusky black, but smoky red forms occur. Most caterpillars with *red-orange dorsal warts* over abdomen. *Lateral tentacles on T1 very long, twice length of those that follow on T2, T3, and A2.* Larva to 5.5cm. Polydamas Swallowtail (*Battus polydamas*) caterpillar has much shorter tentaclelike projections on T1; those over dorsum of T2–A8 noticeably longer than those of Pipevine and of same size as those along sides of body; trunk often marked with numerous oblique lines (*see* opposite). It too eats pipevine; southern Florida and Texas, but straying northward to Missouri and the Carolinas.

OCCURRENCE Forest edges, pinelands, and open dry woodlands from southern Minnesota, Michigan, and central Connecticut south to Florida and Texas. Two generations in North with mature caterpillars from June onward; continuous broods through growing season along Gulf.

COMMON FOODPLANTS Pipevine.

REMARKS The caterpillar of the Pipevine Swallowtail is a most unlikely looking creature whose resemblance to a velvet worm (onychophoran) may be more than accidental. Velvet worms hunt their prey in a bizarre if not somewhat disgusting fashion—by launching strings of slime from a gland in their head that entangles their victim. Velvet worms and *Battus* species are most diverse in tropical forests. Pipevine caterpillars commonly defoliate patches of their foodplant and as a consequence are often seen wandering over the ground in search of food. When viewed from above, the hind end of the Pipevine Swallowtail caterpillar seems to have a set of antennae and well-developed legs. The unpalatable caterpillars are gregarious and considerably more conspicuous in color and habit than those of our other swallowtails.

ORANGE DOG (GIANT SWALLOWTAIL)
Papilio cresphontes

RECOGNITION *Brownish body with three patches of white down each side*: a broad white subdorsal collar that runs just above head back along sides of thorax; white, V-shaped, abdominal saddle that extends down to first proleg; and porcelain-white patch that envelopes caudal end of body. Most have sapphire-blue spots along dorsum. *Osmeterium bright red.* Larva to 5.5cm. Four closely related swallowtails have similar  larvae. Schaus' (*P. aristodemus*) and Bahamian Swallowtails (*P. andraemon*) occur on torchwood, wild lime, and citrus; both are protected species known only from the Florida Keys. In Schaus' Swallowtail all three white patches run along sides of body and do not meet over dorsum except over A8–A10; osmeterium white. Although patterned much like Giant Swallowtail, the Bahamian Swallowtail caterpillar bears small white knobs that extend forward from the prothorax and it has a white osmeterium. Thoas (*P. thoas*) and Ornython Swallowtails (*P. ornython*) occur in southern Texas as strays.

OCCURRENCE Hammocks, citrus orchards, and open woodlands from Michigan, Pennsylvania, and western Connecticut to Florida and Texas.

COMMON FOODPLANTS Citrus, hoptree, prickly ash, torchwood, and other plants in citrus family (Rutaceae).

REMARKS A caterpillar with excellent options in both bird-dropping and snake-mimicry. When viewed head-on the later instar caterpillar passes as a credible snake mimic with scalelike markings all about the thorax. When viewed from the side and top its visage is that of a bird dropping, especially in early instars. Its shiny skin adds to the disguise, giving the larva the character of a freshly deposited dropping.

Papilio glaucus

RECOGNITION Attractive smooth green caterpillar with thickened thorax and tapering abdomen; green ground color wanes below spiracles. *A pair of black, blue, and yellow eyespots sits over T3; note black "eyebrow" toward midline.* Trailing edge of A1 has transverse yellow bar concealed in intersegmental fold while caterpillar is at rest. Lavender subdorsal and supraspiracular spots on A1 and A4–A7. A9 with yellow transverse ridge that bears a low  tooth to either side. Larva to 5.5cm. Caterpillar of Canadian Tiger Swallowtail (*Papilio canadensis*), which has but one generation a year, replaces the Eastern Tiger Swallowtail northward; evidently it is indistinguishable as a mature larva.

OCCURRENCE Wooded streets, shrubby fields, watercourses, woodlands, and forests from lower half of Minnesota, Michigan, and central New England to Florida and Texas. Two broods and often a partial third over much of East with mature caterpillars from mid-June onward; nearly year-round along Gulf.

COMMON FOODPLANTS Especially magnolia, sweetbay, tulip tree (all Magnoliaceae) and cherry; also ash and others.

REMARKS The first three instars are bird-dropping mimics; in the fourth instar the caterpillar acquires its green coloration. The larva rests on the upper side of a leaf, with its crochets engaged in a thin pad of silk. The late instars provide an excellent example of countershading, a common strategy among caterpillars that helps them avoid detection by birds and other visual predators. Countershading is achieved with graded lightening of the sides of the body: those portions of the body receiving the least amount of light, and that would normally appear darkened, end up resembling the dorsum. To find Eastern Tiger Swallowtail larvae, search smaller black cherry, tulip tree, and magnolia trees, especially along fencerows, roads with light traffic, or other edges.

BLACK SWALLOWTAIL
Papilio polyxenes

RECOGNITION Distinctively patterned with green or white, yellow, and black. Most caterpillars *green with black band extending over each body segment.* Six yellow dots are embedded in each black band. Larva to 5cm. Early and middle instars mostly black and white, resembling a bird dropping. Ozark Swallowtail (*Papilio joanae*), a species of Ozark woodlands, has similar caterpillars but its ground color tends to be brighter green, even bluish in some individuals, and the black bands are frequently broken by white, yellow, or orange spots (Opler 1992).

OCCURRENCE Open fields, farmlands, gardens, wet meadows, and other open wetlands from Canada south to Florida and Texas (and Costa Rica). Two or more broods with mature caterpillars from June onward.

COMMON FOODPLANTS Carrot, celery, dill, fennel, parsley, Queen Anne's lace, and other members of carrot family (Apiaceae), also rue and other Rutaceae.

REMARKS The Black Swallowtail, like the American robin and white-tailed deer, flourishes around many types of human activity. In the Northeast it reaches its peak abundance around farmlands and along the coast. The distinctively patterned caterpillars are familiar to all who have spent appreciable time in their gardens. Because females lay just a few eggs in one place, the Black Swallowtail rarely becomes a pest. With the shift away from agriculture and ensuing reforestation of the Northeast, this species is becoming less common—it is sometimes missed on butterfly counts where it was once a regular. In the inset I have provoked an alarm response by gently squeezing the caterpillar with forceps.

Papilio troilus

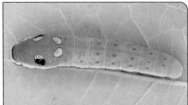

RECOGNITION *Green with large eyespots*: those on T3 largest; yellow eyespots on A1 lacking black "pupil." Blue subdorsal and supraspiracular spots on A4–A7; only supraspiracular spot present on A3 and subdorsal spot on A8. Prepupal caterpillars turn yellow or orange. Larva to 5.5cm. First three instars resemble a bird dropping, shiny green- to chocolate-brown with black eyespots on thorax and white spiracular stripe that may be absent, or more commonly, enlarged to form a saddle over A3 and A8. Palamedes Swallowtail (*Papilio palamedes*) similar, but with smaller eyespots and body more rusty or maroon beneath; on redbay, swampbay, and possibly sassafras. Its breeding range extends from coastal Texas north along Atlantic Coastal Plain to Dismal Swamp, Virginia.

OCCURRENCE Mostly woodlands and swamps, but adults nectaring in fields and gardens. Eastern Nebraska, southern Wisconsin, and New Hampshire south to Florida and Texas. Two broods over much of East with mature caterpillars in June and July, then again from August to October; nearly year-round with at least three generations along Gulf.

COMMON FOODPLANTS Principally sassafras and spicebush.

REMARKS One of our largest shelter-forming insects and perhaps the best snake mimic in North America. The white spot in the false eye is a nice touch—making the eye appear as if it were moist enough to have a reflection spot. While disguised as a bird dropping, the caterpillar rests exposed on the upper side of a leaf. With the change to snake-mimicry the larva forms a leaf shelter, pulling the edges of the leaf up and over its body. The larva remains in the shelter by day, always with the head up. A searching bird, were it to encounter a caterpillar, would see only the anterior "face" of the thorax—the snake.

ZEBRA SWALLOWTAIL
Eurytides marcellus

RECOGNITION Immediately recognizable by both its pattern and foodplant choice. *Body ringed with narrow green, white, blue, yellow, and/or black bands.* In most individuals the green color predominates but largely black forms also occur. *Body widest at leading edge of A1 where body is ringed by tricolored band*: blue-white toward thorax, followed by black ring, which in turn is followed by yellow. Another conspicuous yellow ring immediately behind head and one running over dorsum of each abdominal segment. Larva to 5cm.

OCCURRENCE Watercourses, but also wet woodlands, swamps, and pine flatwoods from eastern Nebraska, southern Wisconsin, and Pennsylvania south to Florida and eastern Texas. Two broods over much of East; three or more along Gulf with mature caterpillars nearly year-round.

COMMON FOODPLANTS Pawpaw and others in custard-apple family (Annonaceae) in Florida.

REMARKS The Zebra Swallowtail is faithful to its foodplant and is seldom seen far from the woodlands where pawpaw grows. Unlike the Eastern Tiger Swallowtail that has adapted so well to rural and city life, the Zebra Swallowtail is a butterfly of the wildlands. Search for eggs and caterpillars along streambeds, roads, powerline cuts, and other edges. The eggs are placed on the underside of new leaves near the tip of a shoot. Evidently the caterpillars are cannibalistic. According to Jeff Boettner (pers. comm.), a good way to see a swallowtail's osmeterium is to catch a wasp, hold one set of wings with forceps and bring the (buzzing) wasp to the caterpillar. The smell is distinctive—at the same time both sweet and putrid.

The vast majority of the world's 1,100 pierids species are tropical, but North America's most species-rich pierid genus (*Colias*) has more than a dozen mostly arctic and sub-arctic representatives. Many, particularly among the sulphurs, are migratory—the movements of *Eurema*, *Phoebis*, and *Zerene* are mostly unidirectional, out of the South northward throughout the summer and fall months. Many pierid caterpillars are a rather inconspicuous and unremarkable lot, more mothlike in appearance than other butterfly caterpillars. Their resemblance to moths may not be entirely coincidental as whites and sulphurs appear to have diverged near the base of the radiation that gave rise to butterflies. Pierids share similarities with several moth groups, especially the Neotropical Hedylidae, from which all butterflies may be derived (photos right and below). But there is a happy ending here—dull pierid caterpillars often yield real head-turning adults.

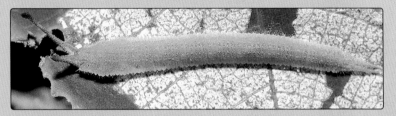

RECOGNITION

The caterpillars are elongate, roughly cylindrical, and often nondescript. An abundance of short setae vest the body and head. Many of the body segments are annulated—commonly, five shallow creases ring each of the midabdominal segments.

LIFE HISTORY NOTES

The upright spindlelike eggs, often orange, pink, or red in color, are laid on leaves, flowers, or buds. Their bright coloration presumably serves as advertisement—female pierids reject plants if previously laid eggs are found. The wisdom is simple enough: many whites and sulphurs are cannibalistic, and smaller (younger) caterpillars are likely to become the soup de jour when two caterpillars meet. Early instars of many species possess secretory hairs that repel ants and other small invertebrate predators (Scott Smedley, pers. comm.). The majority of our whites feed on mustards (Brassicaceae), while our sulphurs are largely dependent on legumes (Fabaceae). The pupa or chrysalis—often quite remarkable in form and coloration—is attached about its middle by a girdle that passes over the wings. Many of our temperate species overwinter in the pupal stage, or, in areas of mild climate, as adults. The caterpillars are rather cold-hardy, tolerating mild freezes. It is fairly easy to obtain livestock by following ovipositing females on sunny days.

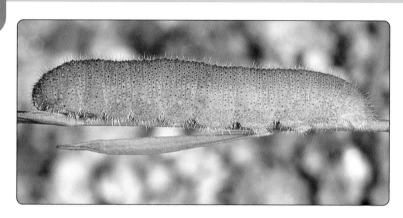

CABBAGE BUTTERFLY
Pieris rapae

RECOGNITION Sea or pea green, with *faint yellow middorsal line*; some individuals also have broken yellow spiracular line that may be represented by just a yellow spot fore and aft of spiracle. *Body and head densely set with short hairs and minute black spots* (visible with lens). Larva to 3cm. Caterpillars of Mustard White (*Pieris oleracea*) and West Virginia White (*P. virginiensis*) lack yellow striping. The double-brooded Mustard White is now restricted to the woodlands of our northern states and Canada; it feeds on toothwort, rock cress, and other mustards. The West Virginia White, another forest species, is found throughout the Appalachian Region westward to Michigan; the caterpillars of this single-brooded insect feed on toothwort from late spring into early summer.

OCCURRENCE Waste lots, gardens, farmlands, fields, and other open, sunny habitats throughout our area. Two to many broods with mature larvae from May until first hard frosts (somewhat cold tolerant).

COMMON FOODPLANTS Both wild and cultivated crucifers (Brassicaceae).

REMARKS For a butterfly, a bit of a wallflower both as a larva and adult, and an unwelcome one at that. The caterpillars too often are found feeding in our vegetable gardens, consuming cabbage, kale, cauliflower, broccoli, brussels sprouts, radish, turnip, and other crucifers. As if this were not enough, its presence in North America may be linked to the decline of the Mustard White, which was formerly a widespread species in the East. Preliminary findings by Roy Van Driesche and his students at the University of Massachusetts suggest that a parasitic wasp (*Cotesia glomerata*), introduced to control the Cabbage Butterfly, has eliminated the Mustard White from much of its former range in New England.

RECOGNITION *Longitudinally striped with alternating smoky gray to steel blue and bright yellow bands.* Subdorsal and spiracular stripes often partially interrupted with white. Numerous *minute setae arise from shiny black spots over head and body.* Larva to 3.5cm.

OCCURRENCE Waste lots, fields, and other dry, open habitats from southern Canada to Florida and Texas, but as a stray or rare non-permanent resident in the north. Two to three broods in New Jersey with caterpillars in May and early June, then again with overlapping broods from July to the first hard frosts; breeds continuously along Gulf.

COMMON FOODPLANTS Wild and cultivated crucifers (Brassicaceae): peppergrass is a favorite in vacant lots and along roads, and cabbage and its cultivars in gardens.

REMARKS The Checkered White was once classified in the genus *Pieris* with the Cabbage Butterfly. If larval coloration is any measure of taxonomic identity then whoever split these two apart has my vote. The overall effect of the larval pattern is similar to that of marbles (*Euchloe*), orange tips (*Anthocharis*), and the Great Southern White (*Ascia*). All of these are principally flower- or fruit-feeders that feed exposed in open inflorescences. Evidently this motif of yellow and white striping over a green to blue-gray ground color is an evolutionary winner. This species has declined precipitously across much of the East in my lifetime—formerly common, the Checkered White is now local and rare along the entire Eastern Seaboard from New England south to the Carolinas. Colonies that were reliable as recently as five years ago have disappeared in West Virginia. It now survives in disturbed habitats such as Jamaica Bay in New York City and along the runways of Newark International Airport. Might *Cotesia glomerata* or other introduced biological control agents be responsible here, too?

GREAT SOUTHERN WHITE
Ascia monuste

RECOGNITION Splendid yellow and black caterpillar not likely to be mistaken for another. *Five prominent yellow stripes run length of body:* middorsal, two subdorsal, and two spiracular stripes. Dorsum between subdorsal stripes may be largely given to yellow. Above each abdominal spiracle look for two shiny blackened plates. Below spiracles, a fringe of whitish setae encircles body. Immediately behind yellow-

orange head, prothorax bears crown of shiny black setae-bearing "thorns." Larva to 5cm.

OCCURRENCE Waste lots, roadsides, salt marshes, and other open, sunny habitats in southern Florida and Texas where mature caterpillars may be found year-round.

COMMON FOODPLANTS Limber caper, peppergrass, and saltwort.

REMARKS Part of the allure of planning field trips to southern Florida is that many species breed year-round. Only at these low latitudes can one follow a female, watch it oviposit, and then have a reasonable chance of finding eggs, young, and older larvae coexisting alongside breeding adults. Such was my reward after watching a female Great Southern White stop to lay eggs on a weed that was growing along a road in Copeland, Florida, where I had stopped for a "five-minute-lookabout" one April morning. The payoff—a full-grown *Ascia* caterpillar—came quickly, followed shortly thereafter by the realization that there were in fact dozens of caterpillars about, and that I had probably walked by many over the course of the day.

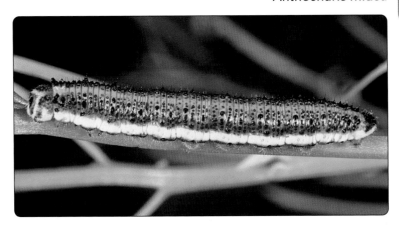

RECOGNITION Green ground color scarcely evident because caterpillar is so lavishly patterned. *Yellow middorsal stripe bounded by faint blue mottling. Broad white spiracular stripe runs length of body*, continuing onto head and around anal plate. Short hairs, arising from small, black, shiny plates, peppered over upper portion of body. Larva to 3cm.

Caterpillars of Olympia Marble (*Euchloe olympia*) similar, but white lateral stripe edged with yellow below and more blue-gray in aspect; it too utilizes rock cress and hairy bitter-cress.

OCCURRENCE In north, exposed hilltops and dry woodlands, elsewhere on shale outcrops, open woodlands, and floodplain forests from eastern Nebraska and Illinois to Connecticut south to northern Georgia and eastern Texas. One brood with mature caterpillars in late spring.

COMMON FOODPLANTS Bitter cress, rock cress, winter cress, and other plants in mustard family (Brassicaceae).

REMARKS Both the adult and larva are exquisitely colored animals. The adults are among the first butterflies to be active in the spring, flying when most naturalists are delighted to see anything that signals winter's retreat. The bright red eggs are usually laid on an inflorescence, where the larvae prefer to take their meals—flowers and fruits are consumed preferentially to leaves. Because a single larva can eat an entire inflorescence and most plants have but a single shoot, the caterpillars are protective about their claim, consuming smaller larvae that they encounter on the same inflorescence. Females are reported to search for previously laid eggs so as to lessen the chances of such encounters. The anterior end of the chrysalis, which may overwinter for two or more years, is drawn well forward into a point. From a distance, it resembles a thorn.

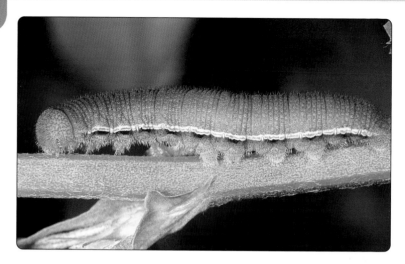

CLOUDED SULPHUR
Colias philodice

RECOGNITION Attractive *green caterpillar with prominent, mostly white spiracular stripe that runs from head to anal plate; stripe may contain lines or bars of pink or orange, and may be edged with dark green or black below.* Yellow subdorsal stripe sometimes present. Secondary hairs, though abundant, scarcely visible without hand lens. Larva to 3.5cm. Caterpillars of Orange Sulphur (*Colias eurytheme*) are similar—you must rear them to adulthood to confirm their identity. The two fly together throughout the East, share the same foodplants, and occasionally hybridize. Toliver (1987) noted that the Orange Sulphur often uses alfalfa when available, while the preferred foodplant of the Clouded Sulphur is clover.

OCCURRENCE Waste lots, roadsides, fields, and other croplands, from Canada south to Florida and Texas. At least three broods in Connecticut with mature caterpillars from late May through the first hard frosts of November; continuous broods along Gulf.

COMMON FOODPLANTS Alfalfa, clover, sweet clover, vetch, and other legumes.

REMARKS The easiest way to see these caterpillars may be to start from the egg. If you know a field where the butterfly is common, it is usually a simple matter to track an ovipositing female and secure two or three eggs in short order. It can be an engaging effort trying to stay far enough from the female so as not to alarm her, but close enough that you have a chance of finding the pale upright eggs, which will be laid near the center of a leaflet. The eggs turn red after a day or two and then gray before hatching. Binoculars are helpful in this endeavor. The adults are active butterflies, and not surprisingly need to tank up with nectar frequently.

RECOGNITION Highly variable in color, ranging from yellow to green, often with *broad yellowish or greenish spiracular stripe. In some forms a dark transverse band runs from spiracle to spiracle; these are best developed over subdorsal area and may have purple-black reflections.* Abdominal segments have six transverse rows of raised shiny black tubercles running over dorsum; black tubercles

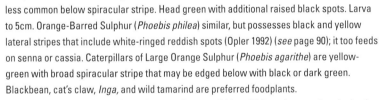

less common below spiracular stripe. Head green with additional raised black spots. Larva to 5cm. Orange-Barred Sulphur (*Phoebis philea*) similar, but possesses black and yellow lateral stripes that include white-ringed reddish spots (Opler 1992) (*see* page 90); it too feeds on senna or cassia. Caterpillars of Large Orange Sulphur (*Phoebis agarithe*) are yellow-green with broad spiracular stripe that may be edged below with black or dark green. Blackbean, cat's claw, *Inga,* and wild tamarind are preferred foodplants.

OCCURRENCE Edges of woods, waste lots, roadsides, thickets, hammocks, pinelands, along watercourses, but also wet woodlands and swamps. Adults migratory and stray into many habitats, especially common along Gulf and Atlantic Coasts. Resident from South Carolina to Texas. Caterpillars found north to New England in the fall, but they do not successfully overwinter.

COMMON FOODPLANTS Cassia or senna.

REMARKS The pupa is bizarre, compressed from side to side, with a greatly distended "chest and belly." Its color, like that of the caterpillar, is highly variable—green, pink, or yellow, banded or otherwise. Adults are migratory and move north to New England (especially along coast) and the Upper Midwest in many years. In their wake, caterpillars turn up on partridge pea, senna, and related legumes, but the species is not cold-hardy and generally fails north of the Gulf States and coastal areas of the Carolinas.

SULPHURS

SOUTHERN DOGFACE *Zerene cesonia*

Resident along Gulf, but
straying northward regularly
to Missouri and Carolinas, and
on rare occasions as far north
as Canada. Mature cater-
pillars through much of
growing season along Gulf.

Indigo bush, lead plant, prairie clover, and other legumes.

LITTLE SULPHUR *Eurema lisa*

Resident in Gulf States north
through Carolinas, but
straying and breeding north
to Minnesota and
southeastern Canada.
Mature caterpillars from July
until first frosts northward;
breeding year-round in Deep
South. Partridge pea, wild
sensitive plant, and other cassias.

SLEEPY ORANGE *Eurema nicippe*

Resident in Gulf States north
into southern Arkansas and
coastal Virginia, but straying
and breeding north to
Nebraska and Connecticut.
Mature caterpillars from July
until first frosts northward;
breeding year-round in Deep South. Cassias.

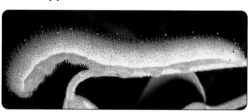

ORANGE-BARRED SULPHUR *Phoebis philea*

Resident in southern Florida,
occasionally straying north to
coastal Georgia and more
rarely to New England and
southern Canada. Breeding
year-round in Keys and lower
Florida. Cassias.

HAIRSTREAKS, BLUES, COPPERS, AND METALMARKS – LYCAENIDAE

This is a large family of butterflies with more than 140 species north of Mexico. While adult lycaenids are surely among the planet's most beautiful animals, their caterpillars are a mundane lot—to my eyes, the larvae of the hairstreaks, blues, and coppers are among the most structurally monotonous large groups of externally feeding Lepidoptera. (There are marvelous exceptions to this claim in South Africa and else-where, but in North America only the metalmarks show great diversity in form.)

RECOGNITION

Head small, retracted into the thorax, except when feeding. Sluglike: body short, wide, and somewhat flattened. Integument densely covered with short setae in blues, coppers, hairstreaks, and very long silky setae in our (Calephelis) metalmarks. In blues, minute star-shaped setae cover thorax and abdomen. Coppers, too, bear unique seta-tion—their minutely plumed ("mushroom") setae appear as tiny white spots over the integument (plumes visible only when viewed with a microscope). The spiracle on A1 is below the level of the others in metalmarks. Coloration may be exceedingly variable within a species, especially among flower- and fruit-feeding hairstreaks and blues. Foodplant associations can be helpful in identification because most species are specialized in diet. Many of our eastern species are figured in Tveten and Tveten (1996), Allen (1997), Allen et al. (2005), and Minno et al. (2005).

LIFE HISTORY NOTES

The highly ornamented eggs are usually laid singly on new growth or near where new growth is expected in the spring. Many hairstreaks and blues specialize on flowers or fruits. Their small heads and extensible necks (prothorax) make it possible for the caterpillars of some species to mine leaves or bore out the inner contents of fruits. The Harvester (Feniseca tarquinius) stands out as our only exclusively predaceous butter-fly; its larva feeds on aphids. Lycaenids usually pupate away from the feeding site, in a concealed location under bark or litter. The chrysalis is short, rounded at both ends, and in most cases cryptically colored.

Nearly half of the world's 5,500 lycaenid species are tended by ants. In some species the association is so tight that the ants may even carry the caterpillars to and from their nests, returning the larvae to a feeding site on the proper foodplant! Ant-tended species have special dorsal glands on the seventh abdominal segment that secrete a sugary sub-stance periodically offered to the attending ants. For the caterpillars, the payoff is pro-tection from natural enemies, especially parasitoids and predators that would otherwise attack unattended larvae. Ant-tended lycaenids have files, scrapers, or other means of producing substrate-borne calls that can be employed to "call" for ants. Nearby ants detect the "singing" caterpillar by the vibrations that emanate through the foodplant. Not all is bliss: some lycaenids are carnivores that grow up in ant nests eating larvae and pupae. Conversely, some ants treat their caterpillars more as cattle, herding and tending their livestock, but consuming larvae in their care when other food sources prove scarce.

HARVESTER
Feniseca tarquinius

RECOGNITION Caterpillar has *moderately long setae that are often cluttered with waxy secretions from their aphid prey and other debris*. Thin, black middorsal stripe, broken between segments, embedded in broad waxy white area that runs length of body. Darker-colored individuals have a deeply toothed subdorsal stripe. Sometimes with yellow or orange spot in center of each of the teeth that make up the subdorsal stripe. Larva less than 2cm.

OCCURRENCE Forest and woodland edges, watercourses, and woody and shrub swamps from southern Canada to central Florida and Texas, but absent from parts of Gulf Coast, Coastal Plain, and Midwest. Two or three generations in Northeast with mature caterpillars from June onward; three to six generations in South.

COMMON "FOODPLANTS" Prey includes at least four genera of woolly aphids. Common hostplants for these aphids include alder, ash, beech, greenbrier, hawthorn, maple, and witch hazel.

REMARKS This butterfly is far more common than most entomologists realize, largely due to the fact that the adults do not come to nectar and are extremely localized, often staying close to the aphid clusters from which they have hatched. Harvesters are doubly dependent on aphids because adults feed principally on the honeydew excretions that accumulate about the aggregations of the aphids. One of the most common prey species is the Woolly Alder Aphid (*Paraprociphilus tessellatus*). An easy time to locate Harvester larvae is in the fall, after alder leaves have fallen and while aphid populations are still high. Large colonies of the Woolly Alder Aphid are sometimes distinct enough to be located even from a car. Harvester caterpillars are often attended by ants—the evolutionary ecology of this ant-aphid-butterfly community is in need of study.

AMERICAN COPPER
Lycaena phlaeas

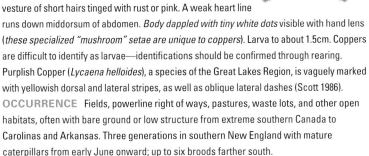

RECOGNITION   In many coppers, anterior end tends to be more rounded than rear; middorsum of T1 shallowly cleft; and body may be more flattened than in blues and hairstreaks. American Copper caterpillar green with vesture of short hairs tinged with rust or pink. A weak heart line runs down middorsum of abdomen. *Body dappled with tiny white dots* visible with hand lens (*these specialized "mushroom" setae are unique to coppers*). Larva to about 1.5cm. Coppers are difficult to identify as larvae—identifications should be confirmed through rearing. Purplish Copper (*Lycaena helloides*), a species of the Great Lakes Region, is vaguely marked with yellowish dorsal and lateral stripes, as well as oblique lateral dashes (Scott 1986).

OCCURRENCE   Fields, powerline right of ways, pastures, waste lots, and other open habitats, often with bare ground or low structure from extreme southern Canada to Carolinas and Arkansas. Three generations in southern New England with mature caterpillars from early June onward; up to six broods farther south.

COMMON FOODPLANTS   Sheep sorrel and less frequently curled dock and other docks.

REMARKS   Opler (1992) presents the argument that our eastern populations of the American Copper (subspecies *L. p. americana*) represent a European introduction whose foodplants are weeds also of European origin. But to date, no one has sequenced the insect's DNA to see what the copper's genes have to say about this matter. Obviously, if Opler's arguments prove correct, his suggested common name of "Little Copper" would be more appropriate. The secretive middle and late instar larvae shelter on lower petioles or in duff at the base of the plant by day and move up onto the leaves to feed at night. It overwinters as a caterpillar.

COPPERS, HAIRSTREAKS, AND ELFINS

BOG COPPER *Lycaena epixanthe*

Southern Canada to New Jersey and Great Lakes States. One generation with mature caterpillars in June. Cranberry.

HOARY ELFIN *Callophrys polios*

Rocky Mountain Region east through southern Canada to New Brunswick south into New Jersey; disjunct population in central Appalachians. One generation with mature caterpillars in May and June. Low heaths, especially bearberry and trailing arbutus.

BRONZE COPPER *Lycaena hyllus*

Southern Canada to West Virginia, Arkansas, and northeastern Oklahoma. Two generations over much of East with mature caterpillars from July to September; three generations southward, caterpillars from May onward. Dock.

SOUTHERN HAIRSTREAK *Fixsenia favonius*

Eastern Kansas to southern Michigan and Massachusetts south to Florida and Texas. One generation with mature caterpillars in February (southward) to June. Oak.

WHITE M HAIRSTREAK *Parrhasius m-album*

Missouri to Massachusetts south to Florida and Texas. At least two generations in Connecticut and four or more in Florida; mature caterpillars more or less throughout the growing season. Oak.

HICKORY HAIRSTREAK *Satyrium caryaevorum*

Great Lakes States, southwestern Quebec, and Massachusetts south to northern Georgia (mountains) and eastern Kansas. One generation with mature caterpillars in June and July. Primarily bitternut (*Carya cordiformis*).

CORAL HAIRSTREAK *Satyrium titus*

Southern Canada to northwestern Florida and central Texas. One generation with mature caterpillars in April (southward) to June. Cherry, chokeberry, and other members of rose family (Rosaceae).

EDWARDS' HAIRSTREAK *Satyrium edwardsii*

Southeastern Saskatchewan to Maine south to northern Georgia and northeastern Texas. One generation with mature caterpillars in April (southward) to June. Scrub oak in northeast, also black and related oaks elsewhere.

Bog Copper

Hoary Elfin

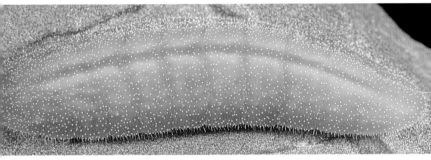

Bronze Copper

Southern Hairstreak

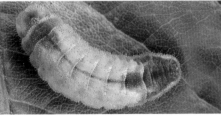

White M Hairstreak

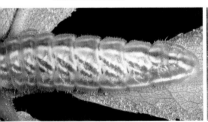

Hickory Hairstreak

Coral Hairstreak

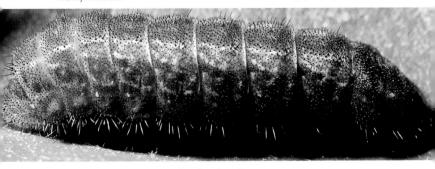

Edwards' Hairstreak

ATALA
Eumaeus atala

RECOGNITION *Bright red-orange larva with raised yellow subdorsal spots on T3–A6.* Body surface shiny, vested with abundant pale, shorter setae and less numerous black spikelike setae from raised warts. Prolegs may also be yellowish. Ground color more yellow-orange at either end of body. Larva to 2.5cm.

OCCURRENCE Hardwood hammocks, tropical pinelands, and gardens in southeastern Florida. Active year-round.

COMMON FOODPLANTS Cycads, especially coontie (*Zamia pumila*) and its varieties; in gardens, on other ornamental cycads.

REMARKS The Atala is very localized, absent from many sites where its foodplants occur. Females raft the eggs in clusters, which sometimes include as many as a few dozen eggs. Only new leaves are eaten by the early instars; older caterpillars consume tough, fully hardened foliage. Because the species is gregarious, individual plants may be defoliated. Evidently concealment is not a problem; even the first instars feed by day, exposed on upper leaf surfaces. The caterpillars have a pungent odor that is not unlike that of decaying lawn clippings. Droplets of a bitter-tasting fluid often occur over the outer surface of the chrysalis. Although nearly extirpated from Florida during the middle part of this century, the Atala is now doing reasonably well, in part because it has taken to life in residential areas from Fort Lauderdale to Homestead. Fairchild Tropical Gardens in Coral Gables is home to a large colony.

RECOGNITION Its *foodplant and large size immediately distinguish this hairstreak.* Caterpillar green, oval with relatively high profile; without the prominent incisures between adjacent segments typical of other hairstreaks. Setae dense, relatively short. *Diamond-shaped bluish white shield over T1.* Oblique lines present or absent. Allen (1997) described the caterpillar as "often striped with yellow laterally, and covered with small yellow tubercles

emitting short orange hairs." The image in Miller and Hammond (2004) is purple with green mottling. Larva to 2.5cm.

OCCURRENCE Woodlands, thickets, mesquite scrub, flatwoods, palmetto forest edges, and stream courses from Texas to southern Ohio to coastal Virginia, breeding north to Delaware in some years; occasionally straying farther north. Three or more generations in Deep South with mature caterpillars through much of growing season.

COMMON FOODPLANTS Mistletoe (on oak).

REMARKS The white eggs are large and easily found by eye. The early instars prefer new leaves and young flowers. Older larvae may mine into leaves. It is often possible to find pupae by peeling up bark flaps from lower trunk sections or flipping debris below trees with mistletoe in the crown. The pupa overwinters.

BANDED HAIRSTREAK
Satyrium calanus

RECOGNITION Exceedingly variable species even by lycaenid standards. Ground color varies from frosted green to gray, reddish, or brown. Usually with set of blurry subdorsal stripes over thorax, which may continue back over abdomen. *Abdominal segments often crossed by two oblique lines that run from subdorsal stripe down to white subspiracular stripe.* White to yellow subspiracular stripe best developed rearward, continued part way around anal plate.

Dorsum of T2–A1 and A6–A10 often marked with darkened patch—in these individuals the space between the oblique lines may also be filled with darker pigments. Larva less than 2cm. Other hairstreaks co-occur on oak. Caterpillar of Edwards' Hairstreak (*Satyrium edwardsii*), a specialist on scrub, black, and related oaks, is dirty brown with area between the subdorsal stripes appreciably darkened and typically has but one oblique line per segment; it shelters beneath a silken sheet at base of an oak stem by day; often tended by ants (*see* page 94). Hickory Hairstreak (*S. caryaevorum*) yellow-green and strongly marked with subdorsal lines; often in leaf shelter (*see* page 94). Southern Hairstreak (*Fixsenia favonius*) green to pinkish with numerous minute pale spots, but otherwise unmarked although variation mostly unstudied; uncommon to rare (*see* page 94). White M Hairstreak (*Parrhasius m-album*) has subdued markings; typically, oblique lines weak, subdorsal and subspiracular stripes absent; larvae larger than those of *Satyrium* (*see* page 94).

OCCURRENCE Woodland and forest edges and clearings, yards, and parks from southeastern Saskatchewan to southern Maine to central Florida and Texas. One generation with mature larvae in late spring, before foliage has hardened up for summer.

COMMON FOODPLANTS Hickory, oak, and walnut.

REMARKS Larvae remain on the leaves by day, resting on leaf undersides. Like other Hairstreaks, they are easily sampled with a beating sheet.

Satyrium liparops

RECOGNITION *Bright emerald green with vague markings.* Faint oblique lines run from middorsal line down to spiracles—three per segment on T3–A6. Dorsum of A7 and A8 sometimes with vague subdorsal stripe and area between darker green. Weak yellowish subspiracular stripe runs below spiracles on A1–A8. Setae somewhat rusty above and pale along sides. Larva less than 2cm. Setae longer and more conspicuous than those of Azures

(*Celastrina*) that feed alongside the Striped Hairstreak on plants in the rose family (Rosaceae). Azure caterpillars are usually less than 15mm long while mature Striped Hairstreaks commonly reach 18mm. Under high magnification, all blues may be immediately recognized by the minute star-shaped setae scattered over their integument.

OCCURRENCE Woodland and forest edges and clearings, fencerows and prairie copses, edges of watercourses, wet meadows, swamps, and bogs from southern Canada to central Florida and eastern Texas. One brood with mature caterpillars in late spring before foliage has hardened for the year.

COMMON FOODPLANTS Many plants mostly in the rose (Rosaceae) and heath (Ericaceae) families. In the former, apple, cherry, chokeberry, hawthorn, plum, serviceberry, and others. Among the heaths, blueberry (especially highbush) and evidently rhododendron are used. American hornbeam, oak, willow, and witch hazel also reported.

REMARKS The larva figured here has been attacked by a parasitic wasp—note the three blackened spots on the abdomen and first thoracic segment. The female wasp pierces the body wall with her ovipositor and lays one or more eggs inside the caterpillar. Many wasps also "host feed" at the wounds, imbibing hemolymph (blood) that leaks from the pierced body wall.

HENRY'S ELFIN
Callophrys henrici

RECOGNITION   Coloration highly variable, commonly green, red-brown, or maroon with *imbricated dorsum* and oblique subdorsal spots that run from T3–A6; these may be white, yellow, or pale green and edged with darker pigment below. Subspiracular stripe extends from T3 to anal plate. Some individuals also marked with faint, blurry middorsal and/or spiracular stripes. Larva less than 2cm. Caterpillar of Brown

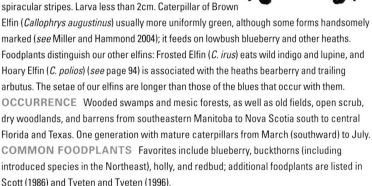

Elfin (*Callophrys augustinus*) usually more uniformly green, although some forms handsomely marked (*see* Miller and Hammond 2004); it feeds on lowbush blueberry and other heaths. Foodplants distinguish our other elfins: Frosted Elfin (*C. irus*) eats wild indigo and lupine, and Hoary Elfin (*C. polios*) (*see* page 94) is associated with the heaths bearberry and trailing arbutus. The setae of our elfins are longer than those of the blues that occur with them.

OCCURRENCE   Wooded swamps and mesic forests, as well as old fields, open scrub, dry woodlands, and barrens from southeastern Manitoba to Nova Scotia south to central Florida and Texas. One generation with mature caterpillars from March (southward) to July.

COMMON FOODPLANTS   Favorites include blueberry, buckthorns (including introduced species in the Northeast), holly, and redbud; additional foodplants are listed in Scott (1986) and Tveten and Tveten (1996).

REMARKS   Henry's Elfin is what Fox and Morrow (1981) labeled a "local specialist, regional generalist." At any one locality it tends to use a single foodplant species, yet over its whole range, it is widely polyphagous. In eastern Texas, Tveten and Tveten (1996) noted that the red form larvae were associated with the fruits of Mexican buckeye (*Ungnadia speciosa*), whereas the green form larvae were only found eating new leaves of the same plant. Efforts to reciprocally transfer larvae between leaves and fruits failed. Henry's Elfin would seem to be a butterfly destined for future evolutionary diversification. The pupa overwinters in elfins.

EASTERN PINE ELFIN
Callophrys niphon

RECOGNITION *Emerald green body with creamy subdorsal and subspiracular stripe*s; the former tending to fade over A8, and the latter continued back to anal plate. Faint, blurry middorsal stripe and often second, poorly defined, spiracular stripe along A1–A8. Larva less than 2cm. Closely related Western Pine (*Callophrys eryphon*) and Bog Elfin (*C. lanoraieensis*) are perhaps inseparable as larvae. The Bog Elfin is strictly associated

with black spruce (*Picea mariana*); it flies in bogs in southeastern Canada and the northeastern United States. In the East, the Western Pine Elfin is limited to a few disjunct populations in the northern United States and southern Canada.

OCCURRENCE Pine balds, barrens, woodlands, and forests from southern Canada to northern Florida and eastern Texas, although absent from many areas in the Midwest. One generation with mature larvae in April (southward) to June.

COMMON FOODPLANTS Both hard and soft pines (*Pinus*), favored species include jack, Virginia, and white pine.

REMARKS Females often lay eggs on saplings and smaller trees, frequently selecting trees less than 7m in height (Allen 1997). Young caterpillars feed only on new growth, initially boring near the base of a needle fascicle and later eating individual needles from the tip back (Scott 1986). Last instar larvae consume older foliage. The background matching that occurs in this genus provides textbook cases of adaptive coloration. Species that feed on broad-leaved plants are essentially green and either unmarked or unceremoniously mottled in browns, pinks, and other pastels. By contrast, the pine-feeders are always boldly striped. In the cedar-feeders, the stripes are broken up into smaller spots, which more closely resemble the reflectance patterns of cedar foliage.

JUNIPER HAIRSTREAK
Callophrys gryneus

RECOGNITION *Prominent white spots to either side of faint middorsal stripe* begin on thorax and run back over abdomen. *White subspiracular stripe*, constricted or broken between segments (especially those of thorax), runs length of body. Often with series of small supraspiracular spots on T2 or T3 to A6. Faint yellow subventral line present on some individuals. Larva less than 2cm. Caterpillars of Hessel's Hairstreak

(*Callophrys hesseli*) very similar, but in my samples, supraspiracular spots absent; it is exclusively associated with Atlantic white cedar (*Chamaecyparis thyoides*) along the Eastern seaboard. An image of the caterpillar is given in Pyle (1981).

OCCURRENCE Old fields, wooded pastures, glades, trap rock ridges and bluffs, powerline right of ways from southern Minnesota, Ontario, and Maine to central Florida and Texas, although absent from many parts of this range. In Northeast one principal generation in May with smaller second brood in midsummer, mature caterpillars in June, August, and September. Two or more full broods from New Jersey southward.

COMMON FOODPLANTS Principally red cedar (*Juniperus virginiana*) in East; occasionally white cedar and other junipers.

REMARKS One of our few lycaenids that is immediately identifiable as a caterpillar. The larvae eat the tips of new foliage. Both their texture and coloration lend much to their ability to match the foliage on which they occur. Probably the most efficient way to find larvae of the Juniper Hairstreak is to employ a beating sheet, although if the caterpillars reside where the adults spend the greater portion of their time, the lion's share will be in canopy foliage.

RECOGNITION Often green with oblique dark green line above each spiracle; pink, red, and brown forms also common. Oblique subdorsal lines edged above with white or cream. Pale subspiracular stripe runs from T3–A7. *Setae over dorsum rather long for a lycaenid, nearly half as long as segment that bears them.* Setae from subdorsal swelling often with minute dark bases. Middorsum of T1 with arrow-shaped plate that may be concealed in fold beneath

T2. Larva to 2cm. Eastern Tailed-blue (*Everes comyntas*) occurs on many of same foodplants. Its setae are shorter and it bears numerous, minute, whitish star-shaped setae over thorax and abdomen (visible only with lens).

OCCURRENCE Fields, gardens, waste lots, croplands, coastal strand communities, and other open habitats from southern Canada to Florida and Texas (to South America). As many as three generations in southern New England with mature caterpillars from June onward; continuous generations in Deep South.

COMMON FOODPLANTS Fruits and flowers of many plants, but foodplants in pea (Fabaceae) and mallow (Malvaceae) families favored. Recorded foodplants represent more than 20 plant families and include corn and cotton.

REMARKS Search for caterpillars by examining the floral heads of legumes and mallows. Be forewarned that many of the larvae that you encounter on legumes will be those of the Eastern Tailed-blue. The scarcity of Gray Hairstreak in the spring, paucity of sightings in some summers, and prevalence of adults along the coast suggest that the Gray Hairstreak may be a migrant in parts of New England. It overwinters as a pupa, at least to New Haven, Connecticut (Dale Schweitzer pers. comm.), but how far north it is able to do so successfully is not understood. It is an occasional pest of beans and other legumes.

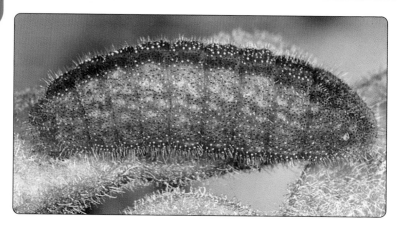

EASTERN TAILED-BLUE
Everes comyntas

RECOGNITION Yet another highly variable and seemingly undistinguished lycaenid; ground color varies from green to yellow-, pink-, green-, rose-, to purple-brown; hairy. *Integument with conspicuous peppering of small white (or sometimes black) star-shaped setae* (best viewed with a lens). Usually with *darkened middorsal line* and prominent subspiracular stripe. The latter may be edged below with pink. *Oblique lines on T3-A6 weakly expressed*. Setae prominent; longest hairs about one-third length of segment that bears them. Larva scarcely exceeding 1cm. Gray Hairstreak (*Strymon melinus*) caterpillars lack the star-shaped setae. Larvae of the Silvery Blue (*Glaucopsyche lygdamus*) lack long setae over the dorsum and have more conspicuous oblique lines above the spiracles.

OCCURRENCE Meadows, waste lots, powerline right of ways, and other open, sunny habitats from southern Canada to northern Florida and eastern Texas. Two or three generations in Connecticut with mature caterpillars from June northward; throughout the growing season southward.

COMMON FOODPLANTS Many herbaceous legumes including bush-clover, clover, lupine, pea vine, sweet clover, tick-trefoil, and vetch.

REMARKS In the right season larvae can be easily found by scanning heads of bush-clover. The larvae normally eat flowers and seeds, but will readily consume new leaves. Allen (1997) notes that ants may tend the caterpillars, although I have not seen ants associated with the larvae that I have found in Connecticut. Like pug moths (*Eupithecia*) (Family Geometridae), many flower-feeding blues are exceptionally gifted at matching the colors of their foodplants. Mature caterpillars overwinter (Tveten and Tveten 1996).

Celastrina ladon species complex

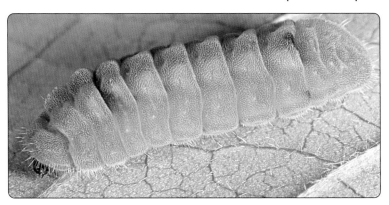

RECOGNITION Blues can be immediately recognized by their *minute, white star-shaped setae*. Like other flower-feeding lycaenids, they are exceedingly variable in color and patterning: ground color may be green (usually), brown, pink, or whitish. Frequently with darkened middorsal area bounded laterally by creamy subdorsal splotches. *Body setae generally very short* except toward rear and along the lower sides. Larva to 1.5cm.

OCCURRENCE Mesic woodlands, forest edges and openings, stream sides, and many other habitats with shrubs and trees from central Canada into northern Florida and Texas. One spring or multiple generations (depending on species) with mature caterpillars from May to at least September—see Remarks.

COMMON FOODPLANTS Favorites of Spring Azure (*C. ladon ladon*) include dogwood and viburnum; subspecies (or species) *C. ladon lucia* on heaths such as blueberry and Labrador tea and less often viburnum and cherry flowers; see also below.

REMARKS The Spring Azure is a complex of several sibling species. Wright and Pavulaan (1999) and Pavulaan and Wright (2000) believe there are at least six species in the *ladon* complex in the East that differ in phenology, dietary preferences, and wing scale characters. Three of these, Appalachian Azure (*C. neglectamajor*), Dusky Azure (*C. nigra*), and Holly Azure (*C. idella*) are single-brooded and their larvae are foodplant specialists on black cohosh (*Cimicifuga racemosa*), goatsbeard (*Aruncus dioicus*), and Atlantic coastal hollies (*Ilex*), respectively. The nominal Spring Azure (*C. ladon*) is now regarded to be a single-brooded insect (spring) that is distinct from the multiple-brooded and broadly polyphagous Summer Azure (*C. neglecta*). The most remarkable entity in this confusing array may be the undescribed Cherry Gall Azure, whose larvae consume the eriophyid mite nipple galls that occur on cherry leaves. Azures overwinter as pupae.

SILVERY BLUE
Glaucopsyche lygdamus

RECOGNITION Pale green to sometimes pinkish caterpillar with dark green or pink dorsal line. *Side of T2 or T3 to A6 marked with pair of oblique lines.* Upper (subdorsal) line more pronounced than that above spiracle. Cream to yellow subspiracular line extending rearward from T2 or T3 but ending before anal plate. Setae very short over dorsum. Larva less than 2cm.

Caterpillars of the Gray Hairstreak (*Strymon melinus*) and Eastern Tailed-Blue (*Everes comyntas*) have longer setae and additional, vague, oblique lines.

OCCURRENCE Shale barrens and open woodlands in Appalachians; to north, a species of bogs, pinelands, roadsides, and other open habitats. Outlying populations in Appalachians and Ozarks, then skipping to Upper Midwest and New England; moving southward in Northeast. In East one generation with mature caterpillars in late May and June.

COMMON FOODPLANTS Vetch, peavine, and other legumes.

REMARKS To find Silvery Blue caterpillars visit stands of vetch and pea vine where the adults have been observed flying, and look for ants. On the caterpillar, pay close attention to the seventh abdominal segment from which a middorsal yellowish honey or nectary organ will be, on occasion, everted for the caterpillar's attentive retinue. Additionally, blues have eversible "tentacular" glands on A8—when exposed nearby ants become more animated and attentive (inset). These glands are commonly displayed when the larva is moving to a new location and signal that the nectary organ might soon be available for "milking." Flowers and fruits are preferred but new leaves are also consumed.

LITTLE METALMARK
Calephelis virginiensis

RECOGNITION *Unmistakable greenish white caterpillar with lateral and addorsal rows of long, white satiny setae.* Addorsal setae directed upward to form "mohawk." Subdorsum of A2–A7 marked with orange-brown to red, lens-shaped spots. Larva to 1.5cm. Our three Eastern *Calephelis* distinguish themselves in diet and preferred habitat. The Northern Metalmark (*C. borealis*) is restricted to shale and limestone barrens, glades, and other woodland openings; larvae feed on roundleaf ragwort (*Senecio obovatus*). True to its name, the Swamp Metalmark (*C. muticum*) haunts wetlands that support populations of thistle (*Cirsium*), the larval foodplant. The subdorsal dots tend to be black or absent in the Northern and Swamp Metalmarks. Three other *Calephelis* occur in south-central and western Texas.

OCCURRENCE Pinelands, open woodlands, salt-marsh meadows, and other open sunny, and often grassy, habitats. Coastal Plain from southeastern Virginia to Houston. Three to five broods with mature caterpillars throughout growing season.

COMMON FOODPLANTS Yellow thistle (*Cirsium horridulum*) commonly; also vanilla-plant or deer's tongue (*Carphephorus odoratissima*) (Bo Sullivan, pers. comm.).

REMARKS Not far into the Neotropics this subfamily explodes into a boundless array of wondrous butterflies. Metalmarks have broken free from the constraints that seemingly impose a regimen of evolutionary uniformity on our blues, coppers, and hairstreaks—they are a study in variation and complexity, both as larvae and adults. Many are tended by ants. Little Metalmark caterpillars are inconspicuous in habit, resting on the undersides of leaves, often in a concealed location (Opler and Krizek 1984). Our *Calephelis* overwinter as partially grown caterpillars.

BRUSHFOOTS – NYMPHALIDAE

About 6,000 species are currently recognized; approximately one in every three butterflies worldwide is a brushfoot. The family is especially diverse in the tropics. About 75 species are resident in the East. Taxonomists are still arguing whether nymphalids should be recognized as a single inclusive family or split into three or even six families. Here I follow the classification of Ackery *et al.* (1999), a conservative stance that even pulls the snout butterflies (Libytheinae) into the brushfoots.

RECOGNITION

Their caterpillars far surpass all other butterfly families in their diversity of form. The only character that will allow the universal recognition of brushfoot caterpillars is thought to be the presence of a minute filiform seta near the base of the scolus on A9 (Harvey 1991). While it is frustratingly difficult to characterize the family in its entirety, each of the six subfamilies treated here is distinctive and easily recognized. All have secondary setae, although these are often tiny and visible only with a lens—they tend to be most obvious above the prolegs. Three subfamilies are armored with stout, branched spines (scoli). In these subfamilies, the head capsule also tends to be spined, sometimes bizarrely so. Brushfoots are usually large-headed, at least relative to the width of the first thoracic segment. The stemmata (lateral eyes) are of unequal size. Occasionally there is a middorsal scolus on A7 (but never on A9 as in some giant silkworm moths). Crochets of one, two, or most commonly, three lengths, are arranged in a series that parallels the body axis.

LIFE HISTORY NOTES

The eggs are laid singly or in groups. A few brushfoots stack their eggs, row upon row, or lay them in short chains. After passing through five or six instars, larvae pupate suspended from a group of hooks (the cremaster) at the rear of the body, anchored in a button of silk spun by the larva. Many are secretive, feeding at night, forming shelters, or in other ways maintaining a low profile. A fair proportion is gregarious, especially through the first three instars. The family includes a substantial number of specialists on low-growing plants, including many plants considered toxic to most generalist caterpillars. The chrysalis is often a complex structure with horns, knobs, and sharp angles. Most chrysalids are cryptically colored, but others—dappled in oranges and reds or with spectacular splashes of silver and gold—are nothing short of gaudy in coloration and surpass both the adult and caterpillar in beauty.

COLLECTING AND REARING TIPS

I encounter brushfoots only occasionally as most are present in low density. Because so many feed on forbs, grasses, and other architecturally inconspicuous plants, it is best to review likely foodplants before a day in the field. Beating works well for those species that feed on vines, shrubs, and trees. I have had limited success holding females for eggs—they are strong flyers that do not take well to confinement.

AMERICAN SNOUT
Libytheana carinenta

RECOGNITION Highly variable in color, but easily recognizable by its posture and foodplant. Green to yellow with brown markings; much of *body splattered with small pale spots that are more or less aligned in transverse rows*. T2 and A8 often marked with subdorsal darkened splotch. Many individuals marked with pale to yellow middorsal, subdorsal, and spiracular stripes. *Frequently, caterpillars arch their thorax and tuck head downward or to side*. Three transverse creases run across dorsum of each abdominal segment. Dark form larvae may occur in high density populations and, possibly as well, if larvae are exposed to high humidities (Edwards 1881; Akito Kawahara, pers. comm.). Larva to 2.5cm.

OCCURRENCE Forests, woodlands, thickets, watercourses, late successional fields, coastal communities, and other habitats. Commonly the Carolinas through Gulf States west to Arizona; migrating north through much of the Midwest and extreme southern New England. Mature caterpillars occur throughout the growing season, but mostly in July and later northward.

COMMON FOODPLANTS Hackberry.

REMARKS The eggs are laid singly on the underside of new growth. The early instars require young leaves. The overall aspect of the larva, at least when viewed from a distance, is not unlike a partially opened hackberry leaf. The American Snout is a regular summer migrant across much of the eastern United States. Massive northward migrations, involving millions of individuals, have been reported. Evidently these populations originate in Texas and Arizona, or to the south in Mexico. Several such accounts are described by Shields (1984) and Tveten and Tveten (1996). No stages are freeze-tolerant, and thus northern localities must be recolonized each summer. The adult overwinters.

GULF FRITILLARY
Agraulis vanillae

RECOGNITION *Warningly colored with orange or red and long, shiny black spines. Integument shiny.* Orange ground color with middorsal and broad, black, purple, or lavender supraspiracular stripes that run length of body. Head orange above and black below. Thoracic legs and plates above prolegs on A3–A7 shiny black. Larva to 4.5cm.

OCCURRENCE Sun-loving adults frequent old fields, thickets, floodplain forests, open woodlands, hammocks, and rural and urban gardens. Resident in Gulf States north to the Carolinas, but migrating north into Midwest and New Jersey. Barring hard frosts, active year-round in southern Florida and Texas and whenever new growth is available for young caterpillars.

COMMON FOODPLANTS Passion-vine.

REMARKS The Gulf Fritillary is a migratory species that establishes transient populations well north of the Gulf States. It is a human-tolerant insect, well known for its ability to maintain colonies in parks and botanical gardens. Many longwings adapt readily to life in greenhouses, perhaps too well, as it doesn't take long before passion-vines are in short supply. In my images of the Gulf Fritillary from Texas the caterpillars have broad purple to lavender stripes, whereas those from Florida have thinner black striping. The chrysalis is an odd construction that resembles a bird dropping in some ways, but in other ways, a dead curled up leaf (inset).

Dryas iulia

RECOGNITION Markings exceptionally variable: often brown or black with *orange head*, but some populations nearly white with darker markings. Another form essentially black except for broken, whitish middorsal and spiracular stripes. *Dorsum and sides bearing long black spines that have many (circa ten) needlelike branches.* Upper portion of body may be transversely marked with fine brown or black lines and spots. Many forms with lateral white patches that begin at legs and extend back and up to subdorsum of following segment. *Head frequently marked with dark splotches to either side of frons.* Prolegs pale orange. Larva to 4.5cm.

OCCURRENCE Scrub thickets, watercourses, pinelands and other open woodlands, edges of hammocks, and gardens where its foodplant has been planted in southern Florida and Texas. In southern Florida mature larvae occur year-round.

COMMON FOODPLANTS Passion-vine.

REMARKS Longwings are certainly candidates for our most intelligent butterflies. Adults trapline, learning a route where they will find flowers, then repeatedly visiting the blooms in the same sequence each day or on consecutive days. The spines of Julia caterpillars are easily broken——the ends snapping off even when caterpillars are handled gently—and leak droplets of greenish hemolymph. Some people break out in a rash after handling the caterpillars (Tveten and Tveten 1996). Heliconiine caterpillars, especially early instars, specialize on new growth. Many longwing caterpillars are cannibalistic, perhaps because new growth is such a precious commodity. Ovipositing females will search a shoot for several seconds and reject plants with previously laid eggs. Interestingly, some passion-vines have evolved egg-mimicking growths (stipules, accessory buds, leaf nectaries, and petioles), presumably to dupe ovipositing females.

ZEBRA
Heliconius charithonius

RECOGNITION Unmistakable: *porcelain white with contrasting, long, black spines and orange or red abdominal prolegs.* Subventer of body dark. Larva to 4.5cm.

OCCURRENCE Edges of hammocks, open woodlands, and gardens where its foodplant has been planted in southern Florida and Texas. Mature larvae may be found year-round.

COMMON FOODPLANTS Passion-vine.

REMARKS Although sometimes placed in their own family, the longwings represent no more than a highly specialized grouping within the brushfoots. Unfortunately, only a handful of these interesting tropical butterflies are resident in our area. As is typical for the subfamily, our species are specialists on passion-vine, a plant that is well defended chemically. Both larval and adult longwings are distasteful as evidenced by their bright colorations and conspicuous behaviors. All of our species have two long black spines on the head and three rows down each side of the abdomen. Whereas butterflies are known to imbibe nectar, Heliconius species are among a select few that also include pollen in their diet. Through their proboscis the adults are able to secrete enzymes that solubilize amino acids on the outside of pollen grains. The butterflies then reverse the direction of flow and ingest the dissolved compounds. They are long-lived butterflies; adults of some species live six months or more. Male Zebras are able to search out and recognize female pupae that are about to hatch. Even before the female has completely emerged, males can break the shell of the chrysalis and mate with the emerging female.

Larval coloration varies considerably across the range of many species and often within a population. Our species have stiff, branched, thickened spines (scoli) over the body and head. Although they appear to have stinging spines, all are harmless to the touch.

EASTERN COMMA
Polygonia comma

RECOGNITION Ground color pale green, yellow, white, or even black. Abdomen sometimes marked with brick red spots above spiracles. *Head bears numerous black and white spines* (inset). *Dorsal scolus very large, much broader at its base than its apex; commonly light-colored with blackened tips.* Pale larvae are often marked with a broad, dark subdorsal stripe. Larva to 4cm. Satyr Anglewing (*Polygonia satyrus*) generally dark below and pale green above, but otherwise similar; both feed within shelters on nettle. The Satyr Anglewing is restricted to localities in central Indiana, our northern tier of states, and southern Canada. Other eastern anglewings—Gray Comma (*P. progne*), Green Comma (*P. faunus*), and Hoary Comma (*P. gracilis*)—occur on a different array of foodplants.

OCCURRENCE Wet meadows, edges of watercourses, woodlands, and disturbed areas from southern Canada to central and eastern Texas. Two generations with mature caterpillars in June, then again in August and September, over much of East.

COMMON FOODPLANTS Nettle, false nettle, hops, and wood nettle; also elm.

REMARKS Caterpillar resides in loose shelter fashioned by folding under the edges of a single leaf.

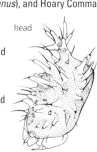

head

QUESTION MARK
Polygonia interrogationis

RECOGNITION Anglewing (*Polygonia*) caterpillars have a pair of dark spiny scoli issuing from top of head and thickened side branches of abdominal scoli that bear black sharpened tips. The Question Mark caterpillar varies from yellow through red and orange (usually) to almost black; *beautifully detailed with white spotting and cream to rusty middorsal, subdorsal, supraspiracular, and subspiracular stripes.* Many forms have an oblique pale line

running beneath spiracle on A4–A8. Bases of the midabdominal prolegs commonly wine red. Larva to 4.5cm. Head of Question Mark has proportionately shorter and sparser spines than Eastern Comma (*Polygonia comma*); many Question Marks have a reddish brown head capsule, while that of the Eastern Comma is more often black. Central shafts of dorsal scoli in Question Mark usually orange; those of Eastern Comma more often pale and with proportionately thicker bases.

OCCURRENCE Woodlands, mesic forests, floodplains, edges of watercourses, roadsides, parks, and yards from southern Canada to central Florida and central Mexico. Two generations over much of range with mature caterpillars in early summer and then again at the end of summer; throughout growing season in Deep South.

COMMON FOODPLANTS Elm and hackberry commonly, but also hops and nettles.

REMARKS Question Mark caterpillars feed without making a shelter, especially on foodplants like elm and hackberry with stiff leaves. On nettle and hops, a lower side shelter may be constructed. I find larvae by searching young elm trees growing along woodland edges and fence rows. Females stack their eggs, sometimes forming chains of eight or more. Thus if you find one larva, it is likely that one or more of its siblings is nearby. The chrysalis bears a strong keel over the thorax and four abdominal pairs of brilliant gold spots. All anglewings (*Polygonia*) overwinter as adults.

RECOGNITION Stunning, *spiny black and red caterpillar* that cannot be confused with any other. Dorsum set with eight red blotches that begin on T3 and end on A7. Body dappled with white spots and armed with long, stout, black spines with relatively short side branches. Prolegs often reddened. Larva to 5.5cm.

OCCURRENCE Wetlands and watercourses, woodland edges and glades, yards, and city parks from northern Canada to northern half of Florida and Texas. One principal brood throughout much of East with mature caterpillars in June and July. Number of generations in South unclarified.

COMMON FOODPLANTS Willows and poplars; also elm, hackberry, and birch.

REMARKS The eggs are laid in a cluster that encircles a twig. The larvae remain together until they are fully-fed and finally move off their foodplant to pupate—they may even leave more or less en masse. As a group they make quite a spectacle with their striking black and red coloration and synchronous thrashing behavior that ensues if the cluster is threatened. They are messy feeders, commonly defoliating branches or small trees. Parasitism may run high, with few larvae surviving from a given cohort. Adults are our longest-lived butterflies; some individuals survive nearly a year. They emerge in midsummer, aestivate until fall, and then seek out a woodpile, shed, or other sheltered site in which to pass the winter. In my experience they rarely use the butterfly hibernation houses sold by nature centers. Adults fly on warm days in the winter and spring; a few seasoned individuals straggle into July.

MILBERT'S TORTOISESHELL
Aglais milberti

RECOGNITION *Dark spiny caterpillar with cream lateral stripes and pale venter.* Sides with series of crescents, just above and below spiracles, that may join to form lateral stripes that run length of body. Body pale below. Stout black scoli, which are not as obviously branched as those of the Red Admiral (*Vanessa atalanta*) and Eastern Comma (*Polygonia comma*), intermixed among numerous pale hairlike setae. Most forms speckled with minute white spots (which under magnification are revealed to be the setal bases). Head set with mixture of black and pale stiff setae. Larva to 3.5cm.

OCCURRENCE Wetlands and watercourses, fields and meadows, weed lots, pastures, and other open habitats from northern Canada south in East to New England, Pennsylvania, and Great Lakes States, but straying southward in boom years. Two principal broods across the southern portion of its range with mature caterpillars in spring, then again in early summer.

COMMON FOODPLANTS Nettle.

REMARKS While this northern butterfly is absent from Connecticut in most years, and sometimes for decades, its numbers were high in both 2003 and 2004, with statewide evidence or reports of breeding. The greenish eggs are laid in huge clusters of 100 or more on the underside of nettle leaves. The young caterpillars feed in dense groups usually from the top of the plant downward, removing all leaf tissue but the veins as they descend leaf by leaf—the damage is diagnostic. Numbers were so high in 2004 in Connecticut that patches of the foodplant were defoliated and many caterpillars starved before they could reach maturity. The adult overwinters in woodpiles, sheds, and under bark.

Vanessa atalanta

RECOGNITION Highly variable species ranging from almost white or yellow-green to black; usually *heavily salted with pale flecking.* A creamy splotch often present on A1–A7 forward and a little below spiracle; in some forms these spots fuse to form a broad, undulating subspiracular stripe. Head dark with pale, stiff hairs and spines (inset); *no scoli* (branched spines). Outer side of prolegs usually pale orange. In darker forms, bases of scoli or surrounding integument may be rusty orange. Larva to 4cm.

OCCURRENCE Meadows, fields, watercourses, swamps; breeding throughout our area in summer months. At least two generations with mature larvae from June onward.

COMMON FOODPLANTS Nettle, false nettle, pellitory, and wood nettle, all in nettle family (Urticaceae).

REMARKS The young caterpillars build nests, tying up the leaves of a shoot tip. Later the larval shelter may consist of a single, folded leaf. Each caterpillar makes a number of shelters. Like the Painted Lady, northern populations are established each spring from migrants from the South. But unlike that species, it is present virtually every year and its numbers rarely climb to the point where they defoliate their foodplants. It overwinters as pupae and adults in the South.

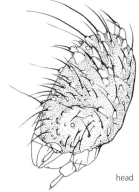

head

PAINTED LADY
Vanessa cardui

RECOGNITION Ground coloration varies from green, yellow, or pink to nearly black. Lavender and yellow morph pictured here makes for an especially attractive combination. Commonly with pale addorsal stripe. Variously colored spiracular stripe often present. *Dark head densely set with long, unbranched hairs.* Each body segment bears prominent dorsal, subdorsal, and lateral scoli (hardened, branched spines). Its *nest building* habit and diet will distinguish it from most caterpillars. Larva to 4.5cm.

OCCURRENCE Extremely generalized; open sunny habitats including waste lots, gardens, grasslands, fields, farmlands, and roadsides, from above timberline to low deserts. Resident in Mexico, and perhaps portions of southwestern United States, frequently migrating throughout our area. Over much of East, adults show up in April and May, and mature caterpillars appear within a month.

COMMON FOODPLANTS Burdock, thistle, and other composites; hollyhock and other members of mallow family; and lupine and other legumes preferred; many other low-growing, mostly non-woody plants are used, especially during outbreaks.

REMARKS In some ways the common name applies better to the caterpillar than to the adult in that two individuals are scarcely ever alike. The caterpillar uses silk to construct a "nest." Occasionally it is common enough to be a pest of crops and garden plants; and in sparsely vegetated landscapes, it can defoliate acres of thistle, globe mallow, and other foodplants. It is a strong-flying cosmopolitan migrant that has no trouble outpacing the monarch in its early sprints to southern Canada each spring, reaching Hudson Bay by June. In many locales, the butterfly may show up in numbers for a single generation and then be gone within weeks; in New England it is scarce in most years.

Vanessa virginiensis

RECOGNITION Although variable in coloration, *usually recognizable by red bases of dorsal abdominal scoli* (branched spines) and thin creamy bands that run across the top of each thoracic and abdominal segment. Most individuals have pairs of white spots over A2–A8. Head black with numerous conspicuous hairs but lacking prominent spines and scoli. Larva to 4cm.

OCCURRENCE Fields, waste lots, powerline right of ways, cemeteries, yards, and other open habitats, breeding throughout our area in summer months. Connecticut with mature caterpillars by mid-June, then again in July and throughout rest of summer.

COMMON FOODPLANTS Cudweed or everlasting, pussytoes, rabbit-tobacco, and related composites.

REMARKS The larvae tie up several leaves and feed within this shelter. A single larva will make a number of shelters, especially on plants with small leaves (like pussytoes). Occupied shelters are inconspicuous, especially if the caterpillar has yet to begin feeding. Because everlasting and pussytoes commonly grow along roadsides, walking paths, and in cemeteries, American Ladies are among our most commonly encountered nymphalid caterpillars. The larvae inevitably turn up in any garden where their foodplants have been planted, often in unwelcome numbers. They are so regular in occurrence, even across our northern tier of states, that it is easy to forget that they, like the Red Admiral and Painted Lady, are migrants. It is an early migrant, establishing in Canada by May.

COMMON BUCKEYE
Junonia coenia

RECOGNITION Coloration highly variable, usually mostly black above and white and/or orange along sides with *metallic blue-black dorsal spines*. Pale stripe runs down dorsal midline. Spines along sides arise from orange wartlike bases. *Head orange above with black bordering frons; short black scolus over each lobe* (inset)*; heavily salted with white tubercles.* Prolegs orange. Larva to 4.5cm. Two closely

related buckeyes occur in southern Florida and Texas. Mangrove Buckeye (*Junonia evarete*) feeds on black mangroves, especially the new growth of young propagules; the body is very dark with white spotting (Opler 1992). Neck (1996) reports other foodplants in the Scrophulariaceae and Acanthaceae as well. The caterpillars of the Tropical Buckeye (*J. genoveva*) are similar to those of the Common Buckeye and share many of the same foodplants. Identification of wild-collected *Junonia* larvae from southern Texas and Florida is probably best based on adult characters.

OCCURRENCE Coastal areas, marshlands, abandoned fields, roadsides, and other open habitats. Resident in Gulf States north through the Carolinas, regularly migrating northward to Great Lakes States, New England, and extreme southern Canada, but increasingly sporadic northward. Over much of East with mature larvae from June until first hard frosts.

COMMON FOODPLANTS Plants in snapdragon (Scrophulariaceae) and acanthus (Acanthaceae) families, including plantain, gerardia, *Ruellia*, snapdragon and toadflax.

REMARKS A superb caterpillar when viewed at those angles where the bases of the dorsal spines reflect metallic blue-black light. No stages of the butterfly are able to withstand freezing temperatures—each year the Buckeye must recolonize its summer range.

head

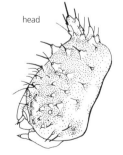

WHITE PEACOCK *Anartia jatrophae*

Resident in lower Florida and Texas. Breeding nearly year-round. *Bacopa*, *Blechum*, lippia, *Phyla*, *Ruellia*, water hyssop, and others.

RED-SPOTTED PURPLE *Limenitis arthemis astyanax*

Nebraska to Wisconsin and southern New Hampshire to central Florida and parts of Texas. Two generations northward with mature caterpillars in May and June, then again in July and August. Cherry, oak, and poplar.

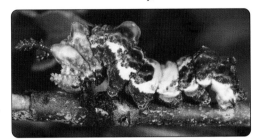

COMPTON TORTOISE SHELL *Roddia vaualbum*

Central Canada south through New England, Great Lakes States, and Upper Midwest, pushing farther southward in irruptive years. One generation with mature caterpillars in June. Aspen, birch, elm, and willow.

GRAY COMMA *Polygonia progne*

Much of Canada to North Carolina (in mountains), Great Lakes States, and into Arkansas (Ozarks). Two generations over much of East with mature caterpillars in June and again in August and September. Commonly currant.

VARIEGATED FRITILLARY
Euptoieta claudia

RECOGNITION *Shiny, orange, black, and white caterpillar. Long, black dorsal scoli of prothorax extend well forward of reddish orange head.* Scoli, thoracic legs, and plate above abdominal prolegs with purple-blue reflections. Middorsum of A1–A8 bears oval footprint-shaped white (and sometimes black) spot over each segment. Broad black subdorsal and spiracular stripes infused with white spotting; in many individuals white more prominent than black. Larva to 5cm.

OCCURRENCE Meadows, fields, and other open habitats. Resident from North Carolina south and west to California, but migrating north into southern Canada and New England. Over much of East with at least two generations; mature caterpillars from July through the onset of winter.

COMMON FOODPLANTS Passion-vine and violet commonly, but also flax, lamb's ears, mayapple, purslane, and others (*see* Howe 1975).

REMARKS A caterpillar handsome enough to kindle interest even in the casual observer. Its bright orange, black, and white colors suggest that it is chemically protected. Females often deposit eggs if held for one or two days under a strong light. Captive adults should be fed once or twice a day and offered violets or passion-vine as an oviposition substrate. Nymphalid chrysalids are among the most beautiful and structurally diverse pupae in the insect world. They would make a beautiful poster or photo essay. That of the Variegated Fritillary is figured in the inset. It overwinters as an adult in the South.

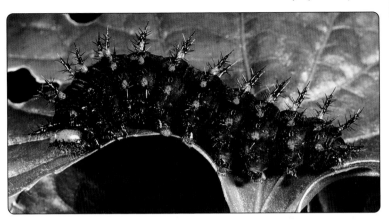

RECOGNITION Large, nearly black caterpillar with *lower half of dorsal scoli orange* (or tan). *Angulate head orange above and black below.* Occasionally with double row of grayish spots running length of abdomen. Larva to 5.5cm. Aphrodite Fritillary (*Speyeria aphrodite*) similar but with dorsal scoli uniformly black and orange patch on head less pronounced (*see* page 124). In Diana Fritillary (*S. diana*)
ground color has orange-brown cast; dorsal scoli proportionately longer and only lower third colored orange; top of head more angulate, almost horned, with orange restricted in extent (*see* page 124). Sometimes with double row of white spots running down dorsum. Regal Fritillary (*S. idalia*) caterpillars have broad, tan middorsal and orange subspiracular stripes; top half of head bright red-orange (*see* page 124).

OCCURRENCE Open woodlands, wet and dry meadows and fields, pastures, powerline right of ways, and yards. Transcontinental in Canada south in East to northeastern Oklahoma, northern portions of Gulf States, and Piedmont areas of Georgia and Carolinas. One generation with mature larvae in May and June.

COMMON FOODPLANTS Violet.

REMARKS The life cycle of our large fritillaries seems ill-conceived. Females lay the eggs in the fall, and only rarely bother to place the eggs on violet leaves. The first instars hatch two to three weeks later, and will drink water, but will not eat for seven to eight months. Few weather the winter. But nature is compensatory—fritillaries are our most fecund butterflies with some species laying over 2,000 eggs. The young caterpillars will starve unless they have access to new violet growth. Fritillaries are secretive, nocturnal, ground-dwelling caterpillars; look for them by turning objects and inspecting brush in the vicinity of violet patches. Last instars are sizable insects capable of consuming two or more grown violet plants.

FRITILLARIES, CHECKERSPOTS, AND CRESCENTS

APHRODITE FRITILLARY *Speyeria aphrodite*
Much of Canada south in East to northern Georgia (mountains), Great Lakes States, and Nebraska. One generation with mature caterpillars in late May and June. Violet.

ATLANTIS FRITILLARY *Speyeria atlantis*
Much of Canada south in East to West Virginia (mountains) and Great Lakes States. One generation with mature caterpillars in late May and June. Violet.

REGAL FRITILLARY *Speyeria idalia*
Mostly tall grass prairies of Midwest. Presently North Dakota, Minnesota, and Illinois south to Arkansas; remnant populations in Pennsylvania and Virginia. One generation with mature caterpillars from late May into June. Violet.

DIANA FRITILLARY *Speyeria diana*
Missouri to West Virginia south to Georgia and Arkansas. One generation with mature caterpillars in late May and June. Violet.

MEADOW FRITILLARY *Boloria bellona*
Much of Canada south in East to North Carolina (mountains), Kentucky, and Missouri. Up to three generations in southern portion of range with mature caterpillars from April to September. Violet.

SILVER-BORDERED FRITILLARY *Boloria selene*
Much of Canada south in East to West Virginia (mountains), Great Lakes States, and Nebraska. Up to three generations in southern portion of range with mature caterpillars from late May to September. Violet.

HARRIS' CHECKERSPOT *Chlosyne harrisii*
Southeastern Saskatchewan to Prince Edward Island south to New Jersey, West Virginia, and Great Lakes States. One generation with mature caterpillars from late May to mid-June. Flat-topped white aster.

PHAON CRESCENT *Phyciodes phaon*
Resident along Gulf north through North Carolina. Multiple generations with mature caterpillars throughout growing season. Fog fruit (*Phyla*).

Aphrodite Fritillary

Atlantis Fritillary

Regal Fritillary

Diana Fritillary

Meadow Fritillary

Silver-bordered Fritillary

Harris' Checkerspot

Phaon Crescent

PEARL CRESCENT
Phyciodes tharos

RECOGNITION *Small, dark brown with numerous white speckles.* Setal warts shiny reddish brown, more or less aligned in ring over dorsum and sides. Broken white subdorsal and subspiracular stripes continue onto head. *Head coloration distinctive: mostly shiny black with white line over each lobe, frons, and lateral line.* Larva to 2cm.

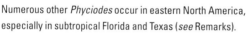

Numerous other *Phyciodes* occur in eastern North America, especially in subtropical Florida and Texas (*see* Remarks).

OCCURRENCE Open fields, powerline right of ways, wet meadows, grasslands, waste lots, and other open habitats from Saskatchewan to southeastern Maine south through Florida and Texas. Two or three generations in Northeast with mature caterpillars from May onward; presumably continuously brooded in Deep South.

COMMON FOODPLANTS Aster.

REMARKS Even though the Pearl Crescent is among the most common butterflies in Connecticut, I have never encountered its caterpillar. Females raft the eggs in clusters of 20–300. The young caterpillars are solitary and do not form a nest. Tawny Crescent (*P. batesii*), a specialist on wavy-leaved aster (*Symphyotrichum undulatum*), is very local and scarce. The first two instars of the Tawny Crescent feed within a silken nest spun on the underside of a leaf blade. The white markings on the head are smaller and the stripes more prominent than those of the Pearl Crescent. The Northern Crescent (*P. cocyta*) largely replaces the Pearl Crescent in Canada and portions of New England and Great Lakes States. Its caterpillar often comes in a reddish-brown to pinkish form that is not known to occur in the Pearl Crescent, but otherwise it is similarly marked. Scott (1986) provides a fine summary of the taxonomy, biology, and the early stages of our crescents. The third instar overwinters.

Chlosyne nycteis

RECOGNITION *Nearly black with dusting of minute white spots on dorsum and sides.* Lateral area frequently bears broad yellow to orange spiracular stripe, which is split into two thinner stripes in some forms. Head black, shiny, cleft, without scoli. Larva to 3cm.

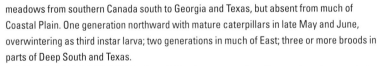

OCCURRENCE Open woodlands, forest clearings, stream courses, trap rock ridges, and, less commonly, wet meadows from southern Canada south to Georgia and Texas, but absent from much of Coastal Plain. One generation northward with mature caterpillars in late May and June, overwintering as third instar larva; two generations in much of East; three or more broods in parts of Deep South and Texas.

COMMON FOODPLANTS Especially wing-stem and sunflowers, but also reported on aster, crown-beard, and black-eyed susan.

REMARKS The female rafts eggs; the young larvae feed together until the third instar. Scott (1986) reports that the third-stage larva hibernates in a "special red-brown skin." Look for the caterpillars on the undersides of plants with damaged leaves. Because the species is gregarious, the feeding damage of a cohort is conspicuous—once you develop a search image for damage you merely need to scan a given patch of foodplant to know if the Silvery Checkerspot is present. The larvae are quick to curl up and drop to the ground if molested. In the Northeast, this species has disappeared—I know of no extant colonies in any of the six New England states. Ranges in Opler (1992) and other works are largely historical and no longer accurate. Curiously, and perhaps not coincidently, Connecticut's colonies of Harris' Checkerspot (*Chlosyne harrisii*) also are in a state of decline. Prepupal larvae of Silvery Checkerspot wander before pupation.

BALTIMORE
Euphydryas phaeton

RECOGNITION Body boldly marked in black and orange. *Each abdominal segment has broad orange band that includes the scoli and which is followed by two sets of alternating black and orange bands. Head, T1, T2, and A9–A10 black.* Larva to 4.5cm. Caterpillars of Harris' Checkerspot (*Chlosyne harrisii*) have T2 and A9 with more orange, the transverse orange bands are interrupted at the level of the spiracles, and small yellow spots follow spiracles on A1–A8. Branches of dorsal scoli needlelike, less than half the height of scolus; in Baltimore branches more hairlike, nearly as long as scolus height.

OCCURRENCE Wet meadows, open floodplains, and less commonly, fields, from southern Canada to Georgia, northern Gulf States, and Ozarks. One generation with mature caterpillars in May and early June.

COMMON FOODPLANTS Turtlehead favored for oviposition, but plantain and yellow foxglove also used. Late instar larvae accept many additional plants, including honeysuckle, lousewort, and viburnum.

REMARKS Stunning as both a larva and an adult, the Baltimore is a perennial favorite among those who take the time to watch and study insects. The female lays all her eggs in a cluster that may contain as many as 700. The reddish eggs hatch after about two weeks. The young larvae form a silken nest and feed from within on new turtlehead leaves. The larvae stop feeding in August, but remain within their communal tent, where they spend the winter. With the onset of springtime temperatures, the larvae leave the nest and wander off to feed individually. The diet is appreciably expanded at this point (*see above*). The Baltimore's chrysalis is also attractive: chalky with raised black and mustard bumps over the abdomen and smeared black spots across the wing.

GOATWEED BUTTERFLY *Anaea andria*

Resident in Gulf States, but straying north to Michigan and southeast Virginia. Two generations in Missouri, somewhat asynchronous generations throughout growing season southward. Croton.

RUDDY DAGGERWING *Marpesia petreus*

Southern Florida and Texas. Mature caterpillars year-round. Fig (*Ficus*).

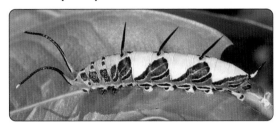

COMMON MESTRA *Mestra amymone*

Resident in southern Texas, straying northward into Midwest. Mature caterpillars year-round in Rio Grande Valley. Noseburn.

MALACHITE *Siproeta stelenes*

Southern Florida. Continuously brooded with mature caterpillars year-round. Blechum, *Ruellia*, and other acanths (Acanthaceae).

VICEROY
Limenitis archippus

RECOGNITION Admirals (*Limenitis*) are immediately recognizable as our only horned bird-dropping mimics. *Dorsum of T2 bears long spined horns that extend over head.* Smaller spined humps occur over T3, A2, A7, and A8. Each side of head drawn into a point that bears a short, brown scolus. Midabdominal segments saddled with white; laterally, saddle merges with white subspiracular stripe that runs from A2–A10. Larva to 5cm. Caterpillars of White Admiral and Red-spotted Purple (each representing different subspecies of *Limenitis arthemis*) similar to Viceroy, but a little less spiny: scolus on head and spine clusters on T2, A2, A7, and A8 proportionately smaller. Additionally, the rounded humps over dorsum of A2 are larger and the "antlers" slightly more clubbed than those of Viceroy (*see* page 121).

OCCURRENCE Wet meadows, edges of watercourses, and other open wet habitats from central Canada south through Florida and much of Texas. Two and a partial third generation over much of East with mature caterpillars from late May onward; continuous broods in parts of South.

COMMON FOODPLANTS Willow, aspen, and poplar.

REMARKS The caterpillar overwinters in a silken hibernaculum. Look for a rolled leaf, sometimes no more than 1cm in length and a fraction of that in width. Like a tiny Promethea Moth (*Callosamia promethia*) cocoon, the petiole of the hibernaculum is secured to a stem with silk so that it stays attached through the winter. The Viceroy's oddly shaped chrysalis is encountered commonly, dangling from a stick, grass blade, or other object. The shiny brown and white chrysalis also resembles a bird dropping; it bears a prominent rounded keel over the base of the abdomen between the wings.

TAWNY EMPEROR
Asterocampa clyton

RECOGNITION   *Pale green caterpillar with enlarged thorny head, narrow neck, and spiny processes extending from rear of body. Head spikelets on dorsal antlers more than half length of longest spikelets issuing from branched spines of "cheeks."* Blue-green middorsal stripe usually continuous.

Larva to 4cm. In Hackberry Emperor (*Asterocampa celtis*) spikelets of dorsal antlers shorter, often half the length of longest ones borne along cheeks; dorsal stripe inconspicuous or absent (Eastern populations) (but not always—*see* Allen 1997) (lower images). Caterpillars of Empress Leilia (*Asterocampa leilia*) tend to have more yellow spotting; well-developed, yellow subdorsal and subspiracular stripes; and proportionately longer antlers. Larvae of this southern Texas butterfly feed only on spiny hackberry (*Celtis pallida*). *See* Friedlander (1987) for additional characters and life history information about Hackberry Butterflies.

OCCURRENCE   Thickets, watercourses, ridge tops, woodland edges and clearings, fencerows, and parks from Minnesota to southern New England to Florida and Mexico. In Northeast with at least a partial second generation with mature caterpillars in May and June, then again in July and August; continuously brooded through growing season in parts of South.

COMMON FOODPLANTS   Hackberry.

REMARKS   The larvae feed communally through the third instar, whereupon they wander off to feed individually, or, in the overwintering brood, roll up a leaf in which to spend the winter. Neither the Hackberry Emperor nor Empress Leilia feed communally. Late instar Tawny Emperors often rest with the body somewhat zigzagged, whereas that of the Hackberry Butterfly is less apt to adopt this position.

Nymphs and Satyrs – Subfamily Satyrinae

Though widespread and common, the spindle-shaped caterpillars are rarely encountered. They are well-camouflaged grass- and sedge-feeders that are active mostly at night. Both the body and head are covered with minute hairs or spines that are frequently borne from whitish granules. A10 is produced into two spurs. One stemma (lateral eye) is greatly enlarged. Our species overwinter as partially grown larvae. Sedge-feeders may accept grasses in captivity.

LITTLE WOOD SATYR
Megisto cymela

RECOGNITION Unlike green ground colors of most satyrids, Little Wood Satyr and its congeners (*Megisto*) tend to be *light brown. Lobes of head but weakly pointed. Vesture of pale, short, hair-tipped spines densely scattered over body.* Sides of body marked with oblique lines and pale subspiracular stripe. Larva to 3cm. Caterpillars of Viola's Satyr (*Megisto viola*) reported to be paler brown (Opler 1992); restricted to parts of South Carolina, Georgia, and northeastern Florida. Red Satyr (*M. rubricata*) caterpillar more conspicuously striped; its darkened middorsal stripe edged with cream; and the dark subdorsal stripe includes whitish dots (Scott 1986). It enters our area in eastern Nebraska, Oklahoma, and Texas.

OCCURRENCE Woods and forest edges, wooded swamps, and brushy fields from southern Canada to southern Florida and central and eastern Texas. Over most of East one protracted (or even staggered) generation with mature larvae in May and early June, overwintering as third or fourth instar (Scott 1986); perhaps two or three broods in Deep South.

COMMON FOODPLANTS Many grasses, including orchard grass and bluegrass.

REMARKS Although this butterfly occurs in yards and around other human habitations, few will ever see the larva. Because the caterpillars are active mostly after nightfall, searches by flashlight can be fruitful.

Enodia anthedon

RECOGNITION Attractive yellow-green larva with *prominent pink to red horns on head and last abdominal segment.* Integument hairy (under a lens), especially above prolegs. The most conspicuous markings are the broad green middorsal and yellow-green subspiracular stripes. A thin, faint subdorsal stripe, green above and yellow below, may run horn to horn. *Head with whitish granules; horn length less than*

head width. Only mandibles and sometimes tips of anterior horns darkly pigmented. Larva to 4.5cm. Caterpillars of Pearly Eye (*Enodia portlandia*) and Creole Pearly Eye (*E. creola*) are closely similar. The Pearly Eye feeds on giant cane and switch cane. The Creole Pearly Eye feeds exclusively on the latter foodplant; its larvae are reported to be paler green in color (Scott 1986). Our Browns (*Satyrodes*) are similar, but have less granulated head capsules, shorter hairs over body, and more conspicuous striping; the horns on the head are essentially as long as the head is broad; they prefer sedges (*see* page 136).

OCCURRENCE Mature woods and open forests, especially if canopy is mostly closed, but enough light penetrates so that there are grassy areas in understory. Southern Canada to northern counties of Gulf States; absent from Coastal Plain. One generation with mature larvae in June, overwintering as third or fourth instar; at least two broods in South.

COMMON FOODPLANTS Many grasses. Scott (1986) lists babel, bottle-brush grass, cutgrass, canary grass, false melic grass, and others.

REMARKS Caterpillars lay down silk each time they move to a new feeding or resting site. The posterior horns are held down and together. When disturbed, both ends of the body are raised and the larva displays its short, blackened mandibles.

COMMON RINGLET
Coenonympha tullia

RECOGNITION *Integument with little white granules, but hairs scarcely visible* even with lens. Ground color usually green, although some individuals tan or brown, particularly those overwintering. *Subdorsal and subspiracular stripes usually well defined.* Broad green middorsal stripe *may be edged with creamy addorsals.* Rounded head unmarked. Pinkish anal spurs proportionately shorter than those of other satyrids treated here. Larva to 2.5cm.

OCCURRENCE Grassy fields and meadows, roadsides, waste lots, yards, and other open habitats. Parts of northern Canada south into entirety of New England, northern tier of Great Lakes States, and Nebraska. Two broods in Connecticut with mature larvae in late May and early June, then again in late July and August.

COMMON FOODPLANTS Many grasses (Poaceae), including bluegrass and needle grass. Also some rushes and sedges, such as cotton grass.

REMARKS In the last two decades this butterfly has been rapidly expanding its range in the Northeast. One thought is that it, like the Silvery Blue (*Glaucopsyche lygdamus*), is using highway corridors to make its southward push. The Ringlet is exceptionally variable in its coloration and life history across its range, which includes northern parts of both North America and Eurasia. Some populations take up to two years to yield a single generation; other populations are single-, double-, or partially triple-brooded. In dry portions of its range, the adults may aestivate over some of the summer months. Seemingly, the Ringlet is evolutionarily poised to fragment into a myriad of distinct species. It overwinters as a young larva.

Cercyonis pegala

RECOGNITION Green to yellow-green caterpillar distinguished from many other eastern nymphs and satyrs by its *large size and rounded head. Short, pink-tipped "tails"* project from A10. A green stripe runs the length of the middorsum. Subdorsal and subspiracular stripes extend length of body; the subdorsal stripe may be absent and often has less of a yellow cast. The *body hairs are comparatively long, fine, and borne from*
inconspicuous granular whitish bases (cf. Northern Pearly Eye, *Enodia anthedon*). *Head "hairy."* Spiracles orange-yellow. Larva to 5cm. Superficially most similar to many satyrs (*Hermeuptychia*, *Cyllopsis*, and *Neonympha*) (*see* page 136), but often distinguished by its habitat (open grassy areas mostly free of trees), larger size, stripes, hairy aspect, and inconspicuous integumental granulations.

OCCURRENCE Grassy meadows, fields, cool season grasslands, powerline right of ways, and open woodlands. Much of southern Canada south to central Florida and central Texas. One generation with mature caterpillars in early summer.

COMMON FOODPLANTS Many grasses (Poaceae), including beard grass, bluegrass, bluestem, oat grass, tall red-top grass, purple-top, and others.

REMARKS Aspects of its life history are similar to those of another grassland butterfly, the Regal Fritillary. Both are long-lived insects that emerge in June and July, but have females that fly into September. Neither species lay eggs until the end of the summer. Both butterflies overwinter as unfed first instars. Perhaps in both cases natural selection has favored individual females that held eggs through the dry weeks of summer, laying eggs at or shortly before the onset of fall rains and cooler weather.

SATYRS AND BROWNS

GEMMED SATYR *Cyllopsis gemma*

Eastern Kansas, southern Ohio, and southeastern Virginia to Florida and Texas. Three to many generations with mature caterpillars throughout year in Deep South. Grass.

CAROLINA SATYR *Hermeuptychia sosybius*

Southeastern Kansas to southern New Jersey (rare) to Florida and Mexico. Three to many generations with mature caterpillars throughout year in Deep South. Grass.

GEORGIA SATYR *Neonympha areolata*

Mostly Atlantic Coastal Plain from southern New Jersey south to Florida and eastern Texas. One generation in New Jersey; two or more southward. Sedge and bulrush.

APPALACHIAN BROWN *Satyrodes appalachia*

Great Lakes States, southern Ontario, and Quebec south to Gulf States and upper Florida. One generation northward with mature caterpillars in early summer over most of range; two broods, at least from Missouri southward. Grass and sedge.

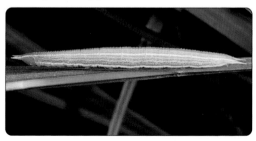

QUEEN
Danaus gilippus

RECOGNITION Bold combination of yellow and white over reddish brown to jet black ground. Three pairs of *whiplike "tentacles" arise from dorsum of T2, A2, and A8.* Dorsum of A3–A7 bears a pair of yellow spots; smaller, white or yellow sets of spots also found over T3 and A1. Creamy transverse lines drop over sides and fuse in puddle of yellow and white below spiracles. Head black and white striped. Larva to 5cm. Immediately separable from Monarch (*Danaus plexippus*) by its extra set of black tentacles on A2. Soldier (*D. eresimus*) has a yellow-green or gray ground color, up to ten pairs of closely situated spots running along dorsum, and some forms possess a broad black or white spiracular line. Literature describing its caterpillar is contradictory, perhaps because it coloration varies geographically. The Soldier breeds from southern Florida and Texas to Brazil, but like other milkweed butterflies it wanders, recently as far north as Connecticut. A good place to search for its caterpillars is in salt marshes and other coastal communities (Minno and Emmel 1993).
OCCURRENCE Hardwood hammocks, pinewoods, thickets, salt marshes, waste lots, roadsides, fields, and other open habitats. Resident from Georgia to Texas, with strays moving north to southern New England and Upper Midwest over summer months. South Carolina with at least two and as many as four broods with mature larvae from May through late summer.
COMMON FOODPLANTS Milkweeds and white vine or rambling milkweed.
REMARKS Like the Monarch, its caterpillars prefer new growth. Frequently it is found in more arid habitats than the Monarch.

MONARCH
Danaus plexippus

RECOGNITION A caterpillar that needs no introduction, second only to the woolly bear in the number of people that recognize it—the *yellow, white, and black banded caterpillars* can be confused with no others in our fauna. Even the head bears bold black and yellow striping. *T2 and A8 with black filaments*. Larva to 5cm.

OCCURRENCE Waste lots, roadsides, fields, croplands, wet meadows, marshes, gardens, and other open habitats. Eastern populations migrating north from roosting sites west of Mexico City into Canada each spring and summer. In Connecticut mature caterpillars occur from June onward; breeding from March until November in Texas.

COMMON FOODPLANTS   Milkweed (*Asclepias*), blue and sand vine (both *Cynanchum*).

REMARKS A favorite in classrooms, as metamorphosis proceeds rapidly—the entire life cycle may transpire in 30 days. The chrysalis is stunning: sea green with fine lines of black and glimmering spots of gold. This coloration gives way to the orange-red, black, and white colors of the adult a day before emergence. The paper thin shell of the chrysalis allows one to watch in detail the "birth" of our most familiar and traveled insect. Search for caterpillars on plants producing young leaves—old growth is ignored by egg-laying females. Isolated patches of milkweed along roadsides, railroads, and other flyways are especially reliable. In late summer, look for a roadside or hayfield that was cut a month or so before—the new growth will have caterpillars. The larvae sequester cardiac glycosides from the milkweed leaves that they consume. Concentrations of these heart toxins in their bodies may be several times higher than those occurring in milkweed leaves. The glycosides consumed by the caterpillars are carried forward both into the chrysalis and adult stages, affording them protection as well.

A small family with just eight Eastern species, four in each of two subfamilies: the Drepaninae and Thyatirinae. The upper part of the head is often lobed or horned. All have an extra seta above and rearward of the spiracle on A1–A8. The crochets are often grouped in two series: the inner set possess larger crochets of one or two lengths; in many hooktips there is an outer set of smaller crochets that are few in number. Many of our species feed from within a loosely tied shelter. The pupa overwinters in a cocoon spun in leaf litter. Hooktip caterpillars lack anal prolegs and possess a pointed anal plate; those treated here have abundant, small to minute secondary setae. Thyatirines are introduced separately below.

ROSE HOOKTIP
Oreta rosea

RECOGNITION Only eastern caterpillar with *long unpaired "tail."* Prominent *middorsal knob over third thoracic segment.* Always variegated in browns and grays with dorsal saddle constricted over A4. Each lobe of head bearing a spined knob. Larva to 3cm.

OCCURRENCE Bottomlands, woodlands, and forests from Canada south to Florida and Texas. At least two generations over much of East with mature caterpillars from late June onward.

COMMON FOODPLANTS Viburnum.

REMARKS The larva is a dead-leaf mimic, its tail presumably has evolved to resemble a leaf petiole. Larvae rest on the upper sides of leaves, exposed, relying on their unusual form and cryptic colors for protection. The moth and its caterpillars are locally common in woodlands where viburnum is common in the understory.

MASKED BIRCH CATERPILLAR (ARCHED HOOKTIP)
Drepana arcuata

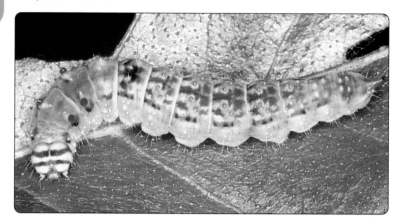

RECOGNITION Somewhat flattened, mostly green but mottled with brown above. *Head with distinctive looped band over top and second parallel brown bar crossing triangle and then bending downward and passing through eyes.* Enlarged reddish setal warts over dorsum of T2 and T3; those over A2 may also be enlarged but usually to a lesser extent.

Larva to 2.5cm. Two-lined Hooktip (*Drepana bilineata*) occurs from Michigan and New Jersey northward; its caterpillar is brown, more warted, and lacks the masking across the face (inset). It too feeds on alder and birch.

OCCURRENCE Northern woodlands and forests from Canada south to Missouri and mountainous areas of South Carolina. Two generations in Northeast with mature caterpillars from late June to July, then again from August to October; possibly a third generation in Missouri (Richard Heitzman, pers. comm.).

COMMON FOODPLANTS Alder and birch.

REMARKS The larva forms a shelter by folding over a leaf edge. At night the caterpillars are active, foraging outside the shelter or exiting to fashion a new bivouac. Jane Yack and colleagues have found that Masked Birch Caterpillars "talk" to one another by scraping their mandibles or beating oar-shaped anal structures against a leaf surface as a means of advertising their presence. In most cases, wandering caterpillars move away from caterpillars with previously established shelters that are drumming out warnings, although occasionally large caterpillars move in and displace smaller residents from their shelters. *Drepana* caterpillars sometimes adopt a dragonesque posture, with the head and hind end raised.

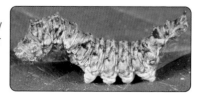

Both adults and larvae resemble cutworms (Noctuidae), yet they are considered geometroids. The head is wider than high and the labrum is deeply incised. Their most distinctive feature is the presence of two extra setae posterior to the spiracle on A1–A8 (visible only with a strong lens). The somewhat reduced anal prolegs bear crochets. Adults come to both light and bait.

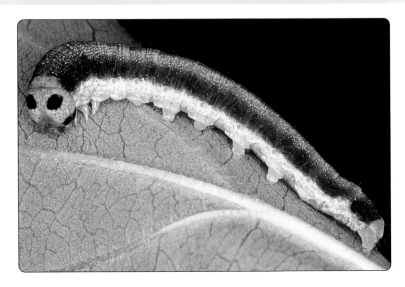

DOGWOOD THYATIRID
Euthyatira pudens

RECOGNITION Gray-green to *smoky above and waxy along sides. Head with prominent black spot over vertex* and smaller black spot that includes eyes. Body widest about T2 then gradually narrowing to rear. Larva to 3.5cm.

OCCURRENCE Woodlands from southern Canada to northern Florida and Texas. One generation with mature caterpillars in May and June.

COMMON FOODPLANTS Dogwood, especially flowering dogwood (*Cornus florida*).

REMARKS The general coloration, waxy bloom, and black spot on the head are reminiscent of a sawfly larva. I have found Dogwood Thyatirid caterpillars in loose shelters and also fully exposed, perched on leaf undersides. A good way to search for caterpillars is to position yourself under a flowering dogwood and then scan lower leaf surfaces. Adults fly early in the year—look for the caterpillars after flowering, but while the foliage is still young.

TUFTED THYATIRID
Pseudothyatira cymatophoroides

RECOGNITION Yellow- to orange-brown with fine reticulate mottling over dorsum and *thin charcoal middorsal stripe.* Thorax swollen. Some forms with pale saddle over T2 and T3; others with white spot over spiracle on A1 or both A1 and A2 (and more rarely A3 and A4). Larva to 3.5cm. Caterpillars of Lettered

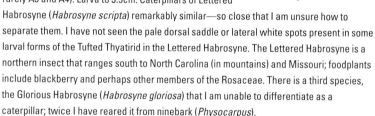

Habrosyne (*Habrosyne scripta*) remarkably similar—so close that I am unsure how to separate them. I have not seen the pale dorsal saddle or lateral white spots present in some larval forms of the Tufted Thyatirid in the Lettered Habrosyne. The Lettered Habrosyne is a northern insect that ranges south to North Carolina (in mountains) and Missouri; foodplants include blackberry and perhaps other members of the Rosaceae. There is a third species, the Glorious Habrosyne (*Habrosyne gloriosa*) that I am unable to differentiate as a caterpillar; twice I have reared it from ninebark (*Physocarpus*).

OCCURRENCE Woodlands and forests from southern Canada to South Carolina, Mississippi, and Arkansas. At least two generations with mature caterpillars from May onward.

COMMON FOODPLANTS American hornbeam, birch, blackberry, serviceberry, and presumably other plants in birch and rose families.

REMARKS The caterpillars of our thyatirines fashion shelters by tying together the edges of one or adjacent leaves. It is curious that caterpillars of the Tufted Thyatirid and Lettered Habrosyne would be so similar given that their adults are so remarkably distinct. A seemingly large proportion of Tufted Thyatirid caterpillars that I find have been attacked by a tachinid fly. The presence of its maggot is easily detected by a black breathing tube (spiracle) that it forces through a lateral wall of the caterpillar's body. The Tufted Thyatirid overwinters as a pupa.

LOOPERS, INCHWORMS, AND SPANWORMS – GEOMETRIDAE

Whether measured in terms of abundance or biomass, loopers are among the most important forest lepidopterans in Eastern North America. They are an especially important component of the spring caterpillar fauna of deciduous forests, where they are the staple in the diets of many forest-nesting birds. They are masters of crypsis, providing many of nature's most marvelous examples of background matching, mimicking a myriad of plant tissues and organs (bark, flowers, buds, twigs, leaves, petioles, etc.). Among their ranks are several outbreak species, whose populations occasionally defoliate large tracts of forest. A sampling of the most common and economically important species is treated here—187 geometrids are illustrated in Wagner *et al.* (2002).

RECOGNITION

Geometrid caterpillars can be immediately distinguished from other Lepidoptera by examining their abdominal prolegs. In all but a handful of species, there are only two pairs of prolegs: an anterior set on A6 and an anal pair on A10. In those species with more than two pairs, the additional prolegs (on A3–A5, or just A5) are reduced in size. Moreover, all geometers loop when they move, underscoring that only the prolegs on A6 are of primary importance. Most are elongate, somewhat cylindrical caterpillars. Anterior abdominal segments are usually greatly lengthened, especially relative to the last four abdominal segments which are sandwiched together. Bright colors are uncommon; most are cryptically colored in greens and browns. Both coloration and pattern can be highly variable, a point to keep in mind when using the images included here to identify caterpillars. The positions of the warts and knobs can be extremely helpful in identification, but the warts, too, vary in their expression, being best developed in the last two instars. Interestingly, both body color and form can be influenced by diet (*see* page 199, Red-fringed Emerald), as well as the lighting of a given caterpillar's surroundings (Poulton 1892).

LIFE HISTORY NOTES

Eggs may be laid singly or in clusters; often they are yellow, orange, or red. First instars of some species are quite active, covering long distances in search of suitable food; a few balloon about on silk strands before settling down to feed. Many are polyphagous, especially among the forest ennomines. The majority overwinter as pupae, although our fauna also includes a number of species that pass the winter as larvae fully exposed on the bark of their foodplant, repeatedly freezing and thawing. Others overwinter as eggs. McFarland's (1988) splendid book on the life histories of Australian geometrids contains a wealth of information on loopers.

COLLECTING AND REARING TIPS

Inchworms are among the easiest caterpillars to rear in captivity, being tolerant of crowding and marginal foodplant quality. A fair number of the spring-active species overwinter as prepupal larvae; for these you will need to provide a deep layer of peat. As noted above, many are dietary generalists, so it is often possible to make substitutions in the larval diets.

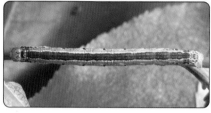

FALL CANKERWORM
Alsophila pometaria

RECOGNITION   Exceedingly variable in coloration, ranging from pale green and yellow to black. Immediately recognizable by *extra, half-sized pair of prolegs on A5*. Body commonly with whitish subdorsal and/or more yellowish subspiracular stripe. Some forms bear a black spot behind each spiracle, especially on the anterior abdominal segments. Larva to 2.5cm.

OCCURRENCE   Yards, orchards, parks, woodlands, and forests from Canada south to northern Florida, west across most of continent. One generation with mature caterpillars in May and June.

COMMON FOODPLANTS   Broad generalist on shrubs and trees: apple, basswood, blueberry, cherry, elm, maple, and oak commonly.

REMARKS   The spring-active caterpillars require young leaves high in nitrogen and water, and low in tannins, to successfully complete their development. Dark forms are prevalent under outbreak conditions—how and when this color polymorphism is induced is not well understood. The species is irruptive, occasionally defoliating thousands of acres of forest. In many populations of the Fall Cankerworm, the adult females mate but discard the male's genes; the resultant offspring are genetically identical to the mother (Mitter *et al.* 1987). The eggs, laid in clutches that are pushed into bark crevices, overwinter. Upon hatching the caterpillars drop down on silken threads to be carried off by spring breezes. "Ballooning" caterpillars move from plant to plant and settle after arriving on a suitable foodplant.

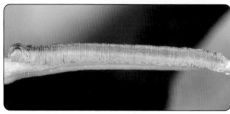 

VIRGIN MOTH
Protitame virginalis

RECOGNITION Yellow- or waxy-green caterpillar with *diffusely edged, reddish brown middorsal stripe*. Stripe dissipates over head, ending before or forking to either side of triangle. Clypeus may share same reddish brown coloration. Subventral flange running between thorax and anal proleg. A1–A5 with two prominent transverse creases over dorsum towards back half of each segment. Paraprocts short and stubby, extending beyond anal plate. Larva less than 2.5cm.

OCCURRENCE Edges of watercourses and wetlands, shrubby fields, woodlands, and forests. Transcontinental in Canada south in East to Virginia (east of the Appalachians) and to Gulf States and northern Texas (west of Appalachians). Two generations over much of East with mature caterpillars from June to July, then again from late August to October.

COMMON FOODPLANTS Aspen, poplar, and willow.

REMARKS The Virgin Moth is a regular in samples from poplar or aspen, especially northward. The red-brown coloration of the dorsal stripe resembles the petiole color of quaking aspen. The caterpillar makes for an especially credible mimic if it happens to come to rest with its anterior end attached to a leaf and the posterior end to a shoot or petiole. Females readily come to light and oviposit if confined for a night or two. The prepupal larva turns brick red (inset). The Virgin Moth overwinters as a pupa.

LESSER MAPLE SPANWORM
Itame pustularia

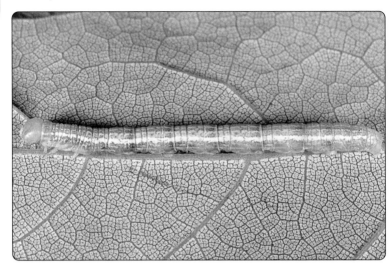

RECOGNITION Yellow-green to pale green caterpillar with *creamy subdorsal stripe*. Green middorsal stripe bounded on either side by broken, white, addorsal stripe; thin, broken supraspiracular stripe often present. Below poorly developed spiracular stripe, ground color may have yellow or orange cast. Pale green to tan head, lobes unmarked; *labrum often white*. A10 stubby with

proportionately small paraprocts, hypoproct, and anal plate. Larva less than 2.5cm.

OCCURRENCE Yards, parks, wooded swamps, woodlands, and forests from Canada to Georgia, Alabama, and Texas. Evidently just one protracted generation over much of East with mature caterpillars principally from late May to July.

COMMON FOODPLANTS Maple, especially red, but presumably silver and other related maples as well.

REMARKS From the end of June through much of August the Lesser Maple Spanworm can be the most abundant moth at lights across southern New England. The caterpillars do most of their feeding at night from the underside of leaves, where they are easily located by flashlight. Prepupal caterpillars become pinkish or even wine-colored. The egg overwinters. Prepupal caterpillars redden (inset).

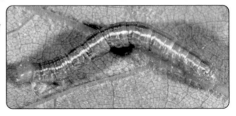

Itame ribearia

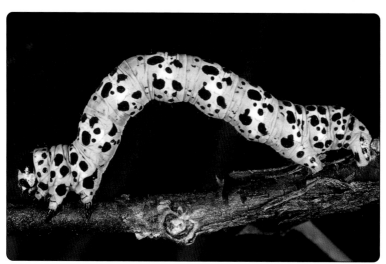

RECOGNITION Warningly colored, *lemon yellow, frosty white, and black inchworm. Each seta arises from large black spot.* White middorsal line extends forward over top of shiny black head then divides and runs down to each antenna; another white line leaves triangle and runs back towards thoracic spiracle (inset). Larva to 3cm.

OCCURRENCE Wooded swamps, woodlands, and forests from Alberta to New Brunswick south to Maryland, West Virginia, and northern Texas but rare or absent from many areas southward. One generation with mature caterpillars from late May through June.

COMMON FOODPLANTS Currant.

REMARKS Formerly more widespread and abundant, the Currant Spanworm was a collateral victim of the currant eradication program that began in the 1920s and continued into the 1960s. Federal and state governments subsidized efforts to remove currant, especially the introduced blackcurrant (*Ribes nigra*), because it was an alternate host in the life cycle of white pine blister rust. The Currant Spanworm is now generally uncommon to rare over many parts of its former range. Where currants are grown commercially, the caterpillar is an occasional pest. When disturbed, the caterpillars drop down from the plant on a strand of silk. The egg overwinters.

WHITE PINE ANGLE
Macaria pinistrobata

RECOGNITION Green and well marked with white stripes. Wild-collected larvae often have a greener aspect than the individual figured above. *Both subdorsal and spiracular stripes relatively broad and well defined*; the latter often yellowish. Immediately below subdorsal stripe a smoky to dull red stripe extends onto head as a dark patch over each lobe. Two fine, wavy, black stripes subtend the

subdorsal stripe. Dorsum often frosted with white (Maier *et al.* 2004). Larva less than 2.5cm. This is a diverse and taxonomically difficult genus with more than a dozen common conifer-feeding species in East (*see* Wagner *et al.* 2002, Maier et al. 2004). Most members of the genus are specialized in diet, and thus foodplant associations are an aid to a caterpillar's identity. Nevertheless, positive identifications are best based on the reared adults.

OCCURRENCE Plantations, woodlands, and forests from Canada south in Appalachians to Alabama and Great Lakes States. At least two generations over much of East with indication of partial third. Mature caterpillars from June to November.

COMMON FOODPLANTS White pine.

REMARKS Wherever white pine grows in abundance, this moth seems to be common. Caterpillars of the pine-feeding *Macaria* are all longitudinally striped. They rest and feed along the axes of needles. The reddish markings on the head, common to many of the pine-feeders, resemble the needle sheath both in color and luster. Perhaps, not surprisingly, caterpillars frequently rest with the head nestled into the base of a needle cluster. The pupa overwinters in all members of the genus.

Digrammia continuata

RECOGNITION Ground color lime green with white spotting; *subdorsal stripe usually well developed, often running uninterrupted over thoracic and posterior abdominal segments*, but occasionally absent. Thin white middorsal stripe, if present, may extend forward onto head, strengthen, and divide over triangle. Dorsal setae frequently borne from darkened bases. Some well-marked individuals with magenta and yellow (or creamy) markings about

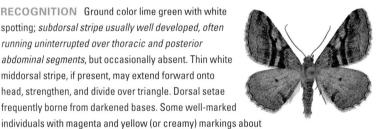

anterior spiracles. *Lateral spots may form broken spiracular stripe that extends to antenna.* Larva less than 2.5cm. Similar to Many-lined Angle (*Macaria multilineata*) which occurs from Missouri to southern Ontario and Massachusetts south to Florida and Texas. In some individuals, the facial triangle tends toward deep green to black and the bases of the dorsal setae are not as prominent as those of Curve-lined Angle. Its preferred foodplants include red cedar and Atlantic white cedar.

OCCURRENCE Pastures, fields, ridge tops, and woodlands, as well as wooded swamps and fens with white cedar northward. Manitoba to Maine south to Florida and Texas. At least two generations with mature caterpillars from May onward.

COMMON FOODPLANTS Red, Atlantic white, and northern white cedar.

REMARKS All of our pine-feeding Angles possess continuous stripes that resemble the reflections that play off the needles upon which they feed. In contrast, those Angles that feed on cedars, with their shorter scalelike leaves, have the stripes broken into dashes. The resemblance is close enough that visual searching for caterpillars of the Curved-lined Angle is essentially futile, especially relative to the numbers that can be obtained by beating. *Digrammia* is a large genus, especially in the West. The pupa overwinters.

FAINT-SPOTTED ANGLE
Digrammia ocellinata

RECOGNITION Ground color yellow-green, gray, or reddish (inset), with pale yellow-orange intersegmental areas, especially rearward. *Often with black spot above spiracle on A2.* Numerous vague wavy stripes, frequently broken into spots and bars, run length of body. Thoracic legs and anterior proleg may be vinaceous. Larva to 2.5cm.

OCCURRENCE Late successional fields, fencerows, parks, and woodlands from southern Canada to Florida, Alabama, and northern Texas. Two or three generations over much of East with mature caterpillars from June until first frosts.

COMMON FOODPLANTS Black locust and related trees.

REMARKS Black locust, the principal foodplant of the Faint-spotted Angle, was formerly restricted to the Ozark and Appalachian Regions. Colonists cultivated the tree, using it as an ornamental, natural fencerow, and as a timber tree. The moth has benefited greatly from the tree's popularity, and now occurs widely throughout the East.

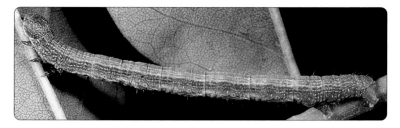

Glena cribrataria

RECOGNITION Cylindrical, greenish to green-brown caterpillar with *modest swelling about spiracle on A2 that is pale anteriorly and darkened posteriorly*. First abdominal spiracle appreciably lower than those that follow. Sometimes with dark middorsal spots along leading edge of each abdominal segment. Each lobe of head may be capped with black; a black line

runs across front of head, over triangle. Small dorsal warts over A8 also may be darkened. Larva to 3cm. Larval characters that distinguish the Dotted Gray from the Blueberry Gray (*Glena cognataria*) are unknown. Both species are illustrated in Wagner *et al.* (2002).

OCCURRENCE Open woodlands, swamps, heathlands, and barrens, often with an open or sparse canopy, from Minnesota and Ontario to Vermont south to Florida and Texas. One generation in North; two or more generations in South with mature caterpillars from June onward.

COMMON FOODPLANTS Birch, blueberry, cherry, maple, oak, poplar, serviceberry, willow, and, probably, other woody species.

REMARKS Most likely to turn up in dry oak woodlands and barrens, whereas the Blueberry Gray is more often seen in heathy wetlands, bogs, and barrens. The second generation adults that emerge in the summer are smaller than those that hatch in the spring. This is somewhat of a paradox because the spring-feeding larvae have access to seemingly superior foliage quality yet yield smaller individuals.

SMALL PURPLISH GRAY
Iridopsis humaria

RECOGNITION Stout, rather wide given its length. One of our most distinctively colored inchworms: *dorsum mostly purple-brown with faint longitudinal striping; sides and venter yellow-green to straw-colored*. A broad, black subdorsal stripe commonly runs from eyes to posterior end of abdomen where it weakens over A8 and A9. *Frequently with dark spot following spiracle on A2* (inset). Head brown above and greenish or yellow below; sometimes with black lateral stripe. Paraprocts and hypoproct relatively small. Larva to 2.5cm.

OCCURRENCE Fields, bogs, woodlands, and forests from Alberta to Nova Scotia south to Florida and Texas; local and uncommon across much of New England. At least two and possibly more full generations from Maryland southward with mature caterpillars from June to October.

COMMON FOODPLANTS Birch, blackberry, blueberry, cranberry, dewberry, hickory, oak, pear, pecan, persimmon, sweet fern, walnut, willow, and other woody species, as well as a number of forbs, including alfalfa, asparagus, clover, goldenrod, nettle, and soybean.

REMARKS Herbaceous legumes appear to be among the Small Purplish Gray's favorites. A reliable way to find this caterpillar is to sweep in fields of soybean in late summer. When alarmed, the caterpillar arches the head backward over the second thoracic segment and offers up a bright green, sticky regurgitant. The pupa overwinters.

Iridopsis larvaria

RECOGNITION Color and pattern highly variable, ranging from green and unmarked (inset) to mostly brown; body smooth and undistinguished. *Often with red to brown spots over dorsum; many forms with diamond-shaped saddle over A2;* some individuals with dark middorsal stripe running length of body. Spiracles white. *Low swelling posterior to spiracle*

on A2; sometimes A3 also has hint of this swelling; and small dorsal warts over A8. Prolegs may be flushed with pink or brown. Front of head flattened and either unmarked or with broad, purple-brown band over top of head that narrows to eyes and frames face. Base of third thoracic leg swollen. Larva less than 3cm. As there are several common *Iridopsis* species in the East, identifications are best based on reared adults.

OCCURRENCE Woodlands and forests across eastern Canada south to Georgia, Gulf States, and Midwest but absent from Texas. Two generations over most of East with mature caterpillars from June onward.

COMMON FOODPLANTS Alder, apple, birch, cherry, currant, dogwood, elderberry, goldenrod, hawthorn, mountain ash, poplar, senna, sweet fern, viburnum, willow, and many other plants.

REMARKS Larvae often rest on leaves with the body looped upward and the head touching the substrate. The Pale-winged Gray (*Iridopsis ephyraria*) caterpillar figured by Ives and Wong (1988) resembles a common color form of the Bent-line Gray. The wild-collected individual figured here (above) did not yield an adult so my identification must be regarded as tentative; the identity of the inset is certain. The pupa overwinters.

LARGE PURPLISH GRAY
Iridopsis vellivolata

RECOGNITION *Corrugated red-brown twig mimic with inconspicuous ridge that connects the two dorsal posterior setae (D2) over A2–A5;* more subtle ridges over A1, A6, and A7. Abdominal spiracles positioned on raised lateral warts that are often pale forward of spiracle and darkened behind. Wavy ridge, often creamy, runs beneath abdominal spiracles. Numerous fine, vague stripes run length of body, especially above level of spiracles; underside mostly pale and unmarked. *Each lobe of head framed by thin cherry-red band.* Crochets in single group. Paraprocts and hypoproct of moderate length. Larva to 3cm. Easily confused with *Caripeta* caterpillars (*see* page 184), but they always have a transverse ridge connecting the posterior dorsal setae on A1–A6 and the crochets are arranged in two groups.

OCCURRENCE Barrens, forests, and woodlands from eastern Canada south to Florida and eastern Texas. One generation in North with mature caterpillars from July to September; two broods in New Jersey and Maryland; three or more in Deep South.

COMMON FOODPLANTS Especially pine, also fir, larch, and spruce.

REMARKS Caterpillars of the Large Purplish Gray are remarkably twiglike in appearance. An interesting aspect of their background-matching repertoire is the textural mimicry of the body—the abdominal bumps and ridges resemble the scars one finds on a conifer twig that has lost its needles. The pupa overwinters.

Cleora sublunaria

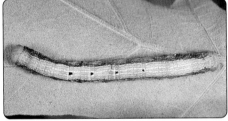

RECOGNITION Body green, brown, yellow, or reddish with distinct *black middorsal spots, edged outwardly with white, near leading edge of A2–A4* (see inset). Faint addorsal, subdorsal, and supraspiracular stripes, and thinner stripes between them. Often with *dark spot behind abdominal spiracles, especially evident on A2*. Black ring encircles each whitish spiracle. Larva less than 3cm. Projecta Gray (*Cleora projecta*), which occurs from southern Manitoba, Ontario, and Maine to Florida and Texas, is indistinguishable as a larva.

OCCURRENCE Woodlands and forests from eastern Kansas to southeastern New York to northern Florida and Texas. One generation with mature caterpillars in late spring.

COMMON FOODPLANTS American hornbeam, cherry, chestnut, oak, sumac, sweet fern, sweet gum, and many other plants.

REMARKS *Cleora* caterpillars are widely encountered on spring foliage throughout the South. In the low elevations of the Smokies they are among the most abundant geometrids in beating samples taken during the latter half of May. There they are commonly attacked by a eulophid wasp (*Euplectrus*) which lays upwards of a dozen eggs in a single caterpillar. The parasitoids develop within the caterpillar, eventually emerging *en masse* from the dorsum of the caterpillar. The cluster of pale blue wasp larvae matures on the outside of the body. The host caterpillar remains active and motile, but is drained of all its life as the wasp larvae put on a final burst of growth. They then disperse and spin their cocoons about the host cadaver, which soon blackens. *Cleora* pupae overwinter.

SADDLEBACK LOOPER (THE SMALL ENGRAILED)
Ectropis crepuscularia

RECOGNITION Body coloration varies from red and purple to brown and tan. Top of T2 and venter of T3 (especially where legs attach) swollen. *Low V-shaped ridge over dorsum of A8 often edged with black*. Head flattened and frequently darkly pigmented about upper portion of triangle. Some individuals have darkened saddle over A4 and black lines beneath spiracles on abdomen. Larva to 3cm.

OCCURRENCE Woodlands and forests. Transcontinental in Canada south in East to Florida and Texas. At least two generations over much of East with mature caterpillars from June onward.

COMMON FOODPLANTS Many hardwoods and softwoods, including apple, ash, birch, blackberry, cherry, cranberry, currant, dogwood, euonymus, fir, hemlock, larch, maple, oak, pear, poplar, spruce, sweet fern, walnut, willow, and witch hazel.

REMARKS An excellent twig mimic in form, coloration, and posture. The caterpillar rests with the anterior end of the body elevated. A strand of silk is laid down wherever the caterpillar goes; at any instant it can drop from its perch on a safety line. I find this caterpillar on many different foodplants and in a variety of habitats, but always as a singleton here and there. The pupa overwinters.

Protoboarmia porcelaria

RECOGNITION Highly variable gray, brown, or reddish caterpillar, variegated with white, brown, and black. *Usually with a subspiracular swelling on A2 that is pale anteriorly and blackened posteriorly.* Middorsal stripe broken, represented by short black bar at front end of each segment (hence the Dash-lined Looper). Prominent creases encircle each segment; these pronounced over thorax. *Minute spines, visible under a hand lens, scattered over body.* Venter pale and mostly unmarked. Each lobe of vertex somewhat angulate. Larva to 3cm.

OCCURRENCE Barrens, woodlands, and forests from British Columbia to Nova Scotia in East south to Florida and Texas. Two generations over much of range with mature caterpillars in late winter and early spring, then again in midsummer; three or more generations in South.

COMMON FOODPLANTS Many trees and shrubs including birch, blueberry, currant, elm, fir, hemlock, larch, maple, mountain holly, oak, poplar, spruce, and willow.

REMARKS The late instar larva overwinters exposed on twigs and bark. It can be common in spring collections, second only to the variants (*Hypagyrtis* species) in many forested habitats. Should a caterpillar show up on your clothing after leaf fall, likely it will prove to be this species or one of our *Hypagyrtis*. The caterpillars are an important winter food source for insectivorous birds, such as kinglets, chickadees, creepers, and nuthatches. The summer-generation caterpillars (and adults) are noticeably smaller than those that result from larvae that overwinter.

TULIP-TREE BEAUTY
Epimecis hortaria

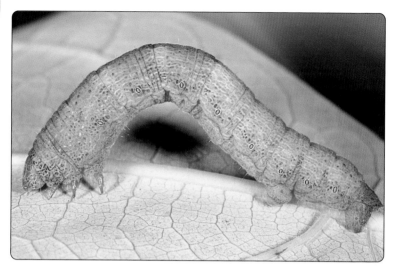

RECOGNITION Stout, oddly proportioned inchworm not likely to be confused with any other in our fauna: *body widest about T3 and A1 and noticeably swollen above last thoracic leg and anterior proleg.* Thoracic segments, short and bunched together, bear comparatively small legs. Ground color highly variable, ranging from nearly yellow to mauve, orange, tan, gray, chocolate brown, and black; frequently with vague pinstripes. Larva to 4cm.

OCCURRENCE Woodlands and forests from southern Ontario to Maine south to Florida and eastern Texas. Two generations with mature caterpillars from June onward.

COMMON FOODPLANTS Magnolia, red bay, sassafras, spicebush, and tulip tree; Bo Sullivan (pers. comm.) has found caterpillars on several occasions feeding on horse sugar.

REMARKS The larva often rests looped, with the anterior abdominal segments raised above the leaf or stem upon which it is perched. Given the shortness of their legs, perhaps it should come as no surprise that caterpillars of the Tulip-tree Beauty are common in beating samples. The pupa overwinters.

Melanolophia canadaria

RECOGNITION Last instar *pale green* and frustratingly nondescript. Integument slightly yellowish where adjacent abdominal segments telescope into one another; approximately nine shallow creases encircling anterior abdominal segments. Sometimes with wavy flange that runs just below abdominal spiracles; it is often highlighted with cream, pink, or red. Occasionally with vague subdorsal stripe, the

vestiges of which may run over thoracic shield. *Head pale green, unmarked, and when extended forward appearing somewhat flattened.* Larva to 3cm. Middle instars yellow-green or even with faint orange flush and more conspicuously striped; most have well-developed subdorsal and yellow spiracular stripes, as well as thinner white addorsal and supraspiracular pinstripes. In addition, the head tends to be more yellow or orange. Caterpillars may not be distinguishable from those of the Signate Melanolophia (*Melanolophia signataria*) with which it co-occurs over most of its range. It is single-brooded, flying in spring only.

OCCURRENCE Woodlands and forests from Canada south to Florida and Texas. Two or more generations throughout much of East with mature caterpillars from late May onward.

COMMON FOODPLANTS Alder, ash, basswood, birch, blackberry, blueberry, buckthorn, cherry, dogwood, elm, hickory, honey locust, larch, magnolia, maple, oak, pine, poplar, sassafras, serviceberry, silver bell, sour gum, spirea, sycamore, viburnum, willow, and many other woody trees and shrubs.

REMARKS The Canadian Melanolophia is one of our most ubiquitous and widely distributed caterpillars. Unfortunately it is so plain and undistinguished as to be difficult to recognize. I often arrive at my determination by eliminating everything else. It feeds mostly at night and rests by day on the undersides of leaves. Individuals may spin down on a short belay line and hang suspended in midair through much of the night. The pupa overwinters.

POWDER MOTH
Eufidonia notataria

RECOGNITION *Emerald green with dark midddorsal, thin yellow to creamy subdorsal, and broad white spiracular stripes.* According to McGuffin (1977) the latter may be edged with pink as in Sharp-lined Powder Moth (*Eufidonia discospilata*), especially about thorax. Often with subventral stripe that runs back from proleg on A6. Anterior abdominal segments have approximately eight annulations. Larva to

2.5cm. Sharp-lined Powder Moth paler green, with several white dorsal stripes, and pronounced red edging along lower edge of spiracular stripe; foodplants include alder, birch, and other deciduous plants. Other than its association with pine, I am unaware of characters that reliably distinguish caterpillars of the Pine Powder Moth (*E. convergaria*) from those of the Powder Moth.

OCCURRENCE Forests from Canada south to Maryland and North Carolina (in mountains), Ohio, and Missouri (as a stray). One generation with mature caterpillars from early July to September.

COMMON FOODPLANTS Fir, hemlock, larch, spruce, and other conifers.

REMARKS Adults fly both by day and night. Females lay their eggs, individually or in groups, at the bases of young needles, which are eaten preferentially by the early instars. The caterpillar rests with its body flattened against a needle. The pupa overwinters.

(PEPPER-AND-SALT MOTH) *Biston betularia*

RECOGNITION Greenish, gray, or brown with *deeply cleft head* (inset). *Minute black spines* (visible with hand lens) *pepper body*. A5 with pair of warts above spiracle. *Spiracles often orange*. Larva to 5.5cm.

OCCURRENCE Barrens, woodlands, and forests. Transcontinental in Canada south to Georgia (in mountains), Texas, Arizona, and California. Presumably one principal (greatly protracted) generation northward; two generations in Missouri (Richard Heitzman, pers. comm.) with caterpillars from late June into November.

COMMON FOODPLANTS Many trees and shrubs, including alder, apple, birch, blueberry, cherry, cranberry, currant, dogwood, elm, hackberry, larch, locust, maple, mountain ash, New Jersey tea, oak, pecan, poplar, redbud, rose, walnut, and willow.

REMARKS The Pepper-and-salt Moth provides one of the most famous examples of microevolution (changes in gene frequencies within a population) (Kettlewell 1973, Howlett and Majerus 1987). The adults, which perch on bark by day, come in both a dark and pale form. The dark (melanic) form often predominates in areas where the trunks of trees are mostly dark, e.g., in forests where lichens have been impacted by pollution or fires. In the presence of lichens and light-colored bark, gene forms (alleles) for lighter coloration are favored. Birds, preying more successfully on the form that is poorly matched to its surroundings, are thought to be the evolutionary operators, controlling which form will tend to leave more offspring and proliferate. The pupa overwinters in litter.

WOOLLY GRAY
Lycia ypsilon

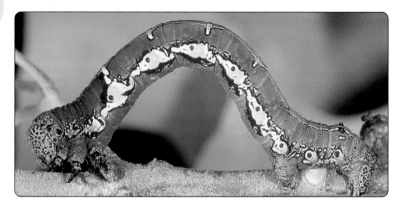

RECOGNITION *Large, marvelously patterned with yellow, maroon, black, and white.* Highly variable in coloration (two forms shown here). Commonly with middorsal stripe sandwiched between two white addorsal stripes that bear spurs that dip down toward spiracles on anterior abdominal segments. Subdorsal and subventral areas often brick-red, maroon, or purplish. Some forms with broadly irregular spiracular stripe composed of alternating white and yellow patches. *Black spots peppered over head*, but no large, blackened patches; anal proleg and anal plate spotted likewise. Midventer often with (yellow) stripe. Larva to 4cm.

OCCURRENCE Barrens, woodlands, and forests from Minnesota to southeastern Massachusetts, south to Florida and Texas. One generation with mature caterpillars in early summer.

COMMON FOODPLANTS Apple, cherry, oak, and likely many other woody plants.

REMARKS The Woolly Gray is one of only a handful of brightly colored inchworms in the East. Although such coloration would suggest that it is chemically protected, there is nothing in its diet that would lend support to this notion. It is locally common along the Atlantic Coastal Plain, especially in the Southeast. The three eastern *Lycia* are among our most handsome eastern forest caterpillars, especially when viewed with a lens. The adult females are odd creatures, wingless and densely scaled. *Lycia* adults are active very early in the spring—northward, all three may fly when snow is still on the ground. The pupa overwinters in *Lycia*.

Hypagyrtis esther

RECOGNITION Highly variable. Brown ground color variously marked with green, yellow, tan, white, and black. In some forms dorsum of abdomen with a series of pale spindle-shaped marks that broadens anteriorly. Laterally, black mottling often heaviest about spiracles; *a pale patch sometimes following these heavily pigmented spiracular areas. Dorsum of A8 slightly raised, and often with minute white subdorsal spot (directly above spiracle).* Larva to 3.5cm. Very closely related to and perhaps conspecific with Pine Variant (*Hypagyrtis piniata*) (*see* below).

OCCURRENCE Pinelands from southeastern Missouri to southeastern Massachusetts to Gulf States and Texas. At least two generations with mature caterpillars from March onward.

COMMON FOODPLANTS Pines.

REMARKS *Hypagyrtis* is a taxonomically difficult genus in great need of study. Molecular characters will be needed to tease apart the species because coloration, genitalia, and other classical character systems have left considerable doubt. As is often the case, there are more available names than there are good species. The assignment of names used here is based on the assumption that the Pine Variant is a northern species with a preference for spruce, hemlock, and related conifers, that gives way to Esther Moth (*Hypagyrtis esther*) in barrens and Coastal Plain communities, where pines are the principal foodplant. In all Variants (*Hypagyrtis*) the larva overwinters exposed on bark or foliage. As in many double-brooded loopers, summer-brood adults are smaller than those of the spring brood.

ONE-SPOTTED VARIANT
Hypagyrtis unipunctata

RECOGNITION Ground color varies from green and yellow-green to gray, brick red, or brown; regardless of ground color, patterning subdued. Body lacking conspicuous bumps or swellings. Many individuals may be recognized by *diffuse pale patch about subdorsum and sides of anterior portion of A5. A8 often with pale subdorsal spot. Venter of body pale and*

weakly mottled, almost powdery in appearance; some individuals with vague, brownish, midventral spot on A4. Under magnification, integument peppered with glossy granules. Larva to 3.5cm (winter generation); summer generation larvae somewhat smaller.

OCCURRENCE Parks and yards, woodlands, and forests. Transcontinental in Canada south in East to Florida and Texas. Two generations, with partial third over much of East; mature caterpillars nearly year-round.

COMMON FOODPLANTS Alder, ash, basswood, birch, blueberry, cherry, dogwood, elm, hazel, hickory, ironwood, maple, oak, poplar, serviceberry, sycamore, walnut, willow, and many other trees.

REMARKS If you plan to do much caterpillar sampling, you must learn this inchworm. Year in and year out, it is among our most ubiquitous and numerically constant caterpillars on shrubs and trees. Unfortunately, it is difficult to recognize—I often identify it by its frosty venter and subtle pale lateral areas on A5 or the white subdorsal dot on A8. The caterpillars often dangle from a thread at night, suspended in the air for hours. Why caterpillars engage in this behavior is not known, although it surely must afford them some protection from predaceous invertebrates, mice, and other animals that glean foliage by night. The caterpillar spends the winter exposed on bark, repeatedly freezing and thawing. They are an important food source for insectivorous birds in winter (Heinrich 2003).

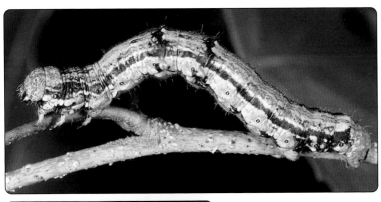

RECOGNITION Most individuals a mix of yellow and brown. *Darkened setal bases slightly raised, especially over A2, A3, and A8.* Side of A2 and A3 bears raised area behind spiracle that is often rust, brown, or black. Usually with hint of broad, pale spiracular stripe running down outer face of A6 proleg. *Dorsum set with vague, narrow striping;* in pale forms distinct addorsal, subdorsal, and supraspiracular stripes. Head brownish with dark spots and occasionally pale patches over and to either side of triangle. Larva to 3cm. I have encountered caterpillars of what I believe were the Toothed Phigalia (*P. denticulata*) only once. These were smoky gray-brown with more subdued markings and less prominent warting. The Toothed Phigalia flies early, sometimes three weeks ahead of our other phigalias. It is a general feeder that occurs from Connecticut southward.

OCCURRENCE Woodlands and forests from Ontario and southern Maine south to Florida and Texas. One generation with mature caterpillars in late spring.

COMMON FOODPLANTS Many woody shrubs and trees including blueberry, chestnut, elm, hazel, hickory, oak, sweet gum, willow, and witch hazel.

REMARKS Phigalias are true winter moths in the South, where they begin flying in January. In New England (or in the mountains elsewhere) the flight is later, lasting into April. The caterpillar in the inset is being fed upon by more than a dozen *Leptus* mites (Family Erythraeidae)—surprisingly, at least to me, it survived this ordeal and continued feeding and reached full size. The pupa overwinters.

THE HALF-WING
Phigalia titea

RECOGNITION *Blue-gray caterpillar with black pinstripes* running length of body. Orange *addorsal stripe edged with black* to either side. Additional *orangish patches occur about spiracles.* Raised warts occur below and behind each spiracle on anterior abdominal segments and A8. *Dorsal abdominal setae borne from black pimplelike bases.* Head peppered with black spots. Larva to 3.5cm.

OCCURRENCE Woodlands and forests from Great Lakes Region to Nova Scotia south to Florida and Texas. One generation with mature caterpillars in late spring.

COMMON FOODPLANTS Many woody shrubs and trees, including American hornbeam, apple, basswood, birch, blueberry, cranberry, elm, hickory, maple, ninebark, oak, and poplar.

REMARKS All of our phigalias are strictly single-brooded, new-leaf specialists that are active early in the spring. Caterpillars will starve if offered only older foliage. Like many other loopers with adults that are active during the cold periods of early spring or late fall, the females are flightless. The Half-wing flies a little later into the spring than our other two phigalias. Eggs are deposited in bark crevices and the first instars crawl or balloon to find suitable foliage. Occasionally The Half-wing is a pest, defoliating local areas of forest. The pupa overwinters in litter or soil.

Paleacrita vernata

RECOGNITION Elongate, slender, and confusingly variable in coloration, ranging from yellow-green through many shades of brown and black. Body smooth, somewhat shiny, with small warts over A8. Most individuals with pale spiracular stripe; addorsal, subdorsal, and supraspiracular stripes sometimes present. Frequently with middorsal spot along anterior edge of A2–A4. *Green-yellow stripe along midventer. Each side of head bears dark transverse bar that extends outward from top third of triangle*; a more diffuse bar runs roughly parallel to first, over each lobe. Paraprocts and hypoproct poorly developed. Larva to 3cm.

OCCURRENCE Yards, orchards, woodlands, and forests. Eastern Canada south to Georgia, Mississippi, and eastern Texas. One generation with mature caterpillars in late spring.

COMMON FOODPLANTS Apple, birch, cherry, elm, maple, oak, and many other trees.

REMARKS Adults emerge, fly, and mate in the early spring on nights too cold for many moths. The wingless females lay their eggs in clutches of 100 or more that are pushed into bark crevices, well ahead of bud break. First and second instars disperse by spinning down on silk threads that allow them to be carried about a forest. Females can be located by searching tree trunks during light rains—sections of bark that are not wet may be those immediately below where females are perched. The caterpillars are new-leaf specialists that complete their development on young spring foliage. Once mature, the caterpillar drops to the ground, tunnels down, and forms an earthen cell in which it will pass the next ten months. Pupation does not occur until late winter or early spring. It is an irruptive species, populations of which sometimes rise to the point where larvae defoliate plantings, orchards, or tracts of forest.

LINDEN LOOPER
Erannis tiliaria

RECOGNITION *Brown dorsum and broad lemon-yellow spiracular stripe* distinguish this caterpillar. Dorsum may be marked with as many as ten dark pinstripes. Venter chalky. In most individuals head pale orange-brown and vaguely spotted or unmarked. Each spiracle ringed in black. Larva to 3cm.

OCCURRENCE Woodlands and forests from Canada south to Georgia and northeastern Texas. One generation with mature caterpillars from late May to early July.

COMMON FOODPLANTS Many woody shrubs and trees, including American hornbeam, apple, ash, basswood, birch, blueberry, cherry, elm, hazel, hickory, maple, oak, poplar, rose, serviceberry, and willow.

REMARKS The adult has been called both the Linden Looper Moth as well as the Winter Moth. The latter name is more often applied to *Operophtera brumata*—a reminder of the danger of unstandardized common names. The caterpillar usually rests with head and T1 elevated above the substrate. It is a boom and bust species, present in low numbers in most years, whose populations sporadically irrupt and cause local defoliations. The Linden Looper is well suited for cold weather; the caterpillars are active early in the spring and the adults emerge late in the fall, mostly in October in New England and November in Kentucky, typically after the first frost. Like many cold-adapted geometrids, the females are wingless (inset). The pupa overwinters in an earthen cell.

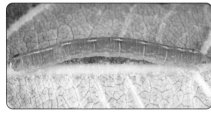

RECOGNITION Elongate, deep- to lime-green caterpillar with ill-defined, creamy subdorsal and supraspiracular stripes. A thin white to yellow stripe runs through spiracles. Underside of body waxy green. *Each lobe of head bears comma-shaped mark with reddish upper portion that gives way to black "tail" which reaches eyes.* Spiracles orange. Larva less than 2.5cm. Bluish Spring Moth (*Lomographa semiclarata*) caterpillar stouter and with yellow middorsal, intersegmental spots that may join to form a stripe (inset).

OCCURRENCE Shrubby fields, woodlands, and forests. Eastern Canada south to northern Florida, east Texas, and Colorado. One principal generation in Connecticut with a partial second; at least two generations in South with mature caterpillars through summer and fall months.

COMMON FOODPLANTS Apple, cherry, hawthorn, mountain ash, ninebark, and other woody members of Rosaceae; but also reported (erroneously?) from hornbeam, maple, snowberry, and viburnum.

REMARKS The White Spring Moth is among the most commonly encountered caterpillars on cherry and apple in late summer. Look for the caterpillar stretched out on a leaf underside. The spring-active adults fly both day and night. The pupa overwinters.

YELLOW-DUSTED CREAM MOTH
Cabera erythemaria

RECOGNITION Both of our common *Cabera* species are easily recognized by their *squarish, forward-projecting head, somewhat flattened body, reddened antenna, cheek line, and in most individuals, the middorsal spots along the leading edge of A1–A7.* Ground color varies from green, blue-green, or yellow-green to brown. Larva to

2.5cm. I am unaware of reliable characters that distinguish caterpillars of Yellow-dusted Cream Moth from those of Pink-striped Willow Spanworm (*Cabera variolaria*). Caterpillars of Yellow-dusted Cream Moth often bear pink to either side of black middorsal spots and pinkish prolegs. Well-marked individuals have prominent subdorsal and narrow, wavy, supraspiracular white stripes. My images of the Pink-striped Willow Spanworm have more subdued spotting and striping (inset). Species identifications should be based on the adult stage.

OCCURRENCE Fields, meadows, swamps, edges of watercourses, woodlands, and forests from Canada south to Georgia (in mountains) and Ozarks. At least two generations over most of range with mature caterpillars from June onward.

COMMON FOODPLANTS Especially willow, but also reported from aspen and poplar.

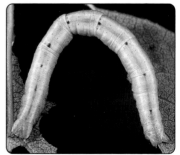

REMARKS Our *Cabera* are readily taken with beating sheets and easily found at night by flashlight. Expect to find caterpillars any time you are searching willow and poplar. The caterpillar rests by day with the head and body flattened against a leaf. The pupa overwinters.

COMMON LYTROSIS
Lytrosis unitaria

RECOGNITION Twig mimic with middorsal black spot along leading edge of T2 and T3. *A1 bears pair of dark subdorsal swellings that fuse over dorsum. Dorsum of A5 with pair of distinctive horns.* An oblique black line runs across anterior proleg up toward dorsum of A8. Paraprocts extend beyond end of abdomen. Larva to 5cm.

OCCURRENCE Woodlands and forests from North Dakota, southern Quebec, and Maine south to Florida and Texas. One generation with mature caterpillars from late April to early June.

COMMON FOODPLANTS Fond of hawthorn, rose, serviceberry, and other plants in the rose family, but also maple, oak, viburnum, and other woody plants.

REMARKS A fantastic twig mimic with remarkably long legs on T3 that are held out from the body when the caterpillar is at rest. The larva angles out from a stem at about 30–40°. Like other twig mimics, it has a "belay" line that it attaches to the stem. If tugged, this single strand can be pulled from the caterpillar's mouth at a rate of several centimeters per second. Presumably this line supports some of the caterpillar's weight as well as serving as a safety line should the caterpillar drop from its foodplant. The elongated leg on T3, grossly enlarged at its base, resembles a persistent stipule. When pinched, the larva makes no attempt to wriggle or escape but rather contracts, increasing turgor within its body, making itself even more twiglike. The pupa overwinters.

OBTUSE EUCHLAENA
Euchlaena obtusaria

RECOGNITION Beige to red-brown stick mimic with *udderlike protuberances over A5. Second set of much smaller warts over A1.* While many euchlaenas have a dark line running forward from the spiracle on A4–A6, these lines are absent more often than not in this species. Obtuse Euchlaena *usually with charcoal dorsal midline that runs from T1 or T2 to leading edge of dorsal transverse ridge on A1*; dorsum may be lightened posterior to dorsal ridges on A1 and A5. Head somewhat flattened, pale in and about triangle; an oblique darkened patch runs from anterior margin of eyes up towards top of triangle. Larva to 4.5cm. Very closely related to (if even distinct from) Muzaria Euchlaena (*E. muzaria*). A dozen euchlaenas occur in the East; until the larval characters are better known, identifications are best based on adults.

OCCURRENCE Woodlands and forests, but especially oak barrens northward. Nebraska and Illinois to New Jersey southward to Florida and Texas. Reports from southern Canada, Maine, and other northerly states represent strays or refer to Muzaria Euchlaena. Two generations over much of range with mature caterpillars in early spring then again in midsummer.

COMMON FOODPLANTS Presumably a general feeder on woody plants; recorded foodplants include rose and touch-me-not or impatiens; captive larvae have been bred on birch and cherry.

REMARKS When handled, *Euchlaena* caterpillars are lethargic and sticklike, shunning quick movement. All overwinter as half- to nearly full-grown caterpillars. It is uncertain as to whether the larvae stay on the foodplant or move down into litter during the winter months. They are difficult to overwinter indoors in containers; caterpillars sleeved on foodplants will fare better (although it may be necessary to protect the larvae from hard freezes).

Xanthotype sospeta

RECOGNITION Although highly variable in coloration, our common Crocus Geometers (*Xanthotype*) are basically one of two colors: pale green or brown. In either case, *body very elongate*, head squarish when viewed from above, and possessing prominent *white spiracular stripe. This stripe is especially pronounced towards rear of body*, occasionally upper portion edged with red or brown, especially

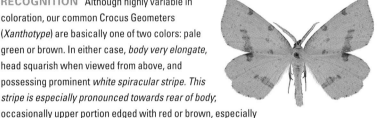

rearward. Often with small, dark middorsal spot along anterior edge of A2–A5. *Paraprocts very long, extending well beyond triangular anal plate.* Larva to 4.5cm. Closely allied to False Crocus Geometer (*Xanthotype urticaria*); definitive identification usually requires genitalic dissection of adult, especially in the Southeast where four members of the genus occur.

OCCURRENCE Fields, wet meadows, other open habitats, and woodland and forest edges from Manitoba to Nova Scotia south to Florida, east central Missouri, and Nebraska. Two generations with mature caterpillars from late April into late summer.

COMMON FOODPLANTS A general feeder, usually on low-growing plants and shrubs, including basswood, blueberry, cherry, chrysanthemum, currant, dogwood, elm, gladiola, hickory, maple, meadow rue, meadowsweet, mint, New Jersey tea, rose, and viburnum.

REMARKS The caterpillar rests on stems in a twiglike fashion, with the body straight and fully extended and its enlarged anal prolegs clamped to the foodplant. The body is secured to vegetation by a belay line as in other ennomines. The caterpillar of the Crocus Geometer is lethargic, seemingly reluctant to move. When settling, modestly perturbed, or moving between perches, it often quavers from side to side. The held larva often feigns death, but, if further molested, will thrash about. *Xanthotype* overwinter as middle to late instars.

HÜBNER'S PERO
Pero ancetaria (= hubneraria)

RECOGNITION Large, mostly cylindrical inchworm, slightly thickened about thorax and A5 and A6. Yellow to brown, often with numerous wavy stripes and darkened setal bases. Thin, dark middorsal stripe usually present, especially rearward. *Squarish head somewhat eared*; face darkened. Look for *small warts anterior to and below spiracle on A2 and low ridge over A8*. Body setae comparatively long, black, and shiny. *More than 20 small setae clustered over outer side of anterior proleg*. Anal plate squared off; hypoproct extends beyond paraprocts. From 40–60 crochets arranged in a single group. Larva to 4cm. Over much of the East, Hübner's Pero co-occurs with Honest Pero (*Pero honestaria*) and Morrison's Pero (*P. morrisonaria*). I am not aware of characters that reliably distinguish the three.

OCCURRENCE Wooded swamps, woodlands, and forests from southern Canada to northern Florida and Texas. Two generations over much of range with mature caterpillars in June and July, then again from September to early November.

COMMON FOODPLANTS Many woody plants including alder, birch, and willow; also reported from conifers, although these records may refer to Morrison's Pero.

REMARKS As noted above there are three widespread eastern *Pero*. The three can be difficult to distinguish without examination of the genitalia and associated anatomy. Like many twig mimics, the caterpillar perches outstretched, attached by a belay line. The pupa overwinters in a sparse cocoon in leaf litter.

Phaeoura quernaria

RECOGNITION *Large*, gray to brown inchworm with *T2 raised and shelflike, especially about the subdorsum. Low ridge spanning dorsum of A2. Fringe of thickened setae running between anterior and anal prolegs*. Top of head notched (inset), but not as deeply as that of Cleft-headed Looper (*Biston betularia*) (*see* page 161). Each primary seta borne from pale yellow to greenish wart. Paraprocts and hypoproct small. Larva to 5cm.

OCCURRENCE Woodlands and forests from Canada south to Florida and Texas. One principal generation over much of East.

COMMON FOODPLANTS Basswood, birch, cherry, elm, oak, poplar, willow, witch hazel, and many other trees and shrubs.

REMARKS Formerly this moth was classified in the genus *Nacophora*. Like other twig mimics, the caterpillars are comparatively lethargic when first handled. One common resting posture is with the head raised and the anterior end of the body, head, legs, and thorax, drawn into a fistlike ball. Occasionally a kink is thrown into the body axis. Analogous subventral fringe setae are found in other bark-dwelling caterpillars such as the underwings (*Catocala*) and the Fringed Looper (*Campaea perlata*). The pupa overwinters.

FRINGED LOOPER (PALE BEAUTY)
Campaea perlata

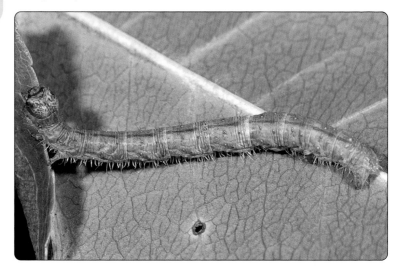

RECOGNITION *The extra set of prolegs on A5 and fringe of thickened pale hairs along the subventer* immediately distinguish this inchworm. Ground color varies from gray to brick red, or less commonly, smoky green. Each spiracle ringed with black. Venter noticeably flattened and pale, green along midventer becoming more waxy towards fringe. Larva to 4cm.

OCCURRENCE Woodlands and forests. Transcontinental in Canada south in East to Georgia (in mountains) and Arkansas. Two generations with overwintering caterpillars maturing from late April into June, and summer generation staggered from late June into September.

COMMON FOODPLANTS Many woody shrubs and trees, including alder, aspen, birch, cherry, hazel, maple, oak, rose, serviceberry, and willow, as well as softwoods such as fir and hemlock.

REMARKS Adults are among the most common moths at light in New England, especially during August. Likewise, the Fringed Looper is a regular in beating samples. The setal fringe along each side of the body may serve to soften the shadow and break up the outline of the caterpillar. Such hairs have evolved convergently among disparate bark-resting caterpillars, the most famous being the underwing (*Catocala*) caterpillars. Similar hairs, although far fewer in number, occur in the Oak Beauty (*Phaeoura quernaria*). Analogous long, downy lateral setae occur in all the lappets (Lasiocampidae) that spend their days on bark. In England, caterpillars of the Light Beauty (*Campaea margaritaria*) overwinter on branches and along trunks, fully exposed to harsh winter conditions (Porter 1997). Probably, our caterpillars do the same.

Ennomos magnaria

RECOGNITION *Very large, elongate, green or brown twig mimic with large swelling over A2 and another smaller one over A5*, and flattened forward-projecting head. A3 warted behind spiracle. A8 with comparatively small dorsal warts. All swellings tend to be darkly pigmented. Long antennae, often reddened, project in front of greenish head. Numerous minute pale bumps scattered over body (visible with lens). Short, thick, conical paraprocts project beyond anal plate. Larva to 5.5cm.

OCCURRENCE Wooded swamps, woodlands, and forests. Transcontinental in Canada south in East to Georgia and Missouri. One generation with mature caterpillars from late June to August.

COMMON FOODPLANTS Many woody shrubs and trees including alder, ash, aspen, basswood, beech, birch, hickory, holly, maple, oak, poplar, and willow.

REMARKS The Maple Spanworm has mastered the art of crypsis both as an adult and caterpillar. The yellow, leaf-mimicking adults fly in late summer–early fall, when maple and other leaves begin changing color and dropping to the ground. The larva is a superb twig mimic in either its green or brown forms. The dark warts, swollen anal prolegs, and posture all add to its deceitful ploy. By flashlight, these enormous loopers are readily discovered—look for them feeding near the end of a shoot. The eggs, which overwinter, are laid in rows.

ELM SPANWORM
Ennomos subsignaria

RECOGNITION Elongate caterpillars that range from yellow-green to brown (inset) or nearly black: greens seem to predominate at low larval densities and darker colors during outbreaks. *A2, A5, and A8 with low ridge that connects bases of the two dorsal (D2) setae at rear of segment*. In pale forms head yellow-green; in dark forms head ranges from brown to red-orange. Head color frequently shared by legs

and anal plate as well. Anal proleg large, sometimes flared outward. Paraprocts and hypoproct well developed. Larva to 4cm.

OCCURRENCE Woodlands and forests from Manitoba to Nova Scotia south to Florida and Texas, but absent to rare from much of Coastal Plain. One generation with mature caterpillars from late May to early July.

COMMON FOODPLANTS Many woody shrubs and trees including apple, ash, basswood, beech, birch, elm, hickory, ironwood, maple, oak, poplar, viburnum, willow, and witch hazel.

REMARKS Populations of the Elm Spanworm periodically irrupt and defoliate acres of broadleaf forest. It rarely becomes a pest in yards and parks. The caterpillars eat holes out of the middle of a blade, leaving the veins and edges intact. Whereas most loopers drop into the litter to pupate, larvae of the Elm Spanworm may form their cocoons among leaves of the foodplant. Females lay the eggs, which will overwinter, on the undersides of twigs.

Selenia kentaria

RECOGNITION Abdominal *girth thickened about A4 and A5*; dorsum of these same segments with raised pimplelike setal bases. *Base of third pair of legs greatly swollen*. Flattened head often streaked with short whitish lines that continue rearward as addorsal and subdorsal stripes. Most individuals have another white line extending back from eyes. Sparse fringe of subventral setae runs between prolegs. Larva to 4cm. Northern Selenia

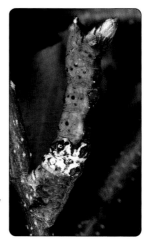

(*Selenia alciphearia*) very similar: Forbes (1948) notes that it has a pronounced pale bar over A2 and larger warts on A4 and A5. Some forms marked with rust-orange about the metathoracic legs. Its caterpillars have been reared from alder, birch, cherry, currant, maple, and willow. It occurs south to North Carolina (in mountains) and Missouri.

OCCURRENCE Woodlands and forests. Transcontinental in Canada south in East to Georgia, Alabama, Mississippi, and Arkansas. One principal generation with mature caterpillars in late June and July, followed by partial second generation with caterpillars maturing in fall.

COMMON FOODPLANTS Basswood, beech, birch, elm, maple, oak, and walnut.

REMARKS The caterpillars are exceptional twig mimics with both barklike coloration and texture; the larval posture adds to the disguise. In some remarkable forms, patterning over A4 and A5 clearly mimics that of foliose lichens. (The caterpillar in the inset, from the central Adirondacks of New York, failed to yield an adult; while it could be either of our two species, it more closely matches characters for Kent's Geometer.) The pupa overwinters in *Selenia*.

PALE METANEMA
Metanema inatomaria

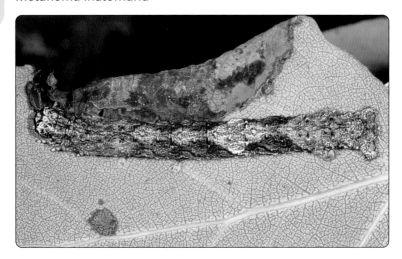

RECOGNITION Flattened bark mimic, usually gray with complex gray, white, and black mottling. Most individuals with *pale diamond over A4 followed by second pale wedge over rear of A5*. This latter wedge open rearward, i.e., pale coloration extends to A10. More subtle pale spots sometimes present over A2 and A3. Venter pale and unmarked.

Paraprocts and hypoproct short. Larva less than 3.5cm. In Dark Metanema (*Metanema determinata*) dorsal setae at rear of A1–A5 borne from darkened pimplelike warts that may be connected by low ridge; dorsal patterning subdued, often with black spiracular stripe. A6 and A7 frequently bearing a thin black addorsal stripe (inset).

OCCURRENCE Edges of watercourses, wooded swamps, woodlands, and forests from British Columbia to Nova Scotia south in East to Maryland, Mississippi, and Texas. Over most of range with two generations with mature caterpillars from May onward.

COMMON FOODPLANTS Especially aspen and poplar, but also willow.

REMARKS The caterpillar's coloration and flattened aspect are well suited for perching on the bark of aspen and poplar, the primary foodplants. The antennae are a bit longer than those of many leaf-feeding inchworms. I frequently encounter caterpillars of the Pale Metanema when beating, especially northward. Both of our metanemas overwinter as pupae in cocoons spun in bark crevices.

RECOGNITION Stout, *cylindrical*, tan, brown, gray, or reddish caterpillars with a *hump over A8*. Posterior half of A1–A6 traversed by set of closely spaced creases. *Frequently dark pigment frames flattened face with each lobe squared off to either side of triangle.* Common Metarranthis often branded with pair of white addorsal spots along leading edge of A2; homologous spots may be faintly expressed on following segments. Larva to 3.5cm. I am unaware of characters that will separate the Common Metarranthis from other eastern members of the genus (*see* Remarks).

OCCURRENCE Shrubby fields, woodlands, and forests. Eastern Canada south to Georgia and Texas. One generation with mature caterpillars in late summer.

COMMON FOODPLANTS Captive caterpillars accept apple, blueberry, and cherry; caterpillars from nature have not been reared.

REMARKS There are more than a dozen named *Metarranthis* species in the East and perhaps two as yet undescribed species. The taxonomy of the group is in need of review because some of these names appear to represent forms or geographic races. Identifications should be based on adults—should you find a caterpillar take pictures and save reared adults. Although metarranthis adults are common at light, as far as I know I have never found a late instar. In a crude sense, the late instars resemble cutworms (Family Noctuidae): the body is plump and the coloration subdued. Perhaps late instars descend from the leaves onto the trunk or move into leaf litter by day (like many cutworms). The Common Metarranthis may prove to be a complex of two or more species—the range given here applies to the entire assemblage. All *Metarranthis* overwinter as pupae.

ALIEN PROBOLE
Probole alienaria

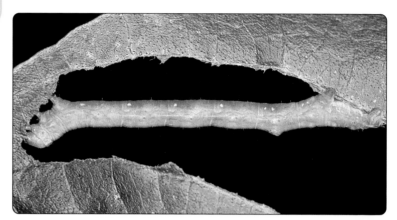

RECOGNITION Green, tan, brown, or brick red with low, *rounded, subdorsal swellings over A5 that are frequently flushed with red or brown. Head often marked with broad red to charcoal stripe* that extends from antenna to subdorsum of T1. Body somewhat thickened about thorax and A5–A6. Many forms and especially middle instars with red or gray middorsal stripe. Paraprocts and hypoproct of average length.

Larva less than 3.5cm. Early instars pale green and frequently bearing a reddened middorsal stripe. Caterpillars may not be separable from those of Red-cheeked Looper (*Probole amicaria*). Both *Probole* and *Plagodis* share swellings over A5. The two may be distinguished by the presence of a cheek stripe in *Probole* (when present); additionally, our eastern *Plagodis* tend to have a more conspicuously swollen T2 and more barklike appearance (*see* images in Wagner et al. 2002).

OCCURRENCE Wetlands, mesic woodlands, and forests from British Columbia to Nova Scotia south in East to Georgia and Arkansas. Over much of its range two generations with mature caterpillars from June onward.

COMMON FOODPLANTS Especially dogwood and sour gum, but also many other hardwoods including basswood, birch, hawthorn, maple, and witch hazel. Its close relative, the Red-cheeked Looper, feeds on dogwood and a broad array of other woody plants, even fir and spruce.

REMARKS The taxonomy of *Probole* is still in flux, in part because the adults are seasonally dimorphic—it would seem there are many more available names than there are good species. McGuffin (1987) considered *P. alienaria* to be just a form of the Red-cheeked Looper (*P. amicaria*). Save reared voucher specimens because species concepts are sure to change in the genus. The pupa of *Probole* overwinters.

Plagodis alcoolaria

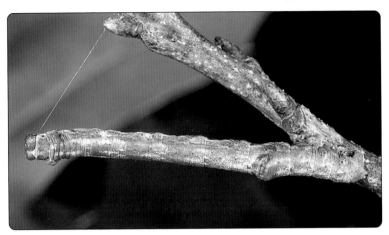

RECOGNITION Tan, gray, reddish, or brown, medium-sized with highly variable patterning—difficult to recognize. *Enlarged T2 and prominent subdorsal swellings on A5* marked with pale and dark markings that contrast with ground. Dorsal setae often borne from black bases. Below, midventral stripe broken into series of lines. Head with dense brown to reddish "snowflaking." Larva to 3.5cm. Early instars pale green, without swellings, occasionally distinguished by reddish middorsal stripe. Four other *Plagodis* occur in the East (*see* Wagner et al. 2002). Caterpillars of Fervid Plagodis (*Plagodis fervidaria*) and Straight-lined Plagodis (*P. phlogosaria*) are especially similar. *Plagodis* caterpillars, particularly early and middle instars, are easily confused with those of *Probole*. Determinations are best based on adults.

OCCURRENCE Woodlands and forests from southern Canada to Georgia and Texas. Two generations over much of East with mature caterpillars from June onward.

COMMON FOODPLANTS Many woody shrubs and trees, including alder, basswood, birch, chestnut, maple, oak, poplar, and willow.

REMARKS Initially *Plagodis* caterpillars are pale green and unwarted, being well suited to remain on leaves by day. The last instar ranks among our most convincing twig mimics. The caterpillars may be beaten from foliage, although usually in low numbers. A female Hollow-spotted Plagodis that I held with a red oak leaf laid her reddish orange eggs in chains, two to seven eggs in length (inset).

NORTHERN PINE LOOPER
Caripeta piniata

RECOGNITION Elongate, strongly corrugated caterpillars that lack distinctive warting. *A low ridge runs between the posterior pair of dorsal setae (D2) on each segment* (especially evident on A1–A6). *Anal plate distinctly squared off.* Our four Eastern species are variable in coloration and difficult to characterize. Northern Pine Looper gray to orange- or red-brown.

Sometimes with an oblique pale patch, edged above with black, in front of spiracle on A1–A6. Crochets arranged in two groups. Larva to 3.5cm. Brown Pine Looper (*Caripeta angustiorata*) sometimes with more pronounced ridging and pale yellow-green markings along dorsum or sides; principally on pines, but also other conifers. Gray Spruce Looper (*C. divisata*) often has reduced warting and is more apt to be found on fir, hemlock, larch, and spruce than pine. I am unfamiliar with Southern Pine Looper (*C. aretaria*), which occurs from Arkansas to Virginia south into Florida. The Large Purplish Gray (*Iridopsis vellivolata*) has the crochets arranged in a single group (*see* page 154).

OCCURRENCE Pine barrens and woodlands from Canada south to New Jersey and Wisconsin. One generation in Connecticut with mature caterpillars in fall; two generations in New Jersey with first being only partial (Dale Schweitzer, pers. comm.).

COMMON FOODPLANTS Pine.

REMARKS *Caripeta* are among the most commonly encountered caterpillars on pine in the fall. The Brown Pine Looper is a denizen of Canadian zone forests. The Northern Pine Looper is more widespread, being found throughout the Northeast, and is the only member of the genus to inhabit the pine woodlands of the Coastal Plain. The Southern Pine Looper replaces the Northern Pine Looper from Virginia southward—the former is uncommon over much of its range. *Caripeta* overwinter as pupae.

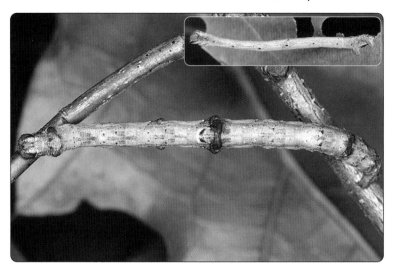

RECOGNITION Excellent twig mimic with *T2 and T3 enlarged, the former about subdorsum and latter where legs attach.* Look for conspicuous subdorsal and lateral swellings on A3 and smaller swellings laterally and subventrally on A2. Variously developed, paired, dorsal warts on A1, A5, A6, and A8. Swellings and warts usually reddened and/or

blackened. Larva to 4cm. Caterpillar of Straw Besma (*Besma endropiaria*), which co-occurs with the Oak Besma over much of East, usually has a more pronounced reddish cast and proportionately smaller warts. Head tending towards red and green in Straw Besma and brown and black in Oak Besma. The Straw Besma has a single generation; often on maple but also reported from alder, birch, and oak.

OCCURRENCE Woodlands and forests. Transcontinental in Canada south in East to Florida and Texas. Two generations through much of East with mature caterpillars from June onward.

COMMON FOODPLANTS Many forest trees including alder, beech, birch, elm, maple, oak, and willow; there are reports from conifers as well.

REMARKS The Oak Besma amply demonstrates the difficulty in characterizing looper caterpillars of different ages. When young, the caterpillars are green and without appreciable warting (inset). In the later instars, the warts and swellings become more developed and the coloration usually includes reds and browns. Both coloration and patterning may be exceedingly variable in this genus, and especially so in the last two instars. The pupa overwinters.

CURVE-LINED LOOPER
Lambdina fervidaria

RECOGNITION *Lambdina* caterpillars are *mosaics of pinstripes and conspicuous gray and black patterning*. Whitish subdorsal stripe often edged below by black. Dorsal and ventral areas decidedly lighter than average shade of lateral coloration. *Lobes of head marked with black spots*. Larva to 3.5cm. Although recognizing the genus is straightforward, assigning species names to *Lambdina* caterpillars based on appearance is not possible. In fact, the taxonomy of the genus is so problematic that having adults may not assure an authoritative identification. A half-dozen names are available for Eastern *Lambdina*—presumably there are more names than valid species. Wagner *et al.* (2002) and Maier *et al.* (2004) figure the caterpillars of common Eastern *Lambdina*.

OCCURRENCE Woodlands and forests. Covell (1984) gives South Dakota to Nova Scotia to North Carolina and Missouri, but until taxonomy of group is revised this is provisional. One generation northward with caterpillars maturing in late summer; two generations from Maryland south with last instars in June then again in September and October.

COMMON FOODPLANTS American hornbeam, birch, eastern hop hornbeam, oak, witch hazel, and other woody species.

REMARKS *Lambdina* caterpillars include some of our slowest-growing inchworms. Eggs of the Eastern Pine Looper (*Lambdina pellucidaria*) hatch in May or June, but it may be September or even October before the caterpillars reach maturity. As noted above, the taxonomy of the genus requires study. Lepidopterists are unclear which, if any, of the foodplant associations (e.g., conifer- versus broadleaf-feeding populations) represent different biological entities. Additional uncertainty surrounds the importance of whether a population is single-brooded or double-brooded. The pupa is thought to overwinter in all *Lambdina* except Hemlock Looper (*L. fiscellaria*), which overwinters as an egg.

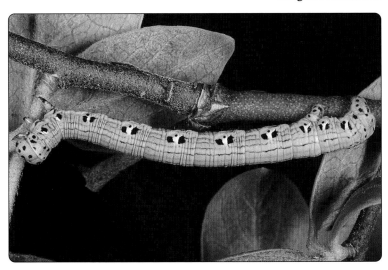

RECOGNITION *Beautiful bright yellow inchworm marked with thin black stripes and black and white spots.* Each *spiracle often embedded in white spot* bounded with black forward and rearward. Dorsum and venter set with three pairs of thin black stripes. Broad yellow stripe runs under spiracles. Yellow head and prolegs prominently spotted with black. Larva to 3.5cm.

OCCURRENCE Barrens, bogs, heathlands, and woodlands from southern Canada to Maryland, Ohio, and Kansas. One generation with mature caterpillars in July and August.

COMMON FOODPLANTS Many trees and shrubs including alder, bayberry, birch, blueberry, bog laurel, cranberry, fir, gale, huckleberry, larch, leatherleaf, maple, northern white cedar, oak, pine, poplar, sweet fern, and willow.

REMARKS In the Northeast, the Chain-dotted Geometer is most likely to be encountered in heathy bogs and along Cape Cod and the offshore islands in huckleberry-dominated heathlands. On Martha's Vineyard and Nantucket, populations often reach high densities following burns. It is a boom and bust species. Tim McCabe (pers. comm.) once saw a flight in the Adirondacks in which adults were so abundant that the scene was reminiscent of a heavy snowfall. Yet most populations across New England are waning—it has been seen just once in the past decade in Connecticut. The cocoon is open and the boldly-patterned pupa is prominently displayed within. Although it seems certain that *Cingilia* caterpillars and pupae are distasteful, their defensive chemistry has not been studied.

FESTIVE PINE LOOPER
Nepytia nr. *pellucidaria*

RECOGNITION *Beautiful orange, yellow, lavender, black, and white striped looper.* Broad, rusty orange middorsal and lemon yellow spiracular stripes especially prominent. White subdorsal stripe subtended by series of black and lavender stripes. Head, prothoracic shield, and legs rusty orange with black spotting. Larva to 3.5cm. The Pine Conelet Looper (*Nepytia semiclusaria*) is found throughout much of the Southeast; its caterpillar is similarly patterned.

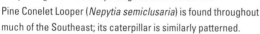

OCCURRENCE Barrens and pine woodlands from New England south to Georgia (in mountains). One generation with mature caterpillars from June to August.

COMMON FOODPLANTS Pine, especially hard pines such as pitch and shortleaf pine.

REMARKS True *Nepytia pellucidaria* is a large, pine-feeding species of eastern Canada and northern New England that flies in late summer. The caterpillar figured here may represent an unrecognized subspecies or species that replaces it to the south. The fall-flying populations of *Nepytia* from the Delmarva Peninsula are also a conundrum, not being readily assignable to this species or *N. semiclusaria*. Brightly-colored looper caterpillars are rare in temperate forests—our geometrid caterpillars tend to be cryptic in their coloration, texture, reflectance, as well as behavior. The significance of the Festive Pine Looper's bright coloration awaits explanation. The egg overwinters. *Nepytia* pupate in rather open cocoons spun among clusters of needles.

RECOGNITION Medium-large, brown, tan, or pinkish cylindrical caterpillar with *many closely set creases running over each segment.* A8 with pair of small warts that are commonly tinted with orange or pink. Subdorsal stripe on thorax often with orange tinge. Subspiracular stripe becomes lighter and wider rearward; in some individuals the stripe is mostly white

from A6 rearward; frequently it is confluent with *white lines that run down outer face of proleg.* Some individuals with whitish spot enveloping spiracle on A2. Spiracles small with black rim and brown center. Larva less than 4cm. *Eusarca fundaria* occurs along the Atlantic Coast from New Jersey southward.

OCCURRENCE Fields and coastal strand communities from Canada south to Florida and Texas. At least two generations from central New England southward; in North Carolina one principal brood in spring yielding mature caterpillars in June and July, but with adults (and mature caterpillars) occurring through rest of growing season.

COMMON FOODPLANTS Aster, dandelion, goldenrod, and other composites; also reported from clover.

REMARKS Females oviposit readily if confined for a night or two. The caterpillar will consume flowers in preference to leaves if they are available. While I reported (Wagner *et al.* 2002) that the Confused Eusarca overwinters as a pupa, I found a nearly mature caterpillar in mid-May in the Smokies (Fontana Village), which would suggest that the caterpillar overwinters, at least some of the time.

WHITE SLANT-LINE
Tetracis cachexiata

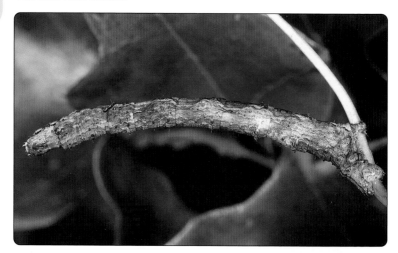

RECOGNITION Brown, gray, or most commonly red-brown caterpillar with *flattened head and conspicuously enlarged T2. Subdorsal swellings on T2 usually blackened at least apically. A4 and A5 with darkened dorsal warts* that are usually connected by a ridge, especially over the latter segment. Wavy black line often above A6 proleg. Lateral areas of anterior abdominal segments may be pinched into

short oblique ridge anterior to each spiracle. Look for *black middorsal line running from A8 over anal plate*. On head, lightly pigmented triangle and dorsal midline often bounded by diffuse field of black that intensifies over each lobe. Paraprocts and hypoproct well developed. Clypeus swollen and yellowish (Maier et al. 2004). Larva to 4.5cm. Caterpillars of the Yellow Slant-line (*Tetracis crocallata*), Variable Antepione (*Antepione thisoaria*), and Large Maple Spanworm (*Prochoerodes lineola*) can be quite similar to those of the White Slant-line.

OCCURRENCE Woodlands and forests from British Columbia to Nova Scotia south to northern Florida and Arkansas. From the Carolinas northward, one principal generation with mature caterpillars from late July to October.

COMMON FOODPLANTS Alder, American hornbeam, ash, basswood, birch, bittersweet, black gum, cherry, elm, fir, gale, hemlock, larch, laurel, maple, ninebark, oak, pine, poplar, spruce, sweet fern, viburnum, willow, and many other woody plants.

REMARKS It is a fine stick mimic endowed with numerous warts and barklike coloration. All three sets of legs are held tightly against the underside of the thorax. I commonly encounter the White Slant-line while beating in August and September. In New England, it overwinters primarily as a pupa.

PURPLISH-BROWN LOOPER
(CURVED-TOOTH GEOMETER) *Eutrapela clemataria*

RECOGNITION Large, brown to purple-brown stick mimic with *eared ridge over A4* and set of small warts over A8. *Anterior of T2 forms raised collar* that frames front end of body (inset). All three of these raised areas often darkly pigmented and *dotted with orange*. Larva to 5cm.

OCCURRENCE Woodlands and forests from Minnesota to Newfoundland south to Florida and Texas. At least two generations from Pennsylvania southward where mature caterpillars may be found from May onward.

COMMON FOODPLANTS Many woody shrubs and trees including ash, basswood, birch, cherry, cranberry, currant, dogwood, elderberry, elm, fir, hemlock, gale, maple, New Jersey tea, oak, poplar, sweet gum, viburnum, walnut, and willow.

REMARKS As in other twig-mimicking inchworms, the venter is colored much like the dorsum and the last four abdominal segments are short and bunched together. When at rest, the Purplish-brown Looper adopts one of two postures. In the first, the legs are held tightly against the thorax and the head is rolled under; the anterior of the body thus resembles a fist. In the second, the swollen legs on T3 are held outward, in such a way as to resemble the scar left after a leaf has dropped from a twig. The pupa overwinters in surface litter.

JUNIPER GEOMETER
Patalene olyzonaria

RECOGNITION *Slender, elongate twig mimic rendered in a complex pattern of diamonds, dashes, and lines.* Darkened dorsum edged with broken black and white stripe that undulates along its length. Side of abdomen bears pale green to cream patches anterior to each spiracle. Pair of minute, black, dorsal spots (D1 pinacula), to either side of midline, over A8. Head with short dark line that carries over vertex, then fades away at about level of triangle; antenna long, pale. Larva to 3cm.

OCCURRENCE Fields, open woodlands, and cedar swamps from Upper Midwest to central New England south to Texas and Florida. At least two or three generations over most of our area with mature caterpillars from June onward.

COMMON FOODPLANTS Atlantic white cedar and eastern red cedar commonly, probably other cedars as well (Maier *et al.* 2004).

REMARKS One could scarcely design a caterpillar to be a better match for a life on juniper. Not only does it match cedar foliage in both color and pattern, but even its texture, shape, and reflectance seem tuned for an existence on cedars and junipers. The caterpillar frequently rests twiglike with the anterior end of the body raised, attached by a safety line. Summer generation caterpillars pupate in a sparse cocoon spun amongst foliage. Brown caterpillars fade to green prior to pupation to yield a green and white pupa that is virtually impossible to locate among the scalelike leaves. The Juniper Geometer overwinters as a pupa.

Prochoerodes lineola (= P. transversata)

RECOGNITION Color and pattern exceptionally variable, although most forms are some shade of tan to purple-brown. *Distinguished by its large size and dorsal warts on A4 and A8. T2 swollen, at least relative to prothorax.* Small pimplelike warts over A5. Often with two black oblique lines that extend from A6 proleg: first short, well defined, and extending less than halfway to spiracle on A5; second longer, ill defined, and directed toward spiracle on A8. Head somewhat flattened, usually with two pale lines across face: upper one running between eyes, and lower between antennae. Larva to 5cm. Some color forms of the Large Maple Spanworm resemble caterpillars of Variable Antepione and Slant-lines (*Tetracis* species) but T2 tends to be less swollen in Large Maple Spanworm and the posterior abdominal segments are rarely marked with the black middorsal stripe common to these two related genera.

OCCURRENCE Woodlands and forests from Great Lakes Region to Nova Scotia south to Florida and Texas. Seasonal phenology remains unclarified in Northeast, where there appears to be a single principal generation, with mature caterpillars from June through August; southward with two to three generations.

COMMON FOODPLANTS Woody shrubs and trees including birch, blueberry, cedar, cherry, currant, dogwood, fir, hemlock, larch, maple, oak, poplar, spruce, viburnum, and willow, but also grasses and ornamental flowers.

REMARKS The Large Maple Spanworm is a showcase example of why coloration should be used guardedly when making larval determinations of geometrids. The frosted forms, i.e., those with a whitish saddle, are striking insects that seem to mimic a twig with exfoliating bark. Frosted forms also occur in slant-lines (*Tetracis*). Over much of New England, the strongly squared-off egg is thought to overwinter.

FILAMENT BEARER
Nematocampa resistaria

RECOGNITION Immediately recognizable by *pale-tipped, eversible tentacles that extend from dorsum of A2 and A3.* Ground color varies from yellow to brown. Pale lateral patch runs from above proleg on A6 back to spiracle on A8. Larva to 2cm. Baggett's Filament Bearer (*Nematocampa baggettaria*) flies with *N. resistaria* from North Carolina (along the coast) south through the Gulf States; presumably its caterpillars are quite similar; it has multiple generations.

OCCURRENCE Parks, meadows, woodlands, and forests from Canada south to Florida and Texas. One generation with mature caterpillars in late spring.

COMMON FOODPLANTS Many hardwoods and softwoods as well as low-growing plants including alder, ash, basswood, birch, blueberry, buckeye, carrot, cherry, chestnut, dogwood, elm, fir, gale, hawthorn, hazelnut, hemlock, hickory, ironwood, larch, maple, mountain ash, New Jersey tea, oak, spruce, strawberry, sycamore, and willow.

REMARKS Ferguson's studies (in prep.) suggest that the Filament Bearer is misplaced here, at the end of the Ennomines, and is properly classified (in the Tribe Cassymini) near the Angles (*Macaria*) (Tribe Macariini). The larva rests exposed on an upper leaf surface with the body thrown into a loop. It is difficult to imagine what the larva is mimicking, but the overall effect is not unlike a fallen brown flower with exerted stamens. Alarmed caterpillars shunt hemolymph into filaments, enlarging them by as much as twice their resting length. The egg overwinters.

COMMON GRAY *Anavitrinella pampinaria*

Transcontinental in Canada, in East south to Florida and Texas. Two to many generations with mature caterpillars from May onward. Generalist on woody species (both broadleaf and conifers), forbs, and even grass.

VARIABLE ANTEPIONE *Antepione thisoaria*

Canada south to Georgia, Alabama, and Mississippi. One generation in Canada; two or more generations southward with mature caterpillars from June onward. Alder, apple, blackberry, cherry, and many other woody plants.

DAINTY GRAY *Glena plumosaria*

Missouri and Illinois to central New Jersey south to Florida and Mississippi. At least two generations with mature caterpillars from June onward. Cedar.

STOUT LOCUST LOOPER (Common Spring Moth)
Heliomata cycladata

Southern Canada to Georgia, Alabama, and Louisiana. One generation with mature caterpillars from May to July. Locust.

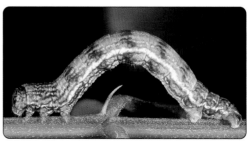

GREEN LARCH LOOPER (Lesser Larch Angle) *Macaria sexmaculata*

Western Canada to Nova Scotia south in East to Connecticut, Maryland, and Great Lakes States. Two generations with mature caterpillars from June to November. Larch.

HOLLY LOOPER (Black-dotted Ruddy) *Thysanopyga intractata*

Missouri to Massachusetts south to Florida and Texas, especially along Coastal Plain. At least three generations in Maryland with mature caterpillars from May to November. Holly.

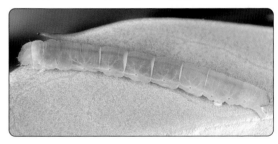

CYPRESS GRAY (Black-shouldered Gray) *Iridopsis pergracilis*

Southeastern Missouri, Maryland, and Delaware south to Florida and Texas. At least three generations with mature caterpillars from May until first hard frost. Occasional defoliator of bald cypress.

GREEN SPANWORM (Sulphur Itame) *Itame sulphurea*

Transcontinental in Canada south in East to southeastern Massachusetts, New Jersey, and Great Lakes States. One generation with mature caterpillars in May and June. Occasional pest of cranberry.

BLACKBERRY LOOPER
Chlorochlamys chloroleucaria

RECOGNITION Slender caterpillar with *forward-projecting horns on T1 and head*. Pale green body generously salted with minute whitish granules; setae small and inconspicuous. Often with red, maroon, or brown middorsal and vague subdorsal, supraspiracular, and spiracular stripes. Each anterior abdominal segment has six or seven annulations. Anal plate strongly pointed. Larva less than 2.5cm. *Chlorochlamys phyllinaria* flies with Blackberry Looper from Georgia westward through Gulf States and northward into Missouri. Except for its smaller size, it is probably indistinguishable from the Blackberry Looper as a larva. The Blackberry Looper may also be confused with other widespread emeralds. The horns on T1 and head are proportionately smaller and less pointed than those of the Pistachio Emerald (*Hethemia pistasciaria*) and related genera.

OCCURRENCE Woodlands, fields, and other open habitats from Canada south to Florida and Texas. At least two generations with mature caterpillars from May until leaf fall.

COMMON FOODPLANTS Blackberry, strawberry, and related plants, including fruits; flowers of goldenrod, yarrow, zinnia, and other composites; leaves of dogbane, sweet fern, and presumably many other plants.

REMARKS The caterpillars eat a curious array of foods, and may be unique among our loopers in their willingness to consume fleshy fruits. It is a member of a diverse guild of caterpillars, containing more than a dozen common species, that feed on goldenrod blossoms in the autumn. The pupa overwinters in a slight cocoon spun among leaf litter.

SHOWY EMERALD
Dichorda iridaria

RECOGNITION Seemingly more trilobite than caterpillar, this unlikely animal cannot be confused with any other looper in eastern North America, where the genus is represented by only a single species. *Winglike dorsolateral flanges extend from last two thoracic and first five abdominal segments. Two large, forward-projecting hooks issue from the dorsum of A8.* A black middorsal stripe runs from thorax back to A8. Larva to 2.5cm.

OCCURRENCE Fields, roadsides, and open woodlands. Southern Canada to Florida and Texas. Over much of East, two generations with mature caterpillars from May into July, then again in late summer and early fall; continuously-brooded through growing season in South.

COMMON FOODPLANTS Sumac and poison ivy.

REMARKS If there is a finite number of search images that a bird can retain while panning vegetation for prey, then surely this insect enjoys a measure of protection just by being so unlike other caterpillars. The caterpillar resembles a withered sumac leaflet. It may rest with the anterior portion of the body raised and looped or crooked to one side, adding to its guise as an aged, browning sumac leaflet. Emerald caterpillars have a single gear—slow. If disturbed, their caterpillars often quaver from side to side, much like loosely attached leaves being pushed about by a light breeze. The pupa overwinters.

Nemoria bistriaria

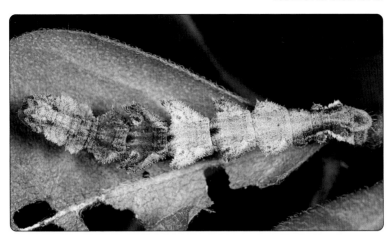

RECOGNITION *Nemoria* are bizarre caterpillars with densely-spined bodies and *winglike lateral extensions* that issue from the anterior abdominal segments. Other conspicuous features include *dorsal spines on A8 and thornlike processes over thorax*. Ground colors range from tan and straw through rust, brick red, brown, and nearly black; some have patches of lime green. In Red-fringed Emerald winglike extensions of A2

and A3 are a bit longer than those of most other common *Nemoria*. Because the caterpillars co-occur with those of the White-fringed Emerald (*Nemoria mimosaria*), Red-fronted Emerald (*N. rubrifrontaria*), and others, identifications should be based on reared adults. Three additional *Nemoria* are figured on page 201. Larva to 2cm.

OCCURRENCE Woodlands and forests from southern Canada to Florida and eastern Texas. Two generations over much of East, perhaps three or more in South, with mature caterpillars from May onward.

COMMON FOODPLANTS Reported from birch, gale, oak, sweet fern, and walnut, but certainly feeding on other woody plants.

REMARKS Interestingly, both larval coloration and patterning are influenced by larval diet (McFarland 1988, Greene 1989). *Nemoria arizonaria* caterpillars fed plant tissues low in tannins develop into a catkinlike form, pale in color with enlarged flanges. (Catkins, the dangling male flowers of oak, are present for only two to four weeks in early spring.) Siblings fed on tannin-rich substrates, such as summer foliage, develop into a form that is grayer in color with appreciably smaller flanges. Behavior too appears to be influenced by diet: the former (spring-brood larvae) prefer to rest among catkins, whereas the latter (summer-brood larvae) occur on twigs and stems. *Nemoria* overwinter as pupae.

CAMOUFLAGED LOOPER (WAVY-LINED EMERALD)
Synchlora aerata

RECOGNITION Our only widespread caterpillar that *adorns its body with plant fragments*. Various debris are attached to projections over the dorsum; integument roughened and setae spinelike. Body brown, black, and white, with oblique white line passing through each spiracle. White lateral stripe running from A6 back to anal proleg; shorter, parallel line below first, extending back to A9. *Synchlora frondaria* begins to replace *S. aerata* from Maryland southward, especially along the Coastal Plain. Five other *Synchlora* occur in Florida and parts of Texas. South of the Mason-Dixon line identifications should be based on reared adults. Larva to 1.5cm.

OCCURRENCE Fields and other open habitats from southern Canada to Georgia (mostly in Piedmont) and Texas. Two generations northward, up to four southward with mature caterpillars from April into October.

COMMON FOODPLANTS Often composite flowers such as ageratum, aster, black-eyed susan, boneset, daisy, goldenrod, ragweed, and yarrow; but also using birch, blackberry, chestnut, raspberry, rose, sage, St. John's wort, and other plants.

REMARKS A Mardi Gras caterpillar that is out of costume only after a molt. The larva fashions its disguise by attaching plant bits (usually flower petals which it has chewed free of its foodplant) to its back. It would be interesting to move a caterpillar from one flower to another to ascertain how many times a caterpillar might change its costume during the course of its development, or to offer a caterpillar scraps of colored paper or different flowers to see if it would use them. I have had good success finding caterpillars by scanning composites for anomalous flowers. The Camouflaged Looper overwinters as a middle instar larva.

PISTACHIO EMERALD *Hethemia pistasciaria*

Southern Canada to Florida and Texas. One generation northward, evidently two from Maryland southward. Basswood, birch, blueberry, ironwood, ninebark, oak, willow, and other woody plants.

WHITE-BARRED EMERALD *Nemoria bifilata*

Long Island south (mostly along Coastal Plain) to Florida and Texas, north to Nebraska. At least two generations with caterpillars from June onward. Oak, sumac, and presumably other woody plants.

CYPRESS EMERALD *Nemoria elfa*

Southeastern Missouri to North Carolina south into Everglades and west into Texas. Two or more generations. Cypress.

OCELLATE EMERALD *Nemoria lixaria*

Atlantic Coastal Plain from New Jersey to Florida west into Texas. As many as three generations in New Jersey and more southward with mature caterpillars present year-round. Oak, red maple, sweet fern, and presumably other woody plants.

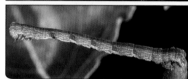

SWEETFERN GEOMETER
Cyclophora pendulinaria

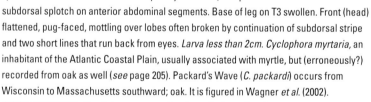

RECOGNITION Exceptionally variable in coloration and patterning with ground color ranging from bright green to yellow, orange, brown, and purple-brown. *Many forms possess a dark lateral spot near spiracle on A1.* Checkered forms frequently with dark, oblique subdorsal splotch on anterior abdominal segments. Base of leg on T3 swollen. Front (head) flattened, pug-faced, mottling over lobes often broken by continuation of subdorsal stripe and two short lines that run back from eyes. *Larva less than 2cm. Cyclophora myrtaria,* an inhabitant of the Atlantic Coastal Plain, usually associated with myrtle, but (erroneously?) recorded from oak as well (*see* page 205). Packard's Wave (*C. packardi*) occurs from Wisconsin to Massachusetts southward; oak. It is figured in Wagner *et al.* (2002).

OCCURRENCE Sandy barrens, woodlands, and edges of watercourses. Transcontinental in Canada south in East to Georgia, Mississippi, and northeastern Texas. At least two generations with mature caterpillars from June until first frosts.

COMMON FOODPLANTS Alder, bayberry, birch, blueberry, cranberry, gale, huckleberry, and sweet fern preferred, but also larch, oak, and presumably other woody species.

REMARKS I have found the caterpillars in virtually every stand of gale and sweet fern that I have searched, often in great numbers. The caterpillar quavers from side to side, especially when changing or moving between perches or if disturbed slightly. The middle instars remove patches of tissue from leaf undersides. The Sweetfern Geometer overwinters as a fully exposed pupa, attached by only a girdle of silk and its cremaster (the set of crochetlike hooks at the terminus of pupa). The girdled pupa is reminiscent of a white butterfly (pierid) chrysalis.

Pleuroprucha insulsaria

RECOGNITION Highly variable; usually some shade of yellow, green, gray, or brown and variegated with white and browns. *T2 and T3 laterally swollen*, especially evident when viewed from above. Anterior abdominal segments with approximately ten annulations. Pale middorsal stripe usually well developed. *Dorsum of each anterior abdominal segment often with pale triangle set within a*

dark chevron. Coloration of prothoracic plate distinctive: often with pale, thin middorsal stripe and broader subdorsal stripes. Many forms with dark spots forming herringbone pattern over each lobe of head. Paraprocts and hypoproct very short. Larva about 1.5cm. Caterpillars of the Common Tan Wave and Common Pug (*Eupithecia miserulata*) feed side by side on flowers throughout late summer and fall. The roughened integument and short peglike setae (best viewed under a lens) help distinguish its larva.

OCCURRENCE Waste places, grasslands, fields, and edges of woodlands from Great Lakes Region to Nova Scotia south to Florida and Texas. Two or more generations with caterpillars from July to first frosts.

COMMON FOODPLANTS Aster, bedstraw, bittersweet, chestnut, coreopsis, corn, false indigo (*Amorpha*), goldenrod, mimosa tree, oak, ragweed, senna (*Cassia*), sweet clover, willow, and many other plants.

REMARKS If you see frass below floral bouquets picked from the garden, it probably belongs to this caterpillar or that of the Common Pug (*Eupithecia miserulata*). Both are flower-loving dietary generalists and virtually ubiquitous. I stayed in a cabin in Goshen,Virginia, where the Common Tan Wave was infesting all of the mimosa trees in our camp—single trees had populations of a thousand or more caterpillars. At night the caterpillar may hang from a short silk thread—presumably to escape the attention of spiders and other nocturnal predators. The pupal stage overwinters.

LARGE LACE-BORDER
Scopula limboundata

RECOGNITION *Extremely elongate with as many as 30 annulations on some abdominal segments* and lateral flange that runs length of abdomen. Truncated anal plate extending beyond base of anal proleg. Ground color varies from green to brown with mature caterpillars tending towards the latter. Caterpillars often with dark middorsal stripe most evident over abdomen. Both lateral

flange and anal proleg often pale, especially anteriorly. Prominent brown stripe running along side of head to antenna. A half-dozen or so other *Scopula* species occur in the East—identifications should be based on adults. Larva less than 3.5cm.

OCCURRENCE Wetlands, swamps, woodlands, and forests from Manitoba to Nova Scotia south to northern Florida and Texas. One generation at northern limits of range, two in New England, and three or more in South.

COMMON FOODPLANTS Woody shrubs, trees, and some herbs including blackberry, blueberry, cherry, chokeberry, clover, dandelion, elm, rhododendron, shrubby cinquefoil, and sweet pepperbush.

REMARKS In Southeast Asia adults of a few *Scopula* feed on blood, sweat, and the eye secretions of cattle and other animals (Bängizer and Fletcher 1985). *Scopula* is one of the world's largest genera of Geometridae with over 700 described species. The few caterpillars I have found have been on woody plants within 2m of the ground, and always as singletons. The fourth instar larva overwinters (McGuffin 1967).

CROSS-LINED WAVE *Timandra amaturaria*

Wisconsin and Massachusetts south to Florida and Texas. Two or more generations with mature caterpillars from June onward. Buckwheat, dock, and knotweed.

WAXMYRTLE WAVE *Cyclophora myrtaria*

Southeast Massachusetts to Florida west to Texas. Many generations with mature caterpillars from late spring onward. Especially common on wax myrtle.

CHICKWEED GEOMETER *Haematopis grataria*

Manitoba to Maine south to Florida and Texas. Many generations with mature caterpillars from spring through first frosts. Chickweed, clover, and other herbaceous plants.

STRAW WAVE *Idaea eremiata*

Southern Michigan to New Jersey to Florida west to Arizona. In New Jersey, one generation with caterpillars overwintering and maturing in spring. Plant detritus such as dead oak leaves.

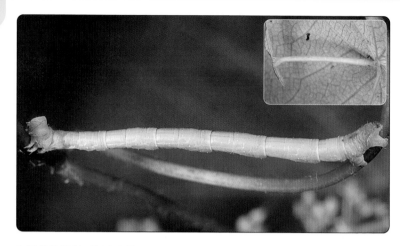

LESSER GRAPEVINE LOOPER
Eulithis diversilineata

RECOGNITION *Elongate, yellow-green to red petiole mimic, with segments A6–A10 very shortened.* T2 often swollen laterally. Cleft head, legs, A6 proleg, and paraprocts sometimes flushed with russet, red, or violet. Additionally, there may be a reddish middorsal stripe or spots over anterior and posterior abdominal segments. Paraprocts conspicuous. Greater Grapevine Looper (*Eulithis gracilineata*) is a brownish twig mimic with darkly pigmented lateral swelling on T2 (Forbes 1948, McGuffin 1958). It, too, feeds on grape and Virginia creeper. The two species have much the same distribution, but the Greater Grapevine Looper ranges farther north through New England into southeastern Canada. Larva to 3.5cm.

OCCURRENCE Roadsides, woodlands, and forest edges from Montana, southern Ontario, and Massachusetts to Florida and Texas. Two generations with mature caterpillars from June onward.

COMMON FOODPLANTS Grape and Virginia creeper.

REMARKS The caterpillar is a superb petiole mimic—its preferred resting posture is with both ends of the body attached to the underside of a leaf, much like a real petiole might be (inset). Caterpillars can be found by searching the underside of grape leaves at night with a flashlight or by beating. I once collected a reddish individual in the fall that so closely matched the fall coloration and curl of a broken grape petiole that my entomology students failed to recognize the insect as a caterpillar (or, for that matter, as any animal life form). The egg overwinters.

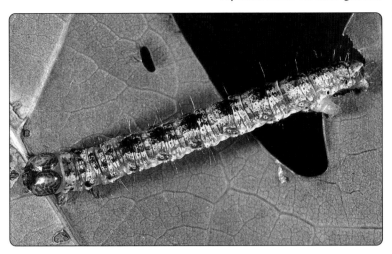

RECOGNITION Hydriomenas are short, stocky inchworms with ill-defined markings and *numerous setae above the anterior A6 proleg*. Coloration of Transfigured Hydriomena variable and the patterning diffuse; ground color ranging from tan to straw. Commonly with dark patches over thoracic shield, dorsum of anterior abdominal segments, and anal plate. Dark coloration of thorax spills down over top of head and may reach into triangle. Paraprocts and hypoproct short. Larva less than 3cm. The caterpillar figured here may be that of the Sharp Green Hydriomena (*Hydriomena pluviata*), a closely related species that also feeds on oak; it is more prevalent over the southern part of the eastern United States.

OCCURRENCE Barrens and oak woodlands from Manitoba to Nova Scotia south to New Jersey and Illinois; records from farther south may refer to the Sharp Green Hydriomena. One generation with mature caterpillars from July into October.

COMMON FOODPLANTS Oak.

REMARKS *Hydriomena* are slow-growing loopers that grind away at midsummer foliage for months. The caterpillar retires by day in a shelter made by folding over a leaf edge and tying it down with silk or securing two overlapping leaves, one atop the other. Within their shelter, they rest looped around to one side. It is not surprising that coloration in *Hydriomena* is subdued—it seems to be a rule among caterpillars that the more time that is spent concealed, the less likely that a caterpillar's coloration will be bright or otherwise distinctive. This is particularly true of internal borers—their caterpillars are especially undistinguished. The wing patterning and coloration of *Hydriomena* adults are bewilderingly variable. Fortunately, genitalic characters are reliable. *Hydriomena* pupae overwinter.

BARBERRY LOOPER (BARBERRY GEOMETER)
Coryphista meadii

RECOGNITION *Plump with broad, white spiracular stripe and red-orange head.* Spiracular stripe frequently infused with yellow or rust about black spiracles. Thin white addorsal and subdorsal stripes run through dark brownish dorsum; venter brown. Larva to 2.5cm.

OCCURRENCE Parks and suburban areas, woodlands, and forests. Transcontinental, south in East to Florida and Texas. Three generations in Connecticut with mature caterpillars from June into November.

COMMON FOODPLANTS Barberry, including introduced Japanese barberry.

REMARKS The native foodplant is thought to have been *Berberis canadensis*. Early instars skeletonize small patches of tissue from leaf undersides, especially about margins. The Barberry Looper is an occasional pest that completely defoliates local stands of its host. By day, the Barberry Looper rests on the underside of a leaf or twig. When disturbed it coils up like a cutworm and drops to the ground. The pupa overwinters in a cell in the soil.

Rheumaptera prunivorata (= *Hydria prunivorata*)

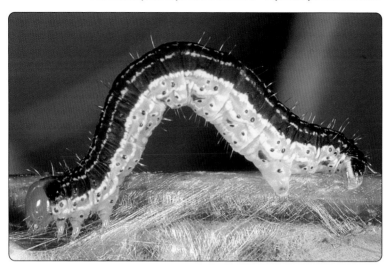

RECOGNITION Its *nest and gregarious habit* immediately distinguish the Cherry Scallop Shell from other Eastern inchworms. *Dark brown dorsum divided into five parts by addorsal and subdorsal white stripes.* White supraspiracular stripe separating darker dorsum from creamy sides. Lateral setae borne from blackened bases. Larva to 2.5cm. Scallop Shell (*Rheumaptera undulata*), scarcely distinguishable as an adult, is

immediately recognizable as a caterpillar by its solitary habit and rather bland coloration—the brown to black colors are essentially absent from the dorsum. This largely Canadian species occurs south to Pennsylvania and the Great Lakes Region. Foodplants include alder, azalea (rhodora), blueberry, poplar, spirea, willow, and presumably other plants.

OCCURRENCE Overgrown fields and woodland edges from southern Canada to Florida and Texas. Two generations in Northeast with caterpillars from May into October.

COMMON FOODPLANTS Black cherry.

REMARKS This occasional pest of black cherry feeds gregariously in a nest fashioned by tying up an entire shoot. The terminal shoot may be killed and thus the growth form of this important tree—wood of which is used in furniture making and cabinetry—may be compromised. There are other insects that make similar elongate, gregarious nests on cherry including two species of web-spinning sawflies (*Neurotoma* species) and the Uglynest Caterpillar (*Archips cerasivoranus*). These are active early in the season, whereas the Cherry Scallop Shell draws greatest attention in late summer when its numbers are highest. The pupa overwinters in leaf litter.

THE BRUCE SPANWORM
Operophtera bruceata

RECOGNITION *Plump, typically pale glossy green, early spring-active caterpillar with proportionately small prolegs.* Under outbreak conditions ground color may be gray-green, smoky, brown, or black. *Whitish subdorsal stripe positioned over weak, mostly broken supraspiracular* stripe; area between sometimes filled with white. Another faint, mostly broken stripe runs beneath yellow-orange spiracles. Setae often borne

from whitish bases. All coloration characters break down in some individuals, especially during outbreaks. Head ranges from pale green to shiny black. *Operophtera* caterpillars have a long and slender spinneret (silk-spinning structure) (visible with lens). Larva about 2cm. The Winter Moth (*Operophtera brumata*) is an introduced pest in the Maritime provinces, the north Pacific Coast between southern British Columbia and Oregon, and most recently, Massachusetts.

OCCURRENCE Forests and woodlands from Pacific Northwest to Nova Scotia south in East to Maryland and Upper Midwest. One generation with mature caterpillars from late April to June.

COMMON FOODPLANTS Many shrubs and trees including alder, aspen, beech, birch, cherry, elm, hazel, maple, oak, serviceberry, willow, and witch hazel.

REMARKS The caterpillar rests on the underside of a leaf, with the body curled to one side. Some fashion a crude leaf shelter in which they pass the day. During outbreaks, the caterpillars may enshroud entire trees in ghostly sheets of silk. *Operophtera* caterpillars are active early in the year, maturing as early as the first week of June in the Northeast. Adults emerge late in the year, usually after the first frost. The males may be seen fluttering about even when temperatures drop near or just below freezing. The orange eggs, laid in bark crevices by the wingless females, overwinter.

Eupithecia miserulata

RECOGNITION Exceptionally variable in coloration, but usually with herringbone pattern of oblique subdorsal lines. These often join over dorsum to form *arrows atop first six or seven abdominal segments*. Pale subspiracular stripe runs from thorax to edge of anal plate. Weak, brownish middorsal and subdorsal stripes often present. *Body*

surface roughened; each segment with seven to nine relatively deep creases. Larva about 1.5cm. There are more than 40 eastern *Eupithecia*—certain identification may require genitalic dissection. Bolte's (1990) monograph of the Canadian fauna includes most of the common United States' species; unfortunately the focus is on adults, caterpillars are neither illustrated nor described. Riley and Prior's (2003) book on the British pug moths is rich in life history information, rearing tips, and larval images.

OCCURRENCE Waste lots, gardens, fields, and woodlands. Transcontinental in Canada south in East to Florida and Texas. Many generations with mature caterpillars from May until the first frosts.

COMMON FOODPLANTS Many woody plants such as gale, grape, holly, oak, viburnum, and willow; also common on herbaceous plants such as dock and St. John's wort; composites such as aster, black-eyed susan, fleabane, goldenrod, joe-pye weed, sunflower, and yarrow also favored.

REMARKS Whereas many pugs are specialized in diet, the Common Pug is remarkably polyphagous. It is a regular in gardens, where it can be seen feeding on the blooms of a variety of plants. The Common Pug accounts for more than 90% of the *Eupithecia* caterpillars that I find—it is to be expected on virtually any herbaceous or woody plant. Caterpillars are especially likely to turn up in late summer and fall. Its coloration frequently blends with that of its foodplant—how the caterpillars come to match their background in coloration is deserving of study. The pupa overwinters.

YELLOW-LINED CONIFER LOOPER
(MOTTLED GRAY CARPET) *Cladara ?limitaria*

RECOGNITION *Green with prominent cream spiracular stripe and thinner, more yellowish subdorsal stripe.* Both stripes tend to be poorly expressed on T1. Base of leg on T3 enlarged. Larva to 2.5cm. Spiracular stripe of *Cladara* ends at spiracle on T1, whereas that of powder moths (*Eufidonia*) continues onto head and may carry forward to antenna. Paraprocts of Yellow-lined

Conifer Looper, though small, are more developed than in powder moths. Another conifer-feeding member of the genus, *C. anguilineata*, occurs with the Yellow-lined Conifer Looper over much of the East. I cannot distinguish caterpillars of the two moths, and in fact this image may represent that species.

OCCURRENCE Forests and woodlands. Transcontinental in Canada south to Georgia (in mountains) and Great Lakes States. One generation with mature caterpillars in early summer.

COMMON FOODPLANTS Fir, hemlock, larch, pine, spruce, and other conifers.

REMARKS The resting posture of the Yellow-lined Conifer Looper (also known as Dotted Line Looper and Green Balsam Looper) is unique among conifer-feeding geometrids (inset): the head is rolled under the thorax. In the extreme, the head is tucked up under the third pair of legs, such that the anterior end of the body resembles a fist. The pupa overwinters.

(POWDERED BIGWING) *Lobophora nivigerata*

RECOGNITION *Waxy green to blue-green, relatively stocky inchworm with elongate anal projections (paraprocts)* (inset). *Whitish subdorsal stripe* thinning and broken over thoracic segments. Elongate swellings form weak ridge below spiracles. Unmarked green head with each lobe raised to either side of midline. *Anal proleg broad*, crudely resembling an elephant's foot. Larva less than 2.5cm.

OCCURRENCE Forests and woodlands. Transcontinental in Canada south to North Carolina, Indiana, and South Dakota. Two generations over much of East with mature caterpillars in late June and July, then again from August to October; common.

COMMON FOODPLANTS Poplar, and, less frequently, willow.

REMARKS The caterpillar rests with the full length of its body held against the underside of a leaf. The Two-lined Aspen Looper's posture and coloration are shared by three *Gluphisia* species (Family Notodontidae) which also perch with their bodies extended on the undersides of poplar leaves by day. Moreover, all are somewhat dorsally flattened, all are waxy green, and all feature a prominent subdorsal stripe. The pupa overwinters.

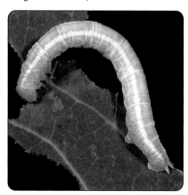

CARPETS

BENT-LINE CARPET *Costaconvexa centrostrigaria* (= *Orthonama centrostrigaria*)

Southern Canada to Florida and Texas. At least two generations with mature caterpillars from April onward. Herbaceous plants.

THE BEGGAR *Eubaphe mendica*

Southern Canada to Florida and Texas. At least two generations with mature caterpillars from June onward. Violet.

WHITE-BANDED TOOTHED CARPET *Epirrhoe alternata*

Transcontinental in Canada, south in East to North Carolina. Two generations with mature caterpillars from June onward. Bedstraw.

BROWN BARK CARPET *Horisme intestinata*

Transcontinental in Canada south in East to Florida and Texas. At least two generations with mature caterpillars from May to November. Clematis.

UNADORNED CARPET *Hydrelia inornata*

Eastern Canada south to North Carolina (in mountains) and Missouri. Two generations with mature caterpillars from May to November. Birch, hop hornbeam, and perhaps other hardwoods.

EARLY JUNIPER CARPET *Thera contractata*

Manitoba to Nova Scotia south to Massachusetts and Great Lakes Region. One generation with mature caterpillars from July to mid-August. Common juniper. Caterpillars of *T. juniperata* mature later, in late August and September.

WHITE-STRIPED BLACK *Trichodezia albovittata*

British Columbia to Labrador south to Georgia (mountains), Missouri, and Kansas. At least two generations with mature caterpillars from June to November. Touch-me-not and other impatiens. Note black line across face.

TISSUE MOTH *Triphosa haesitata*

Transcontinental in Canada south in East to North Carolina (mountains) and Missouri (historic). At least two generations in New York with mature caterpillars from June until first frosts. Buckthorn and evidently other woody species.

Bent-line Carpet

The Beggar

White-banded Toothed Carpet

Brown Bark Carpet

Unadorned Carpet

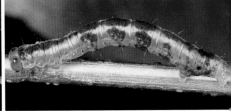

Early Juniper Carpet

White-striped Black

Tissue Moth

SCOOPWINGS – URANIIDAE
(Subfamily Epipleminae)

This small tropical family has but two representatives in our region, both in the Epipleminae. Epiplemine caterpillars are small, inconspicuous, wide-bodied insects. Ours are drab in color with darkened setal bases. Two subspiracular setae arise from a common base (pinaculum) on A1–A3 (setae arise from separate pinacula on A4–A8 in epiplemines and on A1–A8 in other Lepidoptera). Our Eastern species are gregarious, forming a loose silken web, at least in the early instars. The pupa overwinters in litter.

BROWN SCOOPWING
Calledapteryx dryopterata

RECOGNITION *Very small, smoky brown, stout, with proportionately minute prolegs.* Dark setal bases, perched on low warts, ringed by pale area. Usually with *pale patch on side of A8*, contrasting with black spiracle and blackened lateral setal bases. Its small head is peppered with dark spots. Small anal prolegs splay back and away from broadly rounded rump. Larva about 1cm. Gray Scoopwing (*Callizzia amorata*) is more darkly pigmented and feeds on honeysuckle and bush-honeysuckle.

OCCURRENCE Wooded swamps, woodlands, and forests from southern Canada to northern Florida and Arkansas. Over much of East there are two generations with mature caterpillars from late June to mid-July, then again from mid-August to early October.

COMMON FOODPLANTS Nannyberry, wild raisin, and related viburnums.

REMARKS Caterpillars form shelters by silking together adjacent leaves. The cream to green middle and penultimate instars are undistinguished save for their rather lethargic comportment and small prolegs. Like microlepidopterans, Epipleminae drop from their perch on a strand of silk, belaying their way out of danger. The caterpillars are readily obtained by beating—one or two taps on a wild raisin shrub should tell you if this species is present.

Only four sack-bearers occur north of Mexico. The caterpillars are thick-bodied with narrowed thoracic segments. The head is proportionately large and hardened. In our species the posterior abdominal segments are compressed together and angled downward. The caterpillars form open-ended cases by silking together pieces from two or more leaves. Copious silk deposition within greatly fortifies the construction. Caterpillars consume old, hardened summer foliage, leaves that would be impossibly tough for many caterpillars.

MELSHEIMER'S SACK-BEARER
Cicinnus melsheimeri

RECOGNITION This caterpillar cannot be confused with any other: *abdomen seemingly severed or truncated behind spiracle on A8, ending in hard, tan, downward sloping plate. Head bearing two clubbed setae.* Larva to 3.5cm.

OCCURRENCE Barrens and woodlands from Wisconsin to southeastern Massachusetts south to Florida and Texas. One generation with mature caterpillars from August to May.

COMMON FOODPLANTS Oak, especially scrub oak northward.

REMARKS When threatened the caterpillar seals off the entrances of its case by plugging its armored head into one end and jamming the anal plate into the other. When provoked, the caterpillar stridulates, making a high-pitched grinding sound, the noise coming in short bursts in rapid succession (Mike Nelson, pers. comm.). Early instars feed beneath a silken net fortified with feculae. The fully mature caterpillar overwinters in the case, and then pupates in the spring, without feeding again. The thick-bodied adults have a distinctive resting posture: the abdomen is raised and the wings are held below the horizontal (inset).

SCALLOPED SACK-BEARER
Lacosoma chiridota

RECOGNITION Larval *shape diagnostic*; smoky yellow-green with dark conspicuous brownish mottling toward either end of body. When viewed from above, body narrowest about T1 and thickest about A7–A8. *Brown spiracles visible from above.* Head strongly sclerotized with dark reddish brown mottling. Larva to 3cm.

OCCURRENCE Barrens, woodlands, and forests from southern Ontario and New Hampshire south to Florida and Texas. Evidently just one generation with mature caterpillars from June to November.

COMMON FOODPLANTS Oak.

REMARKS Like Melsheimer's Sack-bearer, populations of this species are often restricted to barrens and dry oak woodlands northward, but occur in many forest types southward. The early instar feeds below a coarse network spun over the upper side of a mature oak leaf (insets). Curiously, the caterpillar neatly fastens fecal pellets end to end on the outside of its net. The young caterpillar consumes tissue about the periphery of the shelter, eating entirely through the leaf, but leaving the central area undamaged. At rest it positions itself over its central "green island." Later instars form a shelter, with highly irregular edges, by silking together leaf sections from two or more adjacent leaves.

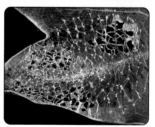

In the New World the Bombycidae are largely tropical—only two species are widespread in our region. The Silkworm, native to China, Taiwan, and Japan, is included due its availability from biological supply houses and its commercial importance. The caterpillars are densely vested in silky setae and have comparatively long prolegs. Even the head bears numerous short secondary (extra) setae. There is no anal point (as in tent caterpillars). The crochets, of two lengths, are arranged in an ellipse whose axis runs parallel to that of the body (similar-appearing caterpillars in other families tend to have crochets of one length).

SPOTTED APATELODES
Apatelodes torrefacta

RECOGNITION Richly endowed with long *unbranched setae* and prominent middorsal lashes; those on *T2, T3, and A8 longest.* Body often with broken, black middorsal stripe and lateral black V-shaped spots. *Abdominal prolegs bright red or orange.* Larva to 4.5cm.

OCCURRENCE Fields and woodlands from extreme southern Ontario to Maine south to Florida and Texas. Two generations with mature caterpillars from June to November.

COMMON FOODPLANTS American hornbeam, ash, blackberry, cherry, hazel, hickory, maple, oak, sassafras, walnut, willow, witch hazel, and other woody species.

REMARKS The caterpillars are conspicuous—white or yellow with contrasting black markings—and rest exposed on foliage. Evidently they are little bothered by birds. Perhaps it is simply the sheer number of setae with which birds must contend that gives the caterpillars license to perch openly. The setae are rather deciduous; caterpillars occasionally lose one or more of the long middorsal lashes. Prepupal larvae are especially apt to lose setae but the red prolegs of the Spotted Apatelodes always reveal their identity. The pupa overwinters.

THE ANGEL
Olceclostera angelica

RECOGNITION Flattened, grayish, mottled, with *long crinkled hair*, especially fore and aft. *Second thoracic segment sporting reddish brown mane* (mostly concealed at rest) (inset). Paired, yellowish addorsal spots bordered by a vague blue and black "W" over dorsum of A1–A7. Larva to 5cm. The Indistinct Angel (*Olceclostera indistincta*) occurs in peninsular Florida and the Seraph (*O. seraphica*) in southern and western Texas; I have not seen their larvae.

OCCURRENCE Fields and woodlands from Wisconsin, southern Canada, and Maine to Florida and Texas. One generation with mature larvae from June to September northward; two or more generations southward.

COMMON FOODPLANTS Ash and lilac.

REMARKS Females, if held for a night or two, will deposit eggs in number. Because the adult mouthparts are vestigial it is not necessary to offer them food. The eggs are curious: round, very flattened, with a central nipple. The handsome caterpillars are hardy and easily reared. By day the caterpillar rests on the trunk, then moves to the leaves to feed at night. The reddish mane over the second thoracic segment (inset) is mostly hidden when the larva is at rest; when alarmed the caterpillar raises its "hackle." revealing its reddish mane. While most bombycids spin a fairly large cocoon, The Angel forgoes the effort and pupates naked in litter or in a cell below ground. The pupa overwinters.

RECOGNITION *Powdery gray-white*, smoothly textured caterpillar with vesture of minute hairs most conspicuous about prolegs and along subventer. A horn issues from A8. Anterior face of hump on T2 bearing "eyespots" (inset). A2 with orange and black subdorsal crescents. Larva to 5cm.

OCCURRENCE Formerly native to China, Taiwan, and Japan; domesticated, no wild populations remain.

COMMON FOODPLANTS Mulberry; osage orange and privet sometimes accepted for short periods (Richard Heitzman, pers. comm.).

REMARKS Our silk ties, sheets, and lingerie come from the cocoons of this caterpillar. Cocoons, if gently unwound, yield a single strand of silk that extends for more than a half mile, and perhaps as much as 1 mile. Many commercial silks are made by entwining four to ten strands into a single thread. Cocoons must be boiled before the silk can be unwound and spun—the pupa is killed in the process. (Boiled pupae are used as feed for chickens and other livestock; they are also eaten by some as a delicacy.) The domestication of the moth and the silk culture antedates written history; the industry was well advanced by the time of the earliest Chinese writings. Eggs can be obtained from biological supply houses. When viewed "head on," the caterpillar looks rather serpentlike (inset). The egg overwinters.

TENT CATERPILLARS AND LAPPET MOTHS – LASIOCAMPIDAE

This small family has only 35 North American species, most of which are found in arid regions of the Southwest. The majority of the world's 1,500 species occur in tropical regions. The Eastern Tent Caterpillar and its congeners are brightly colored, handsome insects that feed openly in the day. Our other lasiocampids are cryptically colored in grays, feed mostly at night, and rest preferentially on bark. Ironically, only two of our Eastern species make sizeable tents. Elsewhere—both in the Neotropics and Old World—many lasiocampids live within communal nests, some of rather unusual shape. Cocoons of some species yield silk in sufficient quantity that it can be spun and carded—silk of the ancient Greeks was probably derived from a lasiocampid. Females are significantly larger than males in many species, so much so that it is often possible to sex prepupal caterpillars by size alone.

RECOGNITION

Our tent caterpillars and lappet moths have an abundance of *long, thin, silky setae, most numerous about the sides of the body and head*; in our Eastern species the *setae are not clustered into conspicuous tussocks and lashes* (some hairs may be grouped into small lashes or tufts elsewhere). Setae are never barbed or plumed, although in two genera (*Artace* and *Tolype*) at least some of the setae are spatulate or scalelike. Many of our lasiocampids are flattened with fleshy lateral lappets. The crochets are of two lengths and arranged in an ellipse whose axis runs parallel to that of the body. All have a fleshy "anal point" between the prolegs on A10, below the anus.

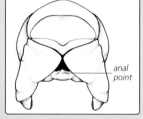

anal point

LIFE HISTORY NOTES

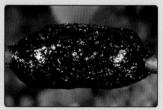

The eggs are covered with specialized scales from the female abdomen or a frothy secretion that dries to a varnishlike covering (inset). Only two of our species form tents although such behavior is common in the West and elsewhere. In *Malacosoma*, foraging "leaders" lay down a trail of pheromone-laden silk that is tracked by "followers." Generally, our species are broadly polyphagous, accepting a variety of woody shrubs and trees. Most overwinter as eggs or larvae. Adults have vestigial mouthparts—they do not feed.

COLLECTING AND REARING TIPS

Tent caterpillars are among our most commonly encountered caterpillars during the spring and early summer. The bark-perching lasiocampids are best found by beating. The adults are strong flyers capable of shredding their wings in short order—release or voucher reared adults before they have a chance to fly.

Tolype velleda

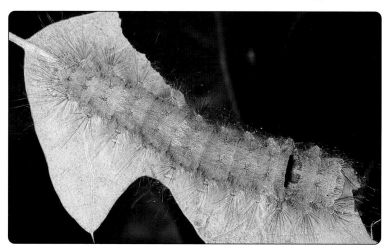

RECOGNITION Body grayish, downy, somewhat flattened with fleshy lateral lappets. Dorsum of *T3 with often reddened knobs immediately followed by black intersegmental area* (concealed at rest). Smaller, paired, addorsal warts run length of abdomen; those on A8 somewhat enlarged and often reddened. Lateral lappets of thorax nearly twice length of those of abdomen. Larva to 5.5cm. Three other lappets (*Tolype*) occur in the East; all are conifer feeders. In the Larch Tolype (*T. laricis*), and presumably also in related conifer feeders, warts on A5 are perched atop protuberances that are larger than those over T3 and the intersegmental "warning bar" includes yellow-orange spots. It is the most northern of the trio. It is replaced by the Small Tolype (*T. notialis*) south of Washington, DC although isolated populations of the Small Tolype occur north to the serpentine barrens in Chester County, Pennsylvania (Dale Schweitzer, pers. comm.). The Southern Tolype (*T. minta*) is associated with pond cypress (Bo Sullivan, pers. comm.) from coastal North Carolina to Florida.

OCCURRENCE Woodlands and forests from southern Canada to central Florida and Texas. One generation with mature larvae from August to September.

COMMON FOODPLANTS Apple, ash, aspen, basswood, beech, birch, cherry, oak, and other woody plants.

REMARKS Caterpillars rest on bark by day where their coloration renders them virtually invisible (inset, head down). The eggs, laid down in a chainlike series along a branch or trunk and covered with black scales from the female's abdomen, overwinter.

DOT-LINED WHITE
Artace cribraria

RECOGNITION Body flattened, mottled with gray, brown, and charcoal, with dense lateral fringe of soft hairs; *some lateral setae broadly spatulate apically.* Collar of setae enveloping head. *Dorsum of A5 with pair of black knobs* that are enlarged relative to those that precede or follow; A8 also with enlarged dorsal knobs. *Intersegmental area between T3 and A1 black and orange* (inset). Lateral lappets on thorax twice the length of those of abdomen. Larva to 5cm. Although superficially similar to Large Tolype (*Tolype velleda*), Large Tolype caterpillar lacks the dark spinose knobs that occur over the dorsum of A5 and A8 present in the Dot-lined White.

OCCURRENCE Fields, woodlands, and forest edges from Kentucky to Long Island south to Florida and eastern Texas. At least two generations with mature larvae from June to November.

COMMON FOODPLANTS Cherry, oak, rose, and presumably other woody plants.

REMARKS The caterpillars feed mostly at night and rest on bark by day. Many caterpillar lineages that rest on bark by day have evolved specialized lateral setae or hairs: e.g., underwing (*Catocala*) (Noctuidae) and Pale Beauty (*Campaea*) (Geometridae) larvae. While these have been called "shadow elimination hairs," I wonder if they have a function in other roles, e.g., serving to break up the outline of the caterpillar or rendering the larvae more texturally cryptic. The egg overwinters.

RECOGNITION *Body variegated in rust, white, and steel blue, densely vested with short downy hairs.* Spiny dorsal knobs absent over both thorax and abdomen. Anal legs elongate and splayed outward. Larva less than 3.5cm. Closest in appearance to the Lappet Moth (*Phyllodesma americana*), but lacking small middorsal hump on A8.

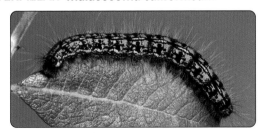

OCCURRENCE Fields and woodlands from Kansas, extreme southern Ontario, and western Pennsylvania south to Florida and Texas. At least two generations with mature larvae from April to October.

COMMON FOODPLANTS Honey locust.

REMARKS The caterpillar's bright colors suggest that it is distasteful or at least unpalatable to many birds. Cuckoos, interestingly, are known to favor hairy caterpillars. Collections of April adults suggest that the pupa overwinters.

WESTERN TENT CATERPILLAR *Malacosoma californicum*

British Columbia to Quebec, south in East to upstate New Hampshire and New York. One generation with mature caterpillars in early summer. Alder, aspen, cherry, oak, willow, and many other woody plants.

EASTERN TENT CATERPILLAR
Malacosoma americanum

RECOGNITION Although mundanely common, it warrants close inspection—the body is lavishly variegated in steel blue, black, orange, and white. Distinguished from other tent caterpillars in our region by its continuous cream-white middorsal stripe. Larva to 4.5 cm. Western Tent Caterpillar (*Malacosoma californicum*) found across much of Canada and into extreme northern United States, has a narrow middorsal stripe, consisting of alternating runs of white and black; its dorsum is marked with irregular orange splotches (*see* page 225).

OCCURRENCE Fields, woodlands, and forest edges from extreme southern Canada to Florida and Texas. One generation with mature larvae from late April through June.

COMMON FOODPLANTS Apple, cherry, hawthorn, and other members of the rose family (Rosaceae) favored; dozens of other woody plants eaten after caterpillars have defoliated the plant on which the eggs were laid.

REMARKS The Eastern Tent Caterpillar spins a communal nest in a crotch between two or more branches. Larvae forage outside the nest, then return to its safety to digest their food. The tent provides protection from natural enemies and serves as a greenhouse on cool days, allowing the caterpillars to raise their body temperatures above the ambient, facilitating digestion and other metabolic processes. The cocoons—flocculent, and infused with a whitish powder—are frequently seen under bark, boards, in garages, and under eaves. The distinctive egg mass contains 150–350 eggs. Curiously, the first instar develops fully in the first summer but holds within the egg through the winter months. Some nine months later, the caterpillar hatches with bud break in the spring.

Malacosoma disstria

RECOGNITION Beautiful bluish caterpillar with white "footprints" that lead towards head. *Orange subdorsal stripe separates blue and black dorsum from mostly blue sides.* Additional fine middorsal and addorsal orange stripes, often broken and/or obliterated, run length of body. *Spiracular stripe thin and more yellow.* Larva less than 4.5cm.

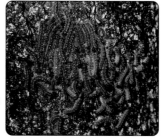

OCCURRENCE Woodlands and forests from southern Canada to Florida and Texas. One generation with mature larvae from late April through July.

COMMON FOODPLANTS Alder, aspen, ash, basswood, birch, blueberry, elm, maple (especially sugar), oak, poplar, sour gum (tupelo), and many other woody species.

REMARKS This is a gregarious species that marches in mass but does not spin a tent. By day the caterpillars gather on the trunks of trees in impressive masses of 100 or more individuals, lined up side by side (inset). Presumably pheromones laid down in the silk trails organize both the foraging sorties and the return to the roosting site. It is an occasional forest pest, especially of sugar maple and aspen. In the Deep South, gums (*Nyssa*) are principal foodplants. The cocoon lacks much of the yellow powder present in that of the Eastern Tent Caterpillar and is usually spun on the foodplant within a folded leaf or two. The egg mass, squared-off at its ends and wrapped around a twig, overwinters.

LAPPET MOTH
Phyllodesma americana

RECOGNITION Body gray or steel blue, with or without darkened abdominal saddle, white dorsal spotting, and vague longitudinal striping. Abundant soft hairs cover head and body; longest setae arising from fleshy "lappets" along sides of body; some lateral setae broadly spatulate (visible with lens). *A8 with small middorsal hump. Orange intersegmental areas behind T2 and T3* (concealed at rest); these often with three black spots, one medially and one to either side. Larva to 4.5cm. The Southern Lappet Moth (*Phyllodesma carpinifolia*) occurs sporadically from Kentucky to South Carolina southward. I have not seen its larva.

OCCURRENCE Woodlands and forests from southern Canada to Georgia and Texas. Two generations with mature caterpillars from May to October northward; evidently just one generation over many parts of Pennsylvania and New Jersey, south through Piedmont and Coastal Plain, but see below.

COMMON FOODPLANTS Alder, apple, birch, cherry, ironwood, oak, poplar, willow, and other woody shrubs and trees.

REMARKS When prodded the larva exposes bright orange intersegmental patches from behind the second and third thoracic segments. I have never found a caterpillar by visual searching. The Lappet Moth is most frequently encountered when beating. It is odd that *Phyllodesma americana* would be double-brooded in Connecticut and other states in the North, but single-brooded in the South. Perhaps two species are confused, each of which is single-brooded. The summer "form" named by Packard as *ferruginea*, tends to be a rustier moth with less gray scaling and more obscure maculation—I associate it with barrens and other dry acid woodlands, at least in the Northeast. Several additional races and forms within *americana* were named by Lajonquière (1969)—this moth would be a good candidate for molecular study. The pupa overwinters.

GIANT SILKWORM AND ROYAL MOTHS – SATURNIIDAE

Saturniids are among the most spectacular insects in eastern North America with caterpillars of the largest sometimes exceeding 10cm in length. They have long been a favorite with collectors and other enthusiasts and are commonly seen on display in insect zoos and nature centers. The North American fauna includes some

Ailanthus Silkmoth (Samia cynthia).

70 species, although the majority of these are Western. Nearly all of the East's 28 species are illustrated or diagnosed here.

RECOGNITION

Caterpillar large to enormous, robust, with secondary setae, especially above the prolegs. The primary setae often arise from hardened plates or are modified as knobs, horns, or branched spines. The anal plate is frequently spinose or heavily armored and the outer face of the anal prolegs often bears a hardened triangular plate. The head is mostly smooth and often shiny. Three subfamilies occur in our area: Royal moths (Ceratocampinae) possess elongate, black, spinose horns on T2 and comparatively thick integument (skin); the buck and day moths (Hemileucinae) are profusely armed with many-branched, poison-filled, stinging spines; giant silkworm moths (Saturniinae) are less distinctive except for their large size. Many saturniines have the head partially drawn into the thorax.

LIFE HISTORY NOTES

Eggs are large, smooth, somewhat flattened, and laid singly or in rafts. Many species are gregarious, especially in early instars. Mature caterpillars may be so large that the prolegs will not support the caterpillar's weight—these feed and rest hanging upside down. They tend to be somewhat generalized in diet, eating a variety of woody species, although many are local specialists that use just a handful of foodplants in any one area. Enormous fecal pellets strewn about porches, cars, and sidewalks often reveal their whereabouts. Each pellet is cut by six distinct channels that run the length of the dropping.

COLLECTING AND REARING TIPS

Because of their grandeur, giant silkworms make for an especially good entry to the world of entomology. Females of most Eastern species come to light. If held in a brown paper bag or styrofoam cooler for a night, eggs may be obtained in good numbers. The mouthparts are vestigial so females need not be fed. There are many books with suggestions for rearing giant silkworms (e.g., Tuskes *et al*. 1996) and considerable information may be gleaned from the Internet. Solitary species do not take well to crowding and do best in well-ventilated containers. Sleeving is advised when raising caterpillars in number. The prepupal caterpillars occasionally turn up on roads and walkways; evidently, many species wander widely in search of suitable pupation sites.

Imperial Moths, Royal Moths, and Oakworms –
Subfamily Ceratocampinae

Ceratocampine caterpillars have the primary setae modified as long, hardened spines. Typically these are black and in turn bear numerous minute denticles—those on the thorax are often greatly lengthened. None sting. All overwinter as a pupa in an earthen cell; no cocoon is spun.

PINE DEVIL
Citheronia sepulcralis

RECOGNITION *Brown or beige with three pairs of thoracic horns* and shorter, yellow to orange, spined, knobs over dorsum of abdomen. *A8 with medial (unpaired) horn* nearly as long as those over T2 and T3. Larva to 8cm. First instars are mostly yellow with black spines and a black saddle over A6 and A7 (inset). The caterpillars in all instars may be distinguished from those of the Imperial Moth by their black spiracles and the absence of any silky hairs.

OCCURRENCE Barrens and pine woodlands from Kentucky to Maine (formerly) south to Florida and Mississippi. One generation northward with mature caterpillars from August to September; two or more generations from Virginia southward.

COMMON FOODPLANTS Pine.

REMARKS Like its congener, the Hickory-horned Devil (*Citheronia regalis*), this species has declined in the Northeast. The pupa passes the winter in an earthen cell excavated by the caterpillar.

(REGAL OR ROYAL WALNUT MOTH) *Citheronia regalis*

RECOGNITION *A behemoth armored with three pairs of stout orange and black thoracic horns* and smaller black spines down dorsum of abdomen. Ground color initially brown but becoming green in last instar. An oblique white band runs below abdominal spiracles on A2–A7. Larva to 12cm.

OCCURRENCE Bottomlands, woodlands, and forests from Missouri to New Jersey south to Florida and eastern Texas. Formerly found north to Massachusetts, but now historic from New England and seemingly declining elsewhere across its range. One generation with mature caterpillars from August to November over most of East; two full broods occur in Louisiana with mature caterpillars in June and early July then again in the fall (Vernon Brou, pers. comm.).

COMMON FOODPLANTS Ash, butternut, cherry, cotton, hickory, lilac, pecan, persimmon, sumac, sweet gum, sycamore, walnut, and certainly others.

REMARKS Devils are so named because of their long thoracic horns, the first pair of which is positioned just behind the head. The thoracic horns are disproportionately large in the early instars, extending the length of several body segments. Although ominous in appearance the caterpillars are harmless to handle. The brown fecal pellets, 1cm in length in mature caterpillars, often reveal the whereabouts of the Hickory Horned Devil. This species has disappeared from the northern portions of its range, which formerly extended at least to the campus of Harvard University in Cambridge, Massachusetts. The prepupal caterpillars change to an attractive blue-green color. Caterpillars are often encountered while they are wandering in search of a suitable pupation site. The pupa passes the winter in a below-ground cell.

IMPERIAL MOTH
Eacles imperialis

RECOGNITION Whether green, salmon, red, cinnamon, tan, brown, or charcoal, *always recognizable by its long silky setae and prominent white spiracles.* Spiny horns issue from T2 and T3. Anal proleg and dorsum of last abdominal segment each bear an armored plate that is edged with tan or yellow. Very different in appearance as an early instar with far more prominent thoracic and abdominal horns, not unlike middle instar devils (*Citheronia* species). Larva to 8cm.

OCCURRENCE Barrens and woodlands from Great Lakes Region to New York and southeastern Massachusetts south to Florida and central Texas. One generation over most of range with mature caterpillars from July to November; two generations in Missouri.

COMMON FOODPLANTS Basswood, birch, cedar, elm, maple, oak, pine, sassafras, sweet gum, sycamore, walnut, and other woody species.

REMARKS The Imperial Moth is aptly named, being one of our most majestic insects, both as a caterpillar and as an adult. Caterpillars feed by locking onto vegetation with their powerful anal prolegs and pulling leaves or needles back over the body. It would be interesting to learn if some of the color forms that seem to appear spontaneously in single clutches of the Imperial Moth are inducible, and if so, what might be the ecological and evolutionary consequences of the various forms. Like the Hickory Horned and Pine Devils this species has declined from many areas within the northeastern portion of its range. The winter is passed as a pupa in an underground cell.

Sphingicampa bicolor

RECOGNITION Splendid caterpillar: lime green with two pairs of thoracic horns and elongated *abdominal horns on A2, A4, and A6–A8. Abdominal horns silvered* over their outer surface. Body speckled with white dots. Red and white supraspiracular stripe. Larva to 5.5cm. Caterpillars of the less common Bisected Honey Locust Moth (*Sphingicampa bisecta*) occur alongside those of *S. bicolor* throughout much of the Midwest. The horns tend to be green in *bisecta* and red in *bicolor*; in addition, the dorsal abdominal horns of *S. bisecta* may be reduced over A2 and A4, and the red portion of the supraspircular stripe is often replaced by a thin blackish line (*see* page 240).

OCCURRENCE Woodlands from Great Lakes Region to western Pennsylvania south to Georgia and Texas, although scarce and local east of Appalachians. Three generations over much of East with mature caterpillars from May onward.

COMMON FOODPLANTS Honey locust and Kentucky coffee tree.

REMARKS The Honey Locust Moth caterpillar appears to be simultaneously cryptic and warningly colored. The overall shape and coloration seem well suited for the legumes on which it specializes: both its ground color and countershading help it blend with foliage. Yet, the red and white lateral stripe would suggest that the caterpillar is also advertising and is in some way protected. Development times in midsummer generations are rapid, with caterpillars maturing in as little as three weeks. Both our locust moths overwinter as pupae below ground. Females of *Sphingicampa* are strongly attracted to lights and oviposit readily if held in a paper bag for an evening.

GREEN-STRIPED MAPLEWORM
(ROSY MAPLE MOTH) *Dryocampa rubicunda*

RECOGNITION *Green with pale blue-green to frosty stripes* and prominent *black horns issuing from T2*; integument roughened. Black dorsal, subdorsal, and subspiracular spines reduced, with longest found in subspiracular row. Head beige to orange-brown. Frequently with subspiracular *rosy patch below spiracle on A7 and A8*. Larva to 5cm. Prepupal larvae may take on a brown coloration.

OCCURRENCE Bottomlands, woodlands, and forests from southern Canada to Florida and Texas. One generation in New England and much of East with caterpillars from July to September, two to three generations southward with mature caterpillars from May to November.

COMMON FOODPLANTS Maple and box elder; also oak.

REMARKS Larvae of the Green-striped Mapleworm are gregarious through the third instar. The caterpillar is an occasional pest, defoliating silver, red, and sugar maples. Ceratocampines are the thickest-skinned of all our caterpillars—the molt that produces the pupa yields a skin that is recognizable, even to species. The pupa overwinters below ground. The adult Rosy Maple Moth is beautifully rendered in yellow and pink. When handled, they feign death, lying on their side, holding the wings over the dorsum, and curling the abdomen under the thorax. After the Luna Moth (*Actias luna*) this may be the runner-up with regard to garnering public interest in moths.

Anisota senatoria

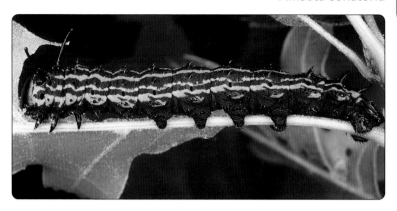

RECOGNITION *Charcoal black ground with orange to yellow-orange addorsal, subdorsal, and lateral stripes;* lowermost (subspiracular) stripe reduced and sometimes represented by just a few spots. Head black. Long, black, tentaclelike extensions issue from T2. Blackened spines run down dorsum with those of A7–A9 somewhat lengthened. Very closely related to, if even distinct from, Peigler's Oakworm (*Anisota peigleri*), which replaces Orange-striped Oakworm from extreme southern North Carolina to northern Florida. In my vouchers, the dorsal, subdorsal, and subspiracular spines are a bit shorter in the Orange-striped Oakworm and the stripes appear to have a purer, brighter orange hue. Larva to 6cm.

OCCURRENCE Oak woodlands and forests from Minnesota to Massachusetts south to North Carolina and east Texas. One generation with mature caterpillars from late July to October.

COMMON FOODPLANTS Chestnut and oak; especially red oak; also reported from birch, hazel, hickory, and maple.

REMARKS The caterpillars are gregarious in early instars and then become solitary. Both Orange-tipped and Peigler's Oakworms are occasional pests of oak. Defoliations in oak woodlands can cover many acres—red oaks are especially hard hit, although so late in the season that the effects are somewhat mitigated. Prepupal caterpillars are commonly seen crossing roads; evidently, the caterpillars may wander considerable distances before selecting a pupation site, where they will entomb themselves in the ground for nine months. Twice I have found numerous mummified larvae affixed to stems and branches, victims of *Hyposoter* (a parasitic ichneumonid wasp). After having consumed the caterpillar's inner contents, the larval wasp spins its cocoon within the body of the vanquished host, and in so doing, mummifies it. Such cadavers may remain affixed to their perch for months. Orange-striped Oakworm pupae may overwinter more than one year.

SPINY OAKWORM
Anisota stigma

RECOGNITION Coloration highly variable: orange, yellow-brown to nearly black (inset), *heavily speckled with white dots. Black dorsal, subdorsal, and subspiracular spines elongate*, longer than those of other *Anisota* (compare those over A1–A7). Tentaclelike extensions on T2 bear whitish granules over their basal portions. Often with smoky spiracular stripe. Head orange-brown. Larva to 6cm.

OCCURRENCE Barrens and woodlands from southern Wisconsin to southeastern Massachusetts to Florida and Texas; restricted to expansive barrens northward. One generation with mature caterpillars from July to October in North; Richard Heitzman (pers. comm.) reports two broods in Missouri.

COMMON FOODPLANTS Oak; also reported from hazel and basswood.

REMARKS The Spiny Oakworm has declined across much of the Northeast where its current strongholds are the oak barrens of New Jersey, Long Island, and Cape Cod. Southward it flies in a variety of oak woodlands. Larval clusters are smaller than those of our other common *Anisota*. For their size, ceratocampine adults are among the smallest-headed moths, possibly indicating that vision (and in particular the compound eyes and optic lobes of the brain) is of modest importance.

Anisota virginiensis

RECOGNITION Handsome *pink and black striped caterpillar with generous sprinkling of white dots*. As in other oakworms long, black tentaclelike extensions arise from T2. Two pink stripes, one subdorsal and one subspiracular, run length of body. Head (inset) and anal plate yellow, caramel, or orange-brown. Larva to 6cm. Black spines over thorax and abdomen reduced in size, shorter than those of Spiny and Orange-striped Oakworms.

OCCURRENCE Oak barrens, woodlands, and forests from Manitoba to Nova Scotia south to Florida and Louisiana. One generation northward, two to three generations in South with mature caterpillars from June to November.

COMMON FOODPLANTS Oak.

REMARKS While some authorities recognize southern populations (north to Virginia) as a separate species, i.e., the Clear Oakworm Moth (*Anisota pellucida*), I am inclined to include both under a single name. Males fly during the day, when virgin females are broadcasting their sex pheromone; mated females also fly at night and come to lights. Females raft their eggs, sometimes placing several hundred in a single cluster.

Buck and Day Moths – Subfamily Hemileucine

Hemileucine caterpillars bear many-branched, poison-filled spines that deliver a painful sting. The eggs are laid in clusters; like oakworms, the larvae are gregarious through the first three instars. Pupation occurs in a flimsy cocoon or naked in the soil.

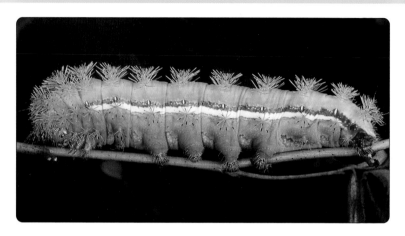

IO MOTH
Automeris io

RECOGNITION *Green with prominent red and white spiracular stripe* along abdominal segments. Spines pale green except for blackened area just below where the fine stinging spines issue. Larva to 6.5cm. The gregarious first instars are dark brown. They molt to a dull orange to orange-brown form. Penultimate instars are tan or beige with a red and white spiracular stripe. The Louisiana Io (*Automeris louisiana*) may be indistinguishable as a larva. It is found in salt marshes where cordgrass, its principal foodplant, grows in abundance from east Texas to southwestern Mississippi.

OCCURRENCE Fields, woodlands, forests, and edges of watercourses from southern Canada to Florida and Texas. One generation in North; two or three in Missouri; at least three generations in Deep South with mature caterpillars from April onward.

COMMON FOODPLANTS Aspen, birch, blackberry, cherry, clover, elm, hackberry, hibiscus, oak, poplar, sassafras, willow, and wisteria, even grasses including corn, and many other plants.

REMARKS The sting is roughly of the same intensity as that of stinging nettle but longer lasting. If the larvae are handled gently they can be picked up with the fingers, although this is not recommended (invariably some people prove highly allergic to insect stings). The ends of the broken spines, embedded in the skin, are mildly irritating for hours after the sting. The Io overwinters as a pupa in a crude, papery cocoon in leaf litter.

Hemileuca maia

RECOGNITION Ground color ranges from mostly black (commonly) to almost white; *thorax and abdomen densely flecked with white dots.* Spines larger and more branched over dorsum. Spiracles pale brown and ringed with black. Larva to 6.5cm. Two other closely related buck moths occur in East—given their variability in coloration it is often easier to identify the caterpillars by their habitat and foodplant preferences. The New England Buck Moth (*Hemileuca lucina*) feeds on meadowsweet in wet meadows, fens, and along powerline right of ways; it is endemic to the Northeast (*see* page 240). The Nevada Buck Moth (*H. nevadensis*) is principally a willow (*Salix*) or buck bean (*Menyanthes*) feeder of fens and marshes eastward, especially of the Upper Midwest, but with isolated colonies found eastward to New York and New Jersey (*see* page 240). In my limited experience, the spines are often shorter in the New England and Nevada Buck Moths. In our populations of the Nevada Buck Moth, the white spiracular band is usually well developed, being broader and almost solid cream in color.

OCCURRENCE Barrens, woodlands, oak forests from Missouri to Maine south to Florida and Louisiana. One generation with mature caterpillars from May to August.

COMMON FOODPLANTS Oaks, especially scrub oak northward (but *see* Remarks).

REMARKS Although *Hemileuca* females are selective about the plant species that they choose for the deposition of their egg rings, after the third instar the caterpillars frequently wander onto and consume a variety of other woody plants. Stings that I received on the back of my hand from a Buck Moth caterpillar were visible 10 days later—each spot where a spine had discharged its poison resulted in a small hemorrhage. Eastern *Hemileuca* normally overwinter as an egg (ring). Additionally, Buck Moth pupae may overwinter for more than a single season.

LOCUST AND BUCK MOTHS

BISECTED HONEY LOCUST MOTH *Sphingicampa bisecta*

Iowa, southern Wisconsin, and Ohio south to northern Georgia and eastern Texas. Two principal generations over most of range with mature caterpillars in early summer then again in fall. Honey locust.

NEW ENGLAND BUCK MOTH *Hemileuca lucina*

New England moving southward and westward. One generation with mature caterpillars in early summer. Eggs and young larvae on meadowsweet, but consuming many woody species in late instars.

NEVADA BUCK MOTH COMPLEX *Hemileuca nevadensis* complex

Great Lakes States and northern New Jersey. One generation with mature caterpillars in early summer. Eggs and young larvae usually on willow, but also bog birch and others.

GROTE'S BUCK MOTH *Hemileuca grotei*

Central Texas. One generation with mature caterpillars in spring. Live oak.

Robust greenish caterpillars with some setae arising from or modified into hardened plates or knobs that are occasionally brightly colored. None sting. Saturniine caterpillars spin a classic "moth cocoon," with a generous allotment of silk. Attempts to develop an industry around American silkmoths have failed miserably. To this day most silk textile products are made much the same way that they have been for more than 4,000 years, from the cocoons of the Silkmoth (*Bombyx mori*), a member of the related family Bombycidae (*see* page 221).

LUNA MOTH
Actias luna

RECOGNITION Beautiful lime-green caterpillar with bright magenta spotting and weak subspiracular stripe on abdomen. A1–A7 with *yellow transverse line that runs across dorsum, near trailing edge of each segment. Anal proleg with dark band at its base that is inwardly edged with yellow,* in a crude fashion resembling a head. Larva to 6.5cm.

OCCURRENCE Woodlands and forests from Canada south to Florida and Texas. One generation northward; three or more from Missouri southward with mature caterpillars from May onward.

COMMON FOODPLANTS Many forest trees but with decided local preferences; favorites include birch, black gum, hickory, pecan, persimmon, sweet gum, and walnut.

REMARKS Regarded by many to be North America's most beautiful insect; a freshly emerged Luna Moth may instill a sense of appreciation even in the most ardent entomophobe. The easiest way to obtain livestock is to confine a gravid female in a paper bag for an evening, then release her after she has deposited some of her brownish eggs. Grocery bags work splendidly; styrofoam coolers work as well, and often yield individuals free of wing damage.

POLYPHEMUS MOTH
Antheraea polyphemus

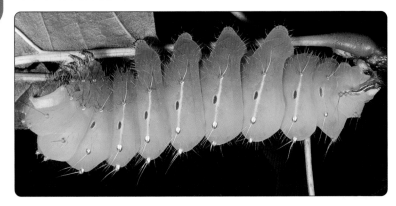

RECOGNITION Magnificent *almost fluorescent green caterpillar, usually with steeply oblique yellow lines that pass through spiracles* of A2–A7. *Dorsum of abdomen with flashy silver and red warts* each of which bears two to five setae; those over thorax mostly orange and without appreciable silver. Orange-brown head partially withdrawn into T1, which is edged with yellow anteriorly (inset). Darkened rim of anal plate continued as a line midway across A9. Larva to 7.5cm.

OCCURRENCE Barrens, woodlands, and forests. Continent-wide except Arizona and Nevada. One generation northward; three in Missouri with mature caterpillars from May to November.

COMMON FOODPLANTS Many shrubs and trees, including apple, ash, birch, dogwood, elm, hazel, hickory, maple, oak, rose, and willow; members of the birch, rose, and willow families especially favored.

REMARKS Polyphemus caterpillars sometimes make a snapping sound with their mandibles, the reason for which has not yet been elucidated. When caterpillars are reared together, snapping by one will incite mandibular snapping in others (Jeff Boettner, pers. comm.). While many caterpillars will descend from the trunk and pupate in leaf litter, others spin their cocoons in a leaf and drop to the ground with other leaves in the fall. Some cocoons, especially southward, are attached by a peduncle, most often in shrubs or on low branches. Occasionally enough silk is deposited about the petiole that the cocoon stays attached to the foodplant through the winter. The cocoon of the Polyphemus Moth is thicker and more evenly elliptical than that of the Luna Moth.

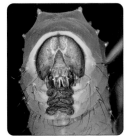

PROMETHEA MOTH
Callosamia promethea

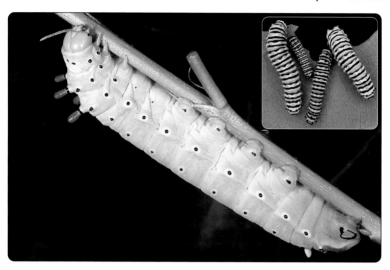

RECOGNITION Pale green with *four elongate, bright red knobs over thorax* and one yellow knob over A8. Legs yellowish. Gregarious early instars transversely banded with yellow and black (inset). Larva to 6cm. The Tulip-tree (*Callosamia angulifera*) and Sweetbay Silkmoths (*Callosamia securifera*) are treated separately below.

OCCURRENCE Fencerows, field edges, woodlands, and forests, doing well in early successional areas from Canada south to Florida and eastern Texas. One principal generation northward; partial second brood in south New Jersey and Pennsylvania; two or more full generations from Missouri southward with mature caterpillars from early June onward.

COMMON FOODPLANTS Many forest trees but with decided local preferences; favorites include ash, buttonbush, cherry, horse sugar, lilac, magnolia, sassafras, silver bells, spicebush, sweet bay, sweet gum, and tulip tree.

REMARKS The female lays from two to about a dozen eggs in a single cluster. The boldly colored early instars feed side by side on the undersides of leaves (inset). Later the caterpillars molt to the greenish form and feed solitarily. The larva spins a cocoon within a leaf, firmly attaching the petiole to the foodplant. Young cherry or sassafras trees growing between plowed fields and along roads make especially good starting points for larval searches or wintertime cocoon hunts. Look on understory plants or low branches—they are seldom out of reach. This species has declined across much of the Northeast. The tachinid fly (*Compsilura concinnata*)—introduced to control the Gypsy Moth—may be implicated in its demise (Boettner *et al.* 2000).

TULIP-TREE MOTH
Callosamia angulifera

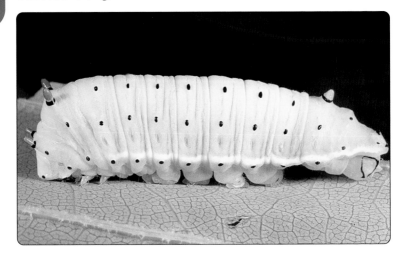

RECOGNITION *Much like preceding but paler or waxier in color with pale stripe running below spiracles on A1–A10 and black dots on abdomen lacking contrasting pale rings.* Yellow abdominal tubercle over A8 short, less than twice as high as broad. Larva to 6cm. Sweetbay Silkmoth (*Callosamia securifera*) similar in appearance but a specialist on sweet bay. Its yellow abdominal tubercle over A8 is nearly three times as long as wide and the red knobs over thorax are cylindrical (*see* page 246).

OCCURRENCE Woodlands and forests from Michigan, southern Ontario, and Massachusetts to northern Florida and Mississippi. One principal generation northward; two broods in South with mature caterpillars from early June onward.

COMMON FOODPLANTS Tulip tree.

REMARKS The larva spins its cocoon within a leaf, but unlike the Promethea Moth the petiole is not secured to the shoot, so the cocoon drops to the ground with leaf fall. The Promethea and Tulip-tree Silkmoths evidently occupy different parts of a forest. The Promethea is a creature of the understory, both as a caterpillar and adult. In contrast, it is not easy to locate Tulip-tree caterpillars because many are high above the ground. The main courtship and mating flight occurs at dusk and lasts for only 15 minutes or so (Dale Schweitzer, pers. comm.). The next time you are in a forest with an abundance of tulip trees, train your eyes upward as the light is fading from the evening sky—if the season is right you will see the males coursing about. To quote Dale Schweitzer, "You could see the males at dusk so easily where I grew up in Pennsylvania, they made the Eastern Tiger Swallowtails (*Papilio glaucus*) using the same trees seem rare by comparison."

Hyalophora cecropia

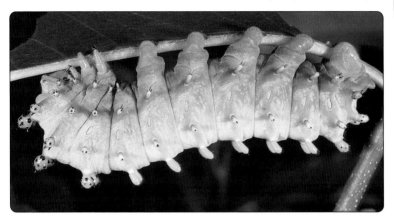

RECOGNITION Frosted green with *shiny yellow, orange, and blue knobs over top and sides of body.* Dorsal knobs on T2, T3, and A1 somewhat globular and set with black spinules. Paired knobs on A2–A7 more cylindrical, yellow; knob over A8 unpaired and rounded. Larva to 10cm. Caterpillars of larch-feeding Columbia Silkmoth (*Hyalophora columbia*) have yellow-white to yellow-pink instead of bright yellow knobs over dorsum

of abdomen and knobs along sides tend to be more white than blue (as in Cecropia) and are set in black bases (*see* page 246).

OCCURRENCE Urban and suburban yards and lots, orchards, fencerows, woodlands, and forests from Canada south to Florida and central Texas. One generation with mature caterpillars from late June through August over most of range.

COMMON FOODPLANTS Frequently apple, ash, box elder, cherry, lilac, poplar, sassafras, and willow, but many other woody plants are used as well, including birch, elm, larch, and maple.

REMARKS Yet another silkmoth that seems to be declining. It is one of many native species suffering from parasitism by a tachinid fly (*Compsilura concinnata*) that was introduced to control the Gypsy Moth. Parasitism rates by *Compsilura* reached 82% in one cohort of 1,400 Cecropia caterpillars placed out in a Massachusetts forest (Boettner *et al.* 2000). Compact, spindle-shaped cocoons are spun on exposed branches and twigs where the larva has little adjacent structure at the time the cocoon is made. In grass at the base of the foodplant—where there is opportunity to attach silk at many contact points—the cocoon is often loose and baglike and considerably larger. For a wintertime outing, try finding "bag cocoons" by running your fingers through grass growing at bases of young isolated cherry and apple trees growing along fencerows and roadsides.

GIANT SILKWORM MOTHS

SWEETBAY SILKMOTH *Callosamia securifera*

Southeastern Virginia to Florida west to Louisiana. Two generations northward and three along Gulf with mature caterpillars from May onward. Sweetbay, but accepting other magnolias and tulip tree.

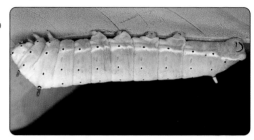

CALLETA SILKMOTH *Eupackardia calleta*

Southern and western Texas. One principal generation with mature caterpillars in late fall, and smaller spring brood with caterpillars in March and April. Purple sage (*Leucophyllum*) and ash; easily reared on privet.

COLUMBIA SILKMOTH *Hyalophora columbia*

Central Manitoba to Nova Scotia south to Maine and Great Lakes States. One generation with mature caterpillars in late summer. Principally larch, but also alder, birch, and cherry.

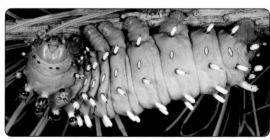

FORBES' SILKMOTH *Rothschildia lebeau forbesi*

Extreme southern Texas. Present year-round, but with two principal generations with mature caterpillars from April to June then again in fall and early winter months. Ash, peach, prickly ash, willow, and others.

HORNWORMS (SPHINX OR HAWK MOTHS) – SPHINGIDAE

Sphinx caterpillars are favorites among those who enjoy looking for and raising caterpillars. The East has some 70 species, although many of these will be encountered only in southern Florida and Texas. Our largest hawk moth, the Giant Sphinx (*Cocytius antaeus*), has caterpillars that may exceed 15cm in length. The long-tongued adults of hornworms are important in the tropics, especially in seasonally dry forests where nearly 10% of the trees may be pollinated by these strong flyers. Sphingids possess the most acute color vision of any animals, discriminating floral colors at light intensities that would appear pitch black to the human eye. Tuttle's (2006) book on the hawk moths of North America is richly illustrated with larval images and contains an abundance of life history information.

RECOGNITION
The caterpillars are large, cylindrical, and usually possess a middorsal horn, eyespot, or hardened button over A8. Setae are absent or inconspicuous, except above the prolegs. Each segment is annulated with 6–8 shallow creases. The anal prolegs are laterally flattened (for tightly engaging leaves, petioles, and twigs). The crochets of two lengths are arranged in series paralleling the body axis. Many (e.g., *Manduca*, *Sphinx*, and *Xylophanes*) come in both a green and brown form—the latter is especially apt to turn up in late-instar captive individuals.

LIFE HISTORY NOTES
The large, smooth, spherical eggs are usually laid on a lower leaf surface. Young sphingid caterpillars start feeding in the middle of the blade, leaving telltale holes in the leaf. Their large, elongate fecal pellets, with six deep grooves, often reveal their whereabouts. Many thrash violently from side to side when disturbed; these same species always seem willing to regurgitate a sticky green fluid as well. Some aggressively nip at their attackers. At least two of our species, Abbot's Sphinx (*Sphecodina abbottii*) and Walnut Sphinx (*Amorpha juglandis*), make sounds when harassed. Most of our hawk moths overwinter as pupae below ground in an earthen cell, but a few spin a cocoon in leaf litter or along the trunk of their foodplant (e.g. *Isoparce* and *Madoryx*).

COLLECTING AND REARING TIPS
The eggs can be found with reasonable frequency. Check especially the underside of terminal leaves. Many hornworms sever the petiole of leaves upon which they have fed and drop these to the ground; a series of two or three adjacent clipped petioles is often a hint that a hornworm is nearby. The most obvious sign of a nearby caterpillar is the accumulation of their enormous feculae. Although caterpillars may be discovered by day, flashlight searches at night are both productive and interesting. Hornworms are easily reared if provided with fresh foliage and ventilated containers. Many fail to pump up their wings properly upon emergence, especially when reared in moist or smallish containers. Mist the pupae periodically and provide rough surfaces for the emerging adults to ascend. Additional notes on finding and caring for larvae are included in the various species accounts.

TOBACCO HORNWORM
(CAROLINA SPHINX) *Manduca sexta*

RECOGNITION Green or brown with *seven oblique white lines that pass above abdominal spiracles*. Anal plate edged with yellow. *Horn orange, pink, or red.* Larva to 9cm. Tomato Hornworm (*Manduca quinquemaculata*) green or less commonly dark brown with *eight* white lines below each spiracle that join those descending from above to form a set of chevrons along side of abdomen (extra set of lines on A8) (*see* opposite); anal plate edged with white; horn usually black or blue or combination of these, sometimes green.

OCCURRENCE Gardens, fields, and waste places from southern Canada to Florida and Texas. One generation northward; evidently two or three in Missouri with mature caterpillars from June onward; nearly year-round in Deep South.

COMMON FOODPLANTS Ground cherry, horse-nettle, nightshade, tobacco, tomato, and other members of nightshade family (Solanaceae).

REMARKS While Covell (1984) and others use the common names Tobacco Hornworm to refer to this species and Tomato Hornworn for *M. quinquemaculata*, I wish it were not so, because it is this sphinx that I invariably find on my tomatoes. In addition to leaves, it also consumes (green) fruits, flowers, and terminal shoots. Caterpillars are attacked by a braconid wasp (*Cotesia congregata*) that lays dozens of eggs within each larva. When fully mature each wasp larva tunnels to the outside of the caterpillar's body and spins a whitish cocoon. The host caterpillar is doomed, consigned to a slow death that may not follow for weeks. To protect your tomatoes allow the wasps to hatch from their cocoons and repeat the process. If you want to protect your caterpillars, sleeve them or bring them indoors and hope that they have not yet been discovered by a female *Cotesia*.

PINK-SPOTTED HAWK MOTH *Agrius cingulatus*

Canada south to Florida and Texas (and Argentina), but only as a fall migrant northward. At least two generations across much of South with mature caterpillars from June into November. Especially sweet potato and morning glory.

RUSTIC SPHINX *Manduca rustica*

Resident in Gulf States, but straying northward to Missouri, Ohio River Valley, and Maine. Present through much of growing season in Deep South. Bignonia, fringe-tree, jasmine, knockaway, matgrass, and others. Note extremely granulated horn.

TOMATO HORNWORM (Five-spotted Hawk Moth)
Manduca quinquemaculata

Canada south to Florida and Texas, but sporadic northward. One principal generation over much of East with mature caterpillars from July to November; year-round in Deep South. Especially ground cherry, potato, tobacco, tomato, and other members of nightshade family (Solanaceae). Both green (above) and brown forms (below) occur.

FOUR-HORNED SPHINX (ELM SPHINX)
Ceratomia amyntor

RECOGNITION Brown or green with *spinulose horns projecting from the second and third thoracic segments.* Scalelike plates run down middorsal line. Much of body bearing white-tipped granules. Larva to 9cm.

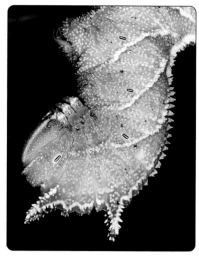

OCCURRENCE Bottomlands, watercourses, woodlands, and forest edges from southern Canada to Florida and Texas. One generation northward; two or more in South with mature caterpillars from late June to November; three or more generations along Gulf.

COMMON FOODPLANTS Principally basswood and elm, also birch; reports from cherry probably erroneous.

REMARKS A spectacular insect that can be found by searching branches of basswood and elm along woodland edges. While at rest, and even more so when alarmed, the larva rears back and draws the head beneath the thorax (a typical hornworm response). Look for the caterpillar on the undersides of leaves or shoots—likely its anal prolegs will be firmly clamped onto the midrib near the leaf base.

Ceratomia catalpae

RECOGNITION Our only common sphinx with larvae that are *gregarious* through the middle instars. Variable pattern ranging from mostly yellow to almost black. Generally more dark coloration found over dorsum. Sides often marked with vertical black lines or spots. Below spiracles body pale or with broad dark stripe that runs length of body. *Horn comparatively long, straight, and black. Head and spiracles black.* Larva to 7.5cm. Some color forms resembling White-lined Sphinx (*Hyles lineata*) (*see* page 275), but easily distinguished by its black head, its longer straighter horn, and specialized diet.

OCCURRENCE Urban areas, parks, yards, woodlands, and forests from extreme southern Canada to Florida and Texas (but rare northward and currently absent from New England). Two or three generations over much of range with mature caterpillars from late June to November.

COMMON FOODPLANTS Catalpa.

REMARKS This boom and bust species is occasionally common enough to defoliate catalpa trees. Females raft the eggs, sometimes laying several hundred in a single cluster. The larvae are gregarious into the third instar; small clusters of caterpillars remain together into the fourth instar. Like many other sphingids, the Catalpa Sphinx is a "barfer" and thrasher. When molested, the larva regurgitates a somewhat viscous green fluid from the foregut and thrashes violently, which, among other things, serves to spread its regurgitant over a potential predator. Catalpa Sphinx caterpillars have been grown and sold commercially as bait in Florida and elsewhere. Evidently they work especially well for largemouth bass. The adult proboscis is short—the adult is not capable of feeding, and as a consequence, provides no pollination services for its host foodplant.

WAVED SPHINX
Ceratomia undulosa

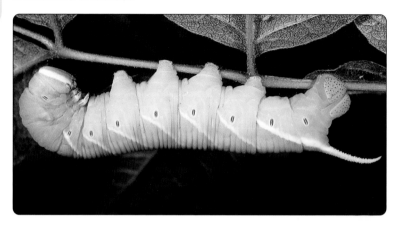

RECOGNITION *Yellow-green above and sea green below spiracles*, sometimes with rust and brown patterning; infrequently with reddened and browned forms. *Head with broad lateral band from vertex to antenna.* Sides of body with seven oblique lines, each mostly limited to single segments (i.e., anterior portion not extending onto preceding segment); last line broad, about same width as line on head. *Convex anal plate and anal prolegs with conspicuous, raised black spotting.* Horn often with pinkish cast. Larva to 8.5cm. Other ash-feeding hornworms are diagnosed below.

OCCURRENCE Bottomlands, watercourses, fields, woodlands, forest edges, including urban environments from Canada to Florida and Texas. One seasonally extended generation northward with mature caterpillars from late June to October; two or more generations in South.

COMMON FOODPLANTS Members of olive family: ash, fringe tree, and lilac; also reported from hawthorn and oak, apparently erroneously.

REMARKS The Waved Sphinx is the most commonly encountered of the six hornworms that occur on ash (*Fraxinus*) in the East. The yellow-green caterpillar of the Ash Sphinx (*Manduca jasminearum*) also has seven oblique lines, but the last one of these is edged with red and dark green. Caterpillar of the Great Ash Sphinx (*Sphinx chersis*) can be readily distinguished by examining the anal plate, which is flatter, longer, and lacks the conspicuous black dotting (*see* page 256). The Canadian Sphinx (*Sphinx canadensis*) inhabits bottomlands dominated by its preferred foodplant, black ash (*Fraxinus nigra*). It is frequently mottled with brown and again lacks the convex, black-dotted anal plate of the Waved Sphinx. Blue-white caterpillar of Franck's Sphinx (*Sphinx franckii*) possesses an unusual addorsal line of raised granules that extends forward from the horn. The Fawn Sphinx (*Sphinx kalmiae*) is treated elsewhere (*see* page 259).

TRUMPET VINE SPHINX (PLEBEIAN SPHINX)
Paratraea plebeja

RECOGNITION Two or more forms: commonly yellow-green above and sea green below; brown form variegated, usually with darkened area above each of the seven oblique lateral lines. Lines long; that on A6 extending back to above spiracle on A7. *Head and body dusted with white granules, those over subdorsum of T2 largest and in some forms connected by subdorsal stripe.* Horn blue, green, sometimes with black above or entirely black. Larva to 6.5cm.

OCCURRENCE Yards, woodlands, and forest edges; Nebraska to southeastern New York to Florida and Texas. At least two generations in New Jersey with mature caterpillars from July to October; nearly year-round with many generations in parts of Deep South.

COMMON FOODPLANTS Trumpet vine and Florida yellow-trumpet (*Tacoma stans*); also reported from lilac and passionflower.

REMARKS This caterpillar was sent by Dale Schweitzer, whom I asked to search the trumpet-creeper vines enveloping his fence. After he searched unsuccessfully for caterpillars by day and night with a flashlight, I encouraged Dale to lay a white bed sheet beneath his vine to catch the droppings of any caterpillars that might be present—three hornworms arrived by mail shortly thereafter. The Trumpet Vine Sphinx is a pollinator of the rare Rocky Shoals spider and Cahaba lilies. Hawk moths are important pollinators, especially in tropical ecosystems. As a general rule any large white flower with a deep corolla is a "sphingid plant." Many have a wonderful aroma. In addition to white flowers, sphinx moths are commonly seen visiting butterfly bush, milkweeds, mimosa tree, and phlox in our region.

PINE SPHINX
Lapara coniferarum

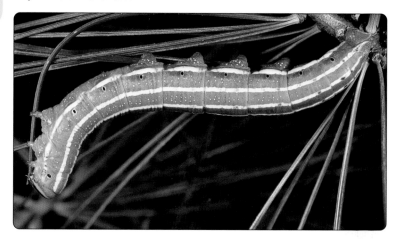

RECOGNITION *Lime green with cream addorsal, supraspiracular, spiracular, and subspiracular stripes.* Subspiracular stripe thickest, running along lower edge of black spiracles. Often with dull red splotches over dorsum, about spiracles, and above prolegs. *Head triangular;* face reddish brown with yellow edging (inset). *Horn absent.* Larva to 5cm. Perhaps indistinguishable as a caterpillar from Northern Pine Sphinx (*Lapara bombycoides*) (*see* Remarks).

OCCURRENCE Pine plantations, barrens, and woodlands from southern Maine south to Florida and Mississippi; widespread in South, including mountains, but mostly coastal and larger pine barrens north of southern New Jersey. One generation in North with mature caterpillars in August and September; at least two generations in South Carolina with mature caterpillars from June onward; multiple generations along Gulf Coast.

COMMON FOODPLANTS Pine, especially loblolly and longleaf in South, and hard pines such as pitch and Virginia northward. Evidently shunning white pine.

REMARKS The Northern Pine Sphinx is common in Canada, the Northeast, and the Appalachians. The Pine Sphinx replaces it southward along the Atlantic Coastal Plain. The two overlap from southern Maine to southern New Jersey and southward in the mountains. In New England, the Pine Sphinx occurs only in a few inland pitch pine barrens and is mostly a Coastal Plain element associated with pitch pine. The Northern Pine Sphinx is widespread across the region and is more frequently associated with white pine.

GIANT SPHINX *Cocytius antaeus*

Southern Florida (and tropical America), straying northward. Pond apple.

PAWPAW SPHINX *Dolba hyloeus*

Wisconsin to Ontario and Maine south to Florida and Texas. One generation northward with mature caterpillars from July to September; several generations along Gulf. Especially inkberry and other deciduous hollies as well as pawpaw.

STREAKED SPHINX *Protambulyx strigilis*

Central and southern Florida. Present year-round. Brazilian pepper.

BALD CYPRESS SPHINX *Isoparce cupressi*

Coastal North Carolina south to Florida and west to Texas. At least two generations with caterpillars from April onward. Bald cypress. Normally green; blue-violet hue in individual figured here possibly indicates its prepupal status.

GREAT ASH SPHINX
Sphinx chersis

RECOGNITION Large greenish or pinkish caterpillar with seven oblique abdominal lines that may be upwardly edged with pink. *Waxy green over abdominal segments* and occasionally T3; lime green below spiracles and over T1–T2 or T3. *Oblique lines long*, continued forward onto preceding segment and rearward to above spiracle on trailing segment. Anal plate more or less flattened and edged with yellow. *Spiracles elongate, central black area ringed with white*. Horn blue or pink. Larva to 10cm. Waved Sphinx (*Ceratomia undulosa*), which shares many of the same foodplants, has an upwardly convex anal plate marked with numerous, raised black dots, black-dotted anal prolegs, and spiracles that are orange anteriorly and posteriorly with a white center. In addition, each of its oblique lines ends abruptly at the back edge of the preceding segment (*see* page 252).

OCCURRENCE Fencerows, woodlands, and forests from Canada south to central Florida and Texas, becoming increasingly rare southward. One generation in North; two or more in South with mature caterpillars from May to November.

COMMON FOODPLANTS Ash, lilac, privet, and other plants in olive family (Oleaceae).

REMARKS Twice I have found caterpillars of this species perched on a leaf-blade underside on small trees. Over much of its range, the Great Ash Sphinx is less common on ash than the Waved Sphinx (*Ceratomia undulosa*). Ben Williams, who has been light-trapping in Connecticut for nearly 40 years, reports that the Great Ash Sphinx is much less common than it was only two decades ago. Another Sphinx in which he has witnessed an appreciable decline is the Wild Cherry Sphinx (*Sphinx drupiferarum*).

Sphinx eremitus

RECOGNITION The "black knight" of
caterpillars: deep chocolate brown with *large black
"eye" over T2 and T3.* Some forms mottled with
green. T2 strongly humped. Oblique striping only
vaguely evident along sides of abdomen. Minute pale
circlets generously scattered over abdominal segments.
Spiracle sometimes surrounded by blackened ring. Larva to 7cm.
Early and middle instars light green, sometimes with brown dorsal splotches, and T2
produced upward into horn (upper left image).

OCCURRENCE Gardens, fields, and wet meadows from Manitoba to Nova Scotia south
to North Carolina (mountains) and Arkansas. One generation northward with mature
caterpillars from July to September; two broods in Missouri with mature caterpillars from
June onward.

COMMON FOODPLANTS Basil, bee-balm, bugleweed, mints, sage, and others in
mint family (Lamiaceae).

REMARKS The best place to start your search for this caterpillar is the garden. The Hermit
Sphinx is more likely to be found as a caterpillar than as an adult, in part because adults seem
to be only weakly attracted to light. If you see a Hermit Sphinx at light it is likely a female;
evidently males fly too early in the evening to be appreciably influenced by lights. To find this
sphinx, go out at dusk and watch for nectaring adults at phlox and milkweed blossoms. It
keeps good company: at the same flowers you may see adults of the Galium Sphinx (*Hyles
gallii*), Fawn Sphinx (*Sphinx kalmiae*), Pawpaw Sphinx (*Dolba hyloeus*), and others. While most
sphingids have cylindrical fecal pellets with six furrows, like those of the Saturniidae, the
droppings of the Hermit and related *Sphinx* are among the most irregular of all Lepidoptera.

APPLE SPHINX
Sphinx gordius

RECOGNITION   Green to blue-green or rarely purple-brown; usually with *numerous minute black circlets over thorax and beneath spiracles*. Oblique lateral lines often edged with magenta or black above; some forms also with yellow edging below. Head broadly triangular; front framed with yellow-green band which may be outwardly edged with black. Spiracles orange. Horn usually green with black lateral line, sometimes mostly black—look for some green on underside near base. Larva to 7.5cm.

OCCURRENCE   Heathlands, savannahs, flatwoods, and other woodlands southward; more generalized northward. Central and eastern Canada south to central Florida and Texas, becoming increasingly rare southward (but *see* Remarks). Evidently a single generation in New Jersey with mature caterpillars from May to September; two generations in the Carolinas.

COMMON FOODPLANTS   Apple, ash, blueberry, gale, huckleberry, larch, leatherleaf, maleberry, rose, spirea, spruce, sweet fern, willow, and other woody species.

REMARKS   The Apple Sphinx may represent a complex of two closely related species. For the purposes of this guide, I ignore the name *Sphinx poecila* (Poecila Sphinx), which purportedly replaces the Apple Sphinx from Pennsylvania, Great Lakes States, and New England northward. In the northern portion of its range, the Apple or Poecila Sphinx is one of the most commonly encountered sphingids. Sweet fern and gale are favored foodplants in sandy areas—most stands in the Northeast and southern Canada will yield larvae. While both sexes may be taken at light, a more sporting alternative is to seek the adults while they are nectaring at flowers at dusk. Pick an evening and park yourself in the back garden, or even better in a large milkweed patch—even if you do not see the Apple Sphinx you are sure to be joined by many other hungry moths.

Sphinx kalmiae

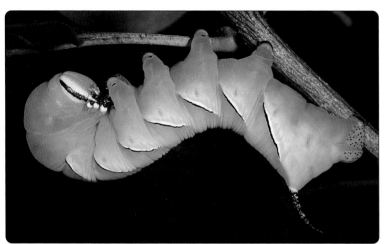

RECOGNITION *Beautiful blue- or yellow-green caterpillar with seven oblique, abdominal lines narrowly edged with black above and usually yellow below*. Head boldly marked with black line that is inwardly bounded with yellow-green. Most individuals recognizable by *blue horn that bears minute black spines*. Spiracles orange. Each midabdominal proleg has shiny yellow band between black crescents. Larva to 8cm.

OCCURRENCE Woodlands, forests, also commonly yards and nurseries from Manitoba to Newfoundland south to northern Florida and Louisiana, becoming uncommon southward. One generation northward with mature caterpillars in August and September; at least two generations southward with mature caterpillars from June onward.

COMMON FOODPLANTS Ash, fringe-tree, lilac, privet, and other plants in olive family (Oleaceae).

REMARKS The widely used name of Laurel Sphinx seems inappropriate given its reliance on plants in the olive family—the common name offered here is merely a suggestion. Caterpillars feed from the underside of shoots, severing the petiole of each leaf upon which it has fed. The most efficient way to locate larvae is to search for clipped leaves under ornamental lilac plants. The inset shows the first 18 *Cotesia congregata* (Family Braconidae) wasp larvae to issue from this Laurel Sphinx caterpillar. Another 175 appeared before the day's end. The caterpillar may live for another two to three weeks before finally succumbing to the damage that has been done to its internal organs.

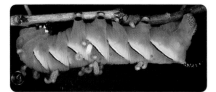

WILD CHERRY SPHINX *Sphinx drupiferarum*

Transcontinental in Canada south
in East to Georgia and north Texas.
One generation with mature
caterpillars mostly in July and
August in Connecticut; two or
more broods in South. Principally
apple, cherry, peach, and plum (all
Rosaceae)

CLEMEN'S SPHINX *Sphinx luscitiosa*

Alberta to Nova Scotia south to New
Jersey (historic), Great Lakes States,
and Nebraska. One generation
northward with mature caterpillars in
August and September. Principally
poplar and willow.

ONE-EYED SPHINX *Smerinthus cerisyi*

British Columbia to
Newfoundland south in East to
Georgia, Arkansas, Tennessee,
and Missouri. One generation
with mature caterpillars from
July through September.
Principally poplar and willow.

HUCKLEBERRY SPHINX *Paonias astylus*

Missouri to Maine south to
Florida and Mississippi. One
generation northward, nearly
year-round along Gulf where
mature caterpillars occur
from April onward. Principally
andromeda and blueberry.

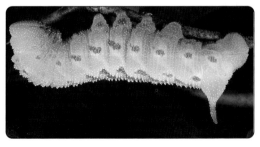

TWIN-SPOTTED SPHINX
Smerinthus jamaicensis

RECOGNITION   Green, yellow-green, or, most commonly, *blue-green* with abundant white granules over head and abdomen. Sometimes with wine-red subdorsal or spiracular spots (inset above). Head broadly triangular; *flattened front framed with cream or yellow.* Thoracic segments with subdorsal line. *Horn with at least flush of blue along sides or top.* Last oblique line descending from horn, ending above proleg on A6. Spiracles with *white center ringed with orange or black.* Integumental granules especially pronounced in earlier instars. Larva to 6cm. Caterpillar of One-eyed Sphinx (*Smerinthus cerisyi*) quite variable: some pale yellow, green, or blue-green; usually recognizable by a *subdorsal stripe that runs from T1–A7*, although it is quite weakly developed in some forms; *head stripe wide*; horn yellow, pink, and/or blue (*see* opposite). Eastern populations of One-eyed Sphinx typically with smaller granules over head and anal plate than those of the Twin-spotted and related *Paonias* species. Caterpillar of Blinded Sphinx (*Paonias excaecatus*) with oblique line that runs forward from base of horn ending near anterior margin of A7, while that of Twin-spotted Sphinx extends to area above proleg on A6. Horn of Blinded Sphinx (and other *Paonias*) lacks blue.
OCCURRENCE   Wet meadows, watercourses, swamps, woodlands, and forests from Canada to central Florida and Texas. Single generation northward with mature caterpillars in August and September; two generations in southern New Jersey; five or more generations in Louisiana.
COMMON FOODPLANTS   Aspen, poplar, and willow preferred (*see* Remarks).
REMARKS   Caterpillars often adopt a serpentlike posture with the front end held upward. Other recorded foodplants, e.g., apple, ash, birch, cherry and elm, require confirmation.

BLINDED SPHINX
Paonias excaecatus

RECOGNITION Bright green with *granulated integument*; some forms with wine-red spots along subdorsum, surrounding spiracle, and/or below level of spiracles. *Front of head flattened, rimmed with thin pale line* that may be outwardly edged with green or red. *Dorsum of thoracic profile roughened, almost serrate in some postures; subdorsal stripe on thorax usually present, although vague. Horn green (no blue), issuing from conical extension of A8*, tending to be straighter, longer, and directed upward at higher angle (about 45°) than that of Twin-spotted Sphinx (*Smerinthus jamaicensis*) (*see* page 261). White spiracles with outer black ring. Larva to 7.5cm. Caterpillars of the Huckleberry Sphinx (*Paonias astylus*) (*see* page 260) are similar but the integumental granules are smaller; the relatively short horn stands more erect and issues from an even more swollen cone-shaped base; the head is not as flattened; and the lateral lines on the head are less well developed.

OCCURRENCE Fields, woodlands, and forests. Transcontinental in Canada south in East to Florida and Texas (and Arizona in Rockies). Evidently one extended generation northward with mature caterpillars from July onward; three generations in Missouri; several generations in parts of Deep South where mature caterpillars occur from May onward.

COMMON FOODPLANTS American hornbeam, apple, basswood, beech, birch, cherry, chestnut, elm, hawthorn, hop hornbeam, oak, poplar, rose, serviceberry, spirea, willow, and undoubtedly many other woody plants.

REMARKS Recently molted caterpillars are conspicuously granulose, especially down each side of the head and over the thorax. This sphinx is highly variable and somewhat difficult to recognize, especially in the earlier instars (lower right image), but the characters given above will work for most individuals. This is the most commonly encountered sphingid caterpillar in many Northeastern hardwood forests.

Paonias myops

RECOGNITION Bright green, frequently with reddish splotches, somewhat pudgy, body widest about A5. Some individuals with subdorsal reddish spots on A2 and A7; others with red spots along subdorsum, about spiracle, and below spiracles.  Subdorsal line on thorax absent. No lateral line on head. *Horn short, greenish, minutely spinulose*, often directed backward, i.e., angle with body axis at apex of horn less than 45º. Larva to 5.5cm.

OCCURRENCE Fields and woodlands. Transcontinental in Canada south in East to Florida and Texas. One or two generations over much of East with mature caterpillars from late May onward; three broods in Missouri; essentially year-round in Gulf States.

COMMON FOODPLANTS Cherry, hawthorn, and serviceberry; other reported foodplants (birch, grape, poplar, willow, etc.) are rarely used or erroneous.

REMARKS Caterpillars are cryptic in habit, feeding mostly at night and excising damaged leaves at their bases. They often avoid the newest leaves, preferring blades back from the shoot apex. One wonders to what extent the red spots in *Paonias* caterpillars are inducible, and if so, are the spots more apt to occur on individuals feeding in the autumn, when such coloration would be particularly adaptive? Both sexes of all our "eyed" sphinxes (*Paonias* and *Smerinthus*) are attracted to light.

WALNUT SPHINX
Amorpha juglandis (= *Laothoe juglandis*)

RECOGNITION Green with *sharply produced head* and comparatively long, straight roughened caudal horn. Some individuals marked with reddish subdorsal patches forward of the oblique lines. Body *conspicuously dotted with white granules arranged in regularly spaced rings*. Head edged with white. Seventh oblique abdominal line thickened—circa three times wider than those that precede it—beginning above last (A6) proleg and extending to caudal horn. *Anal plate with pair of enlarged granules* (excrescences). Small orange spiracles include minute white spot at either end. Larva to 6cm. Head proportionately more elongated in early and middle instars (inset).

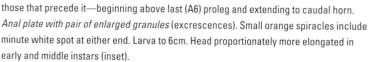

OCCURRENCE Bottomlands, fields, woodlands, and forests from Canada to Florida and Texas. One generation northward with mature caterpillars from July to October; three generations in Missouri; nearly year-round along Gulf.

COMMON FOODPLANTS American hornbeam, butternut, hickory, hop hornbeam, and walnut.

REMARKS The Walnut Sphinx has been previously placed in the genera *Laothoe* and *Cressonia*. When touched, the caterpillar whistles or hisses by forcing air out the spiracles. It is also a thrasher, casting its body violently from side to side when provoked. A good way to see this caterpillar is to go out at night and inspect the lower surfaces of hickory and walnut trees by flashlight—trees where you would be hard pressed to find a single caterpillar by day sometimes yield more than a half-dozen caterpillars at night. The caterpillar often perches over the midrib by day.

RECOGNITION Large, stout, pale to blue-green, or less commonly brown, sphinx with prominent white granules arranged in lines that ring each segment. *Horn shorter than length of segment that bears it.* Thick white oblique line runs from proleg on A7 to tip of horn. Head with broad pink, yellow, or cream line along side. T2 and T3 each have elevated transverse line of whitened granules that are especially prominent in early instars.

Seven oblique lines on abdomen, with those on A2–A4 often more prominent than those fore or aft. Spiracles orange-black with white center. White, cream, or pink ridge running along lower edge of anal proleg. Larva to 9cm.

OCCURRENCE Edges of watercourses, woodlands, and forests. Transcontinental in Canada south in East to Florida and Texas. One generation in Connecticut with mature caterpillars from July to September; up to three in Deep South with caterpillars found from May onward.

COMMON FOODPLANTS Poplar and willow.

REMARKS This caterpillar adopts a question mark posture when at rest: the head is held beneath an elevated thorax, appressed to the forelegs. After a leaf is damaged the caterpillar chews through the petiole, near where it attaches to the shoot, and lets the leaf fall to the ground. In so doing the caterpillar eliminates damaged leaves that might have been used by a bird to locate its position. A good way to start your search for this sphinx and related species is to scan the ground for clipped leaves and/or large feculae.

ELLO SPHINX
Erinnyis ello

RECOGNITION   Body coloration highly variable, often bluish green above subdorsal stripe and emerald green below; other forms green, gray, or brown. Common green form: body marked with yellow subdorsal stripe that extends along body from horn to mandible. Stripe of head edged inwardly with dark line. *Dark eyespot, with brown crescent to either side, over dorsum of T3. Horn reduced to a low point, arising from elevated angular hump.* Each red-orange spiracle with white spot above and below. Tan to pinkish thoracic legs banded with black rings; prolegs with bluish spot near base that may be concealed in fold. Larva to 7cm. Alope Sphinx (*Erinnyis alope*) (*see* page 278) very similar in penultimate instar but with long horn; last instar usually brown and mottled with short, thick, down-curved horn; rump not as prominently angulate as in Ello Sphinx. Obscure Sphinx (*E. obscura*) often with dorsal spots on first six abdominal segments; it prefers climbing milkweeds such as *Cynanchum* and *Philibertia*. Dan Janzen's website for the caterpillars of the Guanacaste Conservation Area in Costa Rica (http://janzen.sas.upenn.edu/) provides dozens of images of *Erinnyis* caterpillars and their seemingly endless variety.

OCCURRENCE   Hammocks, orchards, and yards. Resident in southern Florida and Texas where it breeds year-round.

COMMON FOODPLANTS   Usually on euphorbs such as cassava and poinsettia, also guava, willow bustic, and many other woody species.

REMARKS   In the last instar, the horn is reduced to a nub. Occasionally the Ello Sphinx is common enough to be a pest of poinsettia. The eyespot over third thoracic segment is hidden in the resting caterpillar. The pupa, usually located above the ground in leaf litter, is seemingly aposematic—shiny black with orange spots.

Hemaris diffinis

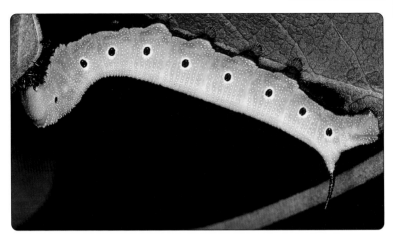

RECOGNITION Blue-green above and yellow-green along sides with *black spots encircling each spiracle* or, less commonly, brown (inset). *Leading edge of thorax yellow, with prominent granules, extended over back of head. Horn long, yellow at base, black from middle to apex.* Each blackened abdominal spiracle bears a minute white spot above and below. Head and body salted with minute white granules. Larva to 4.5cm.

OCCURRENCE Fields, woodlands, and forest edges from northern Canada south to Florida and central Texas. At least two generations over much of East with mature caterpillars from June onward; three generations in Missouri.

COMMON FOODPLANTS Dwarf honeysuckle (*Diervilla*), honeysuckle, and snowberry (all Caprifoliaceae); also *Amsonia* and dogbane (both Apocynaceae).

REMARKS The Snowberry Clearwing is a species of open habitats—isolated honeysuckles in overgrown fields, beneath powerlines, and along fencerows will yield caterpillars. Adults of both the Hummingbird Clearwing (*Hemaris thysbe*) and Snowberry Clearwing resemble large bumblebees. All sphinx moths hover while imbibing nectar, taking it up with their elongate tongues (although many of our species insert their forelegs, perhaps to taste the flower with their feet). By contrast, bumblebees land and crawl inside flowers to gather nectar and pollen.

HUMMINGBIRD CLEARWING
Hemaris thysbe

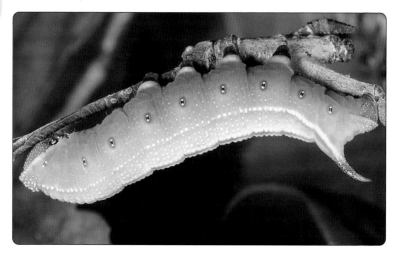

RECOGNITION Lime green, especially along sides, with *leading edge of thorax yellowish and warted*; some individuals yellow-green or pink. *Yellow subdorsal stripe* extends from T1 to horn. Head and body salted with minute white granules; these sparse on A8 and A9. Spiracles orange with white spot at top and bottom. Horn often bluish, curved. Larva to 5cm. Horn of younger caterpillars reddish, straight, and very long (inset).

OCCURRENCE Woodlands and forest edges. Transcontinental in Canada south in East to Florida and Texas. At least two generations over much of our region with mature caterpillars from May onward; three generations in Missouri; present much of year along Gulf.

COMMON FOODPLANTS Viburnum most frequently, but also honeysuckle and snowberry (all Caprifoliaceae); also reported from cherry, hawthorn, and plum (all Rosaceae), but I have never found caterpillars on these plants.

REMARKS An attractive though rather ordinary caterpillar, given that it transforms into one of the East's most distinctive moths. The adults are avid nectarers, frequenting yards, nurseries, and parks. Buddleia is the overall favorite in my garden. Earlier in the summer phlox and sweet rocket receive visits. I have had good success finding caterpillars by searching viburnums at night by flashlight and also beating. It is not uncommon to find a few caterpillars feeding on a single plant. Clearwings (*Hemaris*) pupate in a weak cocoon spun amongst fallen leaves.

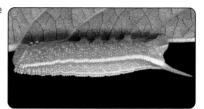

Eumorpha pandorus

RECOGNITION Green, orange, pink, or cinnamon with pale *white to yellow spots enveloping abdominal spiracles on A3–A7* and generous peppering of minute black dots. Head and first two thoracic segments may be withdrawn into greatly swollen T3 (especially when alarmed) (inset). Peculiar thin and coiled horn *of early and middle instars* (upper right image) *replaced by button in last instar*. Larva to 9cm. In Achemon Sphinx (*Eumorpha achemon*) each of the lateral spots on A3–A7 is divided into three parts; often it is more heavily peppered with black dots, especially along the sides of the abdomen.

OCCURRENCE Fields, woodlands, and forest edges from Kansas to Nova Scotia south to Florida and Texas. One generation northward; two or three generations in Missouri; three or more broods in Deep South with mature caterpillars from June onward.

COMMON FOODPLANTS Ampelopsis, grape, and Virginia creeper.

REMARKS The Pandorus Sphinx caterpillar is frequently encountered while it is wandering in search of a pupation site. To find caterpillars search the underside of leaves close to the ground, rock walls, or trees upon which its foodplant is sprawling. The Pandorus Sphinx is one of nearly a dozen hornworms known to use grape and related Vitaceae in the East. If conditions allow, throw a sheet on the ground beneath a suitable vine; the presence of hornworms will be revealed by an accumulation of elongate, deeply furrowed, fecal pellets. Flashlight searches by night, always interesting, may also be productive.

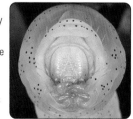

ABBOTT'S SPHINX
Sphecodina abbottii

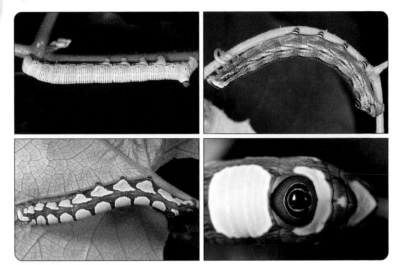

RECOGNITION Last instars come in two color forms. Brown form variegated much like patterns in wood; spotted form with ten pale green saddles over dorsum. *Horn on A8 replaced by raised eyelike button.* Larva to 7.5cm. Middle instars whitish to blue-green with orange raised knob on segment A8 (instead of horn) (upper left image).

OCCURRENCE Fields, woodlands, and forest edges from Minnesota, extreme southern Canada, and Maine south to Florida (rare) and Texas. One generation over much of East with mature caterpillars in June and July; at least two generations along Gulf with caterpillars from May to September.

COMMON FOODPLANTS Ampelopsis, grape, and Virginia creeper.

REMARKS The horn on A8 is lost after the first instar and replaced by a raised orange knob, which in turn is replaced by a convincing false eye in the last instar that closely resembles a vertebrate eye with a black central pupil and encircling iris. Added deception is provided by a "white reflection spot" that makes the eye appear moist and shiny. If the "eye" is poked or pinched, the caterpillar squeaks, reels around, and bites at its attacker. Some believe the spotted form mimics a cluster of green grapes. The brown form resembles grape bark. Adults of this fascinating moth come to light, flowers, and baits of fermented fruit. Males also drink at mud puddles (and soil wetted with urine). The brown adults, at rest, disappear on bark—the abdomen, with its unique arrangement of scale tufts, is raised upwards. The overall effect more closely matches a broken branch than an insect.

Deidamia inscripta

RECOGNITION *Yellow-green with subdorsal stripe that runs from horn forward over head to antenna. Yellow oblique lines pass under spiracles on A1–A7.* Head small relative to swollen thorax. White spiracles enclosed in black "parentheses." Horn yellow, often with downward curve. Larva to 5cm. Early instars more yellow than green with very long black horn that may be yellow at its apex.

OCCURRENCE Fields, woodlands, and forest edges from South Dakota to extreme southern Quebec and Massachusetts south to northern Florida and Mississippi. One generation with mature caterpillars from May to June.

COMMON FOODPLANTS Ampelopsis, grape, sourwood, and Virginia creeper.

REMARKS When disturbed the larva releases its grip and arches the head back over the abdomen; the six legs are held up and splayed outward (inset). It is especially quick to regurgitate. In the Appalachian foothills, Lettered Sphinx caterpillars are locally abundant on sourwood (*Oxydendron*), to the point of damaging much of the foliage on smaller trees. On four occasions I have seen remarkably high densities, with as many as 20–100 caterpillars on a single tree. In 2004 the moth defoliated acres of sourwood along the Foothills Parkway east of Cosby, Tennessee. It is odd that what is reported in the literature as a grape-feeder would be so common on an ericaceous tree. One wonders if there is a unique secondary chemical shared by members of the grape family and sourwood. Adults come to lights, mostly early in the evening and again just before dawn.

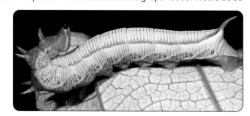

NESSUS SPHINX
Amphion floridensis

RECOGNITION Last instar *unceremoniously mottled in browns with darkened oblique line passing through each spiracle*. Pale line, sometimes inwardly edged with brown, runs from antenna to crown and continues rearward as subdorsal stripe. Horn short, black, slightly curved, and spinulose. Spiracles with white spot above and below. Body with scattered, pale integumental granules that are especially obvious over anal plate and along sides of head.
Larva to 5cm. Middle instars pale green with creamy subdorsal stripe; horn long, straight, and minutely spined (inset).

OCCURRENCE Fields, woodlands, and forest edges from southern Canada to Florida and Texas. One generation northward; three or more generations in South with mature caterpillars from late May through September.

COMMON FOODPLANTS Ampelopsis, grape, and Virginia creeper.

REMARKS The caterpillar of the Nessus Sphinx descends from foliage to rest near the ground by day, a position for which its coloration is well suited. The day-active adults may be seen nectaring at flowers especially in the late afternoon and dusk and just after dawn in hot weather. Like the Abbott's Sphinx, adults visit sap flows, flowers, and bait.

Darapsa myron

RECOGNITION Yellow- to blue-green, green, or brown with *enlarged T3 and smallish head.* Usually with subdorsal stripe running from horn to antenna; *its lower edge may connect with oblique lines that include spiracles on A1–A7.* Subdorsal stripe weakened over T3 and A1 segments. Often with dorsal red-brown splotches over A2–A7. Horn yellow or with flush of blue, frequently peppered with minute black dots above; anal plate edged with yellow. Labrum yellow. Larva to 5.5cm. Azalea Sphinx (*Darapsa choerilus*) also green or brown; its horn somewhat smaller and evidently lacking black flecking. In my images the subdorsal line is more or less absent forward of A6, as is corresponding line on head that extends to antenna in Hog Sphinx (*see page 276*). Hydrangea Sphinx (*D. versicolor*) green or brown with orange to red horn that is often marked with black above; subdorsal stripe well developed over thorax and head but absent over abdomen; oblique stripes more defined, less apt to gradually diffuse (*see page 276*). Our *Darapsa* usually can be identified by their foodplant associations (*see below* and page 276).

OCCURRENCE Woodlands and forest edges from extreme southern Canada to Florida and Texas. Two generations over much of range with mature caterpillars from June onward; three broods in Missouri; four or more in Louisiana.

COMMON FOODPLANTS Ampelopsis, grape, and Virginia creeper (all Vitaceae).

REMARKS All *Darapsa* have a greatly swollen last thoracic and first abdominal segment into which the head and anterior thoracic segments can be withdrawn. Of the 12 or so Eastern sphingids that feed on grape, I encounter this species most often, especially in July and August. Adults are attracted to lights and sugar baits.

GALIUM SPHINX (BEDSTRAW SPHINX)
Hyles gallii

RECOGNITION Highly variable, ranging from green or more commonly brown or black with *bright red or black horn*. Integument *smooth and shiny*. Head, prothoracic shield, anal plate, and prolegs unicolorous, usually reddish but sometimes lavender-purple. *Yellowish subdorsal spots on T3–A8, last often drawn toward base of horn.* Sides of body frequently flecked with small yellow dots that are vertically aligned. Spiracles creamy. Larva to 7cm. The Spurge Hawkmoth (*Hyles euphorbiae*), introduced to control leafy spurge and other invasive *Euphorbia*, is now established in Ontario. Its middorsal stripe is often bright red and each creamy subdorsal spot has a twin below (inset).

OCCURRENCE Fields and waste places from northern Canada south to Virginia (mountains) and Iowa. One principal generation in Connecticut with adults flying from June to August; mature caterpillars common from mid-August to October.

COMMON FOODPLANTS Bedstraw, fireweed, and other plants in the evening primrose family (Onagraceae) preferred, but using many other plants especially in last instar.

REMARKS Look for the caterpillars in hay fields and other open areas with generous patches of bedstraw. Late instars of the Galium Sphinx are typically encountered in late summer, while wandering across driveways and roads. Both of our *Hyles* are avid nectarers.

Hyles lineata

RECOGNITION Yellow and black or bright lime green *with exceptionally variable patterning*; integument smooth. *Head, thoracic shield, and anal plate all one color, either orange or green, and dotted with minute pale spots.* Many forms with subdorsal stripe. In well-marked (blackened) individuals the subdorsal stripe may be represented only by a rounded, creamy spot toward front end of T1–A8. Stout yellow to orange horn, sometimes with black tip or otherwise blackened. Thoracic legs and prolegs usually orange. Larva to 7cm. Catalpa Sphinx has blackened head and prothoracic shield; its horn is black and proportionately longer and more needlelike (*see* page 251).

OCCURRENCE Gardens, fields, rangelands, deserts, and waste places from Canada south to Florida and Texas, but infrequent northward. Two generations over much of East with caterpillars from July onward; three or more generations in Missouri; continuous broods along Gulf.

COMMON FOODPLANTS Frequently plants in evening primrose (Onagraceae) and apple (Rosaceae) families, but consuming many herbs and woody species.

REMARKS *Hyles lineata* is also known as the Morning Sphinx, but this moniker hardly works as the moth is quite active in the evening and through all hours of the night. Occasionally I see adults nectaring in late afternoon. While most of our hornworms are green and cryptic both in color and habit, *Hyles* caterpillars tend to be brightly colored and conspicuous. In the Great Basin and other drier areas of the West, the White-lined Sphinx may reach incredible densities. I have seen outbreaks in Utah where the highways got more use from wandering White-lined Sphinx caterpillars than from cars. I recall a migration while driving west from Salt Lake City one evening, where over a span of 10 miles several hundred adults flew through the beams of my headlights.

HORNWORMS

GROTE'S SPHINX *Cautethia grotei*
Southern half of Florida. Breeding year-round. Milkberry.

BANDED SPHINX *Eumorpha fasciata*
Resident along Gulf north to the Carolinas, straying northward to Michigan and Nova Scotia; caterpillars found northward at least to Connecticut. Two broods in Carolinas, mature caterpillars year-round in Florida. Evening primrose, false loosestrife, and related plants (Onagraceae).

SLENDER CLEARWING *Hemaris gracilis*
Manitoba to Nova Scotia south to Florida and Great Lakes States. One generation from Carolinas northward with mature caterpillars in late June and July; possibly two broods southward. Lowbush blueberry and perhaps laurel and other heaths.

PROUD SPHINX *Proserpinus gaurae*
Missouri to South Carolina to northern Florida and Texas. One generation in Missouri with mature caterpillars in late summer; two or more generations in Deep South. Evening primrose, fireweed, gaura, and stenosiphon.

AZALEA SPHINX *Darapsa choerilus* (= *Darapsa pholus*)
Transcontinental in southern Canada to northern Florida and Texas. Two generations over much of East with caterpillars from May to November; continuous along Gulf. Principally azalea and viburnum; also valerian.

HYDRANGEA SPHINX *Darapsa versicolor*
Michigan to southern Quebec and Maine south to Florida and eastern Texas. One generation with mature caterpillars in late summer northward; at least two generations southward. Buttonbush, hydrangea, and water-willow.

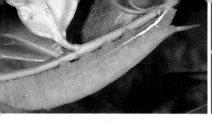

Grote's Sphinx

Banded Sphinx

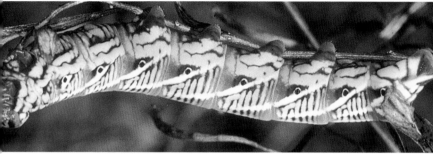

Banded Sphinx (2nd form)

Slender Clearwing

Proud Sphinx

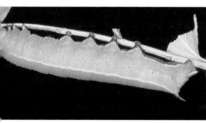

Azalea Sphinx

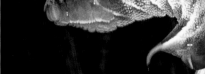

Hydrangea Sphinx

Hydrangea Sphinx (2nd form)

HORNWORMS

ALOPE SPHINX *Erinnyis alope*

Southern Florida (to
South America).
Continuous generations
with mature caterpillars
in all months. Allamanda,
nettlespurge, papaya,
and others.

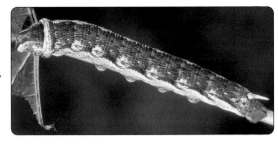

PLUTO SPHINX *Xylophanes pluto*

Southern Texas and Florida (to
Brazil). Continuous generations
with mature caterpillars in all
months. Milkberry, firebush,
cheese shrub (morinda), and other
plants.

TERSA SPHINX *Xylophanes tersa*

Green and brown forms. Resident
along Gulf south to Argentina but
migrating northward to New England
and Ontario. Continuous generations
with caterpillars in all months.
Buttonplant, firebush, *Manettia*,
starclusters, strongbark, wild coffee,
and other woody plants.

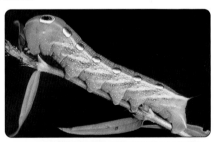

Eastern forests are home to more than 60 species of prominents. They include many of the most handsome and behaviorally interesting caterpillars of the temperate zone. In the tropics they are diverse in both number and form (visit Dan Janzen's caterpillar Web site: http://janzen.sas.upenn.edu/). Perhaps because they are relatively large, common, and stay perched on leaves by day, chronically exposed to the watching eyes of birds, both their morphology and behavior seem to be remarkably specialized and splendidly varied.

RECOGNITION

The body is stout with a proportionately large head, presumably to facilitate feeding on hardened summer foliage. The anal prolegs are modified, being noticeably larger or smaller than those of the midabdominal segments—relatively few notodontids use them for walking or securing their perch. Look for secondary setae above the bases of the prolegs. The crochets are arranged in a single row parallel to the body axis.

LIFE HISTORY NOTES

The smooth, hemispherical eggs are large, nearly 2mm in diameter. First instars skeletonize patches of tissue from upper or lower leaf surfaces. The caterpillars of several genera are gregarious, at least in early instars. Larger larvae feed along a leaf margin, often with the body appressed up against the leaf edge. Fecal pellets are proportionately small and dry. A number of our genera are capable of shooting acid from a neck gland; others regurgitate fluids when disturbed. The winter is passed as a prepupal larva or, more commonly, as a pupa in soil or litter.

COLLECTING AND REARING TIPS

The relatively large eggs may be found by looking on the undersides of leaves. The caterpillar's prolegs are relatively short and rather ineffective at keeping the caterpillar attached to its foodplant. When faced with the sudden jarring of a beating stick, few are able to remain attached; often I find myself individually reattaching caterpillars to their foodplant. Late summer and early fall are especially productive times to look for prominent caterpillars—enjoy the search, prominents are among the most varied and visually striking caterpillars of Eastern forests..

Many of the species illustrated below were reared from eggs obtained from females taken at light. Hold females in smooth-walled containers such as take-out soup containers, new plastic vials, or containers lined with wax paper. Inclusion of sprigs of an acceptable foodplant is usually not necessary; sometimes a touch of moisture in a cotton wick can be helpful. Most prominents lack functional mouthparts and therefore do not need to be fed for the nights that they are held. Often, the most challenging aspect of the process is securing a female—light collections are heavily male-biased. For example, in *Gluphisia* only about 5% of the adults that come to light are females. Unlike most caterpillars, prominents do best on mature leaves (which is not surprising given the size of their heads and late season activity). Provide prepupal larvae with > 2cm of slightly moistened peat.

SIGMOID PROMINENT
Clostera albosigma

RECOGNITION *Solitary. A1 with medial black knob nearly twice length of that over A8.* Dorsum with four indistinct yellow or, more commonly, orange stripes, separated by three poorly differentiated charcoal stripes. In most individuals sides marked by just two broad stripes: a dark subdorsal and an orange spiracular. Secondary setae longer than those of other *Clostera*. Dark head usually with paler brown spot above triangle. Larva to 3cm. *Clostera apicalis* is mostly brown to gray with four wavy white to cream stripes over dorsum; the *primary setal warts are yellowish*, especially over front half of body; enlarged and blackened *middorsal warts on A1 and A8 absent*; head chestnut brown along sides and over vertex; solitary (*see* page 319).

OCCURRENCE Wetlands, fields, woodlands, and forests from Canada to Gulf States but scarce south of New Jersey, Kentucky, and Missouri. At least two generations over much of range with mature caterpillars from May to November.

COMMON FOODPLANTS Especially aspen and poplar; also willow.

REMARKS *Clostera* are nocturnal caterpillars that are easily located by flashlight. By day the caterpillars retreat to leaf shelters formed by tying up a single leaf or drawing together two or more adjacent leaves. As noted above, caterpillars of the Sigmoid Prominent (as well as those of *C. apicalis*) are solitary, whereas those of the next species are gregarious. The pupa overwinters in all *Clostera*.

Clostera inclusa

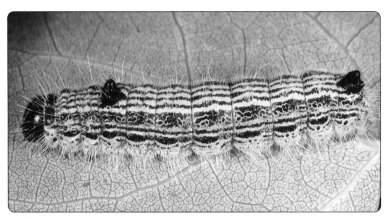

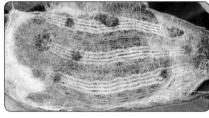

RECOGNITION   *Gregarious*. Four well-defined yellow stripes over dorsum. *Black middorsal knobs on A1 and A8 about equal in size.* Head uniformly black and shiny. Secondary setae finer and shorter than in Sigmoid Prominent (*Clostera albosigma*). Larva to 3cm. *C. strigosus* co-occurs on poplar over much of Canada south in the East to lower New York and Connecticut. Its pale yellow caterpillar lacks any middorsal knobs; the dorsum bears three vague reddish stripes and three stronger lateral stripes, the lowermost being noticeably thickened (Forbes 1948). A photographic slide in the Canadian National Collection suggests that it is gregarious at least in early instars. It is rare—should you find its caterpillar or secure livestock, take notes and images.

OCCURRENCE   Fields, powerlines, wetlands, and forests from southern Canada (rare) to southern Florida and eastern Texas. Two generations over much of the East with mature caterpillars from June onward.

COMMON FOODPLANTS   Aspen, poplar, and willow.

REMARKS   The gregarious caterpillars pass the day in a bivouac fashioned by silking together two to several leaves or rolling a single larger leaf (inset). Clusters contain up to 20 individuals, although two to seven caterpillars are more typical for late instars. They occasionally defoliate small trees and saplings. *Clostera* is a northern genus—five species occur in eastern Canada. The Poplar Tentmaker is the only *Clostera* species likely to be encountered across many mid-Atlantic and southern states.

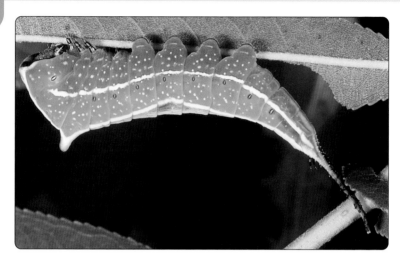

BLACK-ETCHED PROMINENT
Cerura scitiscripta

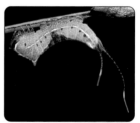

RECOGNITION Lime green with *elevated first abdominal segment that bears a transverse ridge and extremely long, highly modified anal prolegs. White subspiracular stripe edged with pink.* Anal prolegs blue-black (at rest) with extrusible yellow and red distal portion. Prothorax with *black eyespots above magenta "collar"* that frames head (inset). Larva to 4cm.

OCCURRENCE Fields and edges of watercourses from southern Canada to Florida and Texas. At least two generations with mature caterpillars from late May to November.

COMMON FOODPLANTS Willow and poplar.

REMARKS At rest the caterpillar is cryptic; its movements are slow and deliberate. Once alarmed, the warningly colored portions of the anal prolegs are everted and the legs are curled upward over the body and flung about (inset). The caterpillar also rears up to display its false head and separates its shiny black mandibles (inset). Ultimately, the caterpillar may release a spray of acid from a gland on the venter of the first thoracic segment. The pupa overwinters in a cocoon spun along a twig.

Furcula borealis

RECOGNITION   Yellow-green with brown, diamond-shaped saddle over abdomen; lower edges of saddle extend nearly to A4 proleg. Dorsum of thorax with triangular brown patch with spined knob to either side of T1; posterior portion of triangle narrowly extended as middorsal line that joins abdominal saddle over T3. Larva to 4cm.

OCCURRENCE   Fields, edges of woodlands, and forests from Illinois to Maine south to Florida, northern Arkansas, and eastern Kansas. Over much of East, two generations with mature caterpillars from late June to October.

COMMON FOODPLANTS   Cherry.

REMARKS   The exaggerated tails of *Furcula* and other prominents are actually the anal prolegs. When alarmed the larva shunts blood (hemolymph) into the prolegs, greatly increasing their length, raises them over the body, and whips them wildly about. In early instars the length of the distended legs may be over half the length of the body (*see* inset of first instar). The second inset shows nearly 50 braconid wasp larvae issuing from a last instar White Furcula. Furculas overwinter as a pupa in a smooth, spindle-shaped, gray to brown cocoon that is spun along a twig—the finished cocoon is cryptic, not unlike a stem gall in appearance.

GRAY FURCULA
Furcula cinerea

RECOGNITION Green and brown *without pronounced ridge or knobs* on T1 in last instar. *Chocolate brown thoracic and abdominal saddles not connected*. Thoracic saddle triangular with even lateral margins when viewed from above. Abdominal saddle widest over A4, extending to proleg, ending well above proleg on adjacent segments (A3 and A5); note *yellow subdorsal splotches* (within brown saddle). Larva to 4cm. In *Furcula modesta* abdominal saddle often extending to proleg on A3–A5; thoracic and abdominal saddles joined by thin brown middorsal stripe; ground color often more yellow-green; thoracic patch jagged laterally; and two rows of subdorsal spots in abdominal saddle. It occurs across Canada south in the East to Great Lakes States, Pennsylvania, and New Jersey. Caterpillar of *F. scolopendrina* with posterior portion of abdominal saddle more smoothly edged, saddle ending well above proleg on A4, and more subdued subdorsal yellow spotting in abdominal saddle (*see* page 319). It is not clear that *modesta* and *scolopendrina* represent distinct species (Tim McCabe, pers. comm.).

OCCURRENCE Inhabiting fields and wetlands southward, often a forest species northward. Canada to Florida and Texas. At least two generations over much of the East with mature caterpillars from May to October.

COMMON FOODPLANTS Aspen, poplar, and willow.

REMARKS *Furcula* species undergo remarkable changes in coloration and shape as they develop. The first instars are dark and bear enormous spined knobs over the thorax. At each molt green is added and the knobs diminish in relative size. Descriptions provided here apply only to last instars of this interesting genus. It is my experience that this group of species is more apt to be found on poplars, while the Western Furcula (*F. occidentalis*) and Black-etched Prominent (*C. scitiscripta*) often favor willows.

RECOGNITION Although remarkably variable, ranging from nearly all yellow (inset) or green to completely red, always recognizable by *black spots atop head* and low hump over A8. *Second black spot behind antenna* includes stemmata. Four thin stripes along each side of body. Larva to 4cm.

OCCURRENCE Woodlands and forests from Manitoba to extreme southern Quebec to Florida and east Texas. At least two generations over much of East with mature caterpillars from late May to November.

COMMON FOODPLANTS Basswood (linden).

REMARKS The larva rests on the underside of a leaf blade with the head curled back and held alongside the abdomen (inset). When harassed the larva will raise its head and display its bright, shiny black mandibles. The pupa overwinters.

COMMON GLUPHISIA
Gluphisia septentrionis

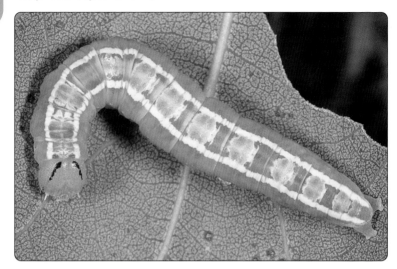

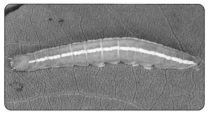

RECOGNITION *Waxy green to blue-green with creamy, broad subdorsal stripe.* Somewhat *flattened*, occasionally with red or yellow patches above. *Prolegs short* and inconspicuous. Larva less than 3.5cm. Two other poplar-feeding *Gluphisia* occur from New England west to Minnesota and Wisconsin. Caterpillar of *G. lintneri* waxy blue-green above and green below yellow spiracular stripe that is thickened fore and aft (*see* page 320); in some individuals the stripe is edged above with pale red (Forbes 1948). I am unaware of features that reliably separate caterpillars of *G. avimacula* from those of the Common Gluphisia. Both *lintneri* and *avimacula* fly early in the year and have but a single spring generation.

OCCURRENCE Fields, meadows, barrens, edges of watercourses, woodlands, and forests from Canada to northern Florida and Texas. Two generations with a partial third in Connecticut; mature caterpillars from May onward.

COMMON FOODPLANTS Poplar.

REMARKS In male caterpillars the yellow-green testes are visible to either side of the dorsal midline in the last (fifth) larval instar. In western North America "septentrionis" is thought to represent a complex of species in need of taxonomic study (Paul Opler, pers. comm.). Gluphisias overwinter as pupae.

Hyperaeschra georgica

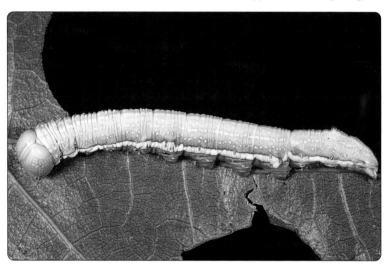

RECOGNITION *Green to frosty blue-green caterpillar with broad, creamy spiracular stripe* that continues along side of head to mandible; stripe often edged with red above and below. Faint white addorsal stripes; subdorsal and supraspiracular stripes broken into spots. *Dorsum of A8 bears pair of small red buttonlike bumps*. T2–A8 may bear an elongate wine to maroon spot below spiracular stripe. Larva to 4cm.

OCCURRENCE Woodlands and forests from Minnesota to southern Quebec to central Florida and Texas. At least two generations over most of East with mature caterpillars from late May to November.

COMMON FOODPLANTS Oak.

REMARKS The Georgian Prominent is one of more than a dozen common Eastern prominents that feed on oak. Although the adults are common at light, the caterpillars are only occasionally encountered in the wild. The young larva feeds from a leaf tip back, removing the blade but leaving a conspicuously protruding midrib. The pupa overwinters.

WHITE-DOTTED PROMINENT
Nadata gibbosa

RECOGNITION Sea-green to waxy blue-green, stocky caterpillar, with weakly developed subdorsal stripe; densely salted with white dots. *Head enlarged, pale green; mandibles yellow with black tips. Anal plate edged with yellow.* Larva less than 5cm.

OCCURRENCE Barrens, woodlands, and forests from Canada southward. Two or three generations over much of East with mature caterpillars from May through November.

COMMON FOODPLANTS Principally oak and other Fagaceae, but also reported from alder, birch, cherry, maple, plum, rose, serviceberry, and willow.

REMARKS The White-dotted Prominent is a common species of oak woodlands and forests throughout our region. When threatened its larva curls up, places its head over the abdomen, and faces its attacker with its bright yellow mandibles (lower inset). The anal prolegs are not appreciably modified as in most prominents and retain the ability to grasp. The upper inset shows a recently molted larva—the old skin, far thinner than paper, lies crumpled under the posterior abdominal segments. The pupa overwinters in peat or soil.

Nerice bidentata

RECOGNITION Pale blue-green body with *coarsely toothed dorsum*. Reddish lateral stripe above thoracic legs often edged with cream above and/or below. Anal prolegs reduced but functional in clasping. Larva to 4cm.

OCCURRENCE Fields, woodlands, and forest edges from southern Canada to Florida and Texas. At least two generations with mature caterpillars from May to November.

COMMON FOODPLANTS Elm.

REMARKS The Stegosaurus of our caterpillar fauna with a doubly toothed dorsal keel that is similar in aspect to the leaf margins of the coarse-leaved elms (e.g., American, rock, and slippery) on which the larvae feed. The caterpillar's oblique subdorsal lines add to the disguise as they are a good proxy for the lateral veins of these same elms, even though they are darker than the surrounding tissue. Like many prominents, the caterpillar feeds along a single leaf edge and carves away a cavity into which the body will be closely appressed. In so doing the dorsal ridge of the Double-toothed Prominent becomes the new "leaf edge," and an especially credible one at that. Young caterpillars consume the blade from the leaf tip back towards the petiole leaving an extended midrib; later this is excised and dropped to the ground. Larvae are especially likely to be encountered on small, isolated seedlings or saplings growing in open fields, fencerows, or along woodland edges. Beating is particularly effective for this small-legged caterpillar. The pupa overwinters.

NORTHERN FINNED PROMINENT
Notodonta simplaria

RECOGNITION Leaf mimic with *sharklike fins over A2 and A3 and strongly humped A8.* Head with pale stripe to either side. Oblique pale line runs down to proleg on A6; behind this mark, ground color decidedly darkened. Larva to 4.5cm. Forbes (1948) noted that caterpillars of the Finned Prominent (*Notodonta scitipennis*) tend to be more strongly marked than the Northern Finned Prominent. In my limited experience, the Finned Prominent often has more yellow-orange along the sides of the terminal abdominal segments (inset). It feeds on willows and poplars across Canada south to North Carolina (in mountains) and northwestern Missouri.

OCCURRENCE Wetlands, woodlands, and forests from Canada south to Great Lakes States and New England. One principal generation in Quebec; two in New York and Connecticut with mature caterpillars from June to October.

COMMON FOODPLANTS Poplar and willow.

REMARKS The characters given above for the separation of our two finned prominents may not be reliable; identifications should be confirmed through rearing. Given the striking differences in adult coloration of our two *Notodonta*, it is only a matter of time before features are found to separate their caterpillars reliably. The pupa overwinters.

RECOGNITION Green, red, gray, or brown *glossy* caterpillar with *twiglike texture and appearance*. Setae reduced and inconspicuous. Mandibles and legs often red-orange or brown. T1 slightly swollen and often lightened in color; *A2 and A8 enlarged and knotlike*. Last abdominal segment often tinted with purple and orange; anal prolegs reduced. Larva to 4.5cm.

OCCURRENCE Watercourses, wetlands, woodlands, and forests from Canada to northern New Jersey and eastern panhandle of Texas. One principal generation in Quebec; two southward with mature caterpillars from June through October.

COMMON FOODPLANTS Poplar.

REMARKS Younger caterpillars are yellow (second instars) (upper inset) or green (third instars) (lower inset) and rest on leaves. The integument is shiny even at this stage. As the caterpillars mature they add markings and swellings that resemble leaf scars. In the last two instars the luster and texture of the body resemble that of poplar and willow bark. The pupa overwinters.

ANGULOSE PROMINENT
Peridea angulosa

RECOGNITION Surprisingly undistinguished
for a prominent: usually lime green (or pinkish red)
with pair of closely set addorsal stripes and *white
and pink spiracular stripe that runs to mandibles* and
continues across labrum. Head bright green, smooth,
as broad as thorax. Thoracic spiracle large, its white
center ringed with black. Larva to 4.5cm. Two related species

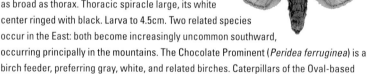

occur in the East: both become increasingly uncommon southward,
occurring principally in the mountains. The Chocolate Prominent (*Peridea ferruginea*) is a
birch feeder, preferring gray, white, and related birches. Caterpillars of the Oval-based
Prominent (*P. basitriens*) (*see* page 320) eat maple, especially sugar and related maples.
Their caterpillars are similar in overall aspect, but lack the pink and red spiracular stripe of
the Angulose Prominent.

OCCURRENCE Barrens, woodlands, and forests from southern Canada to Florida and
Texas. At least two generations over much of East with mature caterpillars from May to
November.

COMMON FOODPLANTS Oak; questionably reported from hickory.

REMARKS The reddish ground color in the inset
occurs in some fall-active larvae, when leaves are
starting to change. If molested the larva will coil and
raise the head over the body in a snakelike fashion,
much like the caterpillars of the White-dotted
Prominent (*Nadata gibbosa*) (*see* inset, page 288). The
pupae of all our *Peridea* overwinter in peat or soil.

FALSE-SPHINX (BLACK-RIMMED PROMINENT)
Pheosia rimosa

RECOGNITION Yellow, lavender, pink, green, brown, or nearly black *with shiny integument and black abdominal horn* on A8. A white ring surrounds each spiracle. Thoracic legs commonly red-orange. Last abdominal segment topped with hardened, spinulose plate, reddened about its edges. Larva to 4.5cm.

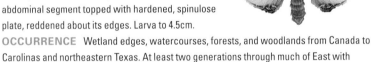

OCCURRENCE Wetland edges, watercourses, forests, and woodlands from Canada to Carolinas and northeastern Texas. At least two generations through much of East with mature caterpillars from May onward.

COMMON FOODPLANTS Poplar principally, but also willow.

REMARKS It is easily mistaken for a young hornworm (Family Sphingidae) caterpillar. The False-sphinx is a tidy feeder that eats along a leaf edge, starting from the leaf base and working toward the tip. Unlike many prominents, the anal prolegs are capable of grasping and aid the caterpillar's effort to establish a new feeding cavity while the rear of the body is clamped to a leaf petiole. The pupa overwinters.

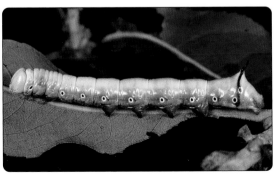

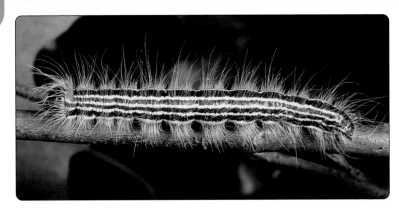

CONTRACTED DATANA
Datana contracta

RECOGNITION *Black- and cream-striped* caterpillar with *long, soft whitish hairs.* Hairs nearly two times longer than segments that bear them. Black middorsal stripe broad with four cream and three black stripes below it; lowermost cream stripe distinctly wider than three above. Prothoracic shield orange. Larva to 4.5cm.

OCCURRENCE Barrens and woodlands from southern Quebec to Florida and Arkansas. One generation northward; at least two generations from Missouri southward with mature caterpillars from June to September.

COMMON FOODPLANTS Chestnut and oak; also reported from blueberry, elm, hickory, walnut, and witch hazel, but perhaps erroneously.

REMARKS All Datanas are gregarious and occur in large clusters, often with dozens to hundreds of individuals (inset). In the Northeast the Contracted Datana is a species of dry oak woodlands and barrens. Datanas are generally hardy in captivity and easily reared. Provide a deep layer of lightly moistened peat as a pupation medium. Some published foodplants for our *Datana* appear to be erroneous or represent exceptional occurrences—if you find a larval cluster on foodplants other than those listed in this guide, photograph the last instar, rear adults, save vouchers, and share your findings. The pupa overwinters in *Datana*—sometimes for two or more years (e.g., *ranaeceps* and *drexelii*) (Dale Schweitzer, pers. comm.).

Datana integerrima

RECOGNITION *Stout, black caterpillar with silky white setae*, those over dorsum especially long. *White subspiracular stripe*; other stripes mostly obsolete or, if present, thin and broken. Younger caterpillars more reddish and glossy, with complete complement of stripes: two subdorsal, one supraspiracular, and thicker subspiracular stripes. Gregarious, sometimes in clusters of 100 or more. Larva to 4.5cm.

OCCURRENCE Orchards, parks, and woodlands from Wisconsin and extreme southern Quebec to Florida and Texas. Often with a partial second generation throughout much of East, probably two full generations from Missouri southward with mature caterpillars from June to October.

COMMON FOODPLANTS Butternut, hickory, pecan, and walnut (all Juglandaceae); uncommonly or falsely reported foodplants include birch, blueberry, oak, and willow.

REMARKS Birds are known to prey heavily on *Datana* aggregations. The Walnut Datana is frequently reported as a pest, defoliating small trees of hickory and walnut. The white eggs, small for a prominent, are deposited by the hundreds in one or more adjacent rafts—each egg bears a small black central spot. Interestingly, molting is synchronized, with nearly all the larvae in a cluster molting at the same time (Johnson and Lyon 1991). Such clusters occur on trunks, well away from foliage. Most curious is the fact that the clusters, with caterpillars stacked two and three deep, often contain larvae of more than one instar (suggesting that the throng draws from more than a single egg mass). Prepupal caterpillars may wander considerable distances in search of a suitable pupation substrate. Provide them with 6–10cm of peat.

YELLOW-NECKED CATERPILLAR
Datana ministra

RECOGNITION *Black with four yellow stripes* down each side and comparatively sparse white setae. *Prothoracic plate behind head orange.* At least four other Eastern *Datana* species have similar caterpillars. Larva to 4.5cm. Angus's Datana (*D. angusii*) has reddish prolegs, black thoracic shield, and a "hairier" aspect (*see* opposite). Drexel's Datana (*D. drexelii*) usually sports an orange rump patch formed from confluence of the orange stripes over A8 and A9 (*see* opposite). Eastern populations of Spotted Datana (*D. perspicua*) have broader yellow stripes and the base of each proleg on A3–A7 is somewhat reddened (*see* opposite). Post-burn Datana (*D. ranaeceps*) distinguished by its orange to red head, broader yellow striping, sparser setae, and orange terminal abdominal segment (*see* opposite). I am not familiar with two of our named southeastern species: *D. modesta* and *D. robusta.*

OCCURRENCE Parks, barrens, woodlands, and forests. Transcontinental across Canada south in East to Florida and Texas. Often with partial second generation over much of our area; probably with two full generations from Missouri southward with mature caterpillars from June to October.

COMMON FOODPLANTS Apple and related Rosaceae and oak; also birch, blueberry, willow, and other woody shrubs and trees.

REMARKS Throughout the Northeast this species and other *Datana* appear to be declining. *Compsilura*, a tachinid parasitoid introduced from Europe to control the Gypsy Moth, may be a factor in its demise. Over one ten-day period *Compsilura* attacked 79% of the fourth and fifth instar larvae that Dylan Parry (pers. comm.) had set out in Massachusetts woodlands.

ANGUS' DATANA *Datana angusii*

Missouri to Nova Scotia south to Florida and Texas. One generation northward; at least two broods in South with mature caterpillars from June to October. Butternut, hickory, and walnut (all Juglandaceae) preferred.

DREXEL'S DATANA *Datana drexelii*

Kentucky to Nova Scotia south to South Carolina. One generation northward; at least two broods in South with mature caterpillars from June to October. Blueberry, other heaths, and witch hazel commonly; also recorded, perhaps falsely, from basswood, birch, and sassafras.

SPOTTED DATANA *Datana perspicua*

In our region from Missouri to southern Ontario and New York south to Florida and Texas. One generation northward; evidently two in South. Principally sumac and smoketree; possibly oak (Richard Heitzman, pers. comm.).

POST-BURN DATANA *Datana ranaeceps*

Pennsylvania to Long Island south along Coastal Plain and southern Appalachians to extreme eastern Texas. Often with partial second generation in North; two broods in South. Staggerbush; also fetterbush and maleberry. This species thrives in barrens that have burned recently.

MAJOR DATANA
Datana major

RECOGNITION Handsome black and yellow-striped caterpillar with *bright red head, prothoracic shield, and legs*. Last instar with *yellow stripes broad and broken* into spots. Whitish body hairs, prominent in related Datanas, relatively inconspicuous. Larva to 4.5cm. Earlier instars resemble caterpillars of Drexel's Datana (*D. drexelii*), Yellow-necked Caterpillar (*D. ministra*), and Post-burn Datana (*D. ranaeceps*).

OCCURRENCE Bogs, acid swamps, barrens, woodlands from Kansas to southeastern Ohio and New Jersey south to Florida and Texas (*see* Remarks). Often a partial second generation in New Jersey with mature caterpillars from July onward; perhaps two or more full generations in Deep South.

COMMON FOODPLANTS Azalea, fetter-bush, leatherleaf, maleberry, staggerbush, and other heaths (Ericaceae), but rarely if ever blueberry.

REMARKS Also known as the Azalea Caterpillar. When disturbed, *Datana* caterpillars hold the ends of the body aloft, and if further agitated, secrete a transparent amber drop from the anus and a glob of regurgitant from the mouth; both droplets are withdrawn back into the body once danger has passed. Ferguson (1955) and Covell (1984) report the Major Datana extending north to Nova Scotia, but because adults are extremely similar to those of Drexel's Datana, this would seem to be a case where records are better based on caterpillars (or molecular evidence). Ferguson commented that there were no reports of the caterpillar from the region and the moth he illustrates appears to me to be that of the Yellow-necked Caterpillar (*Datana ministra*). The species-level taxonomy of the genus is difficult, even with genitalic dissections. However, the last instar larvae of all our *Datana*, or at least those north of the Carolinas, may be readily identified with this guide or the key in Forbes (1948).

WAVY-LINED HETEROCAMPA
Heterocampa biundata

RECOGNITION Light green to blue-green, variably patterned, but usually with dorsal saddle broken by distinct "X" between A4 and A5. *Head dull red-pink to red-purple, produced upward with dark knob to either side of midline*; paler over midline down through triangle. Sides of body often marked with brick red and white splotches on T3, A1, A3–A4, A6, and A8 that resemble necrotic leaf tissue; these spots anastamosing in some individuals. Larva to 4.5cm.

OCCURRENCE Woodlands and forests from Canada south to Florida and Texas. At least two generations with mature caterpillars from late May to November.

COMMON FOODPLANTS Basswood, beech, birch, cherry, hickory, maple, oak, sugar maple, walnut, willow, witch hazel, and other woody plants.

REMARKS This is one of the most commonly encountered prominent caterpillars in Eastern forests, but usually second to the Saddled Prominent (*Heterocampa guttivitta*) in abundance.The young larvae sport spectacular prothoracic "antlers" through the third instar (inset). According to Laplante (1998) the genus overwinters as prepupal larvae, but in the Northeast the pupa overwinters in at least two of our species (Dale Schweitzer, pers. comm.). Many prominents, especially those belonging to the Heterocampinae, turn red prior to pupation.

SADDLED PROMINENT (MAPLE PROMINENT)
Heterocampa guttivitta

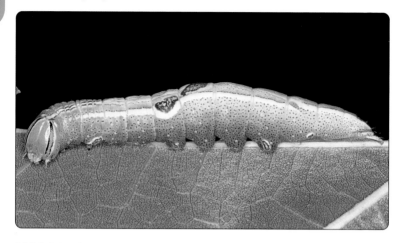

RECOGNITION Pale to lime green (or reddish brown) with creamy, *subdorsal stripe on (T2) T3–A6, continuing on A7–A10 as whiter stripe that is displaced upward.* Red-brown-purple pattern elements absent or highly variable, but often forming *V-shaped saddle over at least A3 and A4. Head usually with three-parted lateral band: central line pink to red-edged with black inwardly and cream outwardly.* Often with dorsal yellow patch on anterior edge of prothorax that bears a pair of tiny yellow to red warts. Top and sides of body bearing numerous minute wine-red dots that do not form lines. Larva to 4cm.

OCCURRENCE Barrens, woodlands, and forests from Canada south to Florida and Texas. Two generations over much of East with mature caterpillars from late May to November.

COMMON FOODPLANTS Apple, beech, birch, blueberry, buckeye, chestnut, dogwood, hazel, hickory, hop hornbeam, maple (especially sugar maple), oak, persimmon, sour gum, sumac, walnut, witch hazel, and many other woody plants.

REMARKS In most years this is the most common summer prominent in my beating samples and can be expected to turn up on almost any shrub or tree. Only the first instar bears prothoracic "antlers." Early instars skeletonize patches of tissue from the underside of leaves; the fourth and fifth (last) instars feed along a leaf margin, often within a cavity that they have excavated. The Saddled Prominent is irruptive and occasionally defoliates large forest tracts in northern New England and eastern Canada. Beech, sugar maple, and yellow birch are among the trees that bear the brunt of these outbreaks. I recall one August evening in eastern Connecticut hearing the steady patter of its hard, dry fecal pellets raining out of the trees overhead.

Heterocampa obliqua

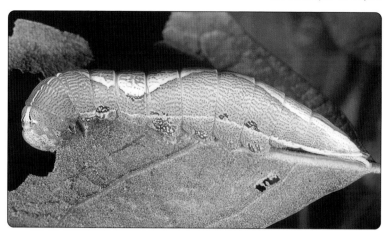

RECOGNITION Green, tan, pink, or reddish brown with abundant wavy mottling formed from *lines of wine-red spots; white diamond saddle over T3–A4*; and body tapered rearward of A5. *Head pale, mottled* with spots sometimes coalescing to form an irregular patch to either side of triangle, drawn into prothorax. *Dorsum of prothorax with white triangular mark, edged outwardly with black and reddish wart in each anterior corner.* Larva to 4.5cm. Caterpillar of *Heterocampa varia*, also an oak-feeder, similarly patterned, but with much more restricted distribution, occurring along the Atlantic Coastal Plain from Nantucket and Long Island south to Florida, west to Texas, north to Missouri; most records from xeric oak habitats. Constriction in saddle over A4 and A5 less pronounced, narrowing only to about half width of posterior white saddle; white prothoracic triangle extending forward over head and reaching antennae; outwardly this pale area bounded by diffuse darker band. In two of my cohorts the minute wine-red spots did not form lines; often with two proximate, wine-colored spots joined by pale spot. Another species, *H. astarte*, occurs from southeastern Virginia south to Florida. Its green or brown caterpillar possesses a middorsal stripe on T1 and T2 that flares outward on T3, widens to A2, and then gradually narrows to A10. Live oak is its preferred foodplant.

OCCURRENCE Barrens, woodlands, and forests from southern Canada to Florida and Texas; absent from Upper Midwest. One generation with mature caterpillars from late June to September in Connecticut; two broods in Missouri; active year-round in parts of Florida.

COMMON FOODPLANTS Oak.

REMARKS The first three instars bear thoracic "antlers," although by the third instar they are scarcely more than short, reddish toothed thorns.

WHITE-BLOTCHED HETEROCAMPA
Heterocampa umbrata

RECOGNITION Green, tan, pink, or reddish brown with a confusing array of patterns. White saddles over T3–A4 (A5) and rear of body separate, rarely joined over dorsum. Prothorax with *pair of raised, shiny reddish knobs* to either side of white middorsal patch. Head uniformly tan-pink to ochre with *black line extending from T1 knob to mandible*, ground color notably paler between black lines. Thoracic legs usually reddened. *Antennal base yellow.* Larva to 4.5cm.

OCCURRENCE Barrens, woodlands, and forests from southern Canada to Florida and Arkansas. At least two generations over most of our region with mature caterpillars from May to November; continuous broods in Florida.

COMMON FOODPLANTS Oak.

REMARKS First instar with long black "antlers" on prothorax and smaller, black, dorsal spines over the abdominal segments (lower inset). Traces of the prothoracic antlers are retained through the last instar and pupa. Caterpillars are splendidly cryptic when feeding, appearing much like a necrotic leaf edge. Prepupal larvae of all *Heterocampa* and *Lochmaeus* turn pinkish red and lose much of their patterning.

Lochmaeus bilineata

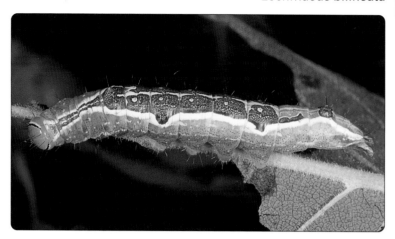

RECOGNITION Like its congener the Variable Oakleaf Caterpillar (*L. manteo*), exceptionally variable in coloration and patterning. Caterpillar of Double-lined Prominent *often has broken yellow supraspiracular stripe (composed of yellow dots)* that is absent in my images of the Variable Oakleaf Caterpillar. Double-lined Prominent caterpillar *rarely has appreciable white on inner side of black head line and lacks blue-green aspect to supraspiracular area* common to many Variable Oakleaf Caterpillars. Red coloration dominates the dorsal area in many forms of Double-lined Prominent, but is commonly limited to spots that border the subdorsal stripe in Variable Oakleaf Caterpillar (*see also* comments under Variable Oakleaf Caterpillar, page 304). Larva to 4cm.

OCCURRENCE Woodlands and forest edges from Canada to Florida and Texas. One generation in New England; at least two generations from Missouri southward with mature caterpillars from May to November.

COMMON FOODPLANTS Elm and basswood seem to be preferred; also reported from beech, birch, oak, and walnut, but some of these records may refer to Variable Oakleaf Caterpillar.

REMARKS Someone with a green thumb and good camera could help to sort out the natural foodplant ranges of our *Lochmaeus*. Caterpillars are common in the fall and easily collected with a beating sheet. As with other prominents, prepupal caterpillars do well if a deep layer (2–5cm) of peat is added to their rearing container. Be watchful at the time of emergence: *Lochmaeus* are strong fliers that soon render their wings featureless when reared in small containers—such adults cannot be identified without resorting to genitalic dissection (or molecular analysis). Take pictures or secure vouchers while the adults are fresh.

VARIABLE OAKLEAF CATERPILLAR
Lochmaeus manteo

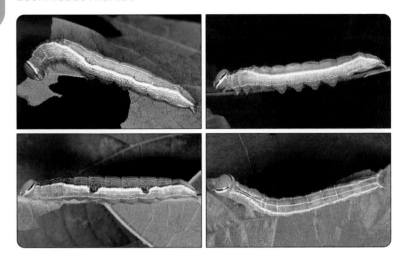

RECOGNITION   True to its name, coloration
and patterning highly variable. Mostly pale lime-
or blue-green (at least along sides of body); dorsum
green or marked with white or brick red saddles.
Usually *whitish subdorsal stripe edged with yellow*
above, although latter may be obscured by wine-red
dorsal saddle. Paired warts on dorsum of A1 and A8 often red.
Yellow spiracular stripe strongest anteriorly, broken into spots both fore and aft. Black line
on head often narrowly edged with white inwardly (and always outwardly). Larva to
4.5cm. Forbes (1948) claimed caterpillars are indistinguishable from those of Double-lined
Prominent (*Lochmaeus bilineata*), and I would not disagree—identifications should be
based on reared adults.

OCCURRENCE   Barrens, woodlands, and forests from southern Canada to Florida and
Texas. One generation in North; at least two generations in South with mature caterpillars
from May to November.

COMMON FOODPLANTS   Beech, chestnut, and oak preferred; also reported on
basswood, birch, elm, hawthorn, maple, walnut and other trees, but some of these records
may refer to Double-lined Prominent.

REMARKS   This is a common prominent in the fall across the Northeast. At times its
numbers are so great as to produce a steady rain of fecal pellets in dry oak woodlands in
late August and September. Reported by Laplante (1998) to overwinter as a prepupa, but I
suspect it overwinters as a pupa under most circumstances.

Hyparpax aurora

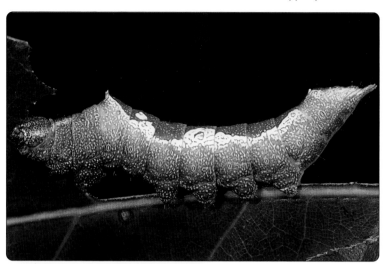

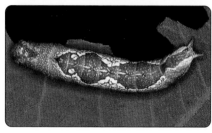

RECOGNITION Bright green saddle above and blue-green along sides; occasionally brown. Entire body splashed with fine white dots. Head strongly mottled, but without distinct lines or stripes. First two thoracic segments with dark red-brown triangle above. *Dorsum of A1 bearing small pair of orange-red horns*; second much smaller pair over A8. Anal prolegs peglike. Larva to 4cm.

OCCURRENCE Barrens and woodlands, and forests. Southern Canada to northern Florida and Texas. In Northeast with one principal generation and partial second; two generations southward with mature caterpillars from June to November.

COMMON FOODPLANTS Oak, especially scrub oak northward; also reported from viburnum, perhaps erroneously.

REMARKS The adults, exquisitely scaled in delicate yellow and pink, are reminiscent of the Rosy Maple Moth (*Dryocampa rubicunda*). It is not known whether this similarity is serendipitous or represents a case of mimicry. To a large measure they occur in different habitats, with the Pink Prominent flying in drier environs. The pupa overwinters.

MOTTLED PROMINENT
Macrurocampa marthesia

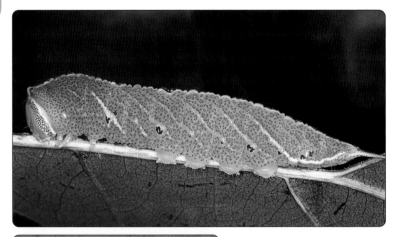

RECOGNITION Pale green body densely mottled with multitude of broken maroon rings and *very elongate, taillike anal prolegs. Body somewhat triangular in cross section* with cream to white and red middorsal stripe. Often with red splotches over midline and about spiracles. Oblique lines run through spiracles on A1–A7; last oblique line on A7 bent abruptly and continuing as subspiracular stripe to A10. Larva to 4.5cm.

OCCURRENCE Barrens, woodlands, and forests from Canada south to Florida and Texas. At least two generations with mature caterpillars from May to November.

COMMON FOODPLANTS Principally oak and other Fagaceae; also reported from maple and poplar (perhaps erroneously).

REMARKS At rest the anal prolegs are held together and positioned against the substrate. When threatened these are hydrostatically enlarged, separated, and raised above the body, presumably to alarm the attacker. If molested further the caterpillars may eject a spray of acid from a "neck" gland on the venter of the first thoracic segment. The horns on the prothorax of early instars suggest common ancestry with members of the genus *Heterocampa*. In the early instars of this species and the next, the anal prolegs are excessively long (inset)—up to two-thirds the length of the rest of the body. The anal prolegs get progressively smaller with each molt. While Laplante (1998) states that the prepupal larva overwinters within its cocoon, I suspect that most individuals overwinter as pupae.

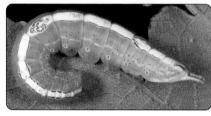 

RECOGNITION Instantly identified by its *"forked tail" and close association with sycamore.* Pale green with broad white dorsal stripe infused with brick-red spots. Head with pair of medial white lines that diverge to follow edges of triangle and conspicuous, broad reddish band, edged below with white that extends to antenna. Larva to 4cm.

OCCURRENCE Edges of watercourses, wetlands, and parks from Missouri to Massachusetts south to northern Florida and Texas. At least two generations with mature caterpillars from May to November.

COMMON FOODPLANTS Sycamore; reports from cottonwood and other foodplants may be in error.

REMARKS This interesting caterpillar is anything but drab—its moniker is derived from the plebian appearance of the adult. The larva rests with its head partially pulled within the thorax (inset). Look for the Drab Prominent on leaf undersides, positioned over the midrib or a strong secondary vein. I have had consistent success searching saplings and young sycamore plants in late summer. In early instars the anal prolegs account for more than half of the body length. Alarmed larvae shunt blood (hemolymph) into their anal prolegs, enlarging them further, and flail them about the body. In each successive instar the anal prolegs become proportionately smaller and lose erectile capacity. The pupa overwinters.

LACE-CAPPED CATERPILLAR
(WHITE-STREAKED PROMINENT) *Oligocentria lignicolor*

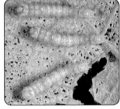  

RECOGNITION Cryptically rendered in green, white, and brown blotching and mottling. *Dorsum of A1 drawn into forward-projecting horn. Head with characteristic mottling* (inset). Thoracic segments and dorsum of posterior abdominal segments lime green. Whitish lateral patch extending from A7 to A10 prolegs. Larva to 4.5cm.

OCCURRENCE Barrens, woodlands, and forests from southern Canada to Florida and Texas. One generation northward; at least two generations over much of East with mature caterpillars from May to November.

COMMON FOODPLANTS Principally beech, chestnut, and oak (all Fagaceae); also reported on birch.

REMARKS The yellow early instars occur in small clusters (inset). The Lace-capped Caterpillar is a marvelously camouflaged insect. Its complex coloration is surprisingly constant among individuals. As in related prominents, the larva chews out a cavity along a leaf margin and holds its body flush against the excavated edge. The collective effect, especially from a distance, is not unlike that of a necrotic herbivore-damaged leaf margin. The brown pattern elements in *Oligocentria* caterpillars, in particular, resemble the abandoned and necrotic feeding refugia of the Oak Leaf Aphid (*Myzocallis*). The Lace-capped Caterpillar turns up frequently in late summer searches of oak foliage. *Oligocentria* overwinters as a prepupal larva.

Oligocentria semirufescens

RECOGNITION Yellow, pink, or brown with extensive network of brown mottling. *A1 with fleshy, forward-projecting horn, cleft at its apex; last thoracic segment also drawn into sizable dorsal horn*; and A5 humped. Head usually with broad, brown stripe running from vertex to antenna. Like *Schizura*, with a whitish dorsal chevron capping A6 and A7, although no *Schizura* sport a horn on T3. Larva to 4cm.

OCCURRENCE Woodlands and forests from Canada to Florida and east Texas. At least two generations over much of East with mature caterpillars from June onward.

COMMON FOODPLANTS Poplar and willow; other reported foodplants include alder, beech, birch, oak, and rose.

REMARKS One of our fauna's most dramatic caterpillars that could easily be dubbed the rhinoceros caterpillar. The Red-washed Prominent, when positioned against a leaf margin, resembles a necrotic or blighted section of leaf—the ruse is first class (inset).

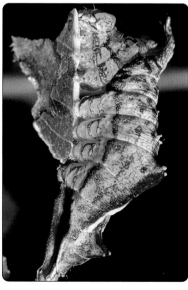

CHESTNUT SCHIZURA
Schizura badia

RECOGNITION Decorated with green, yellow, and purplish markings. Small head bears intricate purple-red mottling, especially about triangle that continues as middorsal stripe over thorax. *Diffuse, bright yellow saddle over dorsum of abdomen.*

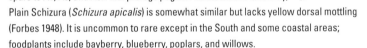

Irregular reddish brown patch along sides of A2–A4 with spurs to A1, A5, and A6. Anal prolegs peglike. Larva to 3cm. Evidently, Plain Schizura (*Schizura apicalis*) is somewhat similar but lacks yellow dorsal mottling (Forbes 1948). It is uncommon to rare except in the South and some coastal areas; foodplants include bayberry, blueberry, poplars, and willows.

OCCURRENCE Woodlands and forests from Canada to Florida and Texas. At least two generations from central New England southward with mature caterpillars from May to November.

COMMON FOODPLANTS Wild raisin and other viburnums.

REMARKS The resting posture is unique: the end of the abdomen is lifted and the anal prolegs splayed apart; the head is held down, appressed to a leaf. Young *Schizura* caterpillars have secretory hairs that protect the first three instars from ants and presumably other small predators (Scott Smedley, pers. comm.). Additionally, *Schizura* caterpillars possess a thoracic neck gland which aids in their defense—older caterpillars can shoot a stream of formic and acetic acid and a medley of other compounds 20cm or more from the gland opening. By craning their heads, the larvae are even able to aim the delivery of the acid jet. The neck gland is impressive in size, occupying some 10% of the caterpillar's internal volume. According to Laplante (1998) Schizuras overwinter as prepupal larvae within their cocoons, but Smedley has noted that many of his lab-reared *Schizura* also wintered as pupae.

Schizura concinna

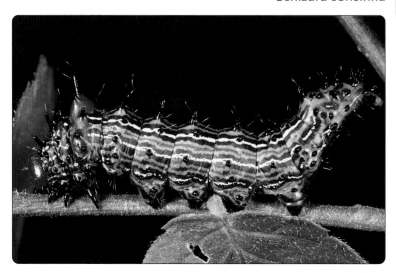

RECOGNITION *Bright red head, red hump over A1, and wavy yellow and white pinstriping* immediately distinguish caterpillar from all others in East. Dorsum, sides below spiracles, and rump mostly orange. Larva to 3.5cm.

OCCURRENCE Fields, yards, barrens, coastal scrub, woodlands, and forests from southern Canada to Florida and California. One generation with a partial second brood in Northeast; two or more generations southward with mature caterpillars from May to November.

COMMON FOODPLANTS Many woody plants: apple, birch, blackberry, blueberry, cherry, dogwood, elm, gale, hawthorn, hickory, locust, maple, oak, persimmon, poplar, rose, serviceberry, sweet gum, viburnum, walnut, willow, and other woody plants.

REMARKS Although occasionally reported as a pest on plantings in parks, yards, and orchards, the adults are rarely seen. Neither sex comes to light with any regularity. The caterpillars occur in aggregations of several dozen individuals, but tend to become solitary prior to maturation. Collective warning displays, with the yellow-orange rears lifted into the air, provide quite a spectacle. Upon further disturbance the caterpillars thrash from side to side and regurgitate a drop of fluid. If left undisturbed they will draw the droplet back into the body. This species can be difficult to overwinter—provide larvae with clean dead leaves over a layer of peat, and some ventilation to discourage mold. The prepupal larva overwinters.

BLACK-BLOTCHED SCHIZURA
Schizura leptinoides

RECOGNITION Brown with *forward-projecting horn on A1 followed by hump on A5 and white "V" over A6 and A7.* Smaller dorsal humps on A4 and A8. *Broad, dark brown spot along dorsum of thorax.* Head intricately mottled, often with dark band to either side of triangle and/or small white to yellow spot crowning each lobe. Occasionally sides of T2 and T3 green, like Checkered-fringe Prominent (*Schizura ipomoeae*) (Forbes 1948). Larva to 4cm. Distinguished from the Checkered-fringe Prominent by its hump over A4. Moreover, the head coloration is diagnostic for all our Schizuras.

OCCURRENCE Barrens, woodlands, and forests from Canada to Florida and Texas. At least two generations with mature caterpillars from May to November.

COMMON FOODPLANTS Hickory and walnut favored, less commonly American hornbeam, hop hornbeam, and oak; also reported from apple, beech, birch, cherry, poplar, rose, sour gum, willow, and other woody plants.

REMARKS The larva chews out a notch along a leaf edge and positions its body within. Frequently, the notch is initiated at the base of the leaf, near where the petiole attaches to the blade. Appressed to an edge, the larva blends into the leaf, with its humps and warts along the dorsum appearing as jagged, damaged sections of the blade. It is not uncommon to find caterpillars with one to several oval, white tachinid fly eggs laid along the top and sides of the body (inset).

Schizura unicornis

RECOGNITION Brown larva with bright *lime green T2 and T3. A1 with forward-projecting horn. White "V" over A6 and A7*. Head with poorly defined brown line to either side of midline. Humps on A4 and A5 low (if present at all), much smaller than that of A8. Dark area over midline of thorax edged with white. Dorsal setae less than one-fourth length of segment that bears them (*see* next species). Larva less than 3.5cm. Caterpillar of Checkered-fringe Prominent (*Schizura ipomoeae*) similar, but easily distinguished by the greater development of the dorsal hump over A5, distinctive patterning on head, longer setae, and larger size.

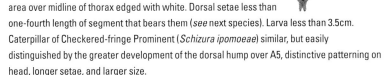

OCCURRENCE Fields, parks, woodlands, and forests from Canada to Florida and Texas. At least two generations with mature caterpillars from May to November.

COMMON FOODPLANTS Apple, beech, birch, blueberry, cherry, dogwood, elm, hawthorn, hickory, hop hornbeam, maple, New Jersey tea, ninebark, oak, persimmon, poplar, rose, sweet pepperbush, willow, witch hazel, and many other woody shrubs and trees.

REMARKS Its unique coloration and body outline distinguish it from all other caterpillars except those of the Checkered-fringe Prominent. Surely a predator would require a special search image to successfully locate Unicorn Caterpillars in a forest with its sea of leaves. Perhaps this is their defense, being at the same time cryptic and unusual—likely the caterpillars are recognized far less than they are seen. The caterpillar in the inset is perched atop a bundle of more than two dozen braconid cocoons—the holes from which the wasps exited are visible in the caterpillar's body wall.

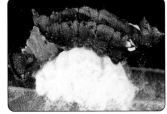

CHECKERED-FRINGE PROMINENT
Schizura ipomoeae

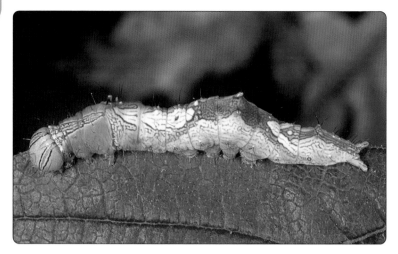

RECOGNITION   Very similar to Unicorn Caterpillar (*Schizura unicornis*) but larger and with A5 *distinctly humped*. White chevrons over A1–A3 and A6–A8. *Each side of head with characteristic band composed of five thin stripes*: gray or steel blue central stripe sandwiched between two whitish lines which in turn are bounded by black lines. Long black, shiny dorsal setae greater than half the length of segment that bears them (cf. Unicorn Caterpillar, *Schizura unicornis*). Larva to 4cm.

OCCURRENCE   Fields, parks and yards, barrens, woodlands, and forests from Canada to Florida and Texas. At least two generations with mature caterpillars from June to November.

COMMON FOODPLANTS   Basswood, beech, birch, blackberry, cherry, chestnut, dogwood, elm, hackberry, hawthorn, maple, oak, rose, and witch hazel, and many other woody plants; probably not morning glory.

REMARKS   The Morning Glory Prominent, the common name for this moth in most texts, strikes me as a misnomer. I offer "Checkered-fringe Prominent" as a replacement, referring to the alternating black and pale scales in the adult forewing fringes. The caterpillar carves out a leaf notch in which it positions itself (inset). From a distance of a few feet the caterpillar resembles a dead, curled-over leaf edge far more than it does food for a clutch of hungry nestlings.

BLACK-SPOTTED PROMINENT
Dasylophia anguina

RECOGNITION Gorgeous *lavender, orange, and yellow striped caterpillar*, evidently also a green form. Integument shiny. Dorsal midline marked by thin black stripe; each side of body with three additional thin, often interrupted, black stripes cutting through lavender lateral area. Dorsum of *A8 set with shiny black button*. Head orange. Larva to 4cm.

OCCURRENCE Fields, barrens, powerline right of ways, and woodlands from Manitoba to southern Quebec to Florida and northeastern Texas. One generation in Connecticut, two or more in South with mature caterpillars from May to November.

COMMON FOODPLANTS Bush clover, clover, lead plant, locust, sweet clover, wild indigo, and other legumes.

REMARKS A spectacular caterpillar well suited for a Salvador Dali landscape. The rear of the body may draw greater attention from predators: it is swollen, bears black "eyespots," and sports elongate prolegs that are not unlike short antennae. Moreover, the rear is often held above the substrate, like a head might be. It seems probable that this brightly colored insect will prove to be chemically protected, at least as a larva. The adult is comparatively plebian, colored much like any other moth. The Black-spotted Prominent is our only Eastern notodontid that routinely feeds on herbaceous plants. The pupa overwinters.

GRAY-PATCHED PROMINENT
Dasylophia thyatiroides

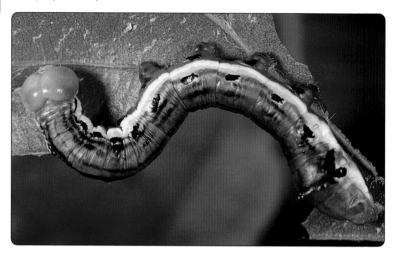

RECOGNITION *Enlarged pink or yellow head and white and lemon spiracular stripe* diagnostic. A8 with shiny, dark, middorsal wart (eyespot?) and often with rosy flush about spiracle. A1–A8 with shiny black spot above spiracle. A8 and A9 much wider than thoracic segments. Integument shiny. Black plate above each proleg on A3–A6. Larva to 4cm. Middle instars decidedly more yellow and striped.

OCCURRENCE Forests from Michigan to Quebec and Nova Scotia south to northern Florida and Arkansas. Two generations over much of East with mature caterpillars from May onward.

COMMON FOODPLANTS Beech.

REMARKS I have searched unsuccessfully for both eggs and caterpillars of the Gray-patched Prominent on several occasions, turning countless leaves and beating dozens of beech limbs. The figured individuals represent two different cohorts, each reared from eggs secured from a gravid female that came to light. The caterpillar is a gorgeous insect— lavender colors such as these are rather rare among North American insects. As noted for the Black-spotted Prominent (*Dasylophia anguina*), the rear of the body makes for a credible false head (inset).

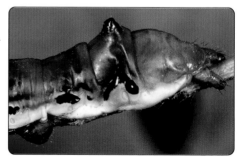

Symmerista canicosta

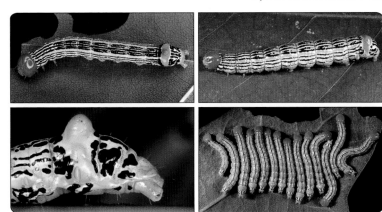

RECOGNITION   *Bright orange head and black, yellow, orange, and white pinstriping* distinguish our *Symmerista. Dorsum of Red-humped Oakworm with five narrow black stripes separated by four white stripes.* Integument smooth and shiny. A8 raised, orange. Larva to 4cm. Distribution broadly overlapping with White-headed Prominent (*Symmerista albifrons*), which becomes increasingly more common southward. Both moths utilize the same foodplants. Specimens and literature records for the two species are mixed, but presumably White-headed Prominent occurs from southern Quebec (Handfield 1999) south along the Coastal Plain and Piedmont to Texas. The caterpillars figured above did not yield adults, so while I believe they represent the Red-humped Oakworm, one or more may, in fact, be the White-headed Prominent—I am unable to separate the two as caterpillars.

OCCURRENCE   Woodlands and forests from southern Canada to Carolinas (mostly in Piedmont and mountains) and Mississippi. One generation in Northeast with mature caterpillars in August and September; two generations from Missouri and New Jersey southward with caterpillars from May to October.

COMMON FOODPLANTS   Beech, chestnut, and oak (all Fagaceae).

REMARKS   The caterpillars are gregarious initially, lining up side by side in clusters of 30 or more on the undersides of leaves. Caterpillars may feed together until the last instar. They are common in the fall, routinely turning up in beating samples. Because the White-headed Prominent has two or more generations south of Long Island, it seems likely that some southern Red-humped Oakworm populations may also have an additional generation. The adults of our two oakworms (*Symmerista*) are closely similar in appearance. At this point only genitalic characters (illustrated in Forbes 1948) provide a reliable means by which to confirm identifications.

ORANGE-HUMPED MAPLEWORM
Symmerista leucitys

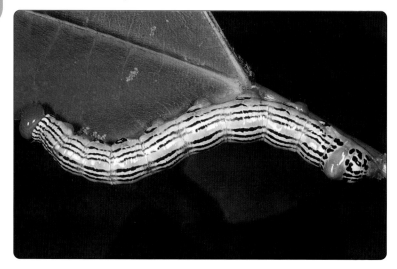

RECOGNITION Similar to Red-humped Oakworm (*Symmerista canicosta*), but more lemon yellow. *Dorsum marked by only three black and two white stripes* in contrast to the oakworms (*S. albifrons* and *S. canicosta*), which bear five black and four white dorsal stripes in the last instar. Always on maple, whereas our other two *Symmerista* eat oak and other Fagaceae. Larva to 4cm.

OCCURRENCE Forests from Manitoba to Nova Scotia south at least to North Carolina and Missouri. One generation with mature caterpillars from July into September.

COMMON FOODPLANTS Maple, especially sugar maple.

REMARKS The Orange-humped Oakworm (*S. canicosta*) and White-headed Prominent (*S. albifrons*) have only three black and two white dorsal stripes prior to the last instar, and thus resemble the last instar of the Orange-humped Mapleworm up until the final larval molt. While feeding, the larva may elevate its rump, displaying what my friend Jane O'Donnell thinks is a false head: it is enlarged, elevated, and bears two short "antennae" (the back prolegs) (*see* previous species). The pupae of *Symmerista* overwinter in a loose cocoon spun amongst leaf litter. Their bright coloration and gregarious habit suggest that *Symmerista* are chemically protected. As handsome as our Eastern prominents are, they are wholly outdone by their Neotropical brethren, which are a study in the wonders of evolution. A guide to notodontid caterpillars of Central and South America would make this chapter seem like little more than an hors d'oeuvre.

TOOTHED CLOSTERA *Clostera apicalis*

Canada south through Connecticut, Great Lakes States, and northern Missouri (also western Texas and California). Two generations in New York and Connecticut. Willow and poplar.

SILVERED PROMINENT *Didugua argentilinea*

Southern Texas. Continuous generations with caterpillars in all months. Serjania and perhaps also balloon vine and *Urvillea*.

WESTERN FURCULA *Furcula occidentalis*

Canada south to Connecticut, Pennsylvania, and northwestern Missouri. Evidently two generations in New England with mature caterpillars in July and again in August and September. Willow.

HOURGLASS FURCULA *Furcula scolopendrina*

Canada south in East to West Virginia (mountains); mostly western. Two generations across southern Canada with mature caterpillars in July and again in August and September. Poplar and willow.

PROMINENTS

LINTNER'S GLUPHISIA *Gluphisia lintneri*

Canada south at least
to Illinois and
Connecticut. One
generation with mature
caterpillars in June.
Poplar.

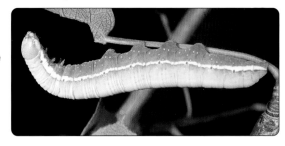

SMALL HETEROCAMPA *Heterocampa subrotata*

Missouri to New York
south to Florida and
Texas. At least two
generations with
mature caterpillars
from May until
November. Hackberry.

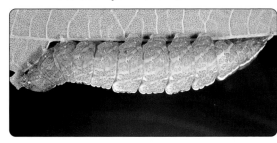

OVAL-BASED PROMINENT *Peridea basitriens*

Transcontinental in Canada
south in East to northeastern
Florida, Alabama, Mississippi,
and eastern Louisiana. At least
two generations over much of
our area with mature
caterpillars from May onward.
Sugar and related maples.

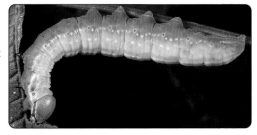

CHOCOLATE PROMINENT *Peridea ferruginea*

Canada south to central
Florida and Texas. At
least two generations
over much of East with
mature caterpillars
from May onward.
White, gray, and related
birches.

OWLETS, CUTWORMS, UNDERWINGS, AND KIN – NOCTUIDAE

This is the largest family of Lepidoptera with more than 35,000 species worldwide. One in every four lepidopterans in North America is an owlet. They are marvelously diverse in form, behavior, and biology. Wingspan is telling enough: they range in size from hypenodines with wingspans of only 13mm to the Neotropical White Witch (*Thysania zenobia*) with an alar expanse occasionally exceeding 300mm. The superfamily Noctuoidea is in a state of taxonomic flux. Long-recognized families such as the tiger moths (Arctiidae) and tussock moths (Lymantriidae) are now known to be of "noctuid stock," so unless the classic concept of the family is redefined, these two well-known families would need to be subsumed within the core of the Noctuidae (reclassified as subfamilies). In the recent treatment by Kitching and Rawlins (1998), groups that were previously classified within the family Noctuidae (e.g., Nolinae and Pantheinae) have been elevated to full family status. Caterpillars of 162 owlets are figured here and another 32 species are diagnosed. Large numbers of Eurasian noctuid caterpillars are illustrated in Sugi (1987), Porter (1997), and Beck (1999); these works can be helpful for making generic-level determinations.

RECOGNITION
No larval characters were identified by Kitching and Rawlins (1998) as being unique to the family. Most owlet caterpillars are smooth and stocky with rounded shiny heads and short, inconspicuous setae, but exceptions are common (e.g., dagger caterpillars possess abundant secondary setae and underwing larvae are often long and gracile). Prolegs are usually present on A3–A6, but those on A3 and A4 are occasionally absent or reduced. Crochets are arranged in a series more or less parallel to the body axis. For the present, the only way to recognize owlet caterpillars is to learn each of the subfamilies, of which there are many.

LIFE HISTORY NOTES
With tens of thousands of species almost anything is possible: some are solitary while others gregarious; most are cryptic but a few are brightly colored; many are foodplant specialists while others are generalists. Some eat detritus and fallen leaves. Curiously, almost none are forest pests, although many, representing different subfamilies (e.g., hadenines, heliothines, plusiines, and noctuines), are injurious to crops and turf. A majority of these pest species are migratory insects that move up from the South each spring and summer. Most pupate in litter or below ground, often with little hint of a cocoon. While adults typically feed on nectar and honeydew like other moths, calpines have a robust, sharpened proboscis that is used to pierce fruit. One Old World species, *Calyptra eustrigata*, has made the evolutionary jump to blood-feeding on mammals.

COLLECTING AND REARING TIPS
This information has been parsed out into the subfamilial, tribal, and generic introductions as well as the species accounts.

Dagger Moths – Subfamily Acronictinae

Daggers derive their name from the sharp black lines present in the forewing markings of many species. The subfamily includes several of eastern North America's most interesting and handsome caterpillars. They are intriguingly variable in form, color, and degree of "hairiness." I am unaware of any characters that assure recognition of the genus given their great morphological diversity. Most are endowed with conspicuous hairlike setae, and in many these arise from tufts. Secondary setae are nearly always present, especially above the prolegs. The head has only primary setae, in all but a handful of our daggers. Some resemble other owlets, tussocks, tigers, and prominents, and likely are mimetic of members of these families.

Several lineages within the subfamily undergo dramatic color changes between the penultimate and ultimate instars (*Acronicta*) or within the last instar (*Polygrammate*). Acronictines, with few exceptions, feed on woody shrubs and trees. While most are foodplant specialists, a handful are generalists. It is often necessary to offer prepupal larvae soft (dead) wood in which to tunnel, especially those that turn red or enter a wandering phase. Some make a hardened cocoon by adding bits of chewed wood to the wall of the cocoon as it is being spun. Acronictines overwinter as pupae, sometimes for more than one winter.

From an evolutionary standpoint the genus *Acronicta* has been remarkably successful: with more than 75 North American species, it ranks as our continent's seventh largest genus of Macrolepidoptera (larger moths and butterflies). Nearly 50 species occur east of the Mississippi. Eight of these are treated individually and another 18 are introduced with abbreviated accounts to whet greater interest in these wonderful insects.

WITCH HAZEL DAGGER MOTH *Acronicta hamamelis* (= *Acronicta subochrea*)

Wisconsin to Nova Scotia south to northern Florida and Kentucky. Two generations over most of East with mature caterpillars from June to November. Witch hazel.

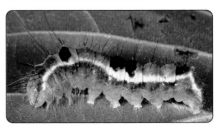

LONG-WINGED DAGGER MOTH *Acronicta longa*

Southern Canada to Florida and Texas. Two or more generations with mature caterpillars from May onward. Birch, blackberry, cherry, oak, rose, and other woody plants.

Acronicta afflicta

RECOGNITION Last instar beige to salmon
with charcoal middorsal stripe and *clubbed, black,
dorsal setae* that are about as long as segment that
bears them. One pair of clubbed setae per segment (D2
setae). Pale spiracles ringed with black. Larva to 4cm.

Acronicta brumosa, a species of xeric oak woodlands and barrens,
has two pairs of black, clubbed dorsal setae per segment (both D setae), which arise from
orange pinacula. Middle instars of Afflicted Dagger Moth with setose warts and pale
middorsal stripe resemble those of Southern Oak Dagger (*A. increta*) complex (inset).

OCCURRENCE Barrens, woodlands, and forests from Colorado to New Jersey south to
Florida and Texas. Two or three generations over much of East with mature caterpillars from
June to November.

COMMON FOODPLANTS Oak.

REMARKS The heads of most daggers, including the Afflicted Dagger, are large,
presumably because the caterpillars feed on mature foliage. Prepupal larvae lose many of
their markings and may turn pink or red (especially those that tunnel into wood to fashion a
pupal chamber). Adults of some daggers, including the Afflicted Dagger, have a melanic
form. The frequency of these dark forms varies considerably among species. The

evolutionary significance of this melanism
and its underlying genetics have not been
studied. It would be interesting to know to
what extent the phenomenon in *Acronicta*
and pantheids parallels that of ennomine
geometrids such as the Pepper-and-salt Moth
(*Biston betularia*)—the latter being one of the
most heralded examples of Darwinian natural
selection (*see* page 161).

AMERICAN DAGGER MOTH
Acronicta americana

RECOGNITION Large caterpillar, densely vested with white or pale yellow setae; *thin, diverging, black dorsal lashes on A1 and A3.* Integument below usually pale green. Thicker, unpaired *tuft of black setae from middorsum of A8.* Head smooth, shiny black, without secondary setae. Larva to 5.5cm. Early and middle instars often a bit more yellow (inset).

OCCURRENCE Woodlands and forests from southern Canada to Florida and Texas. Evidently one principal (extended) generation with mature caterpillars from July to October in Northeast; two or three broods from Missouri southward.

COMMON FOODPLANTS Alder, American hornbeam, ash, basswood, birch, box elder, chestnut, elm, hazel, hickory, horse chestnut, maple, oak, poplar, redbud, sycamore, walnut, willow, and many other woody plants.

REMARKS Daggers are grazers in the first instar, skeletonizing irregular patches of tissue, usually from the lower leaf surface. The American Dagger caterpillar rests with the head wrapped around to one side on a leaf underside. It is frequent in late summer and fall beating samples. I once had what I believe was a dagger caterpillar, excavate a pupal chamber in the cedar siding of my home. It gnawed a trench into the siding some 3cm in length. The exposed outer surface of the cocoon was infused with bits of chewed wood. The finished construction, firm to the touch, somewhat resembled the nest of a mud dauber wasp.

Acronicta funeralis

RECOGNITION A flamboyant dagger: *black and yellow with paddlelike subdorsal setae.* Dorsum of each segment boldly marked with yellow and black—the pattern resembling a set of upside-down cowry shells. Larva to 3.5cm.

OCCURRENCE Fields and woodlands from southern Canada to North Carolina, Mississippi, and Missouri, although absent from many parts of this range. Two to three generations in Missouri with mature caterpillars from June onward.

COMMON FOODPLANTS American hornbeam, apple, alder, birch, blackberry, blueberry, elm, hazel, hickory, oak, poplar, willow, and other woody plants.

REMARKS Dietary staples in our area are mostly in the birch (Betulaceae) and rose (Rosaceae) families. The Paddle Caterpillar is closely similar to the Alder Moth (*Acronicta alni*) of Europe—their last instars are scarcely distinguishable. The gray-splotched, penultimate instar of the Alder Moth resembles a bird dropping, especially at rest when its head is curled along one side of the abdomen. Porter (1997) remarks that the last instar of the Alder Moth (*A. alni*) is warningly colored, but such a claim presupposes that the caterpillar is in some way protected. Although many *Acronicta* are brightly colored, somewhat conspicuous in habit, and sometimes foul-smelling, studies are needed documenting that they are, in fact, manufacturing or sequestering toxic compounds and are unpalatable. Porter (1997) also notes that the Alder Moth caterpillar is thought by some to be more common in canopy foliage than it is on leaves at or near the ground. Prepupal caterpillars tunnel into wood. Unfortunately, this spectacular insect is rather scarce— I've never found its larva.

GRAY DAGGER MOTH
Acronicta grisea

RECOGNITION Yellow- to emerald-green with *dark brown saddle over dorsum. Saddle Y-shaped over thorax, widening and reaching maximum width on A4–A5*, encompassing green middorsal patch over A6 and A7, and finally *narrowing over A8–A10.* Dorsal setae borne from brown, shiny, pimplelike warts that are largest on A1 or A2. Head mostly red to brown except for green triangle and "cheeks." Larva to 3cm. Fragile Dagger Moth (*Acronicta fragilis*) similar but with dorsal saddle darker, more parallel-sided without constrictions (or breaks), more noticeably edged with yellow; head with diffuse black band down each side which reaches antenna. Canada south to North Carolina in mountains and Great Lakes States. Foodplants include alder, apple, birch, cherry, mountain ash, plum, rose, serviceberry, and willow. Caterpillar also resembles Triton Dagger (*A. tritona*), a specialist on blueberry and other heaths (Ericaceae) (*see* page 334).

OCCURRENCE Edges of watercourses, wetlands, woodlands, and forests across Canada, south in East to Massachusetts and Great Lakes States. One generation with mature caterpillars in July and August.

COMMON FOODPLANTS Alder, apple, birch, cherry; also reported from elm, poplar, and willow.

REMARKS The caterpillar of the Gray Dagger may spin its cocoon along a twig or distal branch. Those spun along smaller twigs resemble a gall. The caterpillar is attacked by *Aleiodes quebecensis*, a braconid wasp that "mummifies" it. After the inner contents of the caterpillar have been consumed, the wasp larva chews a hole through the lower portion of the cadaver, glues it in place with a sticky secretion, then spins an elongate cocoon within the body of its host—the mummy remains recognizable as an *Acronicta* caterpillar for months.

(SPEARED DAGGER MOTH) *Acronicta hasta*

RECOGNITION Last instar unmistakable: *charcoal with broken red middorsal stripe* outwardly edged with black. Body with one to few, very long, conspicuous whitish setae, arising from each lateral setal wart. Larva to 4cm. Penultimate instar green with broad red and yellow middorsal stripe that narrows rearward; A8 somewhat humped; vertex and head to either side of triangle cherry red (inset).

OCCURRENCE Fields, powerline right of ways, and woodlands from southern Canada to Florida and Arkansas. Evidently two generations in Northeast with mature caterpillars from June onward; two or three annual broods in Missouri and New Jersey. Second and third broods appear to be partial.

COMMON FOODPLANTS Cherry, especially black cherry.

REMARKS Unlike the vast majority of caterpillars that hide by day or feed from the lower side of leaves, middle to last instars of many daggers perch on leaf uppersides. Larvae spin a thin mesh of silk into which they engage their crochets. The middle and last instars differ so in appearance that few would guess that they represent a single animal. While I have found penultimate instars perched on leaf uppersides on several occasions, I have never seen the black and red final instar except when beating. Evidently it perches on twigs, branches, or along the trunk by day. Cherry has a rich dagger fauna: four species use *Prunus* as a primary foodplant and another half-dozen feed on it occasionally. A thin cocoon of brown silk is spun in leaf litter.

YELLOW-HAIRED DAGGER MOTH
Acronicta impleta

RECOGNITION Easily recognized by its *dense sets of paired tufts over T3, A1, and A2.* Four dense brown to black dorsal tufts over A1 surrounded by six pairs of paler tussocks: one subdorsal tuft on A1, two dorsal tufts on T3, and three dorsal and subdorsal tufts on A2. All of its many color forms with *broad, reddish spiracular stripe.* A8 with pair of diverging brown to black lashes subtended by paler and shorter subdorsal tufts. Larva to 4.5cm.

OCCURRENCE Fields, woodlands, and forests. Transcontinental in Canada south in East to Florida and Texas. Evidently at least two generations over much of range with mature caterpillars from June onward; three or more broods in Deep South.

COMMON FOODPLANTS Hickory and walnut are favorites, but also alder, ash, birch, blueberry, cherry, dogwood, elm, maple, mountain ash, oak, sassafras, sweet gum, willow, and other woody species.

REMARKS Batesian mimicry, where a palatable species mimics an unpalatable or protected species, is generally held to be rare in caterpillars—a curious state of affairs, if true, because mimicry is common among adult butterflies and moths. In fact, the mimicry phenomenon and its evolutionary significance were first recognized by William Bates, based on his studies of Amazonian butterflies. The Yellow-haired Dagger caterpillar would appear to be a promising example for mimicry. It looks remarkably like a tussock caterpillar of the genus *Dasychira*—it has the build, lashes, and tussocks. Moreover, the setae that make up the shorter tufts are densely plumed and downy, very much like those of a lymantriid. Finally, it arches its first two abdominal segments upward, and in so doing more fully displays its tufts, in much the same fashion as a true tussock caterpillar.

Acronicta increta

RECOGNITION *Green, yellowish, pinkish, or salmon to orange with variously developed, paired, white splotches over dorsum of T2–A6.* White spots over T2, T3, and A6 often smaller. Head large, marked with white snowflake spotting. Larva to 3cm. The Southern Oak Dagger is a member of a taxonomically difficult species complex (*see* Remarks). Forbes (1954) regarded the caterpillars within the complex to be largely indistinguishable. The Ovate Dagger Moth (*A. ovata*) is figured on page 337.

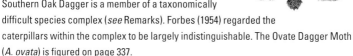

OCCURRENCE Barrens, woodlands, and forests from southern Canada to Florida and Texas. Evidently a single protracted generation with mature caterpillars from late July to November in Northeast; two distinct broods in Missouri.

COMMON FOODPLANTS Chestnut, oak, and probably beech; reports from birch most likely erroneous.

REMARKS *Acronicta increta* is a member of a species complex that also includes *albarufa*, *exilis*, *haesitata*, *modica*, *ovata*, and *tristis*. All feed on oak and other members of the Fagaceae. By day the caterpillar rests on the underside of a leaf or in a leaf shelter with the head alongside the abdomen. Only *A. albarufa* and *A. exilis* are easily identified as adults. It would seem that no two collections have the members of this complex sorted in the same way. Rings *et al.* (1992) provide a set of useful characters for the separation of the adults. There is a great need for someone to rear out cohorts from individual females. The results would establish limits on the levels of variation displayed by families of larvae or adults. Unfortunately, captive females in this complex are reluctant to lay eggs, even when sleeved on an appropriate oak.

GREATER OAK DAGGER MOTH
(LOBELIA DAGGER MOTH) *Acronicta lobeliae*

RECOGNITION Handsome caterpillar with two larval forms (one of which may represent an unrecognized species). *Last instar large, gray to smoky with variously developed pale middorsal and cream subdorsal stripes and skirt of long lateral setae about flanks.* Dorsum of A1 and A8 slightly raised. Look for yellow-orange splotch over each spiracle or about dorsal pinacula.
Body densely peppered with black spots which under a lens can be seen to be bases of minute black spines. One form (Connecticut): charcoal ground color with distinct, pale middorsal and subdorsal stripes, head coal-black above and white below; frons gray-black. Second form (Maryland and New Jersey): gray ground color; primary setal bases black, contrasting with ground; middorsal and subdorsal stripes vague; and head tan with cherry-red dorsal patches and abundant dark "snowflake" spotting over lobes (figured above). Larva to 5cm.

OCCURRENCE Woodlands and forests from southern Canada to Florida and Texas. Two generations over much of East with mature caterpillars from June through November; evidently three broods in Missouri.

COMMON FOODPLANTS Oak.

REMARKS The ultimate instar is well suited for a life on oak bark—its coloration, corona of lateral hairs, and somewhat flattened aspect enable the larva to disappear on an oak limb or trunk. Superficially the caterpillar resembles those of our bark-dwelling lasiocampids, e.g., tolypes and Dot-lined White (*Artace cribraria*). As noted above, I have found two distinctly different caterpillars that key to *Acronicta lobeliae*, one of which may represent a heretofore unrecognized species. The name "Lobelia Dagger" is a misnomer because the moth is an oak specialist—I offer Greater Oak Dagger as a replacement.

Acronicta morula

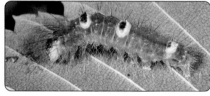

RECOGNITION Last instar *densely vested with brown, black, and white setae*. Setae over dorsum short and mostly of one length; those along sides long, white, and of variable lengths. *Black middorsal warts over A1, A4, and A8. Head black to either side of pale triangle with red over each lobe*; lobes mostly pale with dark spots forming arcs. Larva to 4.5cm. Penultimate instar lime green with yellow-edged, purple-brown spots over A1, A4, and A8; head with reddish patches and darker snowflake spotting (inset).

OCCURRENCE Fields, woodlands, and forest edges from Manitoba to Nova Scotia south to Georgia (mountains) and Texas. At least two generations as far north as Quebec, likely additional broods southward; mature caterpillars from early June through November.

COMMON FOODPLANTS Elm; other reported foodplants include apple, basswood, and hawthorn.

REMARKS Yet another changeling with two stunningly distinct larval forms. In Connecticut this moth is not common in many forested parts of the state even where American elm is relatively common. In upstate New York it does well in open habitats, e.g., along fencerows in agricultural landscapes. Young trees are especially likely to yield caterpillars. Southward, in the Appalachians, I associate it with mid-elevation forests. The penultimate instar perches on the upperside of a leaf blade. The coloration of the last instar suggests that its preferred resting site is over bark.

SMARTWEED CATERPILLAR
(SMEARED DAGGER MOTH) *Acronicta oblinita*

RECOGNITION Highly variable in coloration but nearly always some combination of black, yellow, red, and white, with black usually predominating. Consistently with *yellow lateral blotches that form broad interrupted spiracular stripe.* Often with *raised reddish setose warts over dorsum of thoracic and abdominal segments*, and field of white subdorsal spots that may connect to form stripe. Spiracles white. Setae mostly of one length, somewhat orange above and pale along sides, except for few longer hairs that extend from either end of body. Larva to 4cm.

OCCURRENCE Beaches, barrens, marshes, swamps, and other open habitats from southern Canada to Florida and Texas. At least two generations with mature caterpillars from late May through November over much of East; evidently three or more generations from Missouri southward.

COMMON FOODPLANTS Widely polyphagous with reports from many forbs (including smartweed), shrubs, and trees (softwoods and hardwoods).

REMARKS The Smartweed Caterpillar is occasionally reported as a pest of apple and other orchard trees as well as a variety of field crops. It is hard to imagine any *Acronicta* being so abundant as to cause economic injury; more likely its "pest" status is undeserved. I suspect that the caterpillar has attracted attention from economic entomologists simply because of its splendid coloration. In New England it is common in open wetlands and coastal strand communities. Unlike many other *Acronicta*, the larva forms a simple cocoon in leaves or debris, perhaps reflecting the fact that the Smartweed Caterpillar often lives in early successional habitats devoid of wood into which the caterpillar might bore.

Acronicta radcliffei

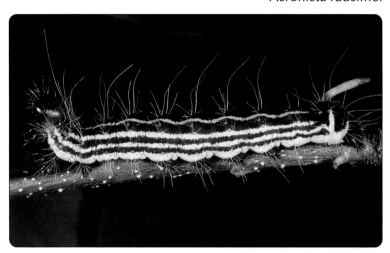

RECOGNITION Dark brown with prominent, *yellow middorsal, subdorsal, supraspiracular, and thickened subspiracular stripes.* Dark rump patch over A8. Thorax and abdomen with long white setae, those over dorsum greater than twice the length of segment that bears them. Larva to 3.5cm. Penultimate instar blue-green with broad, red-brown dorsal stripe, edged with yellow, extending length of body (inset).

OCCURRENCE Fields and woodlands from southern Canada to Georgia and Arkansas, but absent from many areas within this range. At least two generations with mature caterpillars from May through November.

COMMON FOODPLANTS Cherry and other members of rose family (Rosaceae) such as apple, chokeberry (*Aronia*), hawthorn, mountain ash, and serviceberry.

REMARKS Yet another dagger moth with very different middle and last instars. As noted above under the Yellow-haired Dagger, mimicry has been rarely reported as occurring in caterpillars. Last-instar Radcliffe's Daggers resemble many Datanas, so much so that seasoned entomologists and caterpillar aficionados commonly confuse them. One wonders if these two insects, as well as others, such as the Orange-striped Oakworm (*Anisota senatoria*) and Turbulent Phosphila (*Phosphila turbulenta*), have entangled their fates in a mimicry complex.

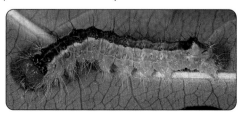

DAGGERS

INTERRUPTED DAGGER MOTH *Acronicta interrupta*

Manitoba to Nova Scotia south to Georgia and Arkansas. At least two broods with mature caterpillars from May onward. Reported from apple, birch, cherry, elm, hawthorn, oak, and silver maple.

STREAKED DAGGER MOTH *Acronicta lithospila*

Southern Canada to northern Florida and Texas. At least two broods with mature caterpillars from late May onward. Usually oak, chestnut, and related species; also reported from hickory and walnut.

RUDDY DAGGER MOTH *Acronicta rubricoma*

Southern Ontario to New York south to central Florida and Texas. At least two broods in South with mature caterpillars from late May until November. Primarily hackberry and elm.

RETARDED DAGGER MOTH *Acronicta retardata*

Manitoba to Nova Scotia south to Florida and Arkansas. At least two broods with mature caterpillars from late May to October. Maple.

SPLENDID DAGGER MOTH *Acronicta superans*

Manitoba to Newfoundland south to North Carolina (mountains) and Great Lakes States. At least two broods with mature caterpillars from early June to October. Principally apple, cherry, hawthorn, mountain ash, and other members of rose family (Rosaceae); also reported from birch and hazel.

TRITON DAGGER MOTH *Acronicta tritona*

Southern Canada to Missouri and Texas. At least two broods in much of South with mature caterpillars from late May onward. Cranberry, blueberry, and rhododendron (azaleas) (all members of the heath family, Ericaceae).

PLEASANT DAGGER MOTH *Acronicta laetifica*

Southern Canada to Florida and Texas. Two generations over much of range with mature caterpillars from May through November. Usually American hornbeam.

NONDESCRIPT DAGGER MOTH *Acronicta spinigera*

Manitoba to Maine south to Florida and Texas. At least two broods with mature caterpillars from late May onward. My lab-reared caterpillars preferred basswood over apple and elm.

Interrupted Dagger Moth

Streaked Dagger Moth

Ruddy Dagger Moth

Retarded Dagger Moth

Splendid Dagger Moth

Triton Dagger Moth

Pleasant Dagger Moth

Nondescript Dagger Moth

DAGGERS

IMPRESSIVE DAGGER MOTH *Acronicta impressa* complex

Transcontinental in Canada south in East to North Carolina (mountains). Two broods over much of range with mature caterpillars from late June to October. Alder, birch, blackberry, blueberry, oak, poplar, serviceberry, willow, and many other woody species.

FINGERED DAGGER MOTH *Acronicta dactylina*

Manitoba to Newfoundland south through Great Lakes States and northern Georgia (Florida record dubious). One generation over much of range with mature caterpillars in August and September. Principally alder, birch, poplar, and willow.

CONNECTED DAGGER MOTH *Acronicta connecta*

South Dakota to extreme southern Canada to Florida and Texas. At least two broods with mature caterpillars from late May to November. Willow.

DELIGHTFUL DAGGER MOTH *Acronicta vinnula*

Extreme southern Canada to Florida and Texas. At least two broods with mature caterpillars from late May to November. Elm.

COTTONWOOD DAGGER MOTH *Acronicta lepusculina*

Canada south to Florida and Texas. Two broods with mature caterpillars from late June onward. Poplar and willow.

NIGHT-WANDERING DAGGER MOTH *Acronicta noctivaga*

Canada south to Florida and Texas. At least two broods with mature caterpillars from late May to November. Usually aspen (and other poplars).

OVATE DAGGER MOTH *Acronicta ovata*

Manitoba to Maine south to North Carolina and Texas. Evidently with just a single brood with mature caterpillars mostly in July to August. Beech, chestnut, and oak.

CLEAR DAGGER MOTH *Acronicta clarescens* (= *A. pruni*)

Ontario to Maine south to Florida and Texas. At least two broods with mature caterpillars from late May to November. Apple, cherry, hawthorn, plum, and other members of rose family (Rosaceae).

Impressive Dagger Moth

Fingered Dagger Moth

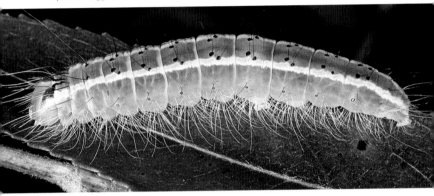

Connected Dagger Moth

Delightful Dagger Moth

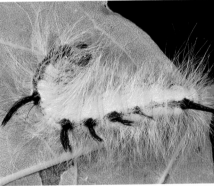

Cottonwood Dagger Moth

Night-wandering Dagger Moth

Ovate Dagger Moth

Clear Dagger Moth

HENRY'S MARSH MOTH
Simyra henrici

RECOGNITION Beautifully patterned in cream and black with *bright orange setal warts*. Dorsum mostly black. Flanks between creamy subdorsal and subspiracular stripes mostly yellow with black mottling. Orange setal warts above level of spiracles with mix of both pale and black setae. Spiracles bright white. Larva to 3.5cm.

OCCURRENCE Wetlands and fields from Canada south to Florida and Texas. Two generations in Connecticut, presumably more southward with mature caterpillars from June through November.

COMMON FOODPLANTS Broad generalist consuming grasses, forbs, and low-growing woody species.

REMARKS This species is common in grassy fields bordering wetlands. My fall semester general entomology students routinely turn up individuals in their sweep samples. The two drably colored caterpillars in the inset are mummies: each contains more than a dozen *Aleiodes stigmator* wasp pupae. The adult braconid wasps issued shortly after this image was taken in mid-July. Forbes (1954) takes note of the unusual cocooning behavior of Henry's Marsh Moth: "The cocoon is made in a distinctive way when a broad grass or sedge blade is available; the blade is sharply folded down near the middle, then after about an inch is sharply folded up again, enclosing a rounded-triangular area in which the fairly strong cocoon is spun." The pupa overwinters.

Polygrammate hebraeicum

RECOGNITION *Lime green with pale subdorsal stripe and creamy addorsal spots at midsegment and middorsal spots along caudal margin of T2–A8.* Dorsal and subdorsal setae longer than segments that bear them. Short anal prolegs extend back from body. Late-stage last instar (bark-tunneling form) blue-gray and mottled with spots and somewhat yellowish pinacula figured in inset. Larva to 3cm. Caterpillar of *Comachara cadburyi*, also a sour gum-feeder, is similar. Its dorsal and subdorsal setae are paler and shorter than segments that bear them and the addorsal spots are missing.

OCCURRENCE Swamps and mesic woodlands from Ontario to Maine south to Florida and Texas. Evidently two generations in Northeast with mature caterpillars from June through October; two or three broods in Missouri.

COMMON FOODPLANTS Sour gum.

REMARKS The pale conspicuously setose early instars "window" leaf blades by removing patches of green tissue from the lower surface, leaving the upper surface intact. The windows that remain are diagnostic. Curiously, two color forms occur in the last instar. The green form described above is the principal feeding stage; it rests on leaves. It is followed by a specialized transitory form whose charge is to excavate a chamber in bark or rotten wood in which pupation will take place—its blue-gray coloration is not unlike that of sour gum bark. The pupa overwinters.

HARRIS' THREE-SPOT
Harrisimemna trisignata

RECOGNITION Unmistakably bizarre: shiny black and white integument. *A8 grotesquely humped. A3 to A7 mounted with white saddle that gives way to streaks along outer face of each proleg.* Thoracic legs long, first two pairs mostly orange. Often with earlier (shed) head capsules adhering to thoracic setae (inset). Larva less than 3.5cm.

OCCURRENCE Wetlands and mesic woodlands from southern Canada to Florida and Texas. Evidently with at least two generations southward with mature caterpillars from July through October.

COMMON FOODPLANTS Apple, ash, blueberry, buck brush (*Ceanothus*), buttonbush, cherry, holly, honeysuckle, lilac, persimmon, viburnum, willow, winterberry, and many other woody species.

REMARKS By almost any measure, this is a strange animal. The caterpillar resembles a bird dropping, a spider, a pile of debris, and who knows what else. The white markings that literally run down the side of the body and shiny integument yield an overall effect of a repulsively gooey, freshly deposited bird-dropping. Yet, and for seemingly ineffable reasons, the caterpillar in life is also spiderlike. When my son Ryan first pointed out a Harris's Three-Spot caterpillar to me, I dismissed the animal as a spider, even after he urged a second look. When disturbed the caterpillar rocks with blurring rapidity from side to side in much the same way as do orb-weaving spiders that violently tug at their webs when alarmed. The caterpillar bores into wood, excavating an elongate chamber where it will pass the winter as a pupa.

Raphiine caterpillars have the first dorsal seta on T2 borne on a small conical process. Like the Pantheidae, they possess characteristics in common with the dagger moths (Acronictinae). Brothers feed on aspens, poplar, and willow. There are two Eastern species.

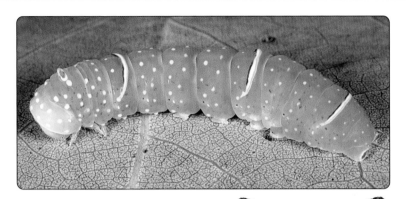

THE BROTHER
Raphia frater

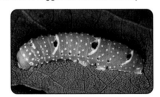

RECOGNITION *Blue-green to bright lime-green with yellow spotting and transverse yellow line running over A1, A5, and A8.* Yellow lines often edged with red or white anteriorly. T2 with rose to red dorsal conical projections that are yellowish at their bases. Abrupt Brother (*Raphia abrupta*) presumably has similar caterpillar. Both moths co-occur across much of East, although Abrupt Brother tends to be more common in Midwest and many areas in South. Larva to 3cm.

OCCURRENCE Edges of watercourses, wetlands, and forests from Canada south to New Jersey and Great Lakes States. Two generations with mature caterpillars from late June to October.

COMMON FOODPLANTS Aspen, poplar, and willow; records from alder and birch may be exceptional or erroneous.

REMARKS The caterpillars rest on the underside of leaves by day and are easily found by turning branches or examining leaves from below. The short-legged larvae are readily dislodged with a beating stick. Over much of the East this is the most common Brother; the Abrupt Brother tends to be local and scarce, especially northward— I have never encountered it. According to McFarland (1964), members of this genus tunnel into pulpy wood to fashion their pupal cells, then overwinter as a pupa.

Litter Moths – Subfamily Herminiinae

Brown, rather undistinguished, slow-moving caterpillars with short, inconspicuous, and often peglike setae. Under magnification, integument appears granulose with minute creases or warts. The first pair of prolegs is sometimes reduced. They consume a wide range of organic matter that includes living foliage, epiphytic growth, senescent leaves, flowers, and fruit as well as fallen leaves. Most overwinter as half-grown caterpillars in leaf litter.

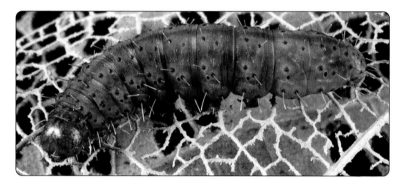

COMMON IDIA
Idia aemula

RECOGNITION Smoky brown with *orangish peglike setae* borne from black bases. Setae lightened at apex. Sometimes with vague charcoal middorsal and subdorsal stripes. "Pseudospiracle" (i.e., a darkened pit) present on T2 and T3. *Proleg on A3 reduced* in all Idias. Larva less than 2cm. There are a dozen or so Idias in the East—identifications should be based on reared adults.

OCCURRENCE Woodlands and forests from Canada south to Florida and Texas. Two or three generations in Northeast with mature caterpillars occurring nearly year-round.

COMMON FOODPLANTS Caterpillars may be reared to maturity on dead oak and cherry leaves.

REMARKS The Common Idia is one of the most abundant moths of Eastern woodlands, yet I have never found its larva in the wild. *Idia* caterpillars are secretive litter grazers that feed on fallen leaves. Female *Idia* will lay eggs in captivity if held in a container with some very lightly dampened peat and dead leaves. Larvae feed on non-vascular leaf tissues. The network of veins left by grazing larvae is lacelike—skeletonized white oak leaves are stunning. Given the numerical dominance of herminiines in woodlands in the East, it seems likely that they play at least a modest role in macrodecomposition of plant litter, nutrient cycling, and soil formation in some forest types—their numbers seem to be especially high in oak woodlands.

RECOGNITION Smoky with granular integument and short, amber peglike setae. *Black (D1) and tan, yellow, or orange (D2) hornlike projections alternate down length of abdomen. Hornlike projections appreciably smaller and in linear band across thoracic segments.* Lateral setae arising from black base perched on low scaly wart that may be somewhat orange in color. Head black, granulose, with conspicuous peglike setae. Larva less than 2.5cm.

OCCURRENCE Woodlands and forests from Canada south to Florida and Texas. Evidently with at least a partial second generation in Northeast with mature caterpillars from May to August; two full broods in Missouri.

COMMON FOODPLANTS Fungi and lichens; perhaps generalized on organic matter of the forest floor: Dale Schweitzer (pers. comm.) has found wild larvae on lower leaves of *Hibiscus syriacus* and reared them through on this foodplant.

REMARKS The setae and dorsal horns may be glandular. While I frequently see adults at my mercury vapor light, it is the bait trap in my yard that gets the greater amount of attention. Underwing hunters who sugar are especially familiar with this moth, as the adults of the Glossy Black Idia peak in abundance at the same season when underwing (*Catocala*) numbers are high. Idia caterpillars will eat fresh leaves but seem to prefer dead leaf litter. Tim McCabe (pers. comm.) has had success rearing herminiines on cherry; I have found dried leaves of white oak to be satisfactory for many herminiines as well. In the wild, caterpillars of the Glossy Black Idia are often found on or close to fallen wood. *Idia* are thought to overwinter as partially grown larvae.

DARK-SPOTTED PALTHIS
Palthis angulalis

RECOGNITION Small, mottled, brown caterpillars with low hump over A1 and *large angulate hump over A8. A7 with oblique white line* that may change to black on A8 and run up outer side of hump. Additional faint oblique white lines on anterior abdominal segments; stripe on A1 usually best developed. Integument with abundant minute spinules. Setal bases black. Larva to 2cm. Larva of Faint-spotted Palthis (*Palthis asopialis*) with larger, more toothlike integumental spinules (visible with lens); these especially evident over white areas on A8 (inset).

OCCURRENCE Woodlands and forests from Canada to Florida and Texas. Two generations with mature caterpillars from June until late fall over much of East; three or more generations from Missouri southward.

COMMON FOODPLANTS Extremely diverse in diet. Forbs, woody shrubs and trees, including conifers: e.g., alder, aster, basswood, birch, chestnut, fir, gale, goldenrod, ninebark, rhododendron, and spruce.

REMARKS The caterpillar eats both live and dead organic matter, be it leaves, flowers, or fruits. The Dark-spotted Palthis has even been reared from the feculae bundles produced by *Pococera robustella* (Family Pyralidae). The caterpillar regularly shows up in low numbers in beating samples. I have also encountered caterpillars of the Dark-spotted Palthis while searching low vegetation at night, especially during the fall. While Forbes (1954) reports that the larva overwinters, I have had some individuals overwinter as pupae in cocoons fashioned in leaf litter.

RECOGNITION   Brown, spindle-shaped with *reticulate red patterning* visible with hand lens. Often with yellow spotting between reddish reticulations. Setae short and inconspicuous. First three thoracic segments with black *setal bases aligned over top of body*, "pseudospiracle" (i.e., a darkened pit) present on T2 and T3. Larva to 2.5cm.

There are more than a dozen *Zanclognatha* in our region, several of which have not been reared. Adults should be reared to verify the identification.

OCCURRENCE   Woodlands and forests from southern Canada to Florida and Texas. One generation northward and two or more in South with mature caterpillars year-round.

COMMON FOODPLANTS   Diet incompletely known; caterpillars have been found on beech, hazel, hemlock, nettle, and red spruce; in captivity easily reared on dead oak leaves. Wilted leaves of herbs are also readily consumed.

REMARKS   John Lill (pers. comm.) has found egg clusters of the Early Zanclognatha containing 2 to 3 dozen eggs on the underside of beech leaves. Presumably the early instars start feeding on foliage, bark, and detritus, then drop to the ground when the leaves are shed. In the fall, caterpillars of the Early Zanclognatha turn up in beating samples from an array of forbs and woody species, including conifers. *Zanclognatha* species overwinter as partially grown larvae.

Zales, Underwings, and Kin – Subfamily Catocalinae

This is the largest owlet subfamily in the East with more than 150 widely distributed species. Dozens of additional species occur in Texas and Florida. Catocalines are especially diverse in the Neotropics. The subfamily is a heterogeneous grouping, possibly derived from more than one ancestral lineage (Kitching and Rawlins 1998). No characters are unique to its members. Many larvae are elongate with reduced or missing prolegs on A3 and a substantial proportion throw a loop into the body while walking. The pupa – the overwintering stage in all but the underwings (*Catocala*) – often has a waxy bloom. Most are foodplant specialists.

CURVE-LINED OWLET
Phyprosopus callitrichoides

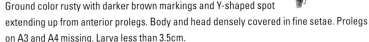

RECOGNITION Fantastically bizarre and wholly uncaterpillarlike: *long tentacular appendage over A2 and smaller recurved extension from dorsum of A3.* Ground color rusty with darker brown markings and Y-shaped spot extending up from anterior prolegs. Body and head densely covered in fine setae. Prolegs on A3 and A4 missing. Larva less than 3.5cm.

OCCURRENCE Woodlands and forest edges from Missouri to Ohio and New Hampshire south to Florida and Texas. Two broods north of Maryland with mature caterpillars from June onward; three broods in Missouri; presumably more southward.

COMMON FOODPLANTS Greenbrier.

REMARKS The caterpillar is a dead-leaf mimic. It quavers from side to side when disturbed, much like a leaf would do in a slight breeze. The pupa overwinters.

Hypsoropha hormos

RECOGNITION *Shape diagnostic.* Lime green and unmarked to heavily mottled in grays and black; green forms often with subdorsal black spots or stripe, especially in later instars. Pinacula often white, especially those over dorsum, with other white spotting inconspicuous or absent. *Note distinctive shape of anal prolegs.* Final instars may be quite barklike with a charcoal ground color that is mottled with whites and grays (inset). Larva to 3cm. Early instars are lime green and unmarked. Penultimates are often spotted with black.

OCCURRENCE Fields, woodlands, and forest edges from Kansas, Ohio, and New Jersey south to Florida and Texas. At least two generations over much of range with mature caterpillars from June onward; breeding year-round in Florida.

COMMON FOODPLANTS Persimmon; reports from sassafras likely erroneous.

REMARKS Caterpillars of the Small Necklace Moth, as well as those of the Large Necklace Moth (*Hypsoropha monilis*), are easily beaten from foliage, especially at night when they are feeding. The larvae of the two moths are easily distinguished: the head of the Small Necklace Moth (*H. hormos*) is green or mostly gray and mottled with black, while that of the Large Necklace Moth is pale orange with two pairs of black spots. The prepupa overwinters in New Jersey (Dale Schweitzer, pers. comm.).

LARGE NECKLACE MOTH
Hypsoropha monilis

RECOGNITION Smoky green to black with broad charcoal middorsal stripe and abundant speckling of white spots along sides of body. *Head pale orange with large black blotch to either side of triangle* and small lateral black spot enclosed by stemmata. Larva to 4cm. Earlier instars dark and with numerous white spots, most of which are aligned into longitudinal stripes (inset).

OCCURRENCE Fields, woodlands, and forest edges from central Missouri, southern Ohio, and southern New Jersey to Gulf. One principal generation with most mature caterpillars in June and July in New Jersey; evidently a partial second generation in Missouri.

COMMON FOODPLANTS Persimmon.

REMARKS The caterpillars are sawfly mimics, even down to the lateral black eyespot. The gregarious larvae leave the foliage at or before dawn and spend the day in litter and surface soil beneath the foodplant. The caterpillars move back up onto the plant at dusk. The response of the caterpillar if poked or pinched is rapid—it reels around and simultaneously bites its attacker and vomits a clear orange liquid. The prepupal larva overwinters in a cocoon in the litter.

Panopoda rufimargo

RECOGNITION Lime green with variously developed *subdorsal stripe and abundant minute, smoky to blue spots*. Middorsal stripe weak and broken or absent. Oblique cream to yellow lines below spiracle on A1–A8. Prolegs on A3 and A4 reduced in size; *prolegs with end splayed fore and aft, reddened*; anal prolegs large and directed backwards. Head rounded, green with abundant dark speckling, usually with transverse yellow line over triangle and red antennae. Larva to 4cm. Brown Panopoda (*Panopoda carneicosta*) caterpillars similar but feeding on hickory (inset); characters given in Forbes (1954) for the separation of panopodas appear to vary within our species. The Orange Panopoda (*P. repanda*), found throughout the Southeast, is thought to feed principally on live oak.

OCCURRENCE Barrens, woodlands, and forests from Minnesota to Maine south to Florida and Texas. One generation in Connecticut; evidently two or more broods in South with mature caterpillars from June onward.

COMMON FOODPLANTS Beech and oak.

REMARKS Caterpillars are common in beating samples from late summer and early fall. While seemingly a rather plain insect when seen from a distance, this caterpillar is quite beautiful when seen with a hand lens. The abundant spotting, not visible to the unaided eye, is often azurite or lapis blue, and the reds of the legs and antennae surprisingly bright. Disturbed larvae may "jump" from their perch, thrashing about wildly for a second or two. The pupa overwinters.

COMMON OAK MOTH
Phoberia atomaris

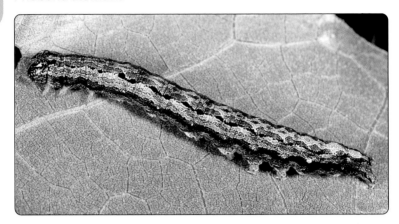

RECOGNITION Variegated pale to deep chocolate-brown with *tapered posterior. Beaded or wavy, black subdorsal stripe* best expressed over abdominal segments. Obscure middorsal "stripe" outwardly edged with doubled, wavy addorsal stripes that may form diamond-shaped spots over abdominal segments. Proleg on A3 about half as large as that on A4,

which in turn is half the size of those on A5 and A6. Dark spiracular stripe, which includes black spiracles, especially prominent rearward. *Often with a whitish spot above and behind spiracle (visible with a lens) with spot on A7 often enlarged.* Head with extensive mottling, especially notable to either side of paler triangle; *many individuals with white comma-shaped spot over each lobe.* Larva to 4cm. *Phoberia orthosioides*, a closely related species mostly of the Atlantic Coastal Plain and Great Lakes Region, probably not distinguishable as a caterpillar. The oak-feeding larva of *Cissusa indiscreta* figured by Miller and Hammond (2004) from the Pacific Coast States has much in common with the *Phoberia* caterpillar figured here. The life history of its Eastern counterpart, the Black-dotted Brown (*Cissusa spadix*), is unknown.

OCCURRENCE Barrens, woodlands, and forest edges from Kansas to Massachusetts south to Florida and Texas. One generation with mature caterpillars in late spring.

COMMON FOODPLANTS Oak.

REMARKS Caterpillars of the Common Oak Moth are not commonly encountered unless you search foliage by night or closely examine bark in late spring and early summer. It is one of the most common caterpillars under burlap bands used to census Gypsy Moth caterpillars in May and June. When mildly alarmed the caterpillar plays dead or draws the head under the body. Agitated caterpillars may hurl themselves from their perch and thrash about, snapping their bodies like wound rubber bands. The pupa overwinters.

Zale is a large and taxonomically challenging genus with some 25 Eastern species. The pine-feeders can be bewilderingly difficult to identify both as larvae and adults. Tim McCabe and Dale Schweitzer, the authorities on the systematics and natural history of the genus, are especially familiar with the Eastern fauna. Forbes (1954) describes many of the caterpillars, although he over-diagnoses several species. Caterpillars of eight of the eastern conifer-feeding zales are figured by Maier *et al.* (2004). Tim McCabe has an excellent collection of larval images.

Zale caterpillars resemble those of underwings (*Catocala*), but lack the subventral fringe (rootlet) setae. The first two pairs of abdominal prolegs are reduced in size. Like underwings, *Zale* caterpillars have dark spots along the venter of the abdomen; however, the venter is never tinted in reds and yellows as is commonly the case in *Catocala*. The pupa shares the same waxy blue bloom present in underwings and other catocalines. Identifications should be based on reared adults or, in some cases, foodplant associations—save vouchers or take images of your adults while they are fresh. *Zale* caterpillars are highly mobile as first instars, often wandering long distances before they begin feeding. Most prefer young leaf tissue, especially in early instars, then consume older leaves and needles in late instars. *Zale* overwinter as pupae in litter. The adults come to light and baits, and can be especially numerous in pine woodlands. Baiting is a productive means of securing females. Other life history information, applicable across the genus, appears in the species accounts.

HORRID ZALE *Zale horrida*

Canada to Florida and Texas. Its long flight season suggests two to three generations with mature caterpillars to be expected from May to November. Viburnum.

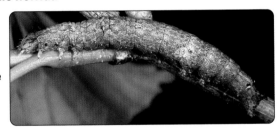

OKEFENOKEE ZALE *Zale perculta*

Southern Georgia and northern Florida. One generation in spring. Climbing fetter-bush (*Pieris phillyreifolia*).

BROWN-SPOTTED ZALE
Zale helata

RECOGNITION Green form with bright white middorsal, white subdorsal, and brick-red spiracular stripes; latter often edged below with white. *Stripes commonly with some black edging over back half of each segment.* Other forms with green ground color replaced with red or brown, but otherwise similarly marked. *A8 without distinct ridge or raised setal warts. Head often with white to yellow "V" over each lobe.* Larva to 4cm. One form of the Pine False Looper (*Zale duplicata*) resembles the individual figured here for the Brown-spotted Zale, but it is distinguished by larger dorsal warts on A8 (Forbes 1954) which are sometimes connected by a low ridge. Additionally, the middorsal stripe is wavy and fragmented (Maier *et al.* 2004) and not as well developed as that of the Brown-spotted Zale. It is believed to be a white pine specialist.

OCCURRENCE Barrens and pine woodlands from Manitoba to Maine south to Florida and Texas. One generation with mature caterpillars from June to July.

COMMON FOODPLANTS Both hard and soft pines.

REMARKS The ground color of most of our pine-feeding *Zale* caterpillars is gray or brown. Caterpillars of the Brown-spotted Zale rest on needles with the head wedged near the base of a needle fascicle (Maier *et al.* 2004), in the same fashion as many of our angles (*Macaria*). Larvae, especially in early instars, consume young needles that are not yet fully hardened. Across much of its range the Brown-spotted Zale is the most widespread and commonly encountered of some dozen pine-feeding eastern zales.

RECOGNITION Highly variable, usually barklike, striped, red- to gray-brown to charcoal or even black with slight hump at rear of A1 and low ridge over A8. Beautiful lichen-mimicking forms occasionally turn up. *Intersegmental area between A1 and A2 often yellow* (only visible when caterpillar is distended or when a loop is thrown into body). Subdorsal and spiracular stripes darkest and becoming more so rearward. Posterior dorsal seta (D2) often borne from low ridgelike wart, which may be subtended by very small elongate white spot. Head with black mottling over vertex and pale brown to white lines over sides and triangle. Larva to 5cm. I cannot reliably separate the caterpillars of Lunate Zale from those of Colorful Zale (*Zale minerea*) (*see* Remarks).

OCCURRENCE Woodlands and forests from southern Canada to Florida and Texas. One or two generations in New England and Upper Midwest, evidently three or four in New Jersey with last emigrating (Ferguson 1991, Dale Schweitzer, pers. comm.); mature caterpillars from May onward.

COMMON FOODPLANTS Apple, blackberry, cherry, plum, sensitive plant (*Cassia*), willow, and wisteria for certain, but evidently also from oak and other woody plants, and occasionally forbs.

REMARKS I have many images of *Zale* caterpillars that are assignable to either the Lunate Zale or Colorful Zale, but am unable to sort them further. I leave it to others to find characters or life history attributes that will insure their proper identification. Such an effort might be aided by including images of the labrum, head patterning, and spots along the venter of the abdomen. Only recently, Ferguson (1991) recognized that the Lunate Zale is a migrant over the northern portion of its range—evidently it overwinters as pupa as far north as New Jersey (Dale Schweitzer, pers. comm.).

WASHED-OUT ZALE
Zale metatoides

RECOGNITION Larva green or mottled in browns and grays with vague striping. Most consistent stripes include beaded middorsal, dark subdorsal, and subtending paler supraspiracular that runs to anal proleg. Usually with *pale lateral patches toward back of A1 and over proleg on A4*. Oblique subdorsal patches, darker forward and paler rearward, over back third of A1–A7. Head with white oval to lens-shaped spot 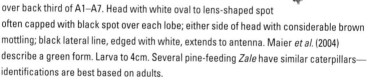 often capped with black spot over each lobe; either side of head with considerable brown mottling; black lateral line, edged with white, extends to antenna. Maier *et al.* (2004) describe a green form. Larva to 4cm. Several pine-feeding *Zale* have similar caterpillars—identifications are best based on adults.

OCCURRENCE Barrens and pine woodlands from Manitoba to Massachusetts south to Georgia and Mississippi. One generation with mature caterpillars from late June to August.

COMMON FOODPLANTS Hard pines such as jack, pitch, red, scrub, shortleaf, and Virginia.

REMARKS Over much of the East the Washed-out Zale is one of the most frequently encountered pine-feeding zales, second only to the Brown-spotted Zale. In the Appalachian foothills in late May and early June, this and Esther Moth (*Hypagyrtis esther*) are among the most common caterpillars in beating samples from Virginia pine. The Washed-out Zale is one of a complex of some dozen eastern pine-feeding zales that vex all but the most-seasoned owlet enthusiasts. Female *Zale* oviposit readily if held with some foodplant foliage. A little sponge square (1cm on each side) or cotton ball soaked in sugar water will serve as a feeding station. Forbes (1954) notes *Zale* caterpillars as being quite muscular, capable of hurling themselves from their perch if threatened—keep this in mind if you plan to handpick your quarry.

GREEN-DUSTED ZALE *Zale aeruginosa*

Missouri to Maine south to Florida and Arkansas. Two generations over much of East with mature caterpillars from June to October. Oak.

BLACK-EYED ZALE *Zale curema*

New York to Maine south to North Carolina (mountains). One generation in Northeast with mature caterpillars from July to August; two broods in Missouri. Pitch and other hard pines.

BOLD-BASED ZALE *Zale lunifera*

Canada to Florida and Texas. One generation range-wide with mature caterpillars from March (Florida) to July. Beach plum and cherry.

ONE-LINED ZALE *Zale unilineata*

Manitoba to Maine south to Georgia and northern Arkansas. One principal generation with mature caterpillars in June and July. Locust.

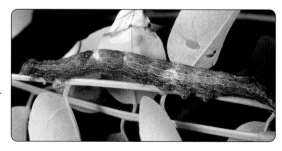

LOCUST UNDERWING
Euparthenos nubilis

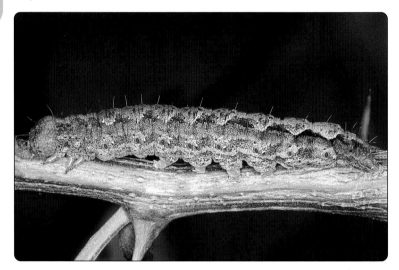

RECOGNITION Broad, crenulate, tan, yellow-brown, or brown stripes alternating with darker stripes. *Stout, more cutwormlike than most catocalines. Often with a pale spot behind each spiracle on A1–A7.* When present, easily recognized by subdorsal, crescent-shaped cluster of four creamy spots on A1. Beaded middorsal stripe often edged with black over posterior abdominal segments. *Prolegs on A3 reduced.* No black spots on venter. Larva to 5.5cm.

OCCURRENCE Abandoned fields, roadsides, and woodlands from Nebraska to southern Ontario and Maine to northern Florida and northern Arkansas. Two generations over much of range with mature caterpillars from June onward.

COMMON FOODPLANTS Locust, especially black locust.

REMARKS The coloration of the Locust Underwing caterpillar would suggest that it spends its days on the lower trunk or on the ground. Early instars are common in beating samples from the foodplant. According to Forbes (1954), the genus represents a basal offshoot of the lineage leading to true underwings (*Catocala*). But as pointed out by my colleague Richard Peigler (in litt.), one would be hard pressed to find evidence of a close association when comparing the larvae of the two genera. Adults are common at light and bait. The pupa overwinters.

RECOGNITION Barklike, elongate, mottled in grays, pinks (inset), and/or browns. Ridge over A8 edged with black posteriorly; black extended laterally as an oblique line toward spiracle. Dorsum and sides of *A1 often noticeably lighter than T3 and A2. Head usually with white spot over each lobe;* fine black line running from eyes to antenna. *Subventral fringe setae (rootlets) absent.* Prominent *brown spot on venter of A3* and less conspicuous spots on A4 and A5. First two prolegs (on A3 and A4) reduced. Larva to 4cm.

OCCURRENCE Swamplands and mesic woodlands from Missouri to southern Maine to Florida and Texas. Two generations through most of East with mature caterpillars from May onward.

COMMON FOODPLANTS Sour gum.

REMARKS Middle and late instars rest on bark by day. Because gum trees are short and their bark is smooth, caterpillars can be located by visual searches, but beating usually yields caterpillars in number. I recall an afternoon in early August along the shores of Lake Michigan where caterpillars of the False Underwing and Hebrew (*Polygrammate hebraeicum*) were so common in my beating samples that I had to individually reattach several in my hopeless search to find caterpillars of Cadbury's Lichen Moth (*Comachara cadburyi*), which, unbeknownst to me at the time, had finished feeding weeks earlier. The pupa overwinters.

MAPLE LOOPER
Parallelia bistriaris

RECOGNITION Highly variable in coloration and
patterning, but usually some shade of tan, brown,
red, or gray; occasionally with alternating dark and
light coloration (inset). *Ridge over A8 edged with
black rearward.* Head diagnostic: *black line from
vicinity of subdorsum of T1 to antenna; narrow black
lateral line also reaching antenna;* and often with dark
coloration to either side of triangle and dorsal midline.

Venter with dark spot on A3 and A4. Anal proleg with fine black line on outer face.
Subventral fringe setae (rootlets) absent. Prolegs on A3 and A4 diminutive. Larva to 4cm.

OCCURRENCE Woodlands and forests from Minnesota to Nova Scotia south to Florida
and Texas. Two or more generations with mature caterpillars from late May onward.

COMMON FOODPLANTS Maple, especially red; other reported hosts include
yellow and white birch, and walnut.

REMARKS All my collections of the Maple Looper have been associated with red and
silver maple. Last instars perch along twigs and branches fully extended lengthwise. The
pupa overwinters.

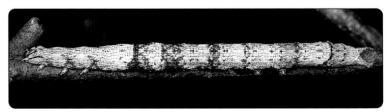

RECOGNITION Coloration and patterning highly variable; often *tan to pale brown, striped; prolegs absent on A3 and A4.* Pale stripe below spiracle a composite of two pale outer stripes and beige inner stripe, runs forward to the antenna. Thin white middorsal stripe edged with tan to reddish-brown stripes that, in turn, are outwardly edged with

prominent white addorsal stripes. All stripes extending onto head. Larva to 4cm. Caterpillars of Forage Looper Moth (*Caenurgina erechtea*) and Vetch Looper Moth (*Caenurgia chloropha*) (inset) are similarly marked. Characters given by Forbes (1954) for the separation of the three species are contradicted by my images. A legume-feeding relative, the Toothed Somberwing (*Euclidia cuspidea*), co-occurs with this trinity over much of the East. Its caterpillar, also striped in a similar fashion, is best recognized by the presence of reduced prolegs on A4. Larval variation within this group of loopers is considerable—identifications are best based on adults.

OCCURRENCE Farmlands, fields, and roadsides from southern Canada to Florida and Texas. Multiple generations over much of East with mature caterpillars from April onward.

COMMON FOODPLANTS Legumes seem to be preferred, but also grasses and many other herbaceous and occasionally woody plants.

REMARKS This caterpillar frequently turns up in sweep samples from fields and meadows in the summer and fall. It and related loopers are especially common in nighttime samples. The Clover Looper Moth is frequently reported as a pest of legumes. The pupa overwinters.

Catocala is the fourth largest genus of macrolepidopteran moths in North America with more than 110 species; approximately 75 of these occur in the East. Their size, beauty, and habits have made them a favorite with collectors. All of our species overwinter as eggs laid in bark crevices or in litter at the base of the foodplant. The caterpillars are elongate with dark spots along the venter; many species possess thickened subventral fringe setae (rootlets). Interestingly, the venter of the last instar may be tinted with the same red or yellow colors that will be found in the adult's hindwing. Larval coloration can be exceedingly variable (*see* The Little Wife, page 364). Some 40 Eastern species are figured in Barnes and McDunnough (1918). Forbes (1954) provides a larval key for nearly all the Eastern species.

Many *Catocala* are new-leaf specialists that starve if forced to feed on older foliage, although most of the hickory-feeders consume mature leaves. They are strong, active crawlers that move many meters each day in search of food or shelter. Late instars rest by day along the trunk, tucked into crevices or crammed under flaps of bark or descend into grasses and other nearby shelters at the base of their foodplant, then move onto foliage to feed at dusk. All are dietary specialists: especially important groups include the legume (Fabaceae), oak (Fagaceae), rose (Rosaceae), walnut (Juglandaceae), wax-myrtle (Myricaceae), and willow (Salicaceae) families.

Beating will yield early and middle instars or late instars if carried out at night. Species that feed on large trees are not so easily secured as few branches are at a height where leaves can be expected or beating is effective. Searches of lower trunks can be very productive about four to six weeks prior to the beginning of the adult flight season. (*See* page 368, Ultronia Underwing, for additional comments about searching for underwing caterpillars.) The larva spins a sparse cocoon, usually in leaf litter.

Baiting is an excellent means of securing females. Eggs may be obtained by holding females in brown paper bags. For most species it will be necessary to feed females over a period of several to many nights and offer a piece of bark or twigs of a suitable food-plant to stimulate egg-laying behaviors. Be patient, some species wait until late summer before they begin laying. Females often push their eggs into what seem to be impossibly tight places such as under the inside seam of a paper bag. Hold eggs out-doors over the winter months and then start checking for the hatchlings about the time of budbreak. It is impossible to do justice to our *Catocala* fauna in a guide of this size. Only 14 species are figured: six in full page treatments and eight additional common or otherwise noteworthy species in abbreviated accounts. Sargent's (1976) "Legion of Night" is a rich source of taxonomic, historical, and biological information about this beautiful group of insects.

Catocala amica

RECOGNITION Small *Catocala* ranging from pale gray to charcoal. *Dorsal setal bases mostly black over thorax becoming red-orange rearwards. A8 humped with conical orange warts.* Body broadest at A5; this segment bears low dorsal hump. Variously developed dark saddle over A5–A6 that reaches to proleg on both segments. Larva to 4cm.

The closely related *Catocala lineella* may be indistinguishable as a larva; it prefers red oaks (*see* Remarks) (inset).

OCCURRENCE Barrens and woodlands from South Dakota, southern Canada, and Maine to Florida and Texas. One generation with mature caterpillars from May to early July.

COMMON FOODPLANTS Oak, especially white oaks.

REMARKS *Catocala lineella*, formerly considered to be a form of the Girlfriend Underwing, has been restored to full species status as had been advocated by early workers. An additional member of the complex that occurs in the Southeast remains undescribed. Members of this species group are among our most abundant underwings. As is generally the case with *Catocala*, burlap banding is an effective method for obtaining late instars. Caterpillars will start showing up under burlap about the time the leaves are fully expanded. Many of our underwings are named after wives, lovers, and girlfriends. For an enjoyable accounting of how many of our *Catocala* got their names, read the first chapter of Sargent (1976).

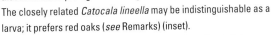

EPIONE UNDERWING
Catocala epione

RECOGNITION Drab, medium-sized *Catocala*, weakly striped in browns, grays, and subdued pale tones; *somewhat plump-looking for a Catocala*. Vague zigzagging subdorsal and spiracular stripes. Body smooth and without knobs or bumps. *Subventral fringe setae lacking.* Dorsal setae borne from small whitened bases. Venter with lance-shaped black spots

(these are more rounded in other hickory-feeders). Front of head with *prominent, black, upside down "W;"* each lobe streaked with reddish brown lines. Larva to 6cm.

OCCURRENCE Woodlands from Wisconsin, southern Ontario, and Maine to Florida and Texas. One generation with mature caterpillars in June and July.

COMMON FOODPLANTS Hickory, principally shagbark (*Carya ovata*), pignut (*C. glabra*), and mockernut (*C. tomentosa*); not bitternut (*C. cordiformis*). Small trees and saplings only.

REMARKS The Epione Underwing is but one of many underwings that feed on hickory. In Connecticut 14 species of *Catocala* feed on shagbark hickory. It makes one wonder if there is any limit to the number of caterpillar species that can share a single resource—in this case the leaves of shagbark hickory. While burlap banding is effective for the collection of *Catocala* caterpillars that feed on trees with smooth bark, the method is ineffective on shagbark hickory and other trees that have an abundance of natural hiding places. The most efficient means by which to acquire late-instar shagbark-feeders is to lay down a set of white bedsheets under saplings and small trees and use a baseball bat (made of hickory, of course) to rap branches and small trunks. Early in the season, searching leaves during the day works for both early and middle instars.

Catocala ilia

RECOGNITION Large *Catocala* with exceptionally variable markings. Usually recognizable by its *rosy red underside* and row of elongate, midventral black spots on A1–A8 (these common to most *Catocala*). Most forms with vague *dark shading over area between A5–A6.* No conspicuous warts or humps, but *rear of A5 with a slightly raised dorsal ridge.* Head with black band enclosing whitish front. Subventral rootlet setae short and stubby. Larva to 7.5cm.

OCCURRENCE Barrens, woodlands, and forests from southern Canada to Florida and Texas. One generation with mature caterpillars from April (Florida) to early July.

COMMON FOODPLANTS Oak.

REMARKS This is one of the East's most abundant underwings. Burlap bands on oak will consistently yield caterpillars about a month after leaf out. While most caterpillars are gray and essentially bark-colored, very occasionally spectacular lichen mimics are encountered. To what extent such forms are inducible has not been studied. Similar "lichen forms" occur in the genus *Zale* as well. Underwings may throw their fecal pellets several body lengths by quickly flicking their rear to one side at the same moment that they release a dropping. Moths, being creatures of the night, are masters of chemical communication, possessing a seemingly endless array of scents and scent-releasing structures. Male underwings (*Catocala*), for example, have a fold on the tibia of the second leg that holds a fascicle of long straw-colored scales that are laden with pheromones. During courtship the male may reveal his scales; when fully displayed they form an impressive brush along the outer face of his tibia.

THE LITTLE WIFE
Catocala muliercula

RECOGNITION Large *Catocala* with several color forms. *Quadri-colored caterpillars smoky above, yellow over subdorsum, rusty to red laterally, and white to cream subventrally. Bicolored larvae dull brick red above with white subventer.* Various combinations link these two forms. Setal bases white. Prolegs on A3–A7 pink to orange with two spots on outer face. Head striped in reds and yellow with or without black "W" mark. Larva to 6.5cm. Caterpillars may be indistinguishable from those of Bay Underwing (*Catocala badia*), which occurs mostly along the coast from New Jersey to Maine.

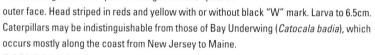

OCCURRENCE Open sandy areas, barrens, and coastal strand communities from Kansas to southeastern Massachusetts south to Florida and Texas, locally common along the Atlantic Coastal Plain. One generation with mature caterpillars from April to July.

COMMON FOODPLANTS Bayberry and wax myrtle (*Myrica*).

REMARKS This species is included to showcase the color polymorphism exhibited by many underwing species. While most members of our *Catocala* fauna are well represented by a single image, there are others, especially those associated with the wax myrtle (Myricaceae) and walnut (Juglandaceae) families that are highly variable such as The Little Wife figured here. Caterpillars are easily obtained by beating bayberry and wax myrtle almost anywhere along the Atlantic coast.

Catocala relicta

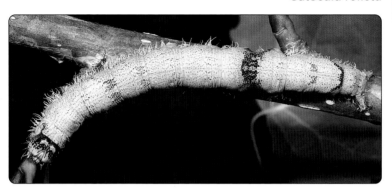

RECOGNITION *Large, pale, smooth caterpillar with dark saddle over A5–A6* that reaches to proleg on both segments. Low ridge over posterior half of A5. *Subventral fringe setae long and numerous.* A8 with low dorsal ridge, edged with black rearward; below ridge, black extends toward spiracle. Head with dark band over top that gives way to black mottling at  about level of triangle; each lobe with white to orange spot above. Midventral black spots present on T2, T3, and A3–A7. Larva to 7.5cm.

OCCURRENCE Forests across Canada south in East to northern New Jersey, western Maryland, and Missouri. One generation with mature caterpillars from late June to early July.

COMMON FOODPLANTS Aspen and poplar; also willow.

REMARKS Both the caterpillar and the adult of the White Underwing are superbly camouflaged for a life on trees with light-colored bark. In addition to the foodplants, the adults also perch on paper birch. The subventral fringe setae characteristic of many *Catocala* and other bark-resting caterpillars are often called "shadow elimination hairs." Such setae are common among bark-resting caterpillars, be these inchworms, owlets, or tent caterpillars. I prefer to think of these as "outline elimination setae," shadow or no shadow. Additionally these fringes make it possible for would-be predators to walk over the top of a hunkered down caterpillar and provide physical separation between predator and the caterpillar's body proper. The markings on the head are a good match for a leaf or bud scar. Underwings are among the most easily photographed caterpillars— they settle quickly if offered a perch on bark.

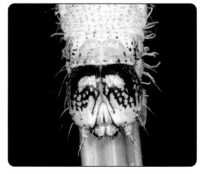

UNDERWINGS

ANDROMEDA UNDERWING *Catocala andromedae*

Great Lakes States, southern Quebec, and Maine to Florida and Texas. One generation with mature caterpillars from late April (Florida) through June. Blueberry and rhododendron.

SWEETFERN UNDERWING *Catocala antinympha*

Canada south to New Jersey, Maryland, and Great Lakes States. One generation with mature caterpillars from June to early July. Sweet fern (*Comptonia*).

SCARLET UNDERWING *Catocala coccinata*

Southern Canada to Florida and Texas. One generation with mature caterpillars from May to July. Especially red oaks.

HAWTHORN UNDERWING *Catocala crataegi*

Manitoba to Nova Scotia south to Florida and Texas. One generation with mature caterpillars from June into early July. Apple and hawthorn.

INCONSOLABLE UNDERWING *Catocala insolabilis*

South Dakota, Ohio, and (historically) southern Ontario and much of New England to Florida and Arkansas. One generation with mature caterpillars in May and June. Pignut and related hickories.

OBSCURE UNDERWING *Catocala obscura*

Missouri, Illinois, southern Ontario, and Massachusetts to northern Gerogia and Arkansas. One generation with mature caterpillars from June into July. Shagbark hickory.

THE BRIDE *Catocala neogama*

South Dakota to Maine to northern Florida and Texas. One generation with mature caterpillars from May to July. Butternut and black walnut (both *Juglans*).

SORDID UNDERWING *Catocala sordida*

Manitoba to Nova Scotia south to northern Florida and Texas. One generation with mature caterpillars from April to July. Blueberry, especially lowbush. Fringe setae nearly absent.

Andromeda Underwing

Sweetfern Underwing

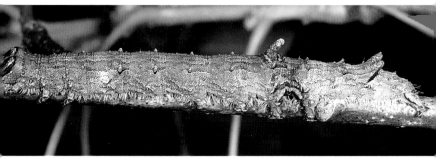

Scarlet Underwing

Hawthorn Underwing

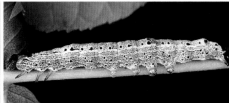

Inconsolable Underwing

Obscure Underwing

The Bride

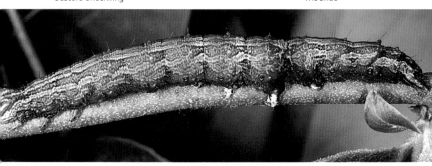

Sordid Underwing

ULTRONIA UNDERWING
Catocala ultronia

RECOGNITION Medium-sized *Catocala* with *elongate fleshy, pointed protuberance from dorsum of A5.* Often with pale lateral patch forward of protuberance and rusty lateral patch rearward. Setal bases along dorsum of body raised: bases shiny black, upper portions orange-red. A8 with prominent dorsal ridge connecting orange setal bases; *flank of ridge marked with black line that ends above spiracle.* "Face" usually framed by contrasting black line that reaches from vertex to eyes. Larva to 5.5cm.

OCCURRENCE Late successional fields, woodlands, and forests from southern Canada to Florida and Texas. One generation with mature caterpillars from April to early August.

COMMON FOODPLANTS Principally cherry and plum (*Prunus*) species, but also reported from apple, hawthorn, and other members of rose family (Rosaceae).

REMARKS Although an occasional ravenous caterpillar may be found feeding during the day, underwing (*Catocala*) caterpillars, as their coloration would suggest, spend most of the day resting on bark. To locate late instars, search branches and the trunk: scrutinize crevices, inspect under flaps of bark, and examine about the trunk where grasses and other low-growing vegetation come into contact with the stem. Inspecting foliage and beating may be productive for early and middle instars which perch on the foliage and twigs and branches. Nocturnal searches, when the caterpillars are feeding, can be especially fruitful. I have collected numerous species of underwing caterpillars from beneath the burlap bands used to census Gypsy Moth caterpillar populations (*see* Finding Caterpillars, page 15).

FIGURE-SEVEN MOTH *Drasteria grandirena*

Wisconsin to Nova Scotia south to Florida and Texas. One generation northward with mature caterpillars in late summer; at least two broods southward. Witch hazel.

THIN-LINED OWLET *Isogona tenuis*

Missouri, southern Ohio, and New Jersey to Florida and Texas. Two generations northward; additional broods southward. Hackberry.

MOONSEED MOTH *Plusiodonta compressipalpis*

Manitoba to Connecticut south to northern Florida and Texas. Two generations northward; additional broods southward. Moonseed vine.

LEGUME CATERPILLAR *Selenisa sueroides*

Southern Georgia south through Florida west to Texas. Breeding year-round in Keys. Various legumes.

Fruit-piercing Moths – Subfamily Calpinae (= Ophiderinae in part)

Adults of this largely tropical subfamily have a unique tongue or proboscis that is highly fortified apically. Calpine caterpillars from two tribes, the Anomiini (*Anomis*) and Gonopterini (*Gonodonta*), bear an additional seta below the second dorsal seta (D2) on A1–A6. In the latter tribe, the crochets at the ends of each series may be reduced in size.

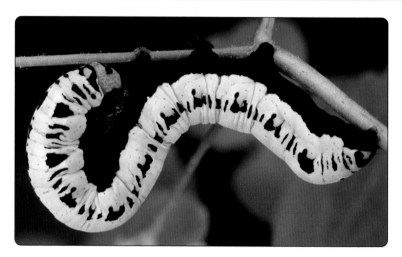

CANADIAN OWLET
Calyptra canadensis

RECOGNITION Dorsum *waxy white with scattered middorsal black spots*. Prothoracic shield yellow and black with middorsal black "H." Broad black supraspiracular band broken into several spots on each segment. Subventer black. Thoracic legs orange-red. Head yellow with three black spots on each side. Larva to 3.5cm.

OCCURRENCE Fields, roadsides, wet meadows, edges of watercourses, and other mesic open habitats from Canada to Georgia (mountains) and Texas. Evidently one generation in Connecticut with mature caterpillars in July; two broods in Missouri.

COMMON FOODPLANTS Meadow rue (*Thalictrum*).

REMARKS When alarmed the caterpillar rolls its head under the venter of the second and third abdominal segments. The larva often loops when it crawls, even though it has a full complement of prolegs. Both its coloration and behavior are reminiscent of a sawfly. The single black lateral spot, which includes the lateral eyes, adds to its "sawfly look." It is not known if and how the Canadian Owlet is chemically protected, but it would certainly appear to be so. The pupa overwinters.

ROSE OF SHARON MOTH *Anomis commoda*

Introduced species (from Japan) ranging widely along Eastern Seaboard, north to at least Massachusetts. Evidently two or three generations with mature caterpillars from late May onward. Hibiscus.

YELLOW SCALLOP MOTH *Anomis erosa*

Resident of South but frequent migrant to southern Canada. Occasionally breeding north to New England in the fall; present year-round in Florida. Cotton, hibiscus, hollyhock, and other mallows (*Malvaceae*).

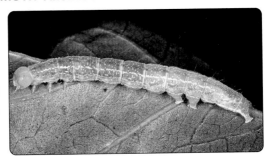

CITRUS FRUIT-PIERCER *Gonodonta nutrix*

Florida. Breeding year-round in southern Florida. Custard apple (*Annona*).

THE HERALD *Scoliopteryx libatrix*

Transcontinental across much of Canada south in East to Georgia and Texas. One generation with mature caterpillars in late summer. Willow.

Hypenines – Subfamily Hypeninae

Elongate green caterpillars with reduced prolegs on A3 and hind prolegs that splay outward from rear of body. Head frequently wider than prothorax. Setae often borne from raised base (pinaculum). Like other caterpillars with reduced or wanting anterior prolegs, they throw a loop into the body when walking.

GREEN CLOVERWORM
Plathypena scabra

RECOGNITION Last instar lime green with *faint subdorsal and strong spiracular stripes*. Setae often rusty to black, long, exceeding length of segments that bear them rearward. Prolegs often with pinkish cast; anal prolegs long and flared out behind body. Head shiny green, unmarked, wider than prothorax (i.e., larva with "neck"). Penultimate instar more strongly striped, many individuals with addorsal stripes to either side of green middorsal stripe (which in fact is the caterpillar's heart). Larva to 3cm.

OCCURRENCE Waste areas, fields, croplands, and woodlands from Canada south to Florida and Texas. Multiple generations with mature caterpillars throughout much of year.

COMMON FOODPLANTS Partial to low-growing legumes (alfalfa, bean, clover, soybean, etc.), but also found on false indigo, locust, and other trees and shrubs such as birch, cherry, elm, New Jersey tea, poplar, ragweed, strawberry, and willow.

REMARKS The Green Cloverworm is a migrant that recolonizes the northern portion of its range every summer. Adults begin showing up in Ohio and New England in very early spring, sometimes as early as February and March. The moths become increasingly common through the summer and early autumn. Like other hypenines the caterpillars hurl themselves from their perch when disturbed, by rapidly contracting and twisting their bodies in a fashion reminiscent of a tightly wound rubber band. It overwinters as an adult north to Missouri and New Jersey.

RECOGNITION Elongate, *emerald green body* with somewhat yellow intersegments; *proleg on A3 about half size of that on A4–A6.* Translucent, tracheal truck visible within body. *Setae long, dark, arising from somewhat orange-red or blackened setal bases.* In some forms, anterior dorsal seta (D1) and that above spiracle (SD1) arise from blackened spots; SD1 pinaculum on A8 largest. Head green and unmarked except for black lateral eyes or with black around setal bases. Larva to 3cm. Several other *Bomolocha* have quite similar caterpillars; foodplant associations often provide the best clue to a Bomolocha's identity (*see* Remarks).

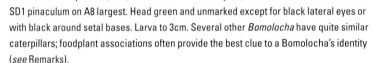

OCCURRENCE Edges of watercourses, swamps, woodlands, and forests from Wisconsin to Nova Scotia south to Florida and Texas. At least two generations in New England and likely more southward with mature caterpillars from May to November.

COMMON FOODPLANTS Red and silver maple.

REMARKS Twelve *Bomolocha* occur in the East, only two of which are figured here. Others include: the Dimorphic Bomolocha (*Bomolocha bijugalis*) on dogwood; the Deceptive Bomolocha (*B. deceptalis*) on basswood; the Flowing-line Bomolocha (*B. manalis*) on false nettle (*Boehmeria*); the Mottled Bomolocha (*B. palparia*) on American hornbeam, hazel, and hop hornbeam; and the White-lined Bomolocha (*B. abalienalis*) on elm. The reported foodplants for Sordid Bomolocha (*B. sordidula*), alder and butternut, are in error—both this species and the Large Bomolocha (*B. edictalis*) feed on wood nettle (*Laportea*). The latter has also been reared from nettle (*Urtica*).

GRAY-EDGED BOMOLOCHA
Bomolocha madefactalis

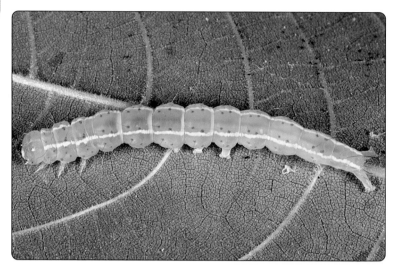

RECOGNITION   Pale green elongate body with *well-developed, yellow subdorsal stripe*; blackened setae borne from minute reddened or blackened pinacula. Body with relatively long, darkened dorsal setae, longer than segment that bears them. Head pale green and unmarked or with two black spots on each lobe. Larva to 3cm. In most

other Bomolochas the subdorsal stripes are lost in the last instar or these stripes are less prominent. Caterpillar of White-lined Bomolocha (*Bomolocha abalienalis*) is similar but it feeds exclusively on elm.

OCCURRENCE   Orchards, floodplains, woodlands, and forests from extreme southern Canada (Quebec) to Georgia and Texas. At least two generations with mature caterpillars from May to November.

COMMON FOODPLANTS   Walnut.

REMARKS   Early instar Bomolochas may have shiny black setal bases and a large conspicuous dark spot on each lobe of the head. *Bomolocha* hurl their feculae by snapping the rear to one side as the pellets are released from the body. Caterpillars are readily sampled with a beating sheet—August and September are especially good months over much of the East to search for *Bomolocha* larvae. Given the subfamily's strong association with the Urticaceae, especially in the Palearctic Region, I suspect that at least one of the two *Bomolocha* that have yet to be reared (*atomaria* and *appalachiensis*) may be associated with pellitory (*Parieteria*). All members of the genus overwinter as pupae in slight cocoons spun amongst leaf litter.

Caterpillars are green with creamy spotting and somewhat spindle-shaped. The anal prolegs are extended backward. The large head is partly withdrawn into the first thoracic segment. This largely tropical subfamily includes seven widespread Eastern species; additional species occur in Florida and southern Texas. Temperate euteliines overwinter as pupae in a cocoon spun in leaf litter.

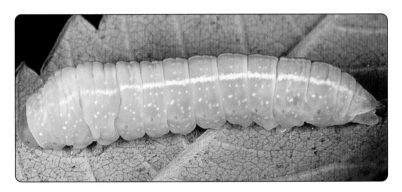

DARK MARATHYSSA
Marathyssa inficita

RECOGNITION Yellow-green with *somewhat swollen thorax*, body appearing smooth and hairless. Speckled with white especially below *subdorsal stripe that begins over T2 and extends rearward*. Thoracic legs small, slender, and unpigmented; prolegs reduced. Larva to 2.5cm. Light Marathyssa (*Marathyssa basalis*) smoky white with bold black spotting and yellow supraspiracular spots; poison ivy.

OCCURRENCE Woodlands and forests from southern Canada to Florida and Texas. At least two generations with mature caterpillars from May to November; three or more broods in Missouri.

COMMON FOODPLANTS Sumac.

REMARKS Search for it by inverting twigs and branches and examining the underside of leaves, especially in late summer. Euteliines are easily taken with beating sheets. Some species have narrow periods of seasonal activity, their caterpillars being common on foliage for only a few weeks each summer. Five of the seven common Euteliines in the East are associated with the plant genus *Rhus* or *Toxicodendron* (sumac and poison ivy). An especially handsome moth, the Beautiful Eutelia (*Eutelia pulcherrima*), feeds on both poison sumac and poison ivy. Presumably its caterpillar resembles that of its European congener (*Eutelia adulatrix*), which is lime green with a white, subdorsal stripe that thickens posteriorly and continues across the anal plate (Beck 1999). At rest the head is deeply retracted into the first thoracic segment.

LARGE PAECTES
Paectes abrostoloides

RECOGNITION *Bright green with prominent yellow spotting* and well-developed, yellow spiracular stripe. *Prolegs reminiscent of elfin boots*, curling upward fore and aft. Spiracles orange. Head pale green, unmarked, drawn into T1. Leading edge of prothorax yellow. Pygmy Paectes (*Paectes pygmaea*) purportedly occurs alongside the Large Paectes on new leaves of sweet gum, although I recently had a clutch of larvae refuse this foodplant; Bo Sullivan (pers. comm.) and I have twice reared the Pygmy Paectes from winged sumac (*Rhus copallina*). The caterpillars of two other Eastern sumac-feeding *Paectes*, *P. abrostolella* and the Eyed Paectes (*P. oculatrix*), are similar; the former feeds on *Rhus* species, and the latter has been reared from poison ivy and poison sumac. Additional species occur in Florida and Texas. Larva to 2.5cm.

OCCURRENCE Woodlands and forests from Missouri to New York south to Florida and Texas. At least two generations with mature caterpillars from May to November.

COMMON FOODPLANTS Sweet gum.

REMARKS The eggs of *Paectes* are odd affairs, with a low hemispherical center that is enveloped by a broad, yolkless ring of clear shell. Prepupal caterpillars redden prior to spinning their cocoons. Like other euteliines, the larvae feed and rest on leaf undersides. Initially the larva skeletonizes patches of tissue, leaving the upper leaf surface intact (creating a characteristic "window"). Later the caterpillar chews holes in central portions of the blade. In July 2003, I asked Eric Hossler to make a random collection of 50 shoot tips of sweet gum from woodlands in eastern Tennessee, in an effort to secure caterpillars of the Pygmy Paectes; while no caterpillars of the Pygmy Paectes were secured, the foliage did yield more than a dozen caterpillars of the Large Paectes over the ensuing weeks that the leaves were kept.

Most of the 50 plusiines that occur in the East can be immediately distinguished by the absence of, or very rudimentary, prolegs on A3 and A4. Typically the caterpillars are green with three (four) pairs of white dorsal stripes and a small head, at least in proportion to girth of the thorax. Crochets are of two lengths except in *Plusia*. Many overwinter as middle instars. Most are foodplant generalists that consume a wide array of herbaceous plants; a subset of these are crop and garden pests. Lafontaine and Poole (1991) illustrate caterpillars of 20 plusiines.

CABBAGE LOOPER
Trichoplusia ni

RECOGNITION Green looper with *minute peglike vestigial prolegs on A3 and A4* (visible with lens) that bear three setae. *Body covered in minute granules* (not elongate spinules). Like many plusiines, setal base above spiracle (SD1) may be black. Spiracular stripe white or yellow, *not edged with black above*, fading rearward of A7, but often continuing to anal proleg. *Three uppermost setal bases on T2 equidistant*. Head green, shiny, *without black lateral line*. Larva less than 3.5cm.

OCCURRENCE Fields, gardens, agricultural lands, and other early successional habitats from southern Canada to Florida and Texas. Three or more generations with mature caterpillars from April onward at least in South.

COMMON FOODPLANTS Many plants, including asparagus, beans, cabbage, corn, tobacco, watermelon, and others.

REMARKS Widely distributed moth, present in both the New and Old Worlds. In recent years it has been curiously scarce in the Northeast. The caterpillars are polyphagous, but most apt to be found on crucifers (plants of mustard family). It is not known how far north the species survives year-round; migrants reestablish northern populations each spring.

COMMON LOOPER
Autographa precationis

RECOGNITION Green looper with roughened integument *densely covered with minute spinules. No vestigial prolegs on A3 and A4.* Scalloped profile. Spiracular stripe black above and white below, fading rearward of A6. First four to six abdominal segments usually with shiny black setal base above spiracle; black base on A3 largest. A8 humped with dorsal setae perched on raised bases. Head green, shiny, with prominent *black bar down each side that extends to antenna.* Larva to 3.5cm. Bilobed Looper (*Megalographa biloba*) with larger spinules covering integument (visible with lens), appearing somewhat fuzzy (*see* page 380). Caterpillar of Soybean Looper (*Pseudoplusia includens*) closely similar—head stripe thinner and not including all (six) lateral eyes (*see* opposite) and with minute vestigial prolegs on A3 and A4.

OCCURRENCE Fields, gardens, agricultural fields, waste places, and other open and early successional habitats from southern Manitoba to Nova Scotia to northern Georgia and Mississippi. Two generations in Connecticut with mature caterpillars from May onward, three or more broods southward.

COMMON FOODPLANTS Many herbaceous plants, including beans, cabbage, clover, dandelion, hollyhock, sunflower, thistle, verbena, and wild lettuce.

REMARKS The caterpillars are "trenchers." When feeding on plants with milky latex, such as dandelion and wild lettuce, the Common Looper and its kin incapacitate the vascular system of the leaf by chewing through the midrib. Upon severing the main vein, often near the leaf base, the caterpillar moves to a distal portion of the leaf to feed. Although commonly reported as a pest in gardens, it rarely does appreciable damage.

Pseudoplusia includens

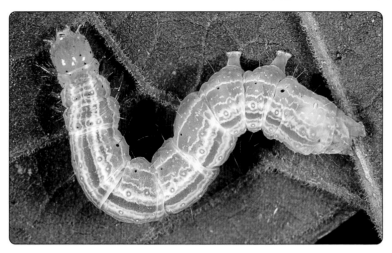

RECOGNITION Green looper with *minute peglike vestigial prolegs on A3 and A4* (only visible with lens) that bear three setae. Integument with minute spinules. *Spiracular stripe white, not edged with black above, often continuing to anal proleg. Two uppermost setal bases on T2 more closely situated to one another than lower one is to setal base below subdorsal stripe.* Head green, shiny; if black lateral line present, it is thin and does not include lateral eyes (stemmata). Larva to 3.5cm.

OCCURRENCE Fields, gardens, greenhouses, agricultural fields, waste places, and other open and early successional habitats from extreme southern Ontario to Maine south to Florida and Texas. Two to many generations with mature caterpillars from May onward.

COMMON FOODPLANTS Many herbaceous plants, including a wide array of crops: alfalfa, bean, cotton, kidney bean, lettuce, mustard, soybean, tobacco, and tomato.

REMARKS Several of the loopers in the East are migratory, flying northward each summer, sometimes in great numbers. Reverse migrations in the fall have not been documented. I once witnessed a mass migration of loopers and armyworms on a high pass in the Great Smoky Mountains. Moths came through by the thousands on the leading edge of a storm that was blowing up from the Gulf. Evidently moths can be so numerous on such occasions that their presence is detectable on radar. Goatsuckers and other birds also move northward on these fronts, feasting on the moths as they go. The Soybean Looper is one of the most abundant plusiines in the East—if it is late summer, there are probably some in your garden now. On occasion the insect is a pest of soybeans and other legumes. It is not known where it is established year-round.

LOOPERS

CELERY LOOPER *Anagrapha falcifera*

Transcontinental in Canada south to northern Georgia and Texas. Two generations in North; three or more in South with mature caterpillars from April onward. Beets, blueberry, celery, clover, corn, dandelion, lettuce, tobacco, and other mostly herbaceous plants.

EPAULETTED PITCHER PLANT MOTH *Exyra fax*

Manitoba to Nova Scotia south to Georgia. One principal generation in Connecticut with mature caterpillars in June; two full broods from New Jersey southward. Pitcher-plant.

BILOBED LOOPER *Megalographa biloba*

Throughout the Americas. Two generations in North; three or more in South with mature caterpillars from April onward. Northern populations annually reestablished or reinforced by southern migrants. Many herbaceous plants including alfalfa, cabbage, dandelion, larkspur, lettuce, and tobacco.

PUTNAM'S LOOPER *Plusia putnami*

Northern Canada south to Pennsylvania and Great Lakes States in East. Two generations over much of range with mature caterpillars in spring then again in midsummer. Bur-reed, grasses, and sedges.

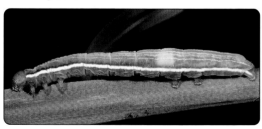

Eastern agaristines are warningly colored, ringed in white and black and often orange. The head is bright orange with black spots. Most of our seven Eastern species feed on members of the grape family (Vitaceae). Prepupal larvae require wood or dense chunks of peat in which to pupate and pass the winter.

GRAPEVINE EPIMENIS
Psychomorpha epimenis

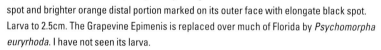

RECOGNITION Body ringed with black and white; *orange limited to prothoracic shield, dorsum of A8, and prolegs.* Head shiny orange with five black spots on each lobe and smaller black spotting about eyes. Base of midabdominal prolegs waxy orange with black spot and brighter orange distal portion marked on its outer face with elongate black spot. Larva to 2.5cm. The Grapevine Epimenis is replaced over much of Florida by *Psychomorpha euryrhoda.* I have not seen its larva.

OCCURRENCE Hedgerows, woodlands, and forest edges from Iowa to Massachusetts south to northern Florida and Texas. One generation with mature caterpillars in late spring.

COMMON FOODPLANTS Grape.

REMARKS The caterpillar forms a shelter in new foliage. The edges of an entire leaf are pulled upward and tied together with silk. Once one learns to spot the characteristic shelters, Grapevine Epimenis caterpillars may be easily located. There is a far more abundant moth, *Geina sheppardi* (Family Pterophoridae), that also makes ties in new grape leaves, but its shelters are smaller and made in partially expanded foliage. Its small (1cm) caterpillars are pale green and quite hairy. The diurnal adults of the Grapevine Epimenis are avid nectarers that visit flowers of apple, redbud, sumac, and others. It flies early with Spring Azures (*Celastrina* species) and the Falcate Orange Tip (*Anthocharis midea*).

EIGHT-SPOTTED FORESTER
Alypia octomaculata

RECOGNITION Body with black, white, and orange rings. Thoracic shield orange. *Dorsum of A1–A8 with orange bands*; bands over A1–A3 broadest. Splotches on A1–A8 below spiracles *white to cream*; that on A8 enlarged, white. Fleshy basal portion of prolegs on A3–A6 orange with single black dot and distal black portion. Larva to 3cm. *Long white setae* distinguish *Alypia* from other Eastern agaristines. In Wittfeld's Forester (*Alypia wittfeldii*), which replaces the Eight-spotted Forester over much of Florida, the white lateral splotch on A8 extends forward onto A7. Kimball (1965) records Japanese persimmon (*Diospyros kaki*) as a foodplant, but this seems improbable; Ben Williams (pers. comm.) has reared Wittfeld's Forester on grape. Two additional Foresters occur along the northern edge of the Eight-spotted Forester's range: Langton's Forester (*Alypia langtoni*) and MacCulloch's Forester (*Androloma maccullochii*). Both have been reared from willow herb.

OCCURRENCE Woodland and forest edges from South Dakota to extreme southern Quebec and Maine to northern Florida and Texas. One principal generation in spring with mature caterpillars from April to July; partial second and third broods occur widely.

COMMON FOODPLANTS Ampelopsis, grape, and Virginia creeper.

REMARKS Look for the caterpillars feeding or perched on the underside of leaves near shoot apices. In addition to leaves the caterpillars consume tendrils and growing stem tissue. Larvae are quick to vomit an orange, mostly clear fluid when disturbed. They may also drop from their perch on a belay line—a behavior commonly associated with inchworms and microlepidopterans. The prepupal larvae will perish if not offered pulpy wood, dense peat balls, blocks of foam, or other materials into which they can tunnel to form their pupal cells.

Eudryas grata

RECOGNITION Similar to the previous species, ringed in black, white, and orange, but *lacking long setae* of *Alypia*. Thoracic shield orange. *Transverse orange band extending down sides of T2–A9. White to cream subspiracular splotches absent*. Fleshy basal portion of proleg on A3–A6 orange with single black spot. Larva to 4cm. Pearly Wood-nymph (*Eudryas unio*) similar, but

with white and black prothoracic shield and fleshy orange basal portion of prolegs with two, offset black spots (inset); it co-occurs with Beautiful Wood-nymph over much of the East. Its larva feeds on evening primose, false loosestrife, loosestrife, water-willow, and willow herb; records from grape and hibiscus require confirmation.

OCCURRENCE Woodland and forest edges from southern Canada to Florida and Texas. Evidently a single protracted generation in Northeast with mature caterpillars from late July to October; two or three generations in Missouri; flying year-round in Florida.

COMMON FOODPLANTS Ampelopsis, grape, and Virginia creeper; reports from hops and buttonbush require confirmation.

REMARKS While most agaristines are diurnal, both of our Wood-nymphs are frequently taken at light. The adults are bird-dropping mimics that perch, often conspicuously, on vegetation during the day. Agaristines have brightly colored caterpillars and all but the Grapevine Epimenis feed and rest exposed on or near new foliage, which suggests that they are chemically protected. The American Southwest has a marvelously rich and varied agaristid fauna—a collection of their larval images would make for a beautiful color publication. Prepupal larvae occasionally bore into cedar siding, fence posts, and other wood structures (Richard Heitzman, pers. comm.).

Bird-dropping Moths – Subfamily Acontiinae

Caterpillar elongate, frequently without prolegs on A3 and A4 and the spinneret reduced. In many acontiines there is only one SV seta on A1 (lens required). Bird-dropping moths are especially diverse in arid regions. Our species overwinter as pupae.

OLIVE-SHADED BIRD-DROPPING MOTH
Tarachidia candefacta

RECOGNITION *Elongate, slender, lime green caterpillar with prolegs absent on A3 and A4.* Body somewhat constricted between anterior abdominal segments; *setae not arising from pimplelike warts.* Dorsum and venter bearing numerous thin wavy white stripes. White spiracular stripe confluent with white line that runs down each proleg. *Abdominal spiracles often with maroon spot above* and, less frequently, with one below. *A8 humped.* Head with mosaic of white mottling; white parabolic lines to either side of triangle. Larva to 2.5cm. Small Bird-dropping Moth (*Tarachidia erastrioides*) brown and with more rounded A8, but otherwise similar (inset), feeding alongside Olive-shaded Bird-dropping Moth on ragweed.

OCCURRENCE Fields, waste lots, roadsides, and other open habitats from lower Canada south in East to Florida and Texas. Two or three generations over much of East with mature caterpillars to be expected from May (southward) until first frosts.

COMMON FOODPLANTS Ragweed.

REMARKS Caterpillars are common in late summer and fall. They do poorly in containers with saturated atmospheres, so provide ventilation and sand into which the prepupal larvae can tunnel and pupate. The caterpillars feed exclusively on flowers if offered.

Members of this subfamily were formerly classified with the bird-dropping moths (Subfamily Acontiinae). Eustrotiines are a heterogeneous (unnatural) assemblage without any shared diagnostic adult or larval characters.

TUFTED BIRD-DROPPING MOTH
Cerma cerintha

RECOGNITION Elongate, somewhat shiny, green and red caterpillar with *long dark setae. Cherry to maroon dorsum edged by prominent white subdorsal stripe.* Sides and subventer lime green to smoky green. Rusty to black setae arise from prominent shiny setal bases. *A8 with pair of prominent dark conical warts.* Bright, shiny, green head with black line that ends short of antenna. Subdorsal stripe broken over A8 then continuing on A9 and A10. Outer face of prolegs sometimes flushed with orange-red. Larva to 3cm. Caterpillar of *Cerma cora* mostly black with broad yellow and black spiracular stripe; lobes of head black. Eric Hossler and I reared this rare species from hawthorn; Rockburne and Lafontaine (1976) report pin cherry as a foodplant in Canada. It occurs from Ontario to Florida.

OCCURRENCE Barrens, fields, and woodlands from Minnesota to Maine south to Florida and Arkansas. One generation over much of East with mature caterpillars mostly in July and August. A second brood occurs from Missouri southward (Richard Heitzman and Vernon Brou, pers. comm.).

COMMON FOODPLANTS Especially cherry, but also reported from apple, hawthorn, and plum.

REMARKS Prepupal *Cerma* caterpillars tunnel into soft wood. Upon completing their tunnels, they turn around and seal off the entrance with a net of silk and wood chips that renders the entrance invisible. The winter is passed as a pupa.

YELLOW-SPOTTED GRAYLET
Hyperstrotia flaviguttata

RECOGNITION *Elongate, pale to lime green with prolegs on A3 absent and those on A4 reduced. Anal prolegs directed backward and splayed outward.* In my photos of this species, the setae arise from smoky (head) or red (body) spots, although this character may vary among species of graylets or even among individuals. Head large and rounded. Four species of graylets occur in our region; identification should be based on reared adults until reliable larval characters are established. Larva to 2cm.

OCCURRENCE Barrens, woodlands, and forests from Missouri and Massachusetts south to Florida and Texas. One principal (summer) generation in the Northeast; two generations in Missouri and New Jersey where mature caterpillars occur from July to September.

COMMON FOODPLANTS Oak.

REMARKS In dry woodlands and barrens, graylet (*Hyperstrotia*) caterpillars are among the most common caterpillars in beating samples from oak during the latter part of summer. The literature suggests that graylets may accept more than a single foodplant. Both the Dotted Graylet (*H. pervertens)* and White-lined Graylet (*H. villificans*) are reported to feed on oak and elm. The Dotted Graylet also uses beech commonly; I have one rearing record of the White-lined Graylet from hickory. Here is yet another group where someone with an interest in rearing and photography could make an immediate contribution. The caterpillars are easily located by turning leaves—they rest fully extended on leaf undersides—and by beating. This caterpillar was obtained by sleeving a female on oak and returning four weeks later to retrieve the larvae. The winter is passed as a pupa.

This subfamily has undergone massive reorganization—most of its previous members have been shifted into the Hadeninae. The spiracular stripe often continues around the anal plate (it does not bend down and continue along the outer face of the anal proleg as in most owlet caterpillars). Crochets are of two distinct lengths. Our common Eastern representatives are mostly flower (and seed) feeders.

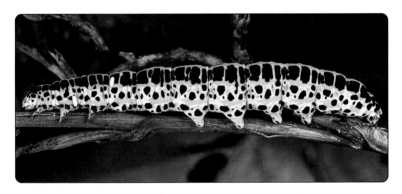

TOADFLAX BROCADE
Calophasia lunula

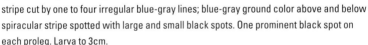

RECOGNITION *Black, yellow, and waxy blue-gray with bright lemon-yellow middorsal, subdorsal, and spiracular stripes.* Black ground color above subdorsal stripe cut by one to four irregular blue-gray lines; blue-gray ground color above and below spiracular stripe spotted with large and small black spots. One prominent black spot on each proleg. Larva to 3cm.

OCCURRENCE Fields, roadsides, waste lots, and other open habitats. Two generations in Connecticut, with mature caterpillars in July then again in September and October.

COMMON FOODPLANTS Butter-and-eggs (*Linaria vulgaris*) and other toadflaxes.

REMARKS The Toadflax Brocade was introduced from Europe into Ontario in 1968 as a biocontrol agent for butter-and-eggs, a naturalized plant that is occasionally invasive. The moth quickly jumped the border and has since spread southward to Ohio and the whole of New England. Caterpillars may be found by searching stems and around the bases of butter-and-eggs. Larvae are most easily found at night when they are feeding on the flowers and upper portions of the plant. The caterpillar figured in the main image bears tachinid eggs on T2 and A1. Prepupal caterpillars should be supplied with cardboard or soft wood in which they can bore and fashion their firm cocoons. The pupa overwinters.

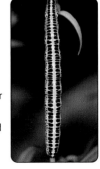

THE ASTEROID
Cucullia asteroides

RECOGNITION Usually *bright green or brown with yellow, black, and white striping*, but exceedingly variable (*see* Remarks). Middorsal stripe yellow, often narrowly edged with white, occasionally flanked by variously developed black subdorsal stripe. If subdorsal is absent, then five or six black pinstripes above level of spiracles. Larva to 4.5cm. I have not seen the caterpillars of three related Eastern *Cucullia*: *postera, omissa,* and *florea*. Likely they are similar.

OCCURRENCE Fields, meadows, and woodland and forest edges from Canada south to Florida and Arkansas. Two generations in Connecticut with mature caterpillars in July and then again from late August into October.

COMMON FOODPLANTS Primarily flowers of aster and goldenrod, at least the numerically more abundant fall generation.

REMARKS The ground color of The Asteroid ranges from green to tan, brown or purple and brown. On several occasions I have had captive green-and-yellow caterpillars of what I believed were The Asteroid switch to a purple-brown morph in the course of the last larval instar. The genus offers great opportunity to someone who has a knack for rearing to take notes and collect images of the color changes that ensue in the last instar. Images and biological observations are especially needed for three of our northern species, *Cucullia postera, C. omissa,* and *C. florae*. All *Cucullia* overwinter in a tough cocoon fashioned below ground. According to Porter (1997), it is important to leave the cocoons intact to insure successful eclosion.

Cucullia convexipennis

RECOGNITION *Stunningly colored in yellow, red, black, and white*; integument shiny. Middorsal stripe orange-red; spiracular stripe bright red. Bright yellow area, edged above and below with white, cut by one thick black line (just behind spiracle) and a few thin black lines. A8 with black hump. Spiracles white. Larva to 4.5cm.

OCCURRENCE Fields, meadows, and woodland edges from southern Canada to South Carolina and Missouri. One principal generation in Connecticut with mature caterpillars from late August into October.

COMMON FOODPLANTS Principally flowers of aster and goldenrod, but presumably other composites as well.

REMARKS This is one of our most beautiful and oft-asked about caterpillars. Each individual appears as if it were hand-painted and then glazed. Larvae are conspicuous by day, usually resting on stems in full view. They move into the flowers to feed. The Brown-hooded Owlet is seldom common enough to warrant stem by stem searches, but certainly sufficiently numerous over most of its range that sweeping could be expected to yield a caterpillar or two. *Cucullia* caterpillars are often attacked by tachinid flies that lay oval white eggs over the body—single individuals sometimes bear more than a half-dozen eggs. Such caterpillars are doomed—the tachinid fly larvae will consume the host caterpillar, feeding at first on non-essential tissues. Then in a final burst of growth, they will finish off the owlet caterpillar.

CUCULLIAS

Cucullia caterpillars are animals of exceptional beauty and variety. The larvae of all nine of the British species are distinctive in their coloration (Porter 1997). Their life history and chemical ecology remain unstudied. Females come to light; to obtain eggs, hold females in containers with flowers of local composites.

CAMPHORWEED CUCULLIA *Cucullia alfarata*

Missouri to southern New York south to Florida and Arkansas. Perhaps only one generation in New Jersey with mature caterpillars in September. Evidently two or three broods in Missouri. Camphorweed and goldenaster.

INTERMEDIATE CUCULLIA *Cucullia intermedia*

Manitoba to Nova Scotia south to Virginia and Great Lakes States. One generation with mature caterpillars from late August through early October. Wild lettuce. Penultimate instar with white lateral stripe (upper); ultimate with orange lateral spots (lower).

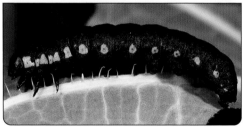

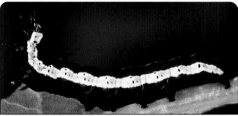

SPEYER'S CUCULLIA *Cucullia speyeri*

Manitoba to Maine south to North Carolina (mountains) and North Dakota. One generation with mature caterpillars from late August through early October in Northeast; two or three broods in Missouri. Horseweed (*Conyza*), perhaps other asters and composites as well.

Formerly a large and unnatural assemblage. As presently defined by Kitching and Rawl-ins (1998), the subfamily includes only the nominate genus.

COPPER UNDERWING
Amphipyra pyramidoides

RECOGNITION Handsome blue-green caterpillar with creamy spots and *conspicuously humped A8. White and yellow spiracular stripe* continues around anal plate; stripe missing across T3. Larva less than 4.5cm.

OCCURRENCE Woodlands and forests from southern Canada to Florida and Texas. One generation with mature caterpillars from May through June.

COMMON FOODPLANTS Many woody plants including apple, basswood, blueberry, cherry, chestnut, currant, grape, greenbrier, hawthorn, hickory, lilac, maple, oak, poplar, raspberry, rhododendron, viburnum, Virginia creeper, and walnut.

REMARKS The caterpillar perches on the underside of a leaf, often with the anterior end of the body raised. Heinrich (1979, 1993) mentioned this species as one that employs a shell-game strategy, i.e., the caterpillar moves away from those leaves upon which it has fed. Hungry birds that focus on damaged leaves as a way to find their quarry are likely to do so fruitlessly with the Copper Underwing. I get great aggregations of pre-reproductive adults in my shutters on my front porch each summer—evidently the adults use an aggregation pheromone to form their assemblies. Lesser numbers of the adults also roost under the seat cushions of our porch furniture. In September the adults become reproductively active and the moths disperse from the aggregations. Gravid females lay eggs into November, which then overwinter.

Psaphidines – Subfamily Psaphidinae

This small subfamily, recently redefined by Kitching and Rawlins (1998), is held togeth-er mostly by male genitalic and pupal features. Caterpillars often bear a hump over A8. There are about ten species in our region; all have only a single generation with adults that fly in the late winter and early spring. Most psaphidines are specialists on young foliage of deciduous trees and shrubs, although *Feralia*, which represents a divergent tribe, eat conifers primarily. Prepupal psaphidine caterpillars may tunnel deeply into lit-ter and soil before forming their cocoons.

ROLAND'S SALLOW
Psaphida rolandi

RECOGNITION Bright lime green with white pinacula and poorly developed stripes. *Somewhat stocky, broadest about A2 and A3*; caudal end dropping off abruptly to anal plate. Middorsal stripe breaking up over thorax. *White spiracular stripe, especially well developed on A7–A10, continuing around rim of anal plate.* Subdorsal stripe vaguely expressed, composed of scattered white spots. Triangle and front of head blue-green; pale snowflakelike markings over vertex. Larva to 3.5cm.

OCCURRENCE Woodlands and forests from southern Ontario to New Hampshire south to central Florida and Texas. One generation with mature caterpillars in spring.

COMMON FOODPLANTS Oak.

REMARKS Gravid females will deposit their pinkish eggs if held in a brown paper bag with oak buds. The caterpillars feed on new, unhardened foliage. Adults are frequently among the most common owlets at my backyard light in Connecticut. Yet, the caterpillars of *Psaphida* and related genera are seldom encountered. One wonders if the caterpillars feed principally on canopy foliage. The pupal stage overwinters (up to seven years, Dale Schweitzer, pers. comm.).

Psaphida styracis

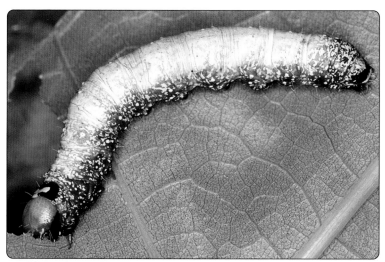

RECOGNITION Coloration variable. Commonly waxy blue-green above, especially over abdomen, and reddish or greenish along lower half of body. Densely speckled with white flecks. *Prothoracic shield shiny black with central white bar.* Head orange and unmarked. Larva less than 3.5cm. Middle instars more reddish to maroon and lacking prominent, pale dorsal area (but *see* Remarks). Gray Sallow (*Psaphida grandis*) is more evenly mottled, lacks a dark prothoracic shield, and has a black head (inset).

OCCURRENCE Dry forests, barrens, and woodlands from southern Ontario to Massachusetts south to Florida and Texas. One generation with mature caterpillars in spring.

COMMON FOODPLANTS Oak.

REMARKS Adults emerge very early in the spring and may fly on rather cold nights, beginning as early as February in the South. The shelter-forming caterpillars feed only on spring foliage. They are somewhat reluctant to leave their shelters once spun, so it is a good idea to transfer larvae or move them in their shelters to new foliage if you are rearing the Fawn Sallow in containers. A better alternative is to sleeve the caterpillars on a shoot with new growth. Evidently, the larva changes color in the last instar, starting off somewhat maroon-red but becoming increasingly greener as it ages. The pupa overwinters.

MAJOR SALLOW
Feralia major

RECOGNITION Deep green with strong, white middorsal and addorsal stripes; *cream spiracular stripe edged with red above.* Subspiracular stripe comprised of yellow bars on thoracic segments and A1–A8 that are nearly connected on A1–A6. Thoracic legs wine red. Larva to 3.5cm. In both Comstock's Sallow (*Feralia comstocki*) and Jocose Sallow (*F. jocosa*) the subdorsal and spiracular stripes are usually broken into lens-shaped spots and the subspiracular spots are reduced or absent. In my photos of Comstock's Sallow the middorsal stripe is sometimes yellowish; yellow is often a prominent component of the spiracular spot coloration; the spiracular spots are nearly fully connected on abdomen; the red spiracular spots are often tinted with rose; and the yellow spots above the prolegs are ovoid. Jocose Sallow has a white middorsal stripe; there is little to no yellow in the spiracular spots; the spiracular spots are often fully separated between segments; the red portion of the spiracular spots is often burgundy; and the spots above the prolegs are oblong, frequently small, or sometimes absent. All three of our Eastern *Feralia* are figured by Maier et al. (2004).

OCCURRENCE Pine barrens, woodlands, and forests from southern Canada to northern Florida and Texas. One generation with mature caterpillars from late April through June.

COMMON FOODPLANTS Principally pine; reports from spruce and other conifers may be erroneous.

REMARKS Our three *Feralia* may co-occur. The Major Sallow is the first on the wing, flying as early as late December and January in the southern part of its range. Comstock's Sallow is the last of the threesome to fly at any one site. The pupa overwinters in *Feralia*, sometimes for more than one year (Dale Schweitzer, pers. comm.).

This heterogeneous subfamily is most diverse in arid areas. Caterpillars frequently have a short, scalelike spinneret. Many of the North American species are flower and seed feeders. Composites are especially favored as foodplants.

GOLD MOTH
Basilodes pepita

RECOGNITION *Distinctly patterned orange, black, and white caterpillar.* Dorsum crossed by alternating smoky black and pale rings. *Each segment with orange supraspiracular spot.* Prothoracic shield and A10 mostly orange with black spots. White subspiracular spots nearly form stripe. Venter pale orange-yellow except for blackened setal bases. Head pale orange and unmarked. Larva less than 4cm.

OCCURRENCE Fields, meadows, and edges of woodlands from eastern Kansas, Illinois, and New York south to Florida and Texas. Evidently just a single generation throughout much of its range with mature caterpillars from August through October.

COMMON FOODPLANTS Crown-beard.

REMARKS Both the coloration and behavior are strongly suggestive of a sawfly. In addition, the Gold Moth caterpillar superficially resembles a Forester Moth caterpillar (Agaristinae). The larva is rather slow-moving and seemingly thick-skinned. When disturbed the larva often stops, rolls the head under, and elevates the anterior abdominal segments. Although the species is not known to be toxic, its coloration, sluggish behavior, and foodplant suggest that the caterpillar enjoys some level of chemical protection. The boldly marked caterpillars are readily found by visual inspection; beating too is effective. Kitching and Rawlins (1998) note that *Basilodes* caterpillars are seed predators in the inflorescences of their respective foodplants. The pupa overwinters.

Flower Moths – Subfamily Heliothinae

Integument bearing numerous, fine spine-tipped granules and often raised (pimplelike) setal bases. On the prothorax the two setae immediately forward of spiracle are usually aligned parallel to the body axis (in most other noctuoids these setae are positioned vertically). Most feed on flowers or seeds; a handful are serious agricultural pests.

CORN EARWORM
Helicoverpa zea

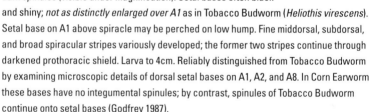

RECOGNITION Highly variable in color, ranging from pale tan to yellow, orange, red, maroon, green, dark brown, or nearly black. *Integument with minute dark spinules* (visible under magnification). Setal bases often black and shiny; *not as distinctly enlarged over A1* as in Tobacco Budworm (*Heliothis virescens*). Setal base on A1 above spiracle may be perched on low hump. Fine middorsal, subdorsal, and broad spiracular stripes variously developed; the former two stripes continue through darkened prothoracic shield. Larva to 4cm. Reliably distinguished from Tobacco Budworm by examining microscopic details of dorsal setal bases on A1, A2, and A8. In Corn Earworm these bases have no integumental spinules; by contrast, spinules of Tobacco Budworm continue onto setal bases (Godfrey 1987).

OCCURRENCE Agricultural fields, gardens, waste lots, and other open habitats from Canada south through Florida and Texas. One principal (fall) generation in North; multiple generations in South with mature caterpillars year-round.

COMMON FOODPLANTS Widely polyphagous, especially on herbaceous plants. Economically important foodplants include beans, corn, cotton, peppers, soybean, tobacco, and tomato.

REMARKS The Corn Earworm has other aliases: the Cotton Bollworm, Soybean Podworm, and Tomato Fruitworm. Individuals that bore into foodplant tissue tend to have more subdued coloration than those caterpillars that feed externally on seeds and flowers. Northern populations are augmented annually by migrants from the Gulf States and Mexico. The pupa overwinters.

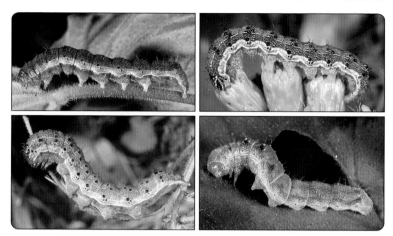

RECOGNITION Extremely variable in coloration, often green but also yellow, red, and other colors. *Integument with rows of minute, whitened spinules* (visible under magnification). *Setae above spiracles arising from white or shiny black pimplelike bases; base over spiracle on A1 enlarged*; setal bases diminish in size rearward. Often with blackened subdorsal patches. Spiracles

tan, rimmed with black, each enveloped by pale halo. Often with broad, lightened spiracular stripe, or at least the upper and lower edges evident as fine white stripes. Larva to 3.5cm. Subflexus Straw (*Heliothis subflexus*) caterpillar similar but with larger black setal bases, three or four of which may enclose each abdominal spiracle (Forbes 1954) (*see* Remarks).

OCCURRENCE Fields, gardens, and waste lots from Nebraska to southern Ontario and Maine south through Gulf States. One principal generation in North, two in New Jersey; breeding continuously in Florida.

COMMON FOODPLANTS Ageratum, cotton, geranium, ground cherry, roses, soybean, tobacco, and many other plants.

REMARKS Caterpillars have a penchant for buds, flowers, fruits, and seeds. Somehow the larvae end up matching the color of their foodplant. The caterpillars found on red geraniums are shades of pink, those on ground cherry yellow, and so on. My colleague Scott Smedley and his students recently discovered that the caterpillars manage to transfer the glandular defensive secretions of their foodplants onto their own setae, and in so doing accrue chemical protection from ants and other natural enemies. If my images of wild-collected *Heliothis* caterpillars are sorted properly, then the integument of *subflexus* is granulose but lacks distinct lines of spinules. The pupa overwinters, but how far northward it is able to do so is unknown. It would certainly appear to be a migrant over much of New England.

PURPLE-LINED SALLOW
Pyrrhia exprimens

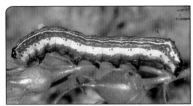

RECOGNITION Exceptionally variable coloration, ranging from almost white, yellow, or green to black with striping variously expressed; *integument shiny with prominent, raised setal bases that are usually blackened.* Spiracular stripe best developed, ranging from a narrow creamy line to a broad, orange to yellow belt that includes the subventral setae. Subdorsal stripe present, although vaguely expressed in many forms. Two sets of faint addorsal stripes variously developed (one along inner side of D1 and other inside of D2). Larva less than 4cm. Co-occurring with American Border Sallow (*Pyrrhia adela*); its caterpillars range from green or pink to olive, brown, gray, and black; usually a broad lemon spiracular stripe is present. It too is a general feeder, although many of the Eastern foodplant records are from sumac and alder. Due to the extreme variability of *Pyrrhia* caterpillars, identifications are best based on adults.

OCCURRENCE Fields, gardens, and mostly open habitats from British Columbia to Newfoundland south to North Carolina and Texas, but mostly in mountains southward. Two generations north to southern Quebec with mature caterpillars from June onward.

COMMON FOODPLANTS General feeder on both forbs and woody species: examples include beggar's ticks, chicory, dogbane, green beans, monkshood, peas, penstemon, poplar, rose, strawberry, sweet fern, and willow.

REMARKS The spectacular coloration and variability of the larvae draw attention whenever the caterpillars are found. Not infrequently the Purple-lined Sallow turns up in flower beds and gardens. The caterpillars consume both leaves and reproductive tissue, but prefer buds, flowers, and fruit; when opportunity allows, the larvae will tunnel into and feed from within these. Its European relative, the Bordered Sallow (*Pyrrhia umbra*), is reported to be cannibalistic (Porter 1997). Females can be collected at light and less commonly bait, and lay their eggs readily in captivity. The pupa overwinters.

Schinia gaurae

RECOGNITION Attractive *yellow to orange, white, and black-ringed caterpillar with orange head.* Bright lemon yellow to orange coloration more or less continuous over dorsum but broken up into patches along sides of thorax and abdomen. Each segment with short black bar toward front and larger black ring that extends below spiracle at mid-segment. Larva to 3cm.

OCCURRENCE Fields, roadsides, prairies, and other open habitats from Nebraska to Ohio south to Florida and Texas. One generation, at least in northern portion of range, with mature caterpillars when gaura is in fruit, mostly September and October in the North.

COMMON FOODPLANTS Gaura.

REMARKS *Schinia* is one of North America's largest moth genera with more than 120 recognized species. The genus is most diverse in arid and semiarid regions, open areas, and early successional habitats. Flower moths (*Schinia*) have very close associations with their foodplants, often nectaring, resting, and laying eggs only on flowers of the foodplant. In contrast to the Clouded Crimson, most of our *Schinia* caterpillars are cryptically colored, rendered in greens and browns. The majority of the 40 or so flower moths (*Schinia*) that occur in our region can be identified simply by knowing the foodplant and then consulting Hardwick (1996). *Schinia* may be difficult to rear, seemingly starving or limping along even when reasonable floral tissue is provided. Sleeve them out when you can, consider using water picks, or take other measures to keep their foodplant fresh. *Schinia* may hold over in the pupal stage for more than a year. To find caterpillars of the Clouded Crimson and other schinias, search inflorescences that are producing seed. All flower moths overwinter as pupae.

FLOWER MOTHS

ARCIGERA FLOWER MOTH *Schinia arcigera*

Southern Manitoba to Nova Scotia south to Florida and Texas. Evidently one extended generation with mature caterpillars from August to October. Aster, horseweed, and related composites.

PRIMROSE MOTH *Schinia florida*

Alberta to Nova Scotia south to North Carolina and Texas. One generation with mature caterpillars from August to September. Buds, flowers, and especially seed capsules of evening primrose.

RAGWEED FLOWER MOTH *Schinia rivulosa*

Minnesota to Massachusetts south to Florida and Texas. One extended generation with mature caterpillars from August to November. Ragweed.

GOLDENROD FLOWER MOTH *Schinia nundina*

Nebraska to Nova Scotia south to central Florida and southern Texas. One generation with mature caterpillars from August to October. Goldenrod.

A small tribe with just seven, largely tropical genera. The caterpillars are often black with bold cream spots and stripes. Many are borers in members of the amaryllis and lily families.

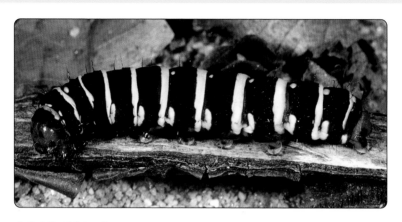

CONVICT CATERPILLAR
(SPANISH MOTH)
Xanthopastis regnatrix

RECOGNITION *Bold black and white-ringed caterpillar with orange head, legs, and rump.* Front of thoracic segments and posterior of abdominal segments ringed with white. White middorsal spots on T3 and (A3)A4–A9. Orange head with black spot on either side of triangle and over eyes. Larva to 4cm.

OCCURRENCE Edges of watercourses, roadside ditches, marshes, and other wetlands from southern Indiana to Long Island south to Florida and Texas, but only as a migrant north of Gulf States. One generation northward with mature caterpillars in August and September; year-round in southern Florida.

COMMON FOODPLANTS Spider lily, narcissus, amaryllis, and other plants in amaryllis, iris, and lily families; many other plants are less commonly reported; caterpillars may be reared on lettuce.

REMARKS Females lay clusters containing hundreds of eggs. Early instars are gregarious. The Spanish Moth breeds as far north as southern Indiana during summer months. Its winter range is probably limited to subtropical Florida and Texas. The caterpillar is almost certainly toxic, although I do not believe its chemical ecology has been studied. The Convict Caterpillar appears to have two heads, with the one at the rear realistic enough to draw initial attention. *Xanthopastis timais*, the name usually applied to North American populations of the moth, more correctly refers to a South American species that is genitalically distinct from our North American populations (Tim McCabe, pers. comm.).

Hadenines – Subfamily Hadeninae

The caterpillars are cutwormlike and rather undistinguished, shaded in brown and other earth tones, but many early spring-active hadenines are green or yellow and, at least to me, border on attractive. The spiracular stripe, when present, often continues down the anal proleg. SD2 seta on A9 often slightly longer and thinner than adjacent setae—but this character is difficult to evaluate without a microscope. This is a large and diverse subfamily with more than 140 Eastern species. The subfamily has undergone consider-able revision and now includes many owlet genera that were formerly classified in the Cuculliinae. As presently defined by Kitching and Rawlins (1998), the subfamily is believed to be an unnatural assemblage destined to be parsed out into different groups. Many pinions and sallows (Xylenini) are foodplant specialists; by contrast the arches, quakers, and kin (Orthosiini) tend to be polyphagous on woody plants. Most treated here have one annual generation. Their caterpillars require new foliage and will gradually starve to death if fed mature leaves. Many pinions and sallows emerge in the fall and have winter-active adults; other hadenines overwinter as pupae. Among the latter group are moths which are among the first Lepidoptera to emerge in the early spring.

Branded Pinion (Lithophane patefacta) *consuming another caterpillar.*

PINIONS AND SALLOWS – TRIBE XYLENINI

This group includes many of our winter moths. All but the Red-winged Sallow (*Xystopeplus rufago*) emerge in the fall. The adults of several genera mate and lay eggs in the fall and early winter; others hibernate, periodically fly on warm nights, but wait until the first warm nights of late winter or early spring to engage in reproductive activities. One of the best methods for observing adults (including females) is to "sugar" or bait with fermenting mix-tures of beer, sugar, and rotten fruit (see Holland 1968: 146 for an engaging essay on bait-ing for moths). Baiting is particularly effective in late winter before red maples have bloomed, and in so doing, providing nectar in abundance. Dale Schweitzer is the North American authority on the biology and taxonomy of the group. I am unaware of larval characters that are unique to the tribe. Many have round, clearly delineated and often pale dorsal pinacula (especially in the pinions, *Lithophane*). Caterpillars of several pinions are facultatively predaceous on other insects, and especially other caterpillars and pupae.

Eupsilia vinulenta

RECOGNITION *Velvety purple-brown* with weak spiracular stripe and prominent glossy shield over T1. Obscure pale middorsal and subdorsal stripes; *spiracular stripe essentially absent on thorax, increasingly expressed rearward.* Lower sides of body often with purple flush; venter mostly bluish green but becoming burgundy below thorax. Head with broad *dark mask over each lobe; triangle paler brown but still darker than maple ground-color of lower and top portions of head.* Five other *Eupsilia* occur on woody vegetation in the East (*cirripalea, morrisoni, sidus, tristigmata,* and an undescribed species near *sidus*). Their separation is difficult both as larvae and adults (*see* Forbes 1954 and Rings et al. 1992). Adults should be reared if certain identification is required; occasionally it will be necessary to microscopically examine the forewing scales and/or genitalia. Larva to 3.5cm.

OCCURRENCE Barrens, woodlands, and forests from southern Canada to Georgia (mountains) and Missouri. One generation with mature caterpillars from May through early July.

COMMON FOODPLANTS Widely polyphagous on woody plants, for example cherry, maple, and oak.

REMARKS *Eupsilia* caterpillars lose much of their distinctive coloration in the last instar—the description above applies best to fifth and early sixth instars. Larvae are new-leaf specialists that fashion crude leaf shelters in young leaves. Provide prepupal caterpillars with a deep layer of lightly moistened peat. Adults emerge in the fall and fly all winter. *Eupsilia* gather by the hundreds at beer and sugar and other baits. Adults are particularly active at dusk and early evening. More often than not, these are the strong-flying moths seen with your headlights over the winter months.

ASHEN PINION
Lithophane antennata

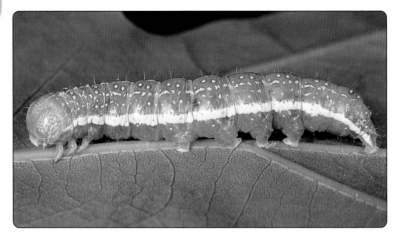

RECOGNITION *Green, somewhat shiny, with broad, creamy spiracular stripe.* Spiracular stripe weakly expressed on T1. Dorsal spots (D1 and D2) circular and well defined. Middorsal stripe thin, creamy, continuous from T2 rearward. Subdorsal stripe white, broken into spots; supraspiracular area also with spots that more or less weakly define a stripe. Head pale green and unmarked, shiny; labrum somewhat whitened; mandibles black. Thoracic legs often black. Larva less than 4cm. Similar to caterpillar of the Broad Ashen Pinion (*Lithophane laticinerea*) which tends to have a more yellow cast to the ground color, a broader middorsal stripe, and a more-developed subdorsal stripe.

OCCURRENCE Woodlands and forests from southern Canada to South Carolina and Mississippi. One generation with mature caterpillars from late May through early July.

COMMON FOODPLANTS Oak; also apple, ash, blackberry, blueberry, cherry, elm, hickory, plum, willow, and other woody plants.

REMARKS Although the caterpillar is commonly known as the Green Fruitworm this is a bit of a misnomer as the Ashen Pinion only occasionally consumes (newly developing) fruit. The caterpillar of Grote's Pinion (*Lithophane grotei*) shares this common name, and to make matters even more confusing, many economic entomologists use "green fruitworm" loosely to refer to many types of green hadenines. In other green fruitworms, e.g., in quakers (*Orthosia*) and genera other than *Lithophane*, the dorsal spots (pinacula) are less clearly delimited. Pinions emerge in the fall and live through the winter, often flying on warm evenings. Mating is delayed until late winter or early spring, hence females may be on the wing six months before pairing. A female's reproductive status may sometimes be determined with a gentle top to bottom pinch of the abdomen—the male's spermatophore within is surprisingly large and firm.

RECOGNITION Light or dark brown to gray or steel blue and *often with reddish brown to rusty middorsal, subdorsal, and spiracular stripes. Dorsum usually marked with dark chevrons that are darkest on A8.* Head brown with darker mottling and dark bar to either side of midline. Larva to 3.5cm. The caterpillars of several other Eastern *Lithophane*, and in particular

Bethune's Pinion (*L. bethunei*) and Hemina Pinion (*L. hemina*), are easily confused with those of the Nameless Pinion. Early instars of all three species somewhat resemble the caterpillar of the Ashen Pinion (*L. antennata*), being green with a broad, pale spiracular stripe.

OCCURRENCE Woodlands and forests across Canada south in East to Georgia (mountains) and Great Lakes States. One generation with mature caterpillars from late May through early July.

COMMON FOODPLANTS Alder, apple, basswood, birch, cherry, fir, hawthorn, hemlock, hornbeam, maple, oak, pine, spruce, willow, and many other woody plants.

REMARKS From the Smokies through much of New England this is often the most frequently encountered *Lithophane* caterpillar. Caterpillars of some pinions, e.g., the related Bethune's Pinion, occasionally attack and consume other caterpillars and soft-bodied insects. It is advisable to house late instar pinions in separate containers. Evidently the pupae of tent caterpillars, loopers, and other owlets are favored as prey. Until a reliable key to pinion larvae has been written, it is best to base identifications on the adults, which are difficult enough. Larval coloration would suggest that members of this group of pinions rest (and perhaps hunt) on bark, at least in the last instar when their markings are most barklike.

BRANDED PINION
Lithophane patefacta

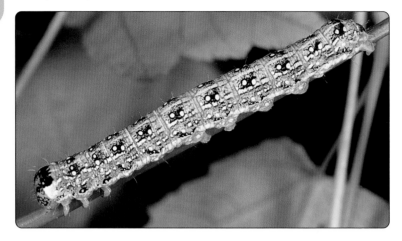

RECOGNITION *Variegated in steel blue, gray, and white, with thin yellow to orange middorsal and subdorsal stripes*; some individuals very pale (inset) while others quite dark (especially southward). *Dorsal pinacula white, prominent.* Pale spiracular stripe, when present, may be edged with black above. Head variable, pale and unmarked to extensively mottled with black. Larva to 3.5cm. The caterpillars of Wanton Pinion (*Lithophane petulca*), a largely northern species, are similarly colored, but have less conspicuous dorsal pinacula. They are commonly found on birch; other foodplants include alder, ash, basswood, elm, poplar, and willow.

OCCURRENCE Woodlands and forests from southern Canada to northern Florida and Kentucky. One generation with mature caterpillars from late May through early July.

COMMON FOODPLANTS Maple commonly, but also blueberry, cherry, and oak.

REMARKS Perhaps the most widespread and abundant pinion in the Southeast, especially in the Piedmont Region. Its propensity to eat other caterpillars (including its own siblings) is curiously variable (*see* page 402). In some collections, especially those from the South, this Pinion like many other pinions is both cannibalistic and predatory. Other cohorts show little interest in carnivory and mature consuming only foliage. It would be interesting to know if and to what degree the predatory behavior of the Branded Pinion is influenced by diet and other environmental factors. Perhaps the darker mottled forms, which appear well suited for a life on bark, are more predatory than the green pale morphs that are especially common northwards.

Lithophane querquera

RECOGNITION *Waxy white with bright yellow markings.* Yellow spiracular stripe broad, sometimes broken below spiracle. *Dorsal yellow patches at anterior and posterior ends of T2 and T3 and caudal end of A1–A7* that may extend laterally to meet spiracular stripe. Prothoracic shield and head pale and unmarked. Larva to 4cm. Caterpillars of Mustard Sallow (*Pyreferra hesperidago*) and other *Pyreferra* species are also white and yellow (*see* page 411), but feed only on witch hazel, American hornbeam, hop hornbeam, and perhaps hazel. In *Pyreferra*, the yellow markings over the dorsum are located centrally or anteriorly on each segment and extend down to the prolegs on the abdominal segments.

OCCURRENCE Woodlands and forests from southern Ontario to New Hampshire south to Georgia, Mississippi, and Missouri. One generation with mature caterpillars from late May through early July.

COMMON FOODPLANTS My students and I have found larvae on apple, ash, cherry, hickory, and oak (*see* Remarks).

REMARKS This is one of our most predatory pinions, consuming other caterpillars and pupae, especially in later instars (Schweitzer 1979). It is perplexing why the caterpillars of *Pyreferra* and the Shivering Pinion should be so similar in appearance—I leave it to others to offer an explanation. Pinions "shiver" prior to taking wing on cold evenings, a behavior that warms the body and in particular the musculature of the thorax. The flight muscles are rapidly stretched, but in such a way that no lift is provided and the moth is able to remain in place. By shivering, pinions are capable of raising their internal thoracic temperatures as much as 30° C (50° F) above ambient temperatures! Once sufficiently warmed, the moths fly off in their search for mates, food, or suitable oviposition sites. The image above was selected to show a caterpillar in the process of molting: the head of the last instar is visible as a bulge above the thoracic legs.

DOWDY PINION
Lithophane unimoda

RECOGNITION *Blue-green especially above yellow spiracular stripe* that runs length of body. Some individuals with mottling of vague cream spots, especially over dorsum. *Spiracles black.* Dorsal spots, common to pinions, only vaguely evident. Larva to 4cm. Penultimate instar more speckled with a dotted subdorsal stripe and thinner spiracular stripe (inset). Caterpillar of George's Pinion (*Lithophane georgii*) similar, but with prominent white middorsal stripe and yellow spiracles ringed in black. This northern species ranges into the high elevations of the southern Appalachians; willow and blueberry are common foodplants.

OCCURRENCE Fields and woodlands from southern Canada to South Carolina, Missouri, and Nebraska. One generation with mature caterpillars from late May through early July.

COMMON FOODPLANTS Cherry and plum preferred; other reported foodplants include apple, aspen, maple, oak, sourwood, and willow, but some of these may represent misidentifications.

REMARKS Gravid females readily oviposit in captivity, especially if offered a solution of sugar water for one or two nights. The caterpillars of most pinions can be reared on cherry. All pinions that feed on deciduous trees require new foliage and will gradually starve if fed only older leaves.

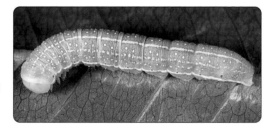

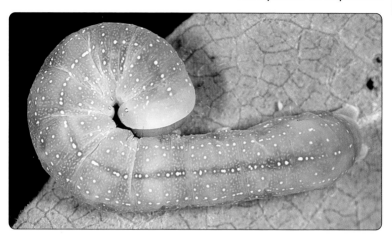

RECOGNITION Lime green with *middorsal, subdorsal, supraspiracular, and spiracular "stripes" of small white spots; subdorsal best developed*. Prothoracic shield waxy blue-green, mostly unmarked. First eight abdominal segments with three small white dorsal spots. Larva to 4cm. Caterpillars of Bailey's Pinion (*Lithophane baileyi*) and Warm Gray Pinion (*L. tepida*) similarly marked and perhaps indistinguishable. Bailey's Pinion occurs from Ontario to Nova Scotia south to Georgia (mountains). Warm Gray Pinion occurs from Manitoba to Nova Scotia south to Georgia, although it is absent from many areas in the southern portion of its range.

OCCURRENCE Shrub swamps, woodlands, and forests from southeastern Massachusetts to northern Florida and west to Texas. One generation with mature caterpillars from May through June.

COMMON FOODPLANTS Lab-reared caterpillars accept cherry, fetter-bush (*Leucothoe*), holly, and blueberry; one wild foodplant record from greenbrier. Probably a generalist on woody shrubs and trees.

REMARKS The caterpillar rests on the underside of new leaves with its head curled to one side. Even though caterpillars of Pale Green, Bailey's, and Warm Gray Pinions are similar, those of the former can usually be identified by their geographic location. The Pale Green Pinion is a species of the Atlantic Coastal Plain, southern Piedmont, and Gulf Coast; in the Northeast it is local and rare, being confined mostly to shrub swamps near Cape Cod and adjacent Coastal Plain sites. By contrast, both Bailey's and Warm Gray Pinions are northern species that are confined to mountains south of New York. Bailey's Pinion is a denizen of northern hardwood forests; the Warm Gray Pinion is associated with woodlands, forests, and wetlands over acidic sandy or granitic soils, flying in both bogs and barrens.

HOLLY SALLOW
Metaxaglaea violacea

RECOGNITION *Tan to flesh ground-color with gray mottling and minute black spotting.* A1 or A2–A8 with black middorsal spot towards front edge of each segment. Setal bases smoky gray to black, contrasting with pale ground; setae very inconspicuous. *Wavy, ill-defined yellow-orange to peach spiracular stripe most pronounced over thoracic segments.* Short peach subdorsal line cuts through prothoracic shield. Head with pale snowflakelike markings over each lobe and directly above triangle; sometimes partially withdrawn into T1. Spiracles black. Larva to 4.5cm. Middle instars creamy and more boldly marked.

OCCURRENCE Woodlands, forests, swamps, parks, and yards from extreme southeastern Massachusetts down Atlantic Coast to northern Florida and Louisiana and inland across extreme southern Pennsylvania and into Kentucky. One generation with mature caterpillars by mid-April in Florida and middle or late May (early June) in New Jersey.

COMMON FOODPLANTS Holly, especially American holly (*Ilex opaca*), but some other evergreen *Ilex* species, notably inkberry, also acceptable in captivity.

REMARKS The gray body color with yellow stripes and black pinacula is diagnostic. The caterpillars feed on new growth and flowers. The more boldly marked middle instars often rest on undersides of old holly leaves where they do not seem cryptic. Last instars can be found by searching litter and surface soil at the base of hollies in late spring. The significance of the larval coloration, which borders on aposematic, is unknown, and a radical departure from that of other *Metaxaglaea* species. Eggs overwinter, but some adults survive winter and continue ovipositing into March.

RECOGNITION *Waxy white with bands of lemon yellow.* Yellow bands absent on T1, A9–A10, and often above spiracle on A8. Amount of yellow coloration on intervening segments highly variable among individuals, usually best developed along subdorsum and at level of spiracles. Larva less than 3.5cm.

Two other *Pyreferra* feed on witch hazel in the East: the Mustard Sallow (*P. hesperidago*) and *P. ceromatica*. I am unable to distinguish caterpillars of the three (*see* Remarks). Shivering Pinion (*Lithophane querquera*) caterpillars are also similar (*see* page 407). *Pyrefera pettiti*, a hop hornbeam-feeder, differs markedly—it is green with white setal bases and pronounced spiracular stripe.

OCCURRENCE Woodlands and forests from Ontario to New Hampshire south to Georgia (mountains). One generation with mature caterpillars in May and June.

COMMON FOODPLANTS Hazel, hop hornbeam, and witch hazel.

REMARKS This genus is in need of study. The Eyed Mustard Sallow is enigmatic. Its recorded foodplants include members of both the witch hazel and birch families, which seems suspicious. Furthermore, there are distinctive larval forms involved—some individuals are yellow-green with the yellow band broken into large subdorsal and spiracular spots that may or not fuse into bands; other individuals have almost complete yellow banding. The latter closely approach my images of the Mustard Sallow. A second conundrum offered by the genus is the mysterious decline of *P. ceromatica*. While formerly widespread across the Midwest and Eastern Seaboard, it is now believed to be extinct from almost all of its former range. It is still reasonably frequent in eastern North Carolina. Forbes (1954) and Crumb (1956) state that its larva resembles that of *P. hesperidago*.

RED-WINGED SALLOW
Xystopeplus rufago

RECOGNITION Mottled, red-brown with *dark, shiny prothoracic shield*. Subdorsal stripe prominent through prothoracic shield, but otherwise weakly expressed, especially rearward. Middorsal stripe vague. *Anal plate black, edged with white, contrasting sharply with rest of rump.* Spiracular stripe continuing to anal proleg, although somewhat

weakened rearward. Penultimate instar somewhat translucent reddish green with thin, white middorsal, subdorsal, and spiracular stripes; neither prothoracic shield nor anal plate darkened or otherwise distinguished. Larva to 3cm.

OCCURRENCE Woodlands and forests from Minnesota to Maine south to Florida and Texas. One generation with mature caterpillars from May to July.

COMMON FOODPLANTS Blueberry, cherry, hazel, oak, poplar, sourwood, and probably many other woody species, but oak seems to be the preferred foodplant. Dale Schweitzer (pers. comm.) has observed late instars avidly feeding on young (green) blueberry fruits in captivity.

REMARKS Pupae from my rearings have yielded adults in the fall, but the majority emerged in the spring. Although seemingly anomalous, because almost all temperate Lepidoptera have a single stage which overwinters, these observations are consistent with museum records for the Red-winged Sallow, i.e., there are fewer collections for fall and winter months relative to the number for spring. The dark color of the late instar suggests that it feeds at night, and moves from foliage into the litter during the day. Caterpillars of the Red-winged Sallow tolerate older foliage better than most xylenines.

BLACK ARCHES
Melanchra assimilis

RECOGNITION Ground color either green or brown (inset) and *boldly striped with yellow. Broad, yellow subdorsal stripe edged with white and black*; spiracular stripe with reduced black edging below. Spiracles white with black outer ring. Head green or brown and mostly unmarked except for short yellow line passing through uppermost eyes. Larva to 3.5cm.

OCCURRENCE Meadows and open wetlands from Canada south to Virginia and Great Lakes States. One generation with mature caterpillars in August and September.

COMMON FOODPLANTS Alder, ash, aster, birch, bracken, goldenrod, mullein, raspberry, St. John's wort, sweet fern, tamarack, willow, and others; primarily a generalist on low-growing plants.

REMARKS Covell (1984) regarded the Black Arches as an uncommon moth, and if I had to judge its abundance based on adult specimens in collections I would agree. Yet as a caterpillar this species can be common. In the fall look for it in open, moist to wet meadows with an abundance of goldenrod. My general entomology students have turned up numerous Black Arches caterpillars in their sweep net samples from the northwestern part of Connecticut, along with larvae of The Asteroid (*Cucullia asteroides*), Common Tan Wave (*Pleuroprucha insulsaria*), and others. The pupa overwinters.

ZEBRA CATERPILLAR
Melanchra picta

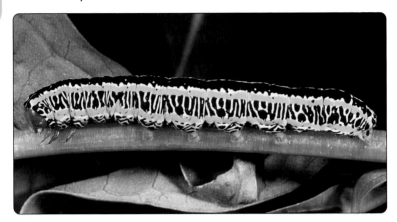

RECOGNITION *Unmistakable black, yellow, and white caterpillar.* Head, legs, and prolegs reddish orange. *Black ground color cut by irregular white lines* (hence Zebra Caterpillar) between *bright lemon yellow subdorsal and spiracular stripes.* Spiracles pale with black outer ring. Larva to 3.5cm.

OCCURRENCE Gardens, fields, meadows, coastal communities, and other open habitats from Canada south to Georgia and northern Texas. One or two generations northward; two or three broods in New Jersey and Missouri and with mature caterpillars from May onward.

COMMON FOODPLANTS Generalist on many low-growing plants including blueberry, cabbage, carrot, clover, dandelion, hazel, knotweed, peas, and willow.

REMARKS The gregarious early instars (inset) sometimes defoliate small plants. The Zebra Caterpillar is occasionally reported as a pest on field crops and in gardens, but rarely is it common enough to be a pest of consequence. While collections of adults at light are not uncommon, the frequency of larval sightings would suggest that the Zebra Caterpillar, like its congener the Black Arches, is not strongly attracted to light as an adult. The pupa overwinters below ground.

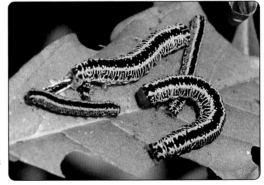

Trichordestra legitima

RECOGNITION *Handsome brown and yellow striped caterpillar.* Dorsum dark brown to black, except for pale narrow "V" over T1 and T2. *Yellow stripes edged with white; black spiracular stripe* contrasting with white spiracles. Head orange-brown, often with funnel-shaped darker brown area over each lobe that reaches eyes. Larva to 3.5cm. Somewhat similar to Black Arches (*Melanchra assimilis*).

OCCURRENCE Fields and other open places from Canada to Florida and Texas. Evidently just a single principal generation with mature caterpillars in late summer and fall.

COMMON FOODPLANTS Many, mostly low-growing plants including aster, beans, butter-and-eggs, dogbane, goldenrod, grasses, milkweed, tobacco, and yarrow.

REMARKS Grass seed heads are a good place to search for the Striped Garden Caterpillar in the fall, but I usually find them feeding in the flowers of goldenrod where their colors seem to be both cryptic and aposematic. A third possibility for their distinctive coloration is mimicry: there are other fall-active caterpillars that are similarly marked such as the Black Arches and forms of The Asteroid (*Cucullia asteroides*). All three of these may be found feeding in goldenrod flowers. Although regarded as a pest, population numbers rarely climb to levels where they cause economic injury. The pupa overwinters in duff or soil.

ARMYWORM
Mythimna unipuncta
(= *Pseudaletia unipuncta*)

RECOGNITION Yellow- to dark chocolate-brown, smooth, with subdued striping. *Thin, white middorsal, subdorsal, supraspiracular, spiracular, and subspiracular stripes separate alternating, darker and paler stripes*; the first two of these stripes pass through the prothoracic shield. *Thin, white subdorsal stripe edged with vague dark patches above, especially over abdominal spiracles*. Head often with black bar to either side of midline and down either side of triangle. Larva to 4cm.

OCCURRENCE Gardens, fields, wet meadows, and other grassy habitats. Distributed worldwide. Two or three generations over much of East with mature caterpillars from April onward. Present year-round in South.

COMMON FOODPLANTS Generalist on grasses (including grains), but consuming many forbs and woody species, including a number of crop and garden plants.

REMARKS The nocturnally active caterpillars are occasionally abundant enough to defoliate entire fields. The mass exodus made by caterpillars from such fields accounts for their common name. Larvae associated with outbreak densities tend to be much darker, almost black in some forms. In the spring, adults migrate northward on the leading edge of storm fronts. One May night, while blacklighting with Doug Ferguson along Clingman's Dome Road in Great Smoky Mountains National Park, we observed a mass migration of adults—hundreds came to our mercury vapor light. Millions of moths must have moved through the park that night. In New England I have seen drowned Armyworm moths wash up by the thousands on beaches of Long Island Sound. The Armyworm overwinters as a larva or pupa below ground, but it is unclear how far northward it is able to do so successfully.

Because so many of the members of this tribe are broadly polyphagous, I have made no attempt to provide exhaustive foodplant listings. For a recent summary of foodplant records see Rings et al. (1992). All overwinter as pupae, but remarkably the adult moths are almost fully formed, save for their wings, within the pupal casing by midsummer, months before they will hatch. Not surprisingly, quakers and other orthosiines are among the first moths to emerge in the spring.

ALTERNATE WOODLING
Egira alternans

RECOGNITION *Brown with broad spiracular stripe that ranges from immaculate white to pale pink-brown.* Thin white middorsal and subdorsal stripes vague and broken. Dark red-brown stripe over spiracle subtly edged along its upper edge with white. A8 somewhat humped. Spiracles black. Head orange and unmarked or more commonly with bar over each lobe and additional mottling. Larva to 3.5cm. Confusingly similar to Subdued Quaker (*Orthosia revicta*) (*see* Remarks).

OCCURRENCE Woodlands and forests from southern Canada to Florida and Texas. One generation with mature caterpillars from late April into early July.

COMMON FOODPLANTS Many woody shrubs and trees including blueberry, cherry, honeysuckle, horse chestnut, oak, rhododendron, silver bells, sourwood, walnut, and willow.

REMARKS Caterpillars of the Subdued Quaker are perplexingly similar, so much so that I am not sure how to separate the two. The coloration differences suggested by Godfrey (1972) do not seem to hold for my collections. One wonders if the similarity of the two caterpillars is due to common ancestry or evolutionary convergence, and if the latter proves to be the case, why such a pattern might be adaptive. The pupa overwinters in soil.

SPECKLED GREEN FRUITWORM
Orthosia hibisci

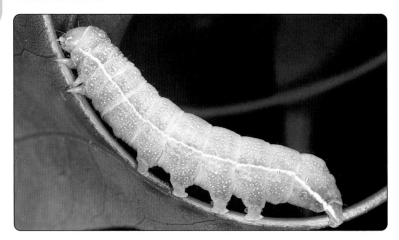

RECOGNITION Green or blue-green with continuous, white, middorsal and spiracular stripes, and broken, subdorsal stripe; creamy specks abundant. *Spiracular stripe running above spiracles on A1–A7 and below spiracles on T1 and A8, especially strong on A7–A10,* sometimes with incomplete dark edging above, particularly in blue-green forms. Spiracles pale with dark rim. Head pale green and mostly unmarked, *with thin white crescent passing through at least top lateral eyes.* Dark-form caterpillars smoky green, especially dark between spiracular and subdorsal stripes. Larva to 3.5cm. Caterpillar of Gray Quaker (*Orthosia alurina*) usually black above spiracular stripe; its green forms frequently bear black plates on outer face of prolegs and blackened anal plate; often with a transverse yellow and black line over dorsum of A8. It is appreciably less common than the Speckled Green Fruitworm. It occurs from Wisconsin to New York southward. Earlier instars of many *Orthosia* resemble the Speckled Green Fruitworm.

OCCURRENCE Woodlands and forests from Canada south to Florida and Texas. One generation with mature caterpillars from late April into early July.

COMMON FOODPLANTS Many woody shrubs and trees including both broadleaf and coniferous species: e.g., apple, ash, autumn olive, cherry, elm, gooseberry, maple, oak, poplar, spruce, and willow.

REMARKS This is one of the most ubiquitous forest insects of spring and early summer. In boom years its caterpillars can be found on almost any tree or shrub. Both the Speckled Green Fruitworm and Gray Quaker have a dark form (*see* Godfrey 1972); perhaps these are induced forms that occur mostly in captive larvae. Analogous dark forms occur in hornworms, snout butterflies, and inchworms.

Orthosia rubescens

RECOGNITION Most mature caterpillars *dark above spiracular stripe*, with white middorsal and broken subdorsal stripes, and abundant white flecking. *Area between spiracular and subspiracular stripes usually white* in all color forms. Frequently with black patches about spiracle and to either side of midline of each segment that meet in dark forms. *Prolegs sometimes with pinkish cast*, especially in paler morphs. Green and blue-green forms usually with ground smokier above spiracular stripe. Most individuals blue-green below subspiracular stripe. Early and middle instars resemble those of Speckled Green Fruitworm (*Orthosia hibisci*) and some pinions such as the Ashen Pinion (*Lithophane antennata*). Larva to 4cm.

OCCURRENCE Woodlands and forests from Wisconsin to Nova Scotia south to Georgia and northern Arkansas. One generation with mature caterpillars from late April into early July.

COMMON FOODPLANTS Many woody shrubs and trees including both broadleaf and coniferous species: e.g., beech, birch, blueberry, cherry, chestnut, elderberry, gooseberry, greenbrier, hemlock, holly, hop hornbeam, maple, oak, and viburnum; less commonly on forbs and other low-growing plants.

REMARKS A very common caterpillar in most years and most places, but because of its variability a difficult species to recognize, especially prior to the last instar which is shown here. While I routinely encounter larvae while searching or beating foliage, I also have found large numbers of last instars under burlap bands while taking censuses of Gypsy Moth larval populations. Certainly the coloration of the dark-form last instars are more cryptic on bark than on foliage. Perhaps the Ruby Quaker and the melanic forms of the Gray Quaker and Green Speckled Fruitworm are "bark resters" by day. Adults of most quakers readily come to bait in the spring, especially before red maple comes into bloom.

NORMAN'S QUAKER
Crocigrapha normani

RECOGNITION Last instar reddish brown to tan-brown without obvious striping and mostly undistinguished. Ground color paler below subtle white spiracular stripe (when present). *Prothoracic shield dark brown, shiny, becoming pale laterally, and with irregular pale spot at posterior end near midline.* A8 somewhat humped with transverse line running over dorsum of posterior end of segment, connecting posterior dorsal (D2) setae. Spiracles maple-colored, rimmed with black. *Head shiny brown with two dark spots that tend to fuse over each lobe.* Larva to 3.5cm. Middle and penultimate instars conspicuously bicolored, dark above and white to cream below; ground color darkest between white subdorsal and spiracular stripes; head with prominent black spot(s) on each lobe (inset).

OCCURRENCE Woodlands and forests from southern Canada to South Carolina and Mississippi. One generation with mature caterpillars from late April through July.

COMMON FOODPLANTS American hornbeam, apple, ash, aspen, birch, blueberry, cherry, elm, hazel, hop hornbeam, maple, oak, rose, willow, witch hazel, and many other woody shrubs and trees.

REMARKS This is one of the more ubiquitous caterpillars that I encounter in my late spring beating samples. Unfortunately, it is rather difficult to recognize, in part because it is variable both within and between instars. The dark spots on the head help to identify most instars. Females raft their eggs. The pupa overwinters.

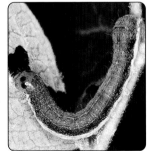

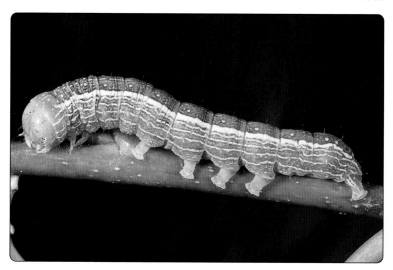

RECOGNITION Pale green with thin, white middorsal stripe; thick, white subdorsal stripe; and *four, creamy, wavy lateral stripes.* Lateral set of stripes includes two supraspiracular, one spiracular, and one subspiracular stripe. Segments T1–A7 with single white spot to either side of midline; A8 with two spots to either side of midline. Spiracles yellow-orange. Head sea-green, shiny, and unmarked. Larva to 3cm.

OCCURRENCE Woodlands and forests from southern Canada to Florida and Texas. One generation with mature caterpillars from late April into July.

COMMON FOODPLANTS Apple, blackberry, blueberry, cherry, elm, hickory, hop hornbeam, oak, viburnum, witch hazel, and many other woody shrubs and trees.

REMARKS A very common species, especially on oak. Many of the hadenines treated in this volume are numerically abundant in Eastern forests during the spring. Based on larval coloration alone one would predict that hadenines as a group are palatable. It is my guess that spring-active hadenines and inchworms are the most important components in the diets of insectivorous birds that forage on caterpillars (e.g., warblers) in Appalachian and Northeastern forests, and that few would nest successfully without them. The pupa overwinters. The individual figured here is especially well marked; occasionally the set of four lateral stripes is considerably paler or the uppermost is more or less fused with the subdorsal stripe, or both. The disproportionately large head and prolegs are indicative that this caterpillar has recently molted into the last instar.

DISTINCT QUAKER
Achatia distincta

RECOGNITION *Sea- or yellow-green with only subdorsal stripe well developed and vague speckling.* Middorsal, spiracular, and subspiracular stripes thin and broken; supraspiracular stripe consisting only of scattered spots. *Dorsum of A1–A8 with single white spot to either side of midline*; many individuals with smaller dorsal spot obliquely situated, at leading edge of segment just above subdorsal stripe. Spiracles yellow-orange. Head sea-green, shiny, and unmarked except for tiny white line through eyes. Larva to 3.5cm.

OCCURRENCE Woodlands and forests from southern Canada to northern Florida and Texas. One generation with mature caterpillars from mid-April to early July.

COMMON FOODPLANTS Apple, ash, birch, blackberry, blueberry, butternut, cherry, hop hornbeam, maple, oak, sour gum, viburnum, walnut, witch hazel, and many other woody shrubs and trees.

REMARKS Caterpillars of the Distinct Quaker are common to abundant in spring across a variety of woodland and forest types. Females lay readily in captivity, especially if provided with a bit of food, a twisted section of paper towel, and a sprig of suitable foliage. The females of *Achatia* and related hadenines lay eggs in rafts, often containing 30 or more. Caterpillars feed mostly at night on new leaf tissue. They may spin a weak shelter in which to hide by day. The pupa overwinters.

Morrisonia confusa

RECOGNITION Last instar very pale to reddish- or orange-brown, densely speckled with minute vague spots. Faint middorsal, subdorsal, spiracular, and subspiracular stripes. Pale spiracles ringed with black. *Head chestnut, shiny, usually with poorly defined dark area over vertex. Antenna with white base and black apex.* Larva to 4cm. Early and middle instars pale green with conspicuous, *maroon supraspiracular spots on T1–A8*; all striping more obvious than in last instar; head without dark patch over each lobe (inset).

OCCURRENCE Woodlands and forests from Canada south to Florida and Texas. One generation with mature caterpillars from June to November.

COMMON FOODPLANTS Many woody shrubs and trees including both broadleaf (e.g., ash, basswood, blueberry, cherry, maple, oak, rhododendron, sycamore, walnut, and willow) and coniferous species as well as forbs such as purple loosestrife and bush clover.

REMARKS The caterpillar fashions a silken nest, often between two leaves, into which it retreats during the day. The shelter of the last instar is substantial, thicker than the pupal cocoon of many other owlets. The red-spotted middle instars draw considerably more attention than the rather homely last instar. Development extends over a long period— I have collected young caterpillars in early June that fed into October. Development in the last instar is curiously protracted, often spanning three months. The pupa overwinters.

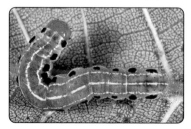

FLUID ARCHES
Morrisonia latex (= *Polia latex*)

RECOGNITION Variably patterned, brown caterpillar with faint middorsal and subdorsal pale stripes. Fine black stripe, running just above spiracles, divides darker upper portion of body from paler venter. *Thin black line connects posterior dorsal setae (D2) on A8.* Darkened subdorsal chevrons run length of abdomen, becoming more prominent rearward. T2–A7 with both dorsal pinacula whitened. *Head usually with dark splotch over each lobe* and additional associated mottling. Larva to 4cm. Early instars pale green to light brown with characteristic darkened patch over each lobe (inset).

OCCURRENCE Woodlands and forests from Canada south to Georgia (mountains) and northern Arkansas. One generation with mature caterpillars from July to September.

COMMON FOODPLANTS American hornbeam, basswood, beech, birch, cherry, elm, hop hornbeam, hazel, maple, oak, poison ivy, willow, witch hazel, and many other woody shrubs and trees. I have found caterpillars that appear to be this species on hemlock.

REMARKS In many Appalachian and Eastern woodlands, caterpillars of the Fluid Arches can be expected to turn up on almost any woody plant. While early and middle instars are green-brown and rest on foliage, the variegated brown late instars are suited for an existence on bark. Nearly all instars can be recognized by the dark spot over each lobe, but the spots may be faint in some individuals, especially those that have molted recently. Norman's Quaker (*Crocigrapha normani*) also bears large dark spots on the head, but the spot on each lobe is paired and its caterpillars are fully mature by early July or earlier. The pupa overwinters.

Nephelodes minians

RECOGNITION Dark brown to greasy black above level of spiracles with *distinctive anal plate: always with tan to white central line and edging.* Body somewhat spindle-shaped, thickest about A4–A5. Integument smooth and shiny. *Prothoracic shield often with middorsal and subdorsal stripes.* Tan middorsal, subdorsal, and spiracular stripes; these are obscure in darker forms (inset). Head orange. Larva to 4.5cm.

OCCURRENCE Gardens, agricultural lands, fields, and yards from Manitoba to Newfoundland south to Georgia and Texas. One generation with mature caterpillars from April to early July.

COMMON FOODPLANTS Grasses, including corn.

REMARKS The Bronzed Cutworm is an occasional pest of turfgrass, corn, and other grains. The caterpillars are largely subterranean. I find them in the spring while turning soil and removing last year's plants from the garden. The eggs hatch in late winter and the larvae feed on roots and leaves as conditions permit. Because they are active early in the growing season, they can be particularly damaging to seedlings. Bronzed Cutworm caterpillars mature and pupate in late spring and early summer, but delay their emergence—over much of the East the adults fly from late July into October.

SPOTTED PHOSPHILA
Phosphila miselioides

RECOGNITION *Lime green with bright yellow spots* (pinacula). Body smooth with very short and inconspicuous setae. *A8 strongly humped.* Intersegmental areas with yellowish hue. Lower and rear portions of body with glaucous bloom. Vague spiracular stripe. Head pale, orange-tan. Larva less than 3.5cm. The prepupal larva turns smoky, almost black, although the dorsal pinacula remain bright yellow (inset).

OCCURRENCE Open woodlands and forest edges from Manitoba to southern Maine south to Florida and Texas. Evidently multiple-brooded with mature caterpillars from May through November.

COMMON FOODPLANTS Greenbrier.

REMARKS The caterpillar preferentially consumes new foliage. The larva rests on the underside of leaves with the head curled back against the abdomen. When disturbed the head is withdrawn into the thorax and held downward out of harm's way. The rear portion of the prothorax gets a deep dimple when the head is withdrawn, indicating that there is muscular attachment that runs from the back of the head to the dorsum of first thoracic segment. The pupa overwinters.

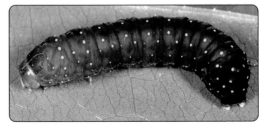

Phosphila turbulenta

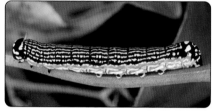

RECOGNITION "Two-headed" last instar marked with prominent black and white pinstriping. *Both ends of body swollen, especially so rearward.* From above, caudal end of body appears more boldly marked. Subspiracular area mostly yellow (inset). Early instar pale green with shiny black head. Larva less than 3.5cm.

OCCURRENCE Open woodlands and forest edges from Illinois to southern Maine to Florida and Texas. At least two generations in North Carolina with mature caterpillars from May to July, then again in the fall (September to November).

COMMON FOODPLANTS Greenbrier.

REMARKS The Turbulent Phosphila is a gregarious defoliator. The caterpillars feed and rest side by side, and not always facing in the same direction, usually on the underside of a leaf blade. The markings at the rear of the body form a striking false head, one that likely draws greater attention than the actual head. The shiny, black, true head is held under the black and white prothoracic shield. Older caterpillars often feed solitarily and exposed. Both their coloration and behavior suggest that the caterpillars of the Turbulent Phosphila are chemically protected. The Turbulent Phosphila is more apt to be found feeding on mature foliage than the Spotted Phosphila. The pupa overwinters.

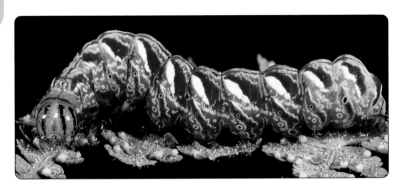

PINK-SHADED FERN MOTH
Callopistria mollissima

RECOGNITION *Emerald green or reddish with whitish, oblique, lens-shaped spots above each abdominal spiracle*; these matched above by an often darkened, mirror-image spot. Finer zigzagging (lightning bolt) lines above each spiracle. A pale halo rings each black spiracle. *Each side of head with two black lines*, one from antenna and other from first stemma, that extend to vertex. Larva less than 2.5cm. The Silver-spotted Fern Moth (*Callopistria cordata*) co-occurs with Pink-shaded Fern Moth over much of East. Its red or yellow-green larva bears well-defined white addorsal stripes and two pairs of strong black lines on head. Caterpillar of Florida Fern Moth (*Callopistria floridensis*) green, brown, black, or reddish; with thin, jagged, cream addorsal and subdorsal stripes; and prominent white spiracular stripes. Sometimes with black, bat-shaped spots over dorsum and small black spots subtending spiracles. This southern species occasionally establishes on ferns in greenhouses. I am familiar with only one form of *C. granitosa*: it is light green with conspicuous longitudinal striping and black spots over the head.

OCCURRENCE Woodlands and forests from Michigan to Nova Scotia south to central Florida and Arkansas. Evidently two generations with mature caterpillars from June to October in Northeast; two or three generations in Missouri.

COMMON FOODPLANTS Ferns, such as New York fern.

REMARKS In captivity I have seen both cinnamon-red and green forms—the pattern elements were essentially the same. All four of our Eastern *Callopistria* are fern-feeders; the extent to which diets are specialized on different fern genera is unexplored. Bracken is a favorite of the Silver-spotted Fern Moth and *Callopistria granitosa*. Fern Moth caterpillars rest on the fronds by day. They may be collected with a beating sheet or by sweeping. The pupa overwinters.

AMERICAN DUN-BAR
Cosmia calami

RECOGNITION Short, stocky, lime green, densely *mottled with irregular cream spots. Body widest through midabdominal segments. Middorsal stripe especially pronounced on A8–A10.* Sometimes with thin, faint subdorsal and spiracular stripes. Head pale sea-green. Larva less than 3cm.

OCCURRENCE Barrens, woodlands, and forests from southern Canada to Florida and Texas. One generation with mature caterpillars from April to June.

COMMON FOODPLANTS Oak (but *see* Remarks).

REMARKS Over many areas of the East, the American Dun-bar is among the ten most common moths seen at light in summer. The caterpillar is active in the spring, feeding on young oak foliage. According to Forbes (1954) the principal diet is other caterpillars. I have reared several caterpillars to maturity on a diet of only foliage. Its European counterpart, the Dun-bar (*Cosmia trapezina*), is also omnivorous, feeding on a variety of woody trees and shrubs as well as other caterpillars. Larvae of the Winter Moth (*Operophtera brumata*) are commonly consumed (Carter and Hargreaves 1986). The egg overwinters.

COMMON HYPPA
Hyppa xylinoides

RECOGNITION Brown, mottled, stout, rather variable in color, with characteristically humped A8. *Pronounced white spiracular line on T1 that* weakens on T2 then enlarges into vague, broad stripe whose upper edge includes spiracle on A8; rearward the stripe becomes constricted and extends

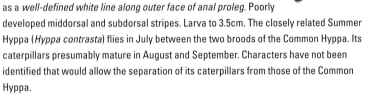

as a *well-defined white line along outer face of anal proleg.* Poorly developed middorsal and subdorsal stripes. Larva to 3.5cm. The closely related Summer Hyppa (*Hyppa contrasta*) flies in July between the two broods of the Common Hyppa. Its caterpillars presumably mature in August and September. Characters have not been identified that would allow the separation of its caterpillars from those of the Common Hyppa.

OCCURRENCE Woodlands and forests from southern Canada to northern Georgia. Two generations with mature caterpillars in June and July, then again from September to November in Missouri and Connecticut.

COMMON FOODPLANTS Broadly polyphagous on forbs and low woody plants.

REMARKS The Common Hyppa may be found at night by searching low vegetation, such as asters and clover. Roadsides running through woodlands and forests can be especially productive. Curiously, the integument collects moisture—at night the caterpillars may accumulate a hoary glaze of condensation over their thorax and abdomen. Adults come to both light and bait. The last instar or prepupa overwinters.

VARIEGATED MIDGET
Elaphria versicolor

RECOGNITION Brown to charcoal, highly variable in pattern; *body swollen about thorax, narrowing to A6, and enlarged again toward rear of A8* (*see* inset). Often with irregular saddle over abdominal segments that ends just above spiracle on A4. Middorsal stripe often with orange, especially over abdominal segments. Usually with small *white subdorsal spot on A8*. Larva less than 2cm.

OCCURRENCE Woodlands and forests from Canada to Florida and Texas. Two or three generations in Missouri with mature caterpillars from June to October.

COMMON FOODPLANTS Many literature records for conifers: fir, hemlock, larch, pine, red cedar, spruce, white cedar, but also birch and other broadleaf plants (*see* Remarks).

REMARKS My students and I have beaten caterpillars from hackberry, hawthorn, and rhododendron. In captivity I had a Variegated Midget caterpillar graze extensively on the green bark of black cherry shoots. The caterpillar fed preferentially on thin bark, stripping centimeters of bark each day, down through the cambium—it showed no interest in foliage. A second larva found on hemlock ate a pupa of the False Hemlock Looper (*Nepytia canosaria*) before the two were to be separated. The Variegated Midget overwinters as a pupa in a shallow chamber carved into tree bark—frass from the excavation is incorporated into the outer surface of the cocoon.

FALL ARMYWORM
Spodoptera frugiperda

RECOGNITION Various shades of brown with subtle markings. *Setal bases shiny black, raised, especially over dorsum and above spiracles; base of anterior dorsal setae (D1) on A8 particularly enlarged.* Vague, tan to yellow-brown middorsal and white subdorsal stripes; supraspiracular area darkened below subdorsal stripe. Broad, pale spiracular stripe often infused with brownish mottling. Prothoracic shield brown, well differentiated, cut by middorsal and subdorsal stripes; sometimes with additional dark spotting. Integument covered with small rounded granules (never with spinules). Larva to 3cm. Beet Armyworm (*Spodoptera exigua*) variable in color; often with spiracular stripe edged above with black, T2 with black lateral spot, and A8 bearing dark subdorsal spot (inset). Occasionally a pest in the West and South, the strongholds for this migratory moth.

OCCURRENCE Fields, waste places, and agricultural lands from southern Canada to Florida and Texas, becoming increasingly common southward. Multiple generations with mature caterpillars through summer and fall months.

COMMON FOODPLANTS General feeder on grasses and low-growing forbs and woody species, including many field crops (e.g., alfalfa, corn, clover, cotton, and tobacco).

REMARKS Frequently a pest in the Deep South. Armyworms, which are a rather heterogeneous group, get their name from the mass marches made by caterpillars when abandoning the fields that they have defoliated. The pupa overwinters, but probably only through Gulf States.

Spodoptera ornithogalli

RECOGNITION Patterning variable: ground color some shade of brown, marked with a variety of colorful stripes. Some individuals with black triangles extending inward from *yellow subdorsal stripe over A1–A8*. Abdominal segments frequently with set of *four, thin, white stripes beneath subdorsal stripe*; these may appear as single, broad, lavender stripe. Often with *black spot on A1 above spiracle*. Many individuals with rusty line beneath each spiracle, which may join to form thin subspiracular stripe. Larva to 4cm. The caterpillar of Dolichos Armyworm (*Spodoptera dolichos*), a tropical species that breeds in the Gulf States, is closely similar. Like the Yellow-striped Armyworm, adults are migratory and occasionally turn up far to the north.

OCCURRENCE Fields and other open habitats from southern Canada to Florida and Texas. Multiple generations with mature caterpillars through summer and fall months.

COMMON FOODPLANTS General feeder on low-growing forbs and woody species, including many field crops and garden plants.

REMARKS Also known as the Cotton Cutworm. This migratory species moves north in the spring with storm fronts that push up from the Gulf of Mexico. One night in late May while blacklighting with Doug Ferguson below Clingman's Dome, North Carolina, we witnessed a massive flight in a pea soup-thick fog—hundreds of adults arrived at our sheets in a matter of a few hours—tens of thousands, perhaps millions, passed over the region that evening. By fall, caterpillars are found well into Canada in most years. The pupa overwinters, but apparently not much north of the Gulf States.

Cutworms and Darts – Subfamily Noctuinae

These are the classic cutworms familiar to farmers and gardeners. The smooth and fleshy caterpillars are usually rendered in various shades of brown. Many tunnel underground by day, emerging after sunset to feed. The subfamily contains more than 100 Eastern species—I treat only a few here since their cryptic colors and habits normally allow them to escape attention. Moreover, larval identifications can be difficult given the variable coloration of noctuines—e.g., White Pine Cutworm (*Xestia badicollis*, *see page 437*). Most feed on grasses, forbs, and low-growing plants. Several genera sever vegetation near ground level and pull it into a vestibule or tunnel where they consume the foliage out of harm's way (hence the name 'cutworms'). Caterpillars of 24 cutworms are figured by Lafontaine (1998).

VARIEGATED CUTWORM
Peridroma saucia

RECOGNITION Stout, smooth cutworm, ranging from gray to brown; frequently with pink to orange markings; many forms more strongly patterned than individual figured here. *Middorsal stripe marked by a small white to orange spot toward rear of abdominal segments A1–A4 (A5–A8).* Poorly differentiated subspiracular stripe, often with shades of orange along its upper edge, runs just beneath black spiracles. *A8 broadly rounded, frequently with yellow to orange rump patch. Vertex marked with a black M; triangle pale tan.* Larva less than 4.5cm.

OCCURRENCE Agricultural lands, fields, and other open habitats. Worldwide. In our area: northern Canada south in East to Florida and Texas. Multiple generations with mature caterpillars from April onward.

COMMON FOODPLANTS General feeder. Economically important foodplants include cabbage, carrot, clover, corn, potato, tomato, wheat, and many others.

REMARKS In most years this is the most economically important cutworm in the Northeast and much of Canada, even infesting greenhouses and cold frames. The pupa overwinters.

BLACK CUTWORM (IPSILON DART)
Agrotis ipsilon

RECOGNITION Tan to brown to virtually coal black with dorsum often lightened between subdorsal stripes. Body pudgy and soft. *Integument smooth, densely peppered with very minute granules and raised blackened setal bases. Posterior dorsal setal base (D2) on abdominal segments A1–A8 twice the diameter of anterior base (D1).* Middorsal and subdorsal stripes most evident in pale individuals. T2 and T3 with upper setal bases aligned in vertical row. Prolegs comparatively small and weak. Head often dark with pale triangle. Larva to 4.5cm.

OCCURRENCE Agricultural lands, waste places, lawns, fields, and grasslands from Canada south to Florida and Texas (and Eurasia). Multiple generations with mature caterpillars from May onward.

COMMON FOODPLANTS General feeder on grasses and low-growing forbs, including many important field and garden crops.

REMARKS Also known as the Greasy Cutworm. Although the integument appears oily, it is not; it is simply smoother than that of other caterpillars. The caterpillar tunnels below ground during the day, emerging after nightfall. It is a pest of many field and garden crops, e.g. clover, lettuce, potato, tomato, and tobacco; the caterpillars also feed on grains, including corn. It may be especially damaging to seedlings in the spring. The Black Cutworm is a migratory species that occurs nearly worldwide—it is not clear what portion (if any) of northern populations represent year-round residents versus migrants from the South. It is one of few migratory moths where a reverse (southward) fall migration has been documented. In the Deep South, the Black Cutworm appears to be continuously brooded or overwinters as a sexually immature adult.

LARGE YELLOW UNDERWING
Noctua pronuba

RECOGNITION Last instar *brown with buff subdorsal stripe bordered inwardly with black hemispheres on A1–A8.* Posterior half of A8 often more pale-colored than anterior half. Body always pale below thin spiracular stripe. Middorsal stripe thin, vague, or absent. Spiracles tan to brown with black outer ring. Head often with black bar over vertex that extends down and runs alongside triangle; short black line under eyes. Larva to 4.5cm. Middle instars bright yellow-green, but otherwise similarly marked (inset).

OCCURRENCE Agricultural lands, waste places, lawns, fields, and grasslands. Transcontinental in Canada south in East to Georgia and Texas. One principal generation with mature caterpillars from late fall through May.

COMMON FOODPLANTS General feeder on grasses and low-growing forbs.

REMARKS This species was accidentally introduced into eastern Canada around 1979 from Europe (Neil 1981). It has since spread very rapidly south and west from its first reported occurrences in the Maritime Provinces of Canada. On Martha's Vineyard, we once had to shut down our mercury vapor light because it was teaming with so many Large Yellow Underwing adults that other moths at the sheet were being pummeled. The caterpillars are active during thaws throughout the winter—commonly turning up on sidewalks, sauntering into garages, or crawling alongside banks of snow. If someone brings you a cutworm in the dead of winter—this is it. The grayish eggs, laid in clusters of several hundred, are deposited on foliage, dead sticks, grass stalks, clothes lines, pine needles, wire fences, or almost any other surface. Pupation occurs below ground in a slight cocoon.

(NORTHERN VARIABLE DART) *Xestia badicollis*

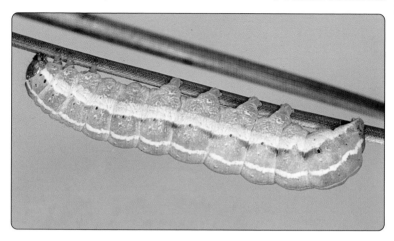

RECOGNITION Ground coloration varies from green to gray and brown; longitudinal striping usually evident. Subdorsal stripe, about twice width of middorsal and half width of subspiracular stripe, ending at A10. *Subdorsal stripe often edged inwardly with darkened oblique lines at mid-segment.*

Subspiracular stripe often edged with black lines that may join to form a black stripe that passes through the spiracles. *Rear low-humped.* Larva to 4cm. Superficially inseparable as a caterpillar from Dull Reddish Dart (*X. dilucida*), Southern Variable Dart (*X. elimata*), and other conifer-feeding members of the genus (*see* Lafontaine 1998).

OCCURRENCE Woodlands and forests. Southern Ontario to Labrador south to West Virginia and Great Lakes States. One generation with mature caterpillars in late spring and summer.

COMMON FOODPLANTS Eastern white pine; less commonly fir, hemlock, larch, other pines, spruce, and perhaps other conifers.

REMARKS While few are likely to encounter this nocturnal caterpillar, I include the White Pine Cutworm in this guide as a precautionary tale of the extreme variablility in ground coloration and patterning in many noctuines. The partially to nearly full-grown caterpillar overwinters.

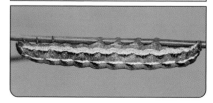

DARTS AND CUTWORMS

SNOWY DART *Euagrotis illapsa*

Southern Canada to
Florida and Texas. Two or
three generations over
most of range with mature
caterpillars occurring
nearly year-round.
Presumably a generalist
on low plants, especially
grasses and sedges.

DARK-SIDED CUTWORM (Reaper Dart) *Euxoa messoria*

Transcontinental in
Canada south in East to
North Carolina and
Missouri. One generation
with mature caterpillars in
spring. General feeder on
forbs and woody plants;
occasional garden and
crop pest.

STRIPED CUTWORM (Tessellate Dart) *Euxoa tessellata*

Manitoba to Newfoundland
south to Great Lakes States
and Florida, although local
southward. One generation
with mature caterpillars in late
spring and early summer.
Generalist on herbaceous and
woody plants; occasional garden and crop pest.

FLAME-SHOULDERED DART *Ochropleura implecta*

Transcontinental in Canada
south in East to North Carolina
and Texas. Two or more
generations with mature
caterpillars occurring nearly
year-round. Clover and other
low plants.

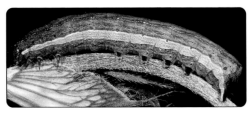

– PANTHEIDAE

Until recently, pantheids were regarded as a subfamily within the Noctuidae. Their body is vested with abundant secondary setae. There is a wart bearing numerous hairs anterior to the spiracle on T1 in our species. Pantheas and yellowhorns share similarities with the dagger moths and their kin (Noctuidae: Acronictinae). Our six or seven Eastern species overwinter as pupae.

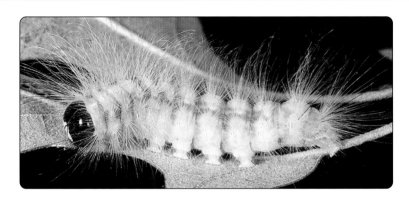

THE LAUGHER
Charadra deridens

RECOGNITION Pale green to smoky (or rarely black) with *abundant long, white wispy setae* not grouped into fascicles or lashes. Ends of longer setae often somewhat curled. Setal warts usually pale. *Head shiny black with bright, lemon yellow triangle and yellow crescent to either side of triangle* (inset). In some forms with few black setae intermixed among white setae at both ends of body. Larva to 4cm.

OCCURRENCE Barrens, woodlands, and forests from southern Canada to Florida and Texas. Two generations over much of East with mature caterpillars from May to November.

COMMON FOODPLANTS Beech and oak most commonly; also reported from birch, elm, and maple.

REMARKS The caterpillar fashions a shelter or uses those of other caterpillars. The Laugher feeds on hardened summer foliage that is too tough for many caterpillars. In the paler forms the yellowish testes of last-instar male caterpillars can be seen through the body wall of A5. Forbes (1954) notes that the larva spins a light cocoon on the foodplant.

CLOSE-BANDED YELLOWHORN
Colocasia propinquilinea

RECOGNITION Coloration ranging from white to rust or black with *conspicuous spreading clusters of white to orange setae. Rust to black subdorsal lashes on T2 and unpaired middorsal lashes present on A1 and (usually) A8.* Head capsule orange or black. Larva to 3.5cm. Co-occurs with Yellowhorn (*Colocasia flavicornis*) over much of East.

Characters suggested by Crumb (1956) for the separation of the two appear to be variable within each.

OCCURRENCE Forests from Canada south to North Carolina, northern Alabama, and Louisiana. At least two generations with mature caterpillars from May to November.

COMMON FOODPLANTS Birch a favorite; American hornbeam, beech, and oak commonly; also reported from elm, maple, and walnut.

REMARKS The caterpillars are shelter formers that silk together adjacent leaves or cut incisions into a leaf edge and then draw over a flap of leaf tissue. In Connecticut the Close-banded Yellowhorn is common throughout the state, while the Yellowhorn tends to be locally common in northern hardwood forests, but curiously scarce over much of the state. It is also local in Louisiana, Missouri, and elsewhere. Yet in the Appalachian foothills and much of Maryland (John Glaser, pers. comm.), the Yellowhorn is often the more common of the two. My only confirmed rearings for the Yellowhorn are from beech. Larval coloration varies within both species, so much so that I cannot yet reliably discriminate the caterpillars of these two moths.

Panthea acronyctoides

RECOGNITION Ground color charcoal, gray, or black with white along sides. In many forms *dorsal setae mostly white and not organized into lashes* as in Eastern Panthea (*P. furcilla*) except rather loosely on enlarged paired tufts over T1, A1, and A8; *paddle-shaped setae absent from dorsal setal clusters.* This description, consistent with my images of *Panthea* caterpillars from Connecticut, Maryland, New Jersey, and Tennessee, does not agree with images provided by Ives and Wong (1988: 19) for *Panthea*. Larva less than 3.5cm. Until this group receives more study, identifications are best based on adults.

OCCURRENCE Forests from Canada south to Great Lakes States and Georgia (mountains). One generation northward; two in southern Appalachians with mature caterpillars from June to October.

COMMON FOODPLANTS Fir, hemlock, larch, pine, and spruce.

REMARKS Although generally regarded as rare in the South, the Black Zigzag is common in hemlock stands of Great Smoky Mountains National Park down to elevations of 500m (1,750ft). Quite possibly it is a glacial relic there because it is quite scarce or absent in many areas to the north (e.g., there are no authenticated records of this moth from Connecticut). Caterpillars from Tennessee reared on hemlock and pine had different color forms—an intriguing study would be to rear caterpillars from a single clutch of eggs on different conifers to see if color variants are inducible. Caterpillars tuck the head under the body and are quick to release their grip and tumble from their perch if molested. *Panthea* overwinter as pupae in leaf litter or soil.

TUFTED WHITE PINE CATERPILLAR
(EASTERN PANTHEA) *Panthea furcilla* (= *P. pallescens*)

RECOGNITION Variegated in orange, red, white, and black. *Conspicuous subdorsal tufts (pencils) of black setae on A1 and A8*; sparser lashes on T1 and T2; subdorsal setal clusters on T3 and A2–A7 variously developed. Longer lashes with at least some setae paddle-shaped, widest near apex. Setal warts often orange. A1–A8 in many forms with oblique white patch below and forward of white spiracle. A geographically and possibly specifically distinct *Panthea* occurs from Long Island south to Florida and Texas (Forbes 1954, Kimball 1965) (*see* Remarks); I suspect that its larva is indistinguishable from that of the Eastern Panthea. Larva to 4cm.

OCCURRENCE Woodlands, pine plantations, and forests from southern Canada to Florida and Texas (but *see* Remarks). One generation northward and two in Connecticut with mature caterpillars from May to October; from New Jersey southward there are at least two broods; moths fly year-round in Florida.

COMMON FOODPLANTS Larch, pine, spruce, and probably other conifers.

REMARKS The thin subdorsal black tufts on T1, T2, and A2–A7 are absent in the images of the Tufted White Pine Caterpillar in Ives and Wong (1988: 19). Perhaps these and other setal tufts are deciduous and frequently lost, or the caterpillars figured by Ives and Wong are misidentified, or more than one (as yet unrecognized) species is involved, or development of the tufts varies geographically. *Panthea furcilla* and *P. pallescens* are synonyms: both names refer to moths from the Northeast with the former name having priority. Populations from the Southeast, should they prove specifically distinct, are as yet unnamed. Adults of all of our Eastern pantheids have melanic forms (*see also* page 323, *Acronicta afflicta*).

TUSSOCK CATERPILLARS

– LYMANTRIIDAE

The family gets its name from the dense setal tufts, the tussocks, that issue from the dorsum of the caterpillar's abdomen. About 20 species occur in our region. Worldwide the family has more than its share of pest species. Identifications can be challenging, even with Ferguson's (1978) monograph in hand. Recent taxonomic studies indicate that tussock moths are closely allied to tiger moths and that both represent specialized groups that evolved from within the owlet moths, or at least from within the broad, classical concept of that family.

RECOGNITION

Tussock caterpillars may be recognized by the disk-shaped yellow, orange, or red middorsal defensive glands on the sixth, and usually the seventh, abdominal segments. Nearly all of our lymantriids bear numerous secondary setae that are gathered into tussocks over the dorsum, although these are absent in the Gypsy and Satin Moths. Many tussock caterpillars have plumed or barbed setae (like tiger moths); in some the setae are so branched as to resemble minute feather dusters. The crochets, of a single length, are arranged in a single series parallel to the body axis. Larvae vary in coloration geographically, especially in *Dasychira*—setal coloration characters given below should be used with caution.

LIFE HISTORY NOTES

The eggs are laid singly, in small groups (*Dasychira*), or in a single large egg mass (*Lymantria* and *Orgyia*). They are frequently overlain with abdominal scales and/or secretions from the mother. Females are wingless or so engorged with eggs that they are rendered flightless in many genera. The principal dispersal stage is the first instar which, like a spiderling, balloons away from the hatch site on a fine strand of silk. The caterpillars are boldly marked, warning of their chemical protection. (They include the only North American caterpillars known to cause, in extremely rare instances, human death.) Tussocks are among the most polyphagous of our caterpillars—more than 140 foodplants are recorded for the White-marked Tussock Moth and the list for the Gypsy Moth exceeds 500. Caterpillars groom themselves by wiping their lashes and other body setae across the defensive glands on A6 and A7. Tussock caterpillars are a cold-hardy lot—one species, the Arctic Woollybear (*Gynaephora groenlandica*), which takes from 9–14 years to complete its development, ranges northward to the shores of Greenland and Ellesmere Island.

COLLECTING AND REARING TIPS

Many tussocks are conspicuous, diurnal feeders that make easy quarry for the caterpillar hunter. The majority are generalists that accept dietary substitutions. A challenge for those interested in rearing tussocks is finding and photographing the newly eclosed males before they have had a chance to beat their wings ragged, there being little time between when males emerge and when they embark on vigorous flights that may descale their forewings and obliterate their identity.

YELLOW-BASED TUSSOCK MOTH
Dasychira basiflava

RECOGNITION *Mostly yellow* but gray and brown forms also reported. Middorsal tufts on A1–A4 tan or brown, always contrasting with adjacent setae; *tuft on A8 black, slightly higher than those over A1–A4. Subspiracular setal clusters mostly pale and bearing one to five (commonly three to five) long, narrow, black setae.* Middorsal glands on A6 and A7 yellow or white. Larva to 4.5cm. Variable Tussock Moth (*Dasychira vagans*) occurs from mountains of southern Appalachians northward into Canada and westward to the Pacific Coast. Its ground color tends to be grayish, or even white, and is distinguished by plumed black setae that extend from the subspiracular setal clusters. Apple, birch, oak, poplar, willow, and many other woody plants are eaten. Southern Tussock Moth (*D. meridionalis*) flies alongside Yellow-based Tussock Moth in the Gulf States; oak is its preferred foodplant. Caterpillars of the Southern Tussock Moth have clubbed, black setae extending from the subspiracular tufts; the clubbed hairs are more numerous than in the Variable Tussock; and it also has clubbed setae arising from the supraspiracular setal tufts. All three tussocks treated here usually have a long black lash extending from the supraspiracular wart on A9 and a comparatively short middorsal tuft (cf. Tephra Tussock Moth, page 447).

OCCURRENCE Barrens and woodlands from Missouri to New England south to Florida and Texas. Evidently just one generation over much of East with mature caterpillars from April to June. Richard Heitzman's (pers. comm.) flight records suggest a second brood in Missouri.

COMMON FOODPLANTS Oak; also blueberry, dogwood, and other woody species.

REMARKS *Dasychira* caterpillars are geographically variable in coloration—the characters provided here may not apply to all populations.

Dasychira obliquata

RECOGNITION Caterpillar immediately distinguished by its *meager caudal black lashes* that range from entirely absent to being only half as long as anterior lashes. *Body dirty brown* and covered with barbed, somewhat plumose setae that make caterpillar appear fuzzy and out of focus (especially under a lens). Blackened *dorsal tufts mostly limited to A1 and A8; those on A2–A3 simply a darker shade of brown.* Larva to 4cm.

OCCURRENCE Barrens, woodlands, and forests from southern Canada to Georgia (mountains) and Arkansas. Evidently one generation over much of East with mature caterpillars from May to July; possibly additional generations southward.

COMMON FOODPLANTS Oak; also beech, birch, blueberry, cherry, elm, hickory, willow, and other woody species.

REMARKS *Dasychira* caterpillars appear regularly under the burlap skirts deployed for monitoring Gypsy Moth caterpillars. The Streaked Tussock Moth is the most common *Dasychira* throughout much of its range. Adults typically fly later in summer than most other *Dasychira*. Its larvae appear to be more tolerant of the Bt (*Bacillus thuringiensis*) applications used by the US Forest Service to control forest pests than many other tussock species. *Dasychira* overwinter as partially grown larvae, 5–10mm in length (as second or third instars), under bark or amongst needles in the conifer-feeders. Getting these diapausing caterpillars through the winter in captivity can be difficult—they seem all too susceptible to both desiccation and mold; sleeving is advised.

MANTO TUSSOCK MOTH
Dasychira manto

RECOGNITION *Conifer-feeding tussock with long middorsal setal tuft over A8.* Body charcoal with whitish mottling and orange lateral warts and subspiracular areas. Head reddish. *Defensive glands on A6 and A7 red.* Larva to 4cm. Closely allied tussocks are distinguished below.

OCCURRENCE Barrens and woodlands from Kentucky to Maryland south to Florida and Texas. At least two generations with mature caterpillars from March to September.

COMMON FOODPLANTS Pine.

REMARKS The Manto Tussock is the only common pine-feeding species of *Dasychira* in southeastern forests. North of Maryland it is replaced by Pine Tussock (*D. pinicola*), which in turn gives way to Northern Conifer Tussock (*D. plagiata*) over much of New England and southern Canada. The Northern Conifer also occurs at high elevations in the Appalachians to North Carolina. The two co-occur in the Great Lakes States. The Pine and Manto Tussocks can sometimes be distinguished by examining the black setae that arise from the subspiracular warts. In the Manto Tussock these are often thickened over much of their length (swordlike), while in the Pine and Northern Conifer Tussocks they tend to be thickened only near their apices (spatulalike). Ferguson (1978) gives other characters for the separation of the three, but implies that the listed larval characters might be expected to vary geographically. Until the caterpillars are better studied, range and adult characters are best used for identification of our pine-feeding *Dasychira*. Cypress swamps from South Carolina to eastern Texas are home to Dominick's Tussock (*D. dominickaria*). The few larval collections available for study suggest that the caterpillar is mostly gray and "more formidably armed with long, black spines than any other species studied" (Ferguson 1978). Of the various conifers offered to caterpillars of Dominick's Tussock by Ferguson, only bald cypress foliage was accepted.

Dasychira tephra

RECOGNITION Distinguished from other oak-feeding *Dasychira* by its *long middorsal tuft on A8*; ground color of setae gray to yellow-brown. Setae from subdorsal cluster often gray or yellow-brown (these usually white in other tussocks). Hairpencils often yellowish or gray over lower half, becoming black at apices. Each subspiracular tuft bears one to several long, black, threadlike setae and *1–3 shorter, thickened (plumed), black setae* with sharp apices. Gray middorsal tufts on A1–A4; *glands on A6 and A7 red*. Larva to 4cm. Replaced northward and in mountains by Sharp-lined Tussock Moth (*Dasychira dorsipennata*), its epithet referring to the long, unpaired hairpencil over A8; it tends to be rendered in grays, black, and white. Although most collections of this Canadian zone species have been made from oak, caterpillars also use elm, hazel, shadbush, willow, and other woody species. It ranges from southern Canada to the mountains of North Carolina.

OCCURRENCE Barrens and woodlands from Missouri, Ohio, and Maryland south to Florida and Texas; uncommon to absent in mountainous areas. Two generations with mature caterpillars from April to September.

COMMON FOODPLANTS Oak.

REMARKS Male tussocks have enormous antennae and are renowned for their abilities to detect trace quantities of the female sex pheromone. Forest Service scientists who work where virgin lymantriids are being reared sometimes complain that male tussock moths follow them around whenever they hike in the woods, or, on occasion, even enter their cars and homes, presumably because their bodies are emitting trace quantities of sex pheromone.

RUSTY TUSSOCK MOTH
Orgyia antiqua

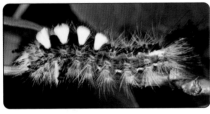

RECOGNITION Handsome caterpillar with jet black dorsal stripe, four straw middorsal tufts, and bright red setal warts. Immediately distinguished from all other tussocks by *long, black, lateral hairpencil on A1 and adjacent white to tan hairpencil on T3*. Black setae in pencils or lashes plumose at their apices. *Glands on A6 and A7 bright red*. Larva to 3cm.

OCCURRENCE Fields, woodlands, and forests across much of Canada (and Eurasia) south to northern Connecticut, central New York, and northern Missouri. One principal generation with mature caterpillars in August and September.

COMMON FOODPLANTS A generalist on many woody species including alder, apple, cherry, elm, fir, hemlock, larch, maple, oak, pine, poplar, spruce, viburnum, and willow.

REMARKS This is one of our most attractive tussocks, especially when viewed with a lens. The complexity of the black setae is impressive—they are among the most deciduous of the caterpillar's plumage. These same setae, or at least those about the head, are pulled across the surface of the defensive glands on A6 and A7 when the caterpillars groom themselves. When threatened, tussock moths arch T3 and A1 upward and draw the head under. The males are principally day flying, although they also come to light. The eggs, each with a black bullseye, are laid in a single layer on the outside of the female's cocoon.

Orgyia definita

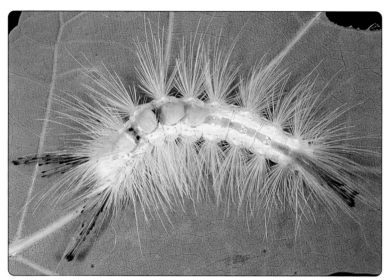

RECOGNITION *Orgyia* caterpillars are comparatively slender tussocks with a long middorsal lash on A8; they lack the paired caudal lashes of many *Dasychira*. Caterpillar of Definite Tussock Moth mostly *bright yellow* with cream to yellow middorsal tufts on A1–A4 and *colorless or blackish middorsal stripe.* Setal warts yellow. Body hair

whitish. *Glands on A6 and A7 whitish or yellowish. Head yellow.* Larva to 3cm.

OCCURRENCE Fields, woodlands, and forests from extreme southern Canada and Maine to Florida and Louisiana. Two generations over much of East with mature caterpillars from April to September.

COMMON FOODPLANTS Basswood, birch, blueberry, elm, hackberry, maple, oak, willow, witch hazel, and other woody plants.

REMARKS This is a very common species. An hour-long sortie any September day should yield a caterpillar or two. Many tussock moth caterpillars are more reliably identified to species than their respective adult stages. The females of *Orgyia* are especially difficult to identify to species because they are wingless. The cocoon contains few larval setae relative to the cocoons of other eastern *Orgyia*. Definite Tussock Moth females lay a single cluster of eggs over the outer surface of their cocoon, cover the eggs with a secretion, and then rub scales from their abdomen over them. The principal dispersal stage is the first instar which balloons about on a fine strand of silk. The egg cluster overwinters.

WHITE-MARKED TUSSOCK MOTH
Orgyia leucostigma

RECOGNITION One of our most distinctive and easily recognized tussock moths. *Bright red head*, white to yellow middorsal tufts on A1–A4, and broad *black middorsal stripe flanked by yellow* subdorsal stripes all diagnostic. *Glands on A6 and A7 bright red*. Larva to 3.5cm. *Orgyia detrita* has similar caterpillars but the sides of the body are

gray and the subdorsal and supraspiracular warts are orange; the black middorsal stripe is flanked by yellow-orange spots on A4–A7. It flies with *O. leucostigma* on the Atlantic Coastal Plain from Long Island south to Florida and west to Texas.

OCCURRENCE Fields, woodlands, and forests from southern Canada to Florida and Texas. Two or more generations with mature caterpillars from May to November.

COMMON FOODPLANTS Apple, birch, black locust, cherry, elm, hackberry, hickory, oak, rose, willow, and a wide variety of other woody plants, including fir, hemlock, larch, spruce, and other conifers.

REMARKS This is one of our most ubiquitous caterpillars—it could turn up on virtually any woody plant in the East. It is often common in late summer when caterpillar activity otherwise seems to be ebbing. White-marked Tussock Moth caterpillars are occasional pests in Christmas tree plantations in the Northeast. The caterpillar may cause allergic reactions, particularly if its hairs come into contact with sensitive skin areas of the back, stomach, and inner arms. The flightless female (inset) lays up to 300 eggs in a single, froth-covered mass over the cocoon from which she has emerged; few to no setae are deposited over the surface of the egg mass. It overwinters in the egg stage.

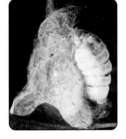

Leucoma salicis

RECOGNITION   *Unique pattern* immediately distinguishes this caterpillar from all others in our fauna. *Dorsum marked with 10–11 white, intersegmental white spots* and *paired, red setal warts on T1–A9*. Broken tan to white subdorsal stripe on abdominal segments. Sides bluish gray. Head black with long hairlike setae. Larva to 4.5cm.

OCCURRENCE   Edges of watercourses, woodlands, and forests of the Canadian zone from Ontario to Nova Scotia south to northwestern Connecticut and central New York. One generation with mature caterpillars in May and June.

COMMON FOODPLANTS   Aspen, poplar, and willow.

REMARKS   Introduced from Europe in the East, the Satin Moth was first reported from the area extending between Boston, Massachusetts, and Hampton, New Hampshire, in 1920. It has since spread west into New York, but appears to have stalled or perhaps may even be declining over much of its previously established range. The Satin Moth overwinters as a third instar, individually or in small groups, in a thin, transparent cocoon or hibernaculum, usually under flaps or in crevices of bark (Ferguson 1978). With the return of warmer springtime temperatures, the caterpillars venture out of the web to feed on nearby leaves and soon strike off on a solitary existence. Disturbed caterpillars are quick to drop from their perches on belay lines. Each caterpillar passes through seven instars before spinning a thin cocoon between leaves or along the bark. The dark, shiny, brown pupa is handsomely set with numerous, erect, bright yellow setae.

GYPSY MOTH
Lymantria dispar

RECOGNITION Recognizable in all instars by *bulging seta-bearing wart to either side of head. Dorsum with five pairs of blue warts followed by six pairs of red warts.* Defensive glands on A6 and A7 small, orange. Larva to 5.5cm.

OCCURRENCE Woodlands and forests from Minnesota to Nova Scotia south to North Carolina and Great Lakes States, expanding range westward and southward. One generation with mature caterpillars in May and June.

COMMON FOODPLANTS Over 500 recorded foodplants; often witch hazel and other understory plants in early instars; beech, hickory, and oak become increasingly important in later instars.

REMARKS All Eastern populations are believed to have originated from a single introduction in Boston in 1869 by E. Léopold Trouvelot, who mistakenly thought the Gypsy Moth would be a good source of commercial silk or could be hybridized with the Silkworm (*Bombyx mori*) to enhance its disease resistance (at that time, both the Gypsy Moth and Silkworm were classified in the same genus, *Bombyx*). Asiatic races of the Gypsy Moth consume both broadleaf plants and conifers, and thus represent an ominous threat to our nation's conifer forests. Early instars balloon on threads of silk, and may be carried up to several hundred meters from the egg mass. Caterpillars often start out on understory vegetation then move into trees to complete their development. Fourth to sixth instars usually descend from foliage to shelter on the trunk by day. The caterpillars are allergenic to many people, especially if the hairs get in the eyes or contact vulnerable areas of the arms, neck, and legs; hypersensitive individuals may react to single hairs and scales from adults. Ballooning early instars in the spring can be problematic, "mysteriously" affecting people well removed from infested plants, e.g., after having dropped into clothing.

Euproctis chrysorrhoea

RECOGNITION Variegated in orange, black, and white with abundant orange setae. Dorsum of abdomen with *paired, closely set, rusty brown tufts over A1–A8. Short white scales arising from subdorsum of A1–A8.* Glands over A6–A7 orange. Larva to 3.5cm.

OCCURRENCE Presently dunes, coastal strand communities, and adjacent woodlands from Maine to Cape Cod (but *see* Remarks). One generation with mature caterpillars in May and June.

COMMON FOODPLANTS Generalist on woody plants, but apple, beach plum, cherry, and other members of the rose family favored; other commonly reported foodplants include beech, oak, and willow.

REMARKS This seemingly innocuous-looking insect is anything but. Its short, deciduous setae (or spicules), tightly packed into the rusty brown tufts over the dorsum, are highly irritating to most people and produce pronounced dermatological reactions if numbers of setae get embedded in the skin. Sensitive individuals may develop severe allergic reactions— two people in Massachusetts are believed to have had fatal exposures to the caterpillars (or their setae). The Browntail Moth was accidentally introduced into Massachusetts from Europe in 1890. Like the Gypsy Moth, it spread quickly across New England and became a serious defoliator and health risk. By 1914 it had spread to the Hudson River Valley and Long Island, but then inexplicably began declining shortly thereafter. Its range has since contracted to the outer beaches of Cape Cod and the vicinity of Portland and Casco Bay in Maine. Data collected by Joe Elkinton and Jeff Boettner of the University of Massachusetts indicate that parasitoids, introduced from Europe, are at least partially responsible for the Browntail's diminished range. Young larvae overwinter in a dense communal web spun about a twig tip.

NOLIDS – NOLIDAE

Nolids include a heterogeneous group, united by their ridged boat-shaped cocoon, which bears a vertical exit slit at one end. Our species fall into two subfamilies. The Nolinae have small, densely hairy caterpillars that lack prolegs on A3. Sarrothripinae are green, somewhat flattened, possess subdorsal stripes, and the lower portion of the prolegs is rolled outward. All are foodplant specialists. The pupa overwinters.

CONFUSED MEGANOLA
Meganola minuscula

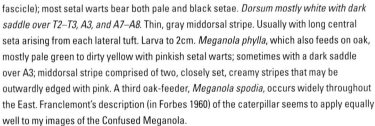

RECOGNITION Small gray, white, and black caterpillar with abundant secondary setae. Setae borne from raised warts and diverging (not grouped into common fascicle); most setal warts bear both pale and black setae. *Dorsum mostly white with dark saddle over T2–T3, A3, and A7–A8.* Thin, gray middorsal stripe. Usually with long central seta arising from each lateral tuft. Larva to 2cm. *Meganola phylla*, which also feeds on oak, mostly pale green to dirty yellow with pinkish setal warts; sometimes with a dark saddle over A3; middorsal stripe comprised of two, closely set, creamy stripes that may be outwardly edged with pink. A third oak-feeder, *Meganola spodia*, occurs widely throughout the East. Franclemont's description (in Forbes 1960) of the caterpillar seems to apply equally well to my images of the Confused Meganola.

OCCURRENCE Barrens, woodlands, and forests from extreme southern Canada to Florida and Texas. At least two generations with mature caterpillars from May to November.

COMMON FOODPLANTS Oak.

REMARKS Nolids were elevated to full family status by Kitching and Rawlins (1998). Larvae of some species retain the head capsules of previous instars, these collecting over the thorax. Coloration of the Confused Meganola suggests that the caterpillars rest on bark by day. Nolids are easily taken with beating sheets.

THREE-SPOTTED NOLA
Nola triquetrana

RECOGNITION Small *densely hairy caterpillar with yellow ground color.* Setae mostly white. *Raised setal warts of dorsum and subdorsum each borne from black spot.* Thoracic shield with shiny black crescent to either side. Lateral setal tufts at end of body with one extremely long seta. Larva to 1.5cm.

OCCURRENCE Mesic woodlands and forests from southern Canada to Florida and Arkansas. One generation with mature caterpillars from May to June over much of East.

COMMON FOODPLANTS Witch hazel.

REMARKS Caterpillars of the Three-spotted Nola live in leaf rolls, sometimes gregariously. The caterpillars roll the new leaves in the spring and then skeletonize the inner tissues. It can be an abundant species in the foothills of the Appalachians. Other *Nola* of woodlands and forests in our region include the Sharp-blotched Nola (*N. pustulata*) on maleberry, Blurry-patched Nola (*N. cilicoides*) on loosestrife, and *N. clethrae* on sweet pepperbush. The former and latter are also shelter-formers. I expect that the Blurry-patched Nola also constructs a leaf shelter. The Three-spotted Nola overwinters as a pupa in a highly cryptic, spindle-shaped cocoon, spun along a twig. The principal character holding nolines with sarrothripines is the presence of a cocoon with a vertical slit at one end. The caterpillars have so little in common that it would appear that the current classification is still in need of emendation—I suspect that nolids branched off near the base of the evolutionary tree for noctuids, while sarrothripines are nested high within, perhaps near the hypenines.

EYED BAILEYA

Baileya ophthalmica

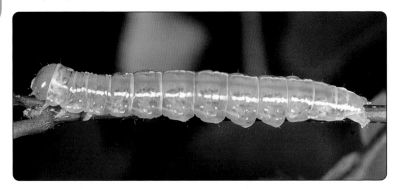

RECOGNITION *Stout lime-green caterpillar with prominent subdorsal stripe. Prolegs short,* caterpillar appearing to rest directly on leaf; anal prolegs directed backward. Supraspiracular stripe represented by 2–3 white spots on each segment; often with additional 1 or 2 cream spots below and behind spiracle. Head green, shiny, rounded, and unmarked. Larva less than 2.5cm.

OCCURRENCE Woodlands and forests from Wisconsin to Nova Scotia south to Florida and Texas. At least two generations with mature caterpillars from May to November.

COMMON FOODPLANTS American hornbeam and hop hornbeam; records from butternut presumably apply to another species; Covell's (1984) record of beech probably refers to blue-beech (= hop hornbeam).

REMARKS Doubleday's Baileya (*Baileya doubledayi*) feeds on alder. The Small Baileya (*B. australis*) is a walnut-feeder. Published foodplant records for the Eyed Baileya and Sleeping Baileya (*B. dormitans*) appear to be confused—while both moths are recorded from hornbeam and hickory, it is my belief that the Eyed Baileya will be shown to feed on American hornbeam and hop hornbeam (both Betulaceae) and Sleeping Baileya on butternut, pecan, black walnut, and hickory (all Juglandaceae). Ex ova Pale Baileya (*B. levitans*) caterpillars accept both walnut and hickory. Baileya caterpillars are easily collected with beating sheets. All members of the genus overwinter in an elongate cocoon infused with chewed leaf fragments (inset shows cocoon of Doubleday's Baileya).

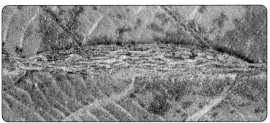

Their bright coloration, moderate size, variety, and chemical ecology have made tiger moths a perennial favorite among moth collectors and watchers. The family is especially varied and diverse in the tropics where 300–400 species may fly together at a single location. In the lowland tropical rainforests of northeastern Costa Rica, they frequently account for 15% of the macro moths in blacklight bucket-trap samples. Despite their taxonomic diversity and ecological importance, rather few tiger moth species are encountered as caterpillars—many are ground-dwellers that hide by day or are otherwise specialized in habit. Hence, only a fraction of the East's 100 or so species are treated in this guide.

RECOGNITION

Our commonly encountered arctiid caterpillars are densely covered with setae that bear microscopic barbs. Many species are warningly colored in some combination of black, white, red, orange, or yellow. The crochets (inset) at each end of a given series are reduced in size. The thoracic claws may possess subtending spatulate setae. Larval coloration frequently changes markedly at molts making identification of early instars difficult.

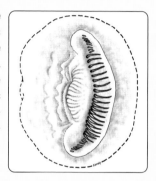

LIFE HISTORY NOTES

The caterpillars of many species are toxic, sequestering biogenic amines (e.g., histamine), pyrrolizidine alkaloids, and/or cardiac glycosides from their foodplants or synthesizing these from dietary precursors. Additional protection is afforded by their abundant setae that range from downy soft to stiff and bristly. Most of our species are broadly polyphagous, consuming both herbaceous and woody species, although significant numbers are specialists. Among the most unusual are the lithosiines, which graze upon the blue-green algae (cyanobacteria) and lichens that grow on tree bark, and other surfaces. Most tiger moths overwinter as a partially grown larva or as a pupa.

COLLECTING AND REARING TIPS

Female tiger moths readily oviposit if held in a bag or vial for a night or two. Because the eggs are so easily obtained, too often one is lured into rearing large cohorts of larvae. Although the caterpillars tolerate crowding and rather messy conditions, they do better if reared under low densities with plenty of ventilation. Generalists can be reared on romaine lettuce from the grocer (assuming it has not been sprayed or genetically engineered to kill insects), plantains, and dandelions, although keeping your rearing containers clean will be made easier if you use honeysuckle, apple, or other drier foliage.

SCARLET-WINGED LICHEN MOTH
Hypoprepia miniata

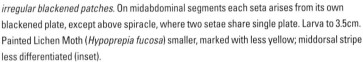

RECOGNITION *Black body mottled with yellow,* especially laterally. *Long, black, shiny spines arise from irregular blackened patches.* On midabdominal segments each seta arises from its own blackened plate, except above spiracle, where two setae share single plate. Larva to 3.5cm. Painted Lichen Moth (*Hypoprepia fucosa*) smaller, marked with less yellow; middorsal stripe less differentiated (inset).

OCCURRENCE Woodlands and forests from southern Canada to Florida and Texas. One generation with mature caterpillars from May to July northward; two or three generations in Missouri with mature caterpillars nearly year-round.

COMMON FOODPLANTS Lichens and blue-green algae (cyanobacteria) growing on tree trunks, fallen logs, and rocks.

REMARKS Adults of eastern *Hypoprepia* vary considerably in different parts of the Southeast, so much so that some lepidopterists feel additional species will eventually be recognized. *Hypoprepia* and other lithosiine arctiids have anal combs that allow them to eject their fecal pellets distances of 30 or more body lengths. The comb, which protrudes from the underside of the anal plate, is hooked under a torus of rectal tissue. Hemolymph (blood) is then forced to the last body segment, where pressure becomes so great that the comb slips and the fecal pellet is ejected with great velocity. "Fecal flicking" foils parasitic and predatory wasps that would use volatiles from the excreta to locate their intended victims. *Hypoprepia* caterpillars are cannibalistic on smaller larvae and pupae. The caterpillar overwinters.

PACKARD'S LICHEN MOTH *Cisthene packardii*

Kansas to Massachusetts south to Florida and Texas. One generation in New England; at least two from Missouri and central New Jersey southward with mature caterpillars from April to September.

LEAD-COLORED LICHEN MOTH *Cisthene plumbea*

Extreme southern New Jersey south to northern Florida and Texas. Two generations in Missouri and New Jersey with mature caterpillars from April to August.

LITTLE WHITE LICHEN MOTH *Clemensia albata*

Transcontinental in Canada south in East to Florida and Texas. One generation in Canada and New England; two or more generations in South with mature caterpillars from April to September.

PALE LICHEN MOTH *Crambidia pallida*

Manitoba to Nova Scotia to South Carolina and Texas. One generation northward with mature caterpillars mostly in July and August; two or more generations southward. Several other *Crambidia* occur in East, at least two of which are unnamed (Forbes 1960).

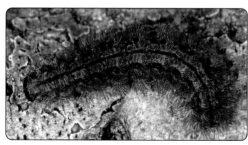

LECONTE'S HAPLOA
Haploa lecontei

RECOGNITION *Mostly black with yellow striping* and large, shiny black warts. Setae comparatively short and sparse; those along sides whitish. *Bright yellow (and white) spots of middorsal stripe* often constricted or broken in middle of abdominal segments. *Spiracular stripe bright yellow and white*, mostly broken into many spots. Larva to 4.5cm. Caterpillar of Clymene Haploa (*Haploa clymene*) tends to have yellow-orange markings (without white components); confluent dull yellow spiracular and subspiracular stripes; and yellow-brown lateral setae (*see* opposite). Caterpillar of Confused Haploa (*H. confusa*) similar to that of LeConte's Haploa: its middorsal stripe averages more uniform in width and evenly bright yellow; broken subdorsal stripe more evident; and broad lateral stripe frequently less developed, i.e., more fragmented (*see* opposite). The Neighbor (*H. contigua*) is distinguished by its thin white middorsal and subdorsal stripes and especially bold and complete yellow lateral stripe (*see* opposite). Two other Haploas that occur in the East, the Colona Moth (*H. colona*) and Reversed Haploa (*H. reversa*) (*see* opposite), both have an orange to red middorsal stripe.

OCCURRENCE Open areas, wetlands, and woodlands from southern Canada to Georgia and Texas. One generation with mature caterpillars from April to July.

COMMON FOODPLANTS Many herbaceous and woody plants, frequently ascending shrubs and trees to feed. I have found caterpillars on apple, thoroughwort (*Eupatorium*), and willow.

REMARKS The yellow lateral bands are especially prominent in the young, overwintering caterpillars. I occasionally find Haploa caterpillars crawling about foundations and buildings on early spring days.

Haploa caterpillars are commonly associated with foodplants in the sunflower and borage families (Asteraceae and Boraginaceae) and other pyrrolizidine alkaloid-rich plants, but forage widely, especially after hibernation. Joe-pye weed and other *Eupatorium* species, growing in wetlands or along watercourses, will often yield Haploa caterpillars. All have only a single generation with overwintering caterpillars maturing in the spring and early summer.

CLYMENE HAPLOA *Haploa clymene*

Kansas, southern Michigan, and Maine to Florida and Texas.

CONFUSED HAPLOA *Haploa confusa*

Manitoba to northern Maine south to Pennsylvania and Great Lakes States. Covell (1984) lists Hound's tongue as a foodplant.

THE NEIGHBOR *Haploa contigua*

South Dakota to Quebec to northern Georgia and Mississippi, and Arkansas.

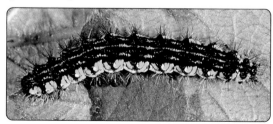

REVERSED HAPLOA *Haploa reversa*

Great Lakes States south to Virginia and Texas.

WOOLLY BEAR (ISABELLA TIGER MOTH)
Pyrrharctia isabella

RECOGNITION Orange and black individuals immediately identifiable, but wholly blond, brown, rust, and tan forms also occur. *All color forms densely covered with stiff bristles of mostly uniform length*, a few slightly longer, softer hairs extend from either end of body. Pale forms with tan or white spiracles. Larva to 5cm.

OCCURRENCE Fields, bottomlands, woodlands, and forests across Canada south to Florida and Texas. Two generations with mature caterpillars throughout most of year over much of East; presumably more broods along Gulf.

COMMON FOODPLANTS Many low-growing herbaceous and woody plants including dandelion, grass, lettuce, meadowsweet, and nettle.

REMARKS The Woolly Bear or Black-ended Bear is among our most familiar caterpillars, especially to children. Caterpillars are often seen crossing roads and driveways. They are most conspicuous around the time of the first frosts. With the return of warmer temperatures in the spring, smaller numbers are again encountered traversing the tarmac. Why they wander is puzzling because the Woolly Bear can eat virtually anything and place themselves at risk when moving about. According to "rural legend," the width of the orange band can be used as a predictor of the severity of the coming winter, with narrower bands forecasting colder winters. In fact, the width is quite a variable character. At each molt, a portion of the black setae is replaced by orange, and hence the orange band is broadest in the last instar. The Woolly Bear and other tiger moth caterpillars are sometimes found at the sugary baits painted on tree trunks to collect moths. It overwinters as a nearly grown caterpillar under leaf litter and boards, usually feeding again in the spring.

Seirarctia echo

RECOGNITION *Fire orange with black and yellow bands across dorsum.* Setae, mostly black, arising from *raised orange warts*. Black dorsal patch interrupted by one or two transverse yellow bands on T2–A8. Spiracles bright white. Head red-orange and unmarked. Larva to 4.5cm.

OCCURRENCE Thickets, scrub, flatwoods, and other open habitats from Georgia south through Florida and west to Mississippi. Multiple generations with mature caterpillars in all months.

COMMON FOODPLANTS Coontie, cabbage palmetto, crotons, lupine, oaks, persimmon, and other woody plants.

REMARKS This is one of only a handful of North American caterpillars known to eat coontie (cycads). Moreover, they seem to do quite well on the older, fully hardened leaves. While coontie is a great place to start your search for this handsome caterpillar, the Echo Moth is wholly polyphagous and apt to turn up on almost any plant. If you are feeling lazy, you can simply drive roads through scrubby areas with an abundance of palmetto and live oak; April is a good time of year in central Florida to search for Echo Moth caterpillars. It is a bit of a mystery why Woolly Bears, Echo Moth caterpillars, and other tiger moth caterpillars wander so widely when they could mature on almost any green plant tissue. Are they collecting dietary precursors for their sex pheromones, or elevating their body temperatures to combat disease or enhance digestion? Perhaps it is simply a matter of wandering away from feculae that might have been deposited at a previous feeding site, volatiles from which are known to attract sundry predators and parasites in other Lepidoptera.

SALT MARSH CATERPILLAR
Estigmene acrea

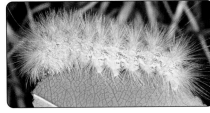

RECOGNITION Exceedingly variable in color, ranging from nearly blond or yellow to black. Body often striped or mottled in black and yellow above and below the *white spiracles. Thoracic and abdominal segments bearing prominent orange or black warts* that bear numerous setae, more or less vertically aligned. Ends of body with very long setae, especially rearward. Setae mostly soft, not bristly. Larva to 5.5cm.

OCCURRENCE Open areas from Canada south to Florida and Texas. At least two generations with mature caterpillars from late June onward; active year-round in southern Florida and Texas.

COMMON FOODPLANTS Many herbaceous and low woody plants including a wide variety of field crops, but also apple, walnut, and a variety of other trees.

REMARKS Early instars tend to be pale and add pigment and dark setae with each molt (penultimate instar figured in inset). The Salt Marsh Caterpillar is an exceedingly rapid crawler. It is reported to occasionally eat other caterpillars, although I have never noted it to be predaceous in my collections when housed with other caterpillars. One wonders if they attack living caterpillars or simply consume tissues of already-dead caterpillars, and whether they engage in such carnage as a means of adding protein or specific substances such as alkaloids to their diet. Tiger moth caterpillars (as well as adults of some species) consume alkaloids not only for their own chemical protection, but also as precursors for their male sex pheromone (scent). The pupa overwinters in a spacious cocoon.

RECOGNITION Exceedingly variable in coloration, ranging from beige or yellow to dark red-brown or nearly black. Body covered in *long, soft setae of variable length.* Most easily recognized by *long hairs— nearly three body segments in length—that extend beyond all others.* Often one long seta, issuing from center of each setal tuft; in pale individuals these

extended setae may have a dark shaft, visible with lens. Spiracles white. Larva to 4.5cm. Early instars pale yellow, hence the common name. Other *Spilosoma* are distinguished below.

OCCURRENCE Fields, gardens, bottomlands, woodlands, and forests across Canada south to Florida and Texas. At least two generations over much of East with mature caterpillars from May through November.

COMMON FOODPLANTS Many low-growing plants, and woody shrubs and trees.

REMARKS The Yellow Bear is among the most common caterpillars on plantings about yards and gardens. I often arrive at my identification of the Yellow Bear by eliminating other possibilities. The Woolly Bear (*Pyrrharctia isabella*), which it may resemble, has decidedly stiffer setae. The caterpillar of the Agreeable Tiger Moth (*Spilosoma congrua*) has shorter, more bristly setae—those of the midabdominal segments scarcely exceed the lengths of segments that bear them (*see* page 478); its caterpillars are not present in the fall, at least northward. My examples of the Pink-legged Tiger Moth (*Spilosoma latipennis*) are pale caramel to reddish brown with setae of intermediate length and have fewer of the long setae extending from either end of the body; the lower half of its head is yellow-brown. The pale early instars of *Spilosoma* are gregarious; later instars are solitary. Yellow Bears start out as cream or yellow, but darken as they age, especially in the last instars when yellow larvae may turn red-brown overnight, following a molt. The pupa overwinters.

FALL WEBWORM
Hyphantria cunea

RECOGNITION Highly variable in coloration, ranging from pale yellow to charcoal. *Cream subdorsal stripe borders darkened dorsal area* in most forms; second more developed stripe runs below spiracles. *Some hairs extremely long, greater in length than four or five body segments.* Spiracles white. Black setal warts over dorsum; those above and below spiracle often red or orange. Larva to 3cm.

OCCURRENCE Yards and parks, fields, fencerows, woodlands, and forests from southern Canada to Florida and Texas. One principal generation in central New York and New England, two generations in New Jersey, and at least four generations in parts of Florida. In Connecticut mature caterpillars in August and September, but found much earlier southward; year-round in Florida.

COMMON FOODPLANTS Recorded from over 400 species of woody plants; commonly seen on apple, ash, cherry, elm, hickory, maple, pecan, poplar, sour gum, walnut, and willow, also consuming herbaceous plants.

REMARKS This frequent defoliator is often misidentified as the Gypsy Moth (*Lymantria dispar*) or the Eastern Tent Caterpillar (*Malacosoma americanum*). Webworm larvae live communally in a silken nest that may envelop whole branches. Nests of the Eastern Tent Caterpillar are smaller and confined to crotches in trees, do not include terminal leaves, and are present only in the spring. Over much of its range, as implied by its name, *Hyphrantia* tends to be a pest in the fall months when its nests may enshroud limbs or even entire trees. The caterpillar is a "parasitoid hotel" hosting more than 50 species of parasitic flies and wasps. When disturbed the larvae often wag in unison, providing a curious collective display. This is one of the few caterpillars likely to be encountered in cities. It overwinters as a pupa.

Hypercompe scribonia

RECOGNITION *Large, black, and densely set with stiff bristles. Intersegmental rings dull red.* Stiff, black, sharply pointed bristles arise from prominently raised warts. Spiracles dull red. Larva to 7.5cm. Middle instars with conspicuous orange patches (inset).

OCCURRENCE Forests and woodlands from extreme southern Canada to Florida and Texas. One generation in New England with nearly mature caterpillars overwintering and occurring through spring northward; two or more broods in South with caterpillars nearly year-round.

COMMON FOODPLANTS Broadly polyphagous, consuming an array of forbs and woody plants, including cherry, dandelion, oak, plantain, sunflower, violet, and willow.

REMARKS The nearly full-grown caterpillars are frequently encountered in the fall and spring, when people are raking leaves or cleaning up their yards. Overwintering caterpillars also shelter under logs and beneath bark. The caterpillars are frequently attacked by a tachinid fly, much to the disappointment of those interested in raising this handsome moth. The caterpillar, reclusive by day, hides in leaf litter and under loose bark, then emerges at night to feed, sometimes ascending saplings and trees. When disturbed, the caterpillar rolls up and, in so doing, exposes its red intersegmental rings. While its stiff, barbed setal bristles afford the caterpillar some physical protection, the bold markings of the adults suggest that both the caterpillars and adults are chemically protected as well. While males are commonly seen around lights, it is unusual to draw females to light. According to Richard Heitzman the caterpillar is also known as the "Fever-worm" in Missouri.

GREAT TIGER MOTH
Arctia caja

RECOGNITION Large with hairs of two distinct lengths. *Entire body vested in layer of bristles, but dorsum also with long, soft, whitish setae, twice the length of others.* Setae on first thoracic segment and subventral tufts decidedly orange-red. Integument black; spiracles white. Larva to 6cm. St. Lawrence Tiger Moth (*Platarctia parthenos*), similar in size and distribution, readily distinguished by its more uniformly dark coloration, brown spiracles, and warty setal tufts (*see* page 476).

OCCURRENCE Arctic alpine zone and boreal forests of northern Canada south to Massachusetts, Pennsylvania, and Great Lakes States. One generation with overwintering caterpillars maturing from May to July.

COMMON FOODPLANTS Broadly polyphagous, consuming a wide array of forbs and woody plants, including alder, cherry, honeysuckle, lilac, poplar, and willow.

REMARKS This densely hairy behemoth is the entomological equivalent of a musk ox. It is a denizen of northern latitudes and alpine habitats that is rarely encountered south of our northern tier of states. Although eggs are easily obtained, rearing this species can be a challenge to even the most attentive caterpillar wrangler because the middle instars enter a sustained diapause and require an extended period of low temperatures (winter) before they will complete their development in the spring. Mirroring natural conditions is difficult; too often captive caterpillars end up succumbing to mold or desiccation. Given the highly polymorphic coloration of adult Great Tiger Moths, it would not surprise me to learn that the caterpillar's coloration varies considerably across its range.

Grammia arge

RECOGNITION Purple- to charcoal-black with *prominent middorsal and subdorsal whitish stripes; these often infused with orange.* Dorsal setal warts smoky to black; lateral ones with orange, at least above. Setae *downier* than those of most other *Grammia.* Lateral warts with at least one very long seta. Larva to 4.5cm. Caterpillars of Doris Tiger Moth (*G. doris*) very similar. In the few photos that I have for comparison, the dorsal setae of the Arge Moth are black, while those of the Doris Tiger Moth tend towards white; in addition there is less orange in the middorsal stripe of Doris Tiger Moth, but these differences may represent no more than individual variation. Forbes (1960) states that in the Doris Tiger Moth the stripes tend to be narrower and that the subdorsal stripe is broken into spots.

OCCURRENCE Dunes, sand plains, grasslands, waste lots, and other dry open areas from Minnesota to southern Quebec and Maine south through Florida and Texas. Two generations over most of East with mature caterpillars from March onward; three or more broods in Deep South.

COMMON FOODPLANTS Many herbaceous plants.

REMARKS This is a local species in the Northeast, confined principally to sandy and open grassy habitats; the moth is common from New Jersey southward. Mike Singer (pers. comm.) has clocked a related *Grammia*, *G. genura*, sprinting at speeds of 10cm/s. In absolute speed this is far from impressive, only 0.36kmph, but in terms of body lengths, this is a feat (so to speak) as mature caterpillars are racing at twice their own body length per second. Caterpillars of the Arge Moth are even faster, ramping up to 1.4kmph in short bursts (James Adams, pers. comm.). The Arge Moth overwinters as a nearly full-grown caterpillar.

VIRGIN TIGER MOTH
Grammia virgo

RECOGNITION *Large, black, bristly*, with orange-brown spiracles. Frequently with *middorsal line*, although this may be pale in some forms. T2–A8 with enlarged *tan warts* bearing numerous setae. Setal clusters *without longer, fine projecting hairs*. Setae often black over dorsum and orange below spiracles. Larva to 5.5cm.

OCCURRENCE Fields and meadows, edges of wetlands, pastures, other open areas, and woodlands from southern Canada to northern Florida and Kansas. One generation with mature caterpillars from May to July; late-flying individuals in South may represent second brood.

COMMON FOODPLANTS Many herbaceous and low woody plants; evidently bedstraw is a favorite.

REMARKS There are more than a dozen other *Grammia* in the East, and there are no keys that can be used to identify the caterpillars with reliability. The Virgin Tiger Moth is the largest among them—most members of the genus grow only to a length of 4cm. Where the Virgin Tiger Moth is common, I often find wandering caterpillars crossing roads and driveways in late spring and early summer. Adults, when gently squeezed, may bubble generous amounts of their yellow "blood" out of the front corners of the thorax, yielding a frothy mass that contains alkaloids that the caterpillar has consumed (inset). All *Grammia* overwinter as caterpillars.

Halysidota tessellaris

RECOGNITION Yellow-brown to gray-black with conspicuous black and white lashes extending from anterior end of body. *T1 and T2 each bear pair of black (inner) and white (outer) lashes*; those of prothorax often held forward over top of head (inset). *A8 with long black lash above spiracle.* Caterpillar to 4.5cm. Sycamore Tussock Moth (*Halysidota harrisii*), a sycamore specialist, co-occurs with the Banded Tussock throughout much of East. Its anterior lashes are rust and white, and the posterior lashes over the spiracle on A8 are white (*see* page 476). Florida Tussock Moth (*Halysidota cinctipes*) largely replaces the Banded Tussock Moth in central and southern Florida. Its caterpillars are general feeders on woody plants; pigeon plum is a favorite. Other *Halysidota* occur in Texas.

OCCURRENCE Woodlands and forests from Canada to central Florida and Texas. One principal generation in North with mature caterpillars from July onward; two broods in Missouri.

COMMON FOODPLANTS Alder, ash, birch, blueberry, chestnut, elm, grape, hackberry, hazel, hickory, oak, walnut, willow, and many other woody shrubs and trees.

REMARKS Caterpillars are conspicuous in habit, frequently resting on upper leaf surfaces in full view. Moreover, they make little effort to move away from the damage inflicted by their own feeding, which suggests that most birds regard Banded Tussock Moth caterpillars as unsuitable prey. I occasionally encounter individuals that have lost many of their setae, presumably during a scuffle with a predator. The pupa overwinters in a cocoon that is laced with dozens of the caterpillar's setae.

HICKORY TUSSOCK MOTH
Lophocampa caryae

RECOGNITION *White with prominent black middorsal tufts* and black warts bearing numerous setae. *Long black subdorsal lashes on A1 and A7.* First eight abdominal segments with black transverse middorsal tuft followed by oval black subdorsal spot to either side; these may be flanked by beige tufts. Larva to 4.5cm.

OCCURRENCE Woodlands and forests from southern Ontario to North Carolina (in mountains) and Nebraska. One generation with mature caterpillars from late July to September.

COMMON FOODPLANTS Hickory, pecan, and walnuts are favorites; other common foodplants include American hornbeam, ash, elm, oak, and willow, but to be expected on almost any woody species.

REMARKS Eggs laid in large batches. Early instars remain in clusters of 100 or more caterpillars (inset). Populations occasionally irrupt and cause noticeable local defoliation. Sensitive persons get rashes and associated itching when exposed to the hairs; severe allergic reactions are rare. The winter is spent as a pupa in a loose cocoon spun in leaf litter. Like other tiger moths, the caterpillars weave their setae into the cocoon.

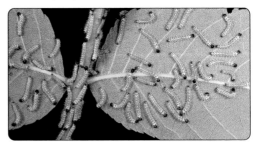

Lophocampa maculata

RECOGNITION Densely hairy with approximately five *yellow-orange to red segments bounded by black segments at either end of body.* Orange segments with *black middorsal tufts.* Numerous *long white lashes* extend from body fore and aft. Bright white spiracles visible through stiff lateral bristles. Larva to 4cm. Middle instars with black at either end of body reduced or absent; middorsal tufts typically red. While superficially similar to Woolly Bear (*Pyrrharctia isabella*), the white lashes at ends of body and the black middorsal tufts immediately distinguish the two.

OCCURRENCE Northern wetlands, edges of watercourses, and forests. Transcontinental in Canada south in East to Great Lakes States and North Carolina (mountains, but absent from many intervening states). Principally single-brooded with mature caterpillars from July to September, although Handfield's (1999) records suggest at least a partial second generation north into southern Canada, hence with mature caterpillars to be expected from late June to October.

COMMON FOODPLANTS Alder and willow are favorites; also reported from basswood, cherry, elm, hazel, maple, oak, poplar, and many other woody species.

REMARKS In North Carolina this is a glacial relict—from its colonies in the high Appalachians, the Spotted Tussock skips to northeastern Massachusetts and the Adirondacks. In Canada the moth occurs north into Labrador. Another means to distinguish the caterpillar of the Spotted Tussock from the Woolly Bear is to note where it is resting or feeding. The Spotted Tussock feeds up on woody shrubs and trees whereas the Woolly Bear feeds close to the ground, and frequently on forbs. The Spotted Tussock is gregarious, at least in early instars. The pupa overwinters.

MILKWEED TUSSOCK CATERPILLAR
Euchaetes egle

RECOGNITION *Densely hairy caterpillar with numerous black, orange (or yellow), and white tufts and lashes.* Prominent black lashes extend from ends of body and sides of anterior abdominal segments. Long white lashes issue from sides and subdorsum anterior and posterior to orange tussocks. Orange

tussocks curve upward over abdomen and meet over midline. Larva to 3.5cm. A dozen other *Euchaetes* occur in Texas and the Southwest.

OCCURRENCE Fields and open areas from Minnesota to Maine south to Florida and Texas. One generation in Canada; at least two generations over much of range with mature caterpillars from June onward.

COMMON FOODPLANTS Milkweed.

REMARKS Females lay rafts of eggs. The caterpillars, which are gregarious through the third instar, often defoliate individual plants, especially in gardens and nurseries. In some years populations of the Milkweed Tussock irrupt and lay bare patches of milkweed. It is often school teachers who first alert me to such infestations, in part alarmed because they fear that there will be no leaves left for their real interest, Monarch caterpillars. Yet, in my experience, the two insects commonly affect different sorts of plants. I associate Monarchs with young, vigorously growing shoots, while Milkweed Tussock Moths are content to eat older foliage, sometimes that which has already started to yellow. The pupa overwinters in a cocoon that Forbes (1960) described as felted.

RECOGNITION *Pink-red, scarlet or fiery red-orange* with long, but relatively sparse black setae. Immediately *recognizable by pair of very long white hairs that issue from dorsal warts on T2.* Setal warts on A1, A2, and A5–A7 metallic blue or purple and black. Larva to 5.5cm.

OCCURRENCE Hardwood hammocks, woodlands, and other subtropical communities of southern Florida including Keys.

COMMON FOODPLANTS Plants in the spurge (Euphorbiaceae) family, especially devil's potato or rubber vine (*Echites*), but also bay bean, leafless cynachum, and others.

REMARKS While the larva is strikingly handsome in its own right, the adult is one of North America's most beautiful insects. The mostly black adult has enough red, white, and blue to warrant its second common name, the "Uncle Sam Moth." Both larva and adult are highly conspicuous and diurnal in habit. Presumably all stages are chemically protected—even the pupa is boldly marked and clearly visible within its thin-walled cocoon. This is our region's only pericopine arctiid—a group of modest diversity but great splendor in the American tropics. Pericopines are often models for other mimetic insects or themselves are members of (Müllerian) mimicry complexes. Adults can be found flying in the day as well as at lights.

TIGER MOTHS

UNEXPECTED CYCNIA *Cycnia inopinatus*
South Dakota to southeastern Massachusetts to Florida and Texas. Two generations in New Jersey with mature caterpillars from May into November. Primarily butterfly weed.

DELICATE CYCNIA *Cycnia tenera*
South Dakota to Nova Scotia south to Florida and Texas. Two or three generations over much of range with mature caterpillars from June to November. Dogbane (especially *A. cannabinum*). Oregon Cycnia (*C. oregoniensis*), another dogbane feeder, has somewhat sparser and coarser blond setae.

ORANGE VIRBIA *Virbia aurantiaca* (= *Holomelina aurantiaca*)
Canada south to Florida and Texas. Two or more generations with mature caterpillars from May to November. Dandelion, pigweed, plantain, and other forbs.

PHYLLIRA TIGER MOTH *Grammia phyllira*
Especially sandy areas. Manitoba to Maine south to Florida and Texas. Two principal generations over much of East with overwintering caterpillars maturing in spring and second generation caterpillars in summer. Forbs and grasses.

SYCAMORE TUSSOCK MOTH *Halysidota harrisii*
Southern Michigan and New England to Florida and Texas. Two generations over much of range with mature caterpillars from May onward. Sycamore.

CHARLOTTE'S TIGER MOTH *Apantesis carlotta*
Nebraska to southern Wisconsin, Michigan, and Maine to Georgia and Texas, but absent along Gulf. Two or more generations with mature caterpillars throughout much of the year. Forbs.

ST. LAWRENCE TIGER MOTH *Platarctia parthenos*
Transcontinental in Canada south in East to North Carolina (mountains). One generation with overwintering caterpillars maturing in June and July. General feeder.

YELLOW-WINGED PAREUCHAETES *Pareuchaetes insulata*
Florida to Texas. Mature caterpillars occur year-round. Eupatorium. Captive larvae accept many plants.

Unexpected Cycnia

Delicate Cycnia

Orange Virbia

Phyllira Tiger Moth

Sycamore Tussock Moth

Charlotte's Tiger Moth

St. Lawrence Tiger Moth

Yellow-winged Pareuchaetes

TIGER MOTHS

RUBY TIGER MOTH *Phragmatobia fuliginosa*

North Dakota to Newfoundland south to New Jersey, Pennsylvania, and Great Lakes States. One generation with overwintering caterpillars maturing in spring. General feeder.

AGREEABLE TIGER MOTH *Spilosoma congrua*

Canada south to Florida and Texas. One generation northward; two broods in Missouri and Tennessee with mature caterpillars from June to November. General feeder. Two forms shown: upper right from Connecticut. Second row from Great Smoky Mountain National Park.

DUBIOUS TIGER MOTH *Spilosoma dubia*

Transcontinental in Canada south in East to Florida and east Texas, but absent from southern New England and many mid-Atlantic States. Evidently just one generation with mature caterpillars from May to August. General feeder.

BELLA MOTH *Utetheisa bella*

Minnesota to Nova Scotia (as stragglers) south to Florida and Texas. A migrant and transient colonist over much of East. Two generations in New Jersey, breeding continuously in South. Principally legumes, such as rattlebox.

SCARLET-BODIED WASP MOTH *Cosmosoma myrodora*

Gulf States. Breeding year-round. Climbing hempweed.

BLACK-WINGED DAHANA *Dahana atripennis*

Southern Georgia and Florida. Breeding year-round. Spanish moss.

EDWARDS' WASP MOTH *Lymire edwardsii*

Central and southern Florida. Breeding year-round. Fig (*Ficus*).

Ruby Tiger Moth

Agreeable Tiger Moth

Agreeable Tiger Moth (2nd form)

Dubious Tiger Moth

Bella Moth

Scarlet-bodied Wasp Moth

Black-winged Dahana

Edwards' Wasp Moth

YELLOW-COLLARED SCAPE MOTH
Cisseps fulvicollis

RECOGNITION Yellow to brown or nearly black with comparatively sparse, silky setae. Black middorsal stripe. *Broad black spiracular stripe edged with yellow to orange subdorsal and subspiracular stripes.* Subdorsal stripe often with red or orange aspect, especially along its upper edge. *Dorsal setal warts without pigment; those over T2, T3, and A9 enlarged, oval.* Most body setae dirty white, of essentially one length, splaying out from warts. Barbs along setal shaft long, visible with hand lens. Ends of body with some setae greatly lengthened and darkened. Most caterpillars have dark markings about eyes or in line across face, but otherwise head pale orange-brown, shiny, and unmarked. Prolegs pale. Larva less than 3cm.

OCCURRENCE Open fields and meadows from Canada south to Florida and Texas. In Connecticut evidently with two principal generations; three or more generations southward with mature caterpillars nearly year-round.

COMMON FOODPLANTS Grasses and sedges.

REMARKS Although locally abundant in open grassy habitats, the caterpillars are not commonly encountered because they feed close to the ground and are primarily nocturnal. Occasionally they appear in sweep-net samples. Success will also be obtained by searching grassy meadows by flashlight—and even if none is seen, other interesting caterpillars will be encountered during the search. Open fields, with abundant goldenrod and asters upon which the adults nectar, are a good place to start. There is great variation in the size of the larvae that overwinter. Evidently the Yellow-collared Scape Moth is a migratory species. Dale Schweitzer (pers. comm.) has noted flights moving northward through New Jersey from July through September. How far north the caterpillars are able to overwinter successfully is not known.

Ctenucha virginica

RECOGNITION *"Tussocked" with row of black middorsal abdominal tufts;* first and last tufts longer than those of intervening segments. *Flanking white, blond, or yellow setal tufts may obscure black middorsal tufts.* Beneath tufts, body nearly black with broken, cream subdorsal and white subspiracular stripes. *Prolegs usually reddened.* Head to either side of triangle blackened; remainder of head orange to red. Larva to 4cm. Middle instars without dense coat of pale setae; middorsal tufts especially evident (inset). Caterpillars of Veined Ctenucha (*Ctenucha venosa*), which enters our range in Texas, scarcely exceed 3cm in length.

OCCURRENCE Moist, open grassy fields and meadows from southern Canada to Nebraska and northern Pennsylvania. My records from Connecticut suggest one generation with mature caterpillars in May and early June.

COMMON FOODPLANTS Grasses (Poaceae), but also consuming other plants.

REMARKS Caterpillars of the Virginia Ctenucha are most often encountered in the fall and early spring in grassy fields. Like many other tiger moths, the larva curls into a ball if disturbed, and, in so doing, reveals its white stripes and reddish prolegs. Sweeping, especially at night, may yield a caterpillar or two. The larva overwinters; those that I have found in Connecticut over the fall months range upward to 1.5cm in length.

SPOTTED OLEANDER CATERPILLAR
Empyreuma affinis

RECOGNITION *Pale orange with sparse, long setae and white subdorsal and subventral spotting.* Dorsum of *T2, T3, and A8 with pair of narrow black lashes, each of which has an especially long, white-tipped hair that extends beyond others.* White subdorsal spots, vaguely edged with black, often fused. Each proleg with "anklet" ring of pale setae. Head capsule shiny pale orange. Larva to 4.5cm.

OCCURRENCE Yards, cities, and other planted areas in southern Florida. Active year-round.

COMMON FOODPLANTS Oleander.

REMARKS This native to Cuba and other Antilles was first recorded from Boca Raton in Palm Beach County in 1978; it has since spread through the southern portion of the state. The foodplant, oleander, is a hardy perennial with showy flowers that is extensively used in landscaping. Highway departments seem to be especially enamored with the plant. No doubt, both the Spotted Oleander and Oleander Caterpillars (*Syntomeida epilais*) have benefited from the popularity of their foodplant, and it seems that both will eventually spread to other southern states. If the larvae are half as toxic as their foodplant, then they are well equipped to deal with birds and other predators. A few leaves of oleander can poison a child. The caterpillar passes through six instars, usually over a period of four weeks. Caterpillars are solitary; those of the Oleander Caterpillar are gregarious.

(POLKA-DOT WASP MOTH) *Syntomeida epilais*

RECOGNITION *Bright orange with smoky black setae.* Setae arise from shiny black bases. *Some setal clusters adjacent to spiracles as well as those at front and rear of body lashlike,* extending well beyond body; those over top of abdomen shorter and splayed. Head bright orange and unmarked. Larva to 4.5cm. Yellow-banded Wasp Moth (*Syntomeida ipomoeae*) has dense, white dorsal tufts on A3–A7 in last instar; distinguished in earlier instars by absence of lateral setal lashes and shorter, denser dorsal tufts over abdomen. Although catholic in diet (morning glory, grapefruit, and thistle), morning glory and other latex-bearing plants may be preferred.

OCCURRENCE Scrub woodlands, fields, and other open areas in Florida. Mature caterpillars occur year-round.

COMMON FOODPLANTS Oleander and devil's potato.

REMARKS The caterpillars have three of the classic earmarks of unpalatability: bright orange and black coloration, conspicuous diurnal activity, and they feed gregariously. Larvae are often encountered while moving about the plant or crossing open ground in search of young leaves. They are highly animated in their movements, undulating forth at what are, by other caterpillars' standards, impossible speeds. Females deposit the eggs in clusters, some of which may contain upwards of 70 eggs. The caterpillars are gregarious through the third instar, feeding in groups from leaf undersides. Curiously, this species may form pupal aggregations that contain numerous individuals. The cocoon, whether spun by one or several individuals, is a wispy construction—the aposematically orange-brown and black pupae are clearly visible within. Both females and males use ultrasound to locate one another and carry out courtship duets.

MEXICAN JUMPING BEAN
CATERPILLAR – TORTRICIDAE
Cydia deshaisiana

While Mexican jumping beans are familiar to many, few realize that the occupant is a microlepidopteran caterpillar, related to the Codling Moth (*Cydia pomonella*) that infests apples. The caterpillar hollows out the seed into which it has bored and is able to make it bounce by craning its head backward then rapidly snapping it forward, against the opposite wall of the seed. Some hypothesize that the caterpillar "jumps" to move its location into more favorable environments or as a means of avoiding predation by seed-eating vertebrates. Common foodplants in Mexico and the Southwest include euphorbs in the genera *Sebastiana* and *Sapium*. The beans may be so numerous (and active) that the jumping beans make an audible rustle while they are tumbling about in the leaves below their foodplant. Señor Joaquin Hernandez, "King of the Jumping Beans," is said to be responsible for the collection and distribution of some 20 million beans each year from his home town of Alamosa, Mexico. The caterpillar passes the winter within the seed, holding off on pupation until the following season. The adult emerges through a circular exit hatch at one end of the "bean" made by the caterpillar prior to pupation.

MESCAL, AGAVE, OR MAGUEY WORM – COSSIDAE

Comadia redtenbacheri

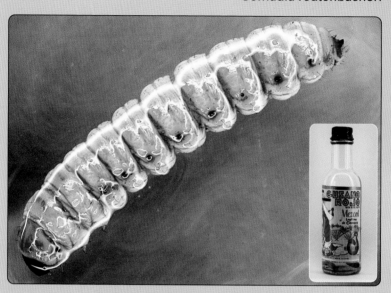

An insect surrounded in considerable legend, lore, and misconception, native to the American Southwest and Mexico, where it is known as Gusano Rojo or "red worm." While all the larvae that I have seen (all being, of course, well preserved) have been largely devoid of color, I wonder if the prepupal caterpillars turn red. Many Lepidoptera, especially among the microlepidopterans, daggers (*Acronicta*), and prominents, redden prior to pupation. A common misunderstanding, at least among lepidopterists, is that the worm swirling around in the bottom of a mescal bottle is that of a giant skipper (*Megathymus*), another agave-feeder. Every bottle that I have seen has contained a *Comadia* caterpillar, an abundant borer in the heart of agaves. While the swallowing of the worm will not get you any higher, imbue you with great sexual prowess or superhuman powers, or bring you good luck, you may consider your act a rite of passage, but to what I am most uncertain. Both tequila and mescal are distillates of a fermented mash made from agave (or in Spanish, *maguey*) hearts. They differ in their origin and the species of agave that is used. Tequila is made only from blue agave in the tequila district of Jalisco, and more recently Tamaulipas, while mescals are made everywhere else and use other agaves; tequila is never bottled with a worm. A credible account as to how worms came to be associated with mescal is given on the Del Maguey website (http://www.mezcal.com/worms.html).

GLOSSARY

abdomen: ten segments of body that immediately follow leg-bearing thoracic segments.

addorsal: to either side of dorsal midline (Fig. 6, page 11).

aestivate: to enter period of summer inactivity.

anal plate: dorsal shield atop last abdominal segment (A10) (Fig. 1, page 9).

anal point: medial fleshy spur located below anus in lappet moths.

anal proleg: proleg arising from last abdominal segment (A10) (Fig. 1, page 9).

annulations: shallow creases that ring each segment, perpendicular to body axis; they may be incomplete.

antenna: elongate sensory structure forward from eyes (Fig. 2, page 10).

antepenultimate instar: instar preceding penultimate instar.

anterior proleg: proleg of sixth abdominal segment of inchworms.

aposematic: warningly colored; boldly colored in yellows, oranges, and reds, often with black or white markings as well; less commonly with only black and white pattern elements.

band: pattern running around segments, perpendicular to body axis; broader than rings.

beating: method of obtaining caterpillars by abruptly striking branches over a sheet, umbrella, or other collection surface (*see* page 14).

caterpillar: larval stage of butterflies and moths.

chaetotaxy: distribution of larval setae; and in particular primary setae (= those present in first instar). Chaetotaxy is important in classification and identification of larval lepidopterans.

chrysalis: exposed pupal stage of butterflies and some moths; often angulate and sculptured; usually attached by cremaster.

clypeus: elongate plate between antennae, immediately below frons or frontal triangle (Fig. 2, page 10).

cocoon: construction of silk fashioned by caterpillar prior to pupation; often incorporating frass, wood chips, larval setae, feculae, etc.

cremaster: set of hooklike spines on terminus of pupa used to lock anal end of pupa in place.

crochets: distal hooklike structures on abdominal prolegs (Figs 3, 4, page 10).

detritus: partly decomposed organic matter.

diapause: period of hormonally controlled inactivity. Often induced by shortening day lengths in late summer and fall and broken by warm temperatures in spring.

distal: away from body (cf. proximal).

dorsal: along back or upper side.

dorsum: back or upper side.

eclosion (eclose): the act of emergence from an egg or pupa.

facultative: brood that may or may not happen; used here to refer to a partial generation; antonym of obligatory.

feculae: pelletlike larval excrement.

frass: larval scrapings, for example, from a larval excavation; used by some authors to refer to feculae or excrement.

frons: triangular area in center of head, also called frontal triangle (Fig. 2, page 10).

hairpencil: fascicle of long setae.

heart stripe: middorsal stripe resulting from visibility of heart through larval cuticle.

hemolymph: clear green fluid that fills an insect's body, sharing some functions of blood, but differing in that it does not transport oxygen.

hypoproct: fleshy spur ventral to anus in inchworms; well developed in many species that rest on twigs (Fig. 5, page 10).

instar: one of the larval stages between molts.

integument: body surface, cuticle, or skin.

intersegmental: between adjacent segments.

labrum: upper lip; plate below clypeus that rests over jaws; it is often cleft (Fig. 2, page 10).

larva: feeding stage of insects with complete metamorphosis; in this book used synonymously with caterpillar.

lateral: along sides, especially at level of spiracles.

lobe: rounded area of head above eyes, to either side of midline.

medial: running along or near body midline.

melanic: dark (charcoal or black) forms; melanic forms are commonly seen in ennomine geometrid adults such as the Pepper-and-salt Moth (*Biston betularia*) and others.

middorsal: along dorsal midline of body; cf. heart stripe.

midline: (imaginary) line that divides left and right sides of body; that above is the dorsal midline and that below the ventral midline.

midventral: along ventral midline of body.

paraproct: small, fleshy protuberance to either side of anus in inchworms, often best developed in those species that rest on stems and twigs (Fig. 5, page 10).

parasitoid: predator that lives internally or externally in close association with its host. Parasitoids are parasitelike in that they are minute to small, feed from within or on the host body, and often do so over a period of weeks or months. Functionally they are predators because they almost always kill the host.

penultimate instar: instar preceding last or ultimate larval instar.

phenology: seasonal progression of life cycle.

pheromone: chemical released by one individual that brings about a response in a second individual of the same species; intraspecific odor or scent.

pinaculum (pinacula): base plate from which a seta is borne. Often pigmented, shiny, or in some other way distinguished from adjacent cuticle.

polyphagous: eating plants from several plant families.

prepupa: last portion of larval stage; typically applied to post-feeding portion of last instar. Coloration changes frequently occur in the prepupa: most species lose patterning and color, and a few turn bright red.

primary setae: setal complement present in first instar; primary setae have a standardized nomenclature (Fig. 7, page 11). The positions of the primary setae are often used in identification and classification of Lepidoptera.

prolegs: fleshy "legs" located on abdominal segments three, four, five, six, and ten; usually bearing hooklike spines called crochets (Figs 1, 3–5, pages 9 and 10).

prothoracic shield: dorsal plate over first thoracic segment (Fig. 1, page 9).

proximal: closer to body (cf. distal).

pupa: stage between caterpillar and adult; often enclosed in cocoon. A largely immobile stage, but one of great physiological activity in which larval tissues are replaced by those of adult. *See* chrysalis.

rootlet setae: thickened setae that form fringe along subventer of underwing caterpillars (*Catocala*) and other bark-resting species. Sometimes greatly modified, more fleshy than hairlike.

scolus: branched spine.

secondary setae: setae that appear in the second to final larval instars (in excess of primary setae).

seta (setae): hairlike outgrowth from head or body.

setal base: hardened plate at base of seta; pinaculum (pinacula).

skeletonize: to remove all leaf tissue except for underlying network of veins.

spatulate: resembling a spatula; here referring to seta that broadens distally.

specialist: feeding on one species in a single plant genus or two closely related genera.

spermatophore: reproductive packet delivered to female during copulation; in addition to sperm it may contain carbohydrates, protein, salts, steroids, defensive substances, and other compounds. These may enhance female's survival or reproductive efforts. The spermatophore can be ephemeral or persistent; in many species it may interfere with the ability of the female (or other males) to obtain additional copulations.

spinneret: elongate silk-producing structure on the lower surface of head (*see* page 9).

spinule: minute spine.

spinulose: covered with minute spines; referring to surface texture of integument or a larger spine.

spiracles: lateral, oval to round openings of respiratory system found on first thoracic and first eight abdominal segments (Fig. 1, page 9).

spiracular: adjacent to or passing through spiracles (Fig. 6, page 11).

stripe: marking that runs (longitudinally) along body axis.

subdorsal: below level of addorsal and above supraspiracular areas (Fig. 6, page 11).

subspiracular: below level of spiracles and above subventer (Fig. 6, page 11).

supraspiracular: above level of spiracles and below subdorsal area (Fig. 6, page 11).

subventral: area above legs and prolegs but below subspiracular area (Fig. 6, page 11).

thoracic: of or pertaining to the thorax.

thorax: body area consisting of three segments immediately behind head that bears true, claw-bearing legs.

trachea (tracheae): principal tube in respiratory system of insects (*see* tracheal trunk).

tracheal trunk: principal respiratory duct connecting spiracles, often visible through body wall.

transverse: running from side to side, perpendicular to body axis.

triangle: triangular area between eyes (Fig. 2, page 10); also called frontal triangle or frons.

truncate: appearing cut or squared off.

venter: underside or "belly."

vertex: dorsal or top portion of head (Fig. 2, page 10).

HELPFUL AND CITED LITERATURE

Ackery, P. R., R. de Jong, and R. I. Vane-Wright. 1999. The Butterflies: Hedyloidea, Hesperioidea and Papilionoidea. pp. 263–300. *In* N. P. Kristensen (ed.), *Lepidoptera, Moths and Butterflies. Volume 1: Evolution, Systematics, and Biogeography. Handbook for Zoology. Volume IV. Arthropoda: Insecta.* Walter de Gruyter, Berlin.

Allen, T. J. 1997. *The Butterflies of West Virginia and Their Caterpillars.* University of Pittsburgh Press, Pittsburgh, Pennsylvania.

Allen, T. J., J. P. Brock, and J. Glassberg. 2005. *A Field Guide to Caterpillars.* Oxford University Press, Oxford.

Bängizer, H. and D. S. Fletcher. 1985. Three new zoophilous moths of the genus *Scopula* (Lepidoptera: Geometridae) from South-east Asia. *Journal of Natural History*, **19**: 851–860.

Barnes, W. M. and J. McDunnough. 1918. *Illustrations of the North American Species of the Genus Catocala.* Memoirs of the American Museum of Natural History, New Series, Volume III, Part 1.

Beck, H. 1999. *Die Larven der Europäischen Noctuidae—Revision der Systematik der Noctuidae.* Herbipolianna 5. Volumes 1, 2. Verlag Dr. Ulf Eitschberger, Marktleuthen, Germany.

Beck, H. 2000. *Die Larven der Europäischen Noctuidae—Revision der Systematik der Noctuidae.* Herbipolianna 5. Volumes 3, 4. Verlag Dr. Ulf Eitschberger, Marktleuthen, Germany.

Boettner, G. H., J. S. Elkinton, and C. J. Boettner. 2000. Effects of a biological control introduction on three nontarget native species of saturniid moths. *Conservation Biology*, **14**: 1798–1806.

Bolte, K. B. 1990. *Guide to the Geometridae of Canada (Lepidoptera). VI. Subfamily Larentiinae. 1. Revision of the genus* Eupithecia. Memoirs of the Entomological Society of Canada, No. 138.

Brou, V. A. and C. D. Brou. 1997. Distribution and phenologies of Louisiana Sphingidae. *Journal of the Lepidopterists' Society*, **51**: 156–175.

Carter, D. J. and B. Hargreaves. 1986. *A Field Guide to the Caterpillars of Butterflies and Moths in Britain and Europe.* Collins Press, London.

Covell, C. V., Jr. 1984. *A Field Guide to the Moths of Eastern North America.* Houghton Mifflin Co., Boston, Massachusetts.

Crumb, S. E. 1956. *The Caterpillars of the Phalaenidae.* Technical Bulletin 1135. USDA Forest Service, Washington, DC.

DeVries, P. J. 1997. *The Butterflies of Costa Rica and Their Natural History. Volume II. Riodinidae.* Princeton University Press, Princeton, New Jersey.

Dunn, G.A. (ed.). 1993. *Caring for Insect Livestock: An Insect Rearing Manual.* Young Entomologists' Society, Inc., Lansing, Michigan.

Dyar, H. G. and E. L. Morton. 1895–1896. The life-histories of the New York slug caterpillars, Parts I–II. *Journal of the New York Entomological Society*, **3**: 145–157, **4**: 1–9.

Dyar, H. G. 1896–1914. The life-histories of the New York slug caterpillars, parts III–XX. *Journal of the New York Entomological Society*, **4**: 167–190, **5**: 1–14, 57–66, 167–170, **6**: 1–9, 94–98, 151–158, 241–246, **7**: 61–67, 234–253, **15**: 219–226, **22**: 223–229.

Edwards, W. H. 1868–1897. The Butterflies of North America, 1st series, 218 pp., 52 color pls., Philadelphia, 1868–1872; 2nd series, 357 pp., 51 color pls., Boston and New York, 1884; 3rd series, 431 pp., 51 color pls., Boston and New York, [1887]–1897.

Epstein, M. E. 1996. Revision and phylogeny of the limacodid-group families, with evolutionary studies on slug caterpillars (Lepidoptera: Zygaenoidea). *Smithsonian Contributions to Zoology*, No. 582.

Ferguson, D. C. 1955. *The Lepidoptera of Nova Scotia*. Part 1. Macrolepidoptera. Bulletin No. 2. Nova Scotia Museum of Science, Halifax, Nova Scotia.

Ferguson, D. C. 1978. Lymantriidae, Noctuoidea. *In* Dominick, R. B., *et al.* (eds), *The Moths of America North of Mexico. Fasc. 22.2*. Wedge Entomological Foundation, Washington, DC.

Ferguson, D. C. 1991. An essay on the long-range dispersal and biogeography of Lepidoptera, with special reference to the Lepidoptera of Bermuda. pp. 67–79. *In* Ferguson, D.C., D. J. Hilburn, and B. Wright (eds), *The Lepidoptera of Bermuda, Their Foodplants, Biogeography, and Means of Dispersal*. Memoirs of the Entomological Society of Canada, 158: 1–106.

Ferguson, D. C. in prep. Geometroidea. Geometridae (Part). Ennominae (Part—Abraxini, Cassymini, Macariini). *In* Dominick, R. B., *et al.* (eds), *The Moths of America North of Mexico*. Wedge Entomological Foundation, Washington, DC.

Forbes, W. T. M. 1923. *The Lepidoptera of New York and Neighboring States. I. Primitive forms, Microlepidoptera, Pyraloids, Bombyces*. Memoir 68. Cornell University Agricultural Experiment Station, Ithaca, New York.

Forbes, W. T. M. 1948. *The Lepidoptera of New York and Neighboring States. II. Geometridae, Sphingidae, Notodontidae, Lymantriidae*. Memoir 274. Cornell University Agricultural Experiment Station, Ithaca, New York.

Forbes, W. T. M. 1954. *The Lepidoptera of New York and Neighboring States. III. Noctuidae*. Memoir 329. Cornell University Agricultural Experiment Station, Ithaca, New York.

Forbes, W. T. M. 1960. *The Lepidoptera of New York and Neighboring States. IV. Agaristidae Through Nymphalidae, Including Butterflies*. Memoir 371. Cornell University Agricultural Experiment Station, Ithaca, New York.

Fox, L. R. and P. A. Morrow. 1981. Specialization: Species property or local phenomenon? *Science*, **211**: 887–893.

Friedlander, T. P. 1987 [1986]. Taxonomy, phylogeny, and biogeography of *Asterocampa* Röber, 1916 (Lepidoptera, Nymphalidae, Apaturinae). *Journal of Research on the Lepidoptera*, **25**: 215–338.

Friedrich, E. 1986. *Breeding Butterflies and Moths: A Practical Handbook for British and European Species* [translation by S. Whitebread; ed. A.M. Emmet]. Harley Books, London.

Godfrey, G. L. 1972. *A Review and Reclassification of Caterpillars of the Subfamily Hadeninae (Lepidoptera: Noctuidae) of America North of Mexico*. USDA Technical Bulletin 1450, Washington, DC.

Godfrey, G. L. 1987. Noctuidae (Noctuoidea). pp. 549–578. *In* F. W. Stehr (ed.), *Immature Insects*. Kendall/Hunt Publ. Co., Dubuque, Iowa.

Greene, E. 1989. A diet-induced developmental polymorphism in a caterpillar. *Science*, **243**: 643–645.

Handfield, L. 1999. *Le guide des papillons du Québec*. Broquet Inc., Boucherville, Quebec.

Hardwick, D. F. 1996. A *Monograph to the North American* Heliothentinae *(Lepidoptera: Noctuidae)*. Privately published, Almonte, Ontario.

Harvey, D. J. 1991. Higher classification of the Nymphalidae. pp. 255–273. *In* H. F. Nijhout, *The Development and Evolution of Butterfly Wing Patterns*. Smithsonian Institution Press, Washington, DC.

Heinrich, B. 1979. Foraging strategies of caterpillars: leaf damage and possible predator avoidance strategies. *Oecologia*, **42**: 325–337.

Heinrich, B. 1993. How avian predators constrain caterpillar foraging. pp. 224–247. *In* N. E. Stamp and T. M. Casey (eds), *Caterpillars. Ecological and Evolutionary Constraints on Foraging*. Chapman and Hall, New York.

Heinrich, B. 2003. *Winter World: The Ingenuity of Animal Survival*. Harper Collins Publishers, New York.

Heitzman, J. R. 1964. The early stages of *Euphyes vestris*. *Journal of Research on the Lepidoptera*, **3**: 151–153.

Hodges, R. W. 1971. Sphingoidea. *In* Dominick, R. B., *et al.* (eds), *The Moths of America North of Mexico. Fasc. 21*. E. W. Classey Ltd., London, England.

Hodges, R. W., *et al.* (eds). 1983. *Checklist of the Lepidoptera of America North of Mexico*. E. W. Classey, London, England.

Holland, W. J. 1968. *The Moth Book: A Guide to the Moths of North America*. Dover Publications, New York.

Howe, W. H. 1975. *The Butterflies of North America*. Doubleday and Co., Garden City, New Jersey.

Howlett, R. J. and M. E. N. Majerus. 1987. The understanding of industrial melanism in the peppered moth (*Biston betularia*) (Lepidoptera: Geometridae). *Biological Journal of the Linnean Society*, **30**: 31–44.

Ives, W. G. H. and H. R. Wong. 1988. *Tree and Shrub Insects of the Prairie Provinces*. Information Report NOR-X-292. Canadian Forestry Service, Northern Forest Centre, Edmonton, Alberta.

Kettlewell, H. B. D. 1973. *The Evolution of Melanism*. Clarendon Press, Oxford.

Kimball, C. P. 1965. *The Lepidoptera of Florida*. State of Florida Division of Agriculture, Gainesville, Florida.

Kitching, I. J. and J. E. Rawlins. 1998. The Noctuoidea, pp. 355–401. *In* N. P. Kristensen (ed.), *Lepidoptera, Moths and Butterflies. Volume 1: Evolution, Systematics, and Biogeography. Handbook for Zoology. Volume IV. Arthropoda: Insecta*. Walter de Gruyter, Berlin.

Klots, A. B. 1951. *A Field Guide to the Butterflies*. Houghton Mifflin, Boston, Massachusetts.

Knudson, E. C. and C. W. Bordelon. 1999. *Checklist of the Lepidoptera of Texas*. Privately published by authors, Houston, Texas.

Kristensen, N. P. (ed.). 1998. *Lepidoptera, Moths and Butterflies. Volume 1. Evolution, Systematics, and Biogeography. Volume IV. Arthropoda: Insecta*. Walter de Gruyter, Berlin.

Lafontaine, J. D. and R. W. Poole. 1991. Noctuidae, Plusiinae. *In* Dominick, R. B., *et al.* (eds), *The Moths of America North of Mexico. Fasc. 25.1*. Wedge Entomological Foundation, Washington, DC.

Lafontaine, J. D. 1998. Noctuoidea. Noctuidae (Part), Noctuinae (Part—Noctuini). *In* Dominick, R. B., *et al.* (eds), *The Moths of America North of Mexico. Fasc. 27.3*. Wedge Entomological Foundation, Washington, DC.

Lajonquière. 1968 [1969]. Révision du genre *Phyllodesma* (=*Epicnaptera auctorum*), IIe partie— Espècies néarctiques [Lep. Lasiocampidae]. *Annales de la Société Entomologique de France*, Nouvelle série, **4**: 781–851.

Laplante, J.-P. 1998. *Papillons et Chenilles du Québec et de l'est du Canada*. Book Art, Inc., Montréal, Québec.

Leverton, R. 2001. *Enjoying Moths*. T. and A. D. Poyser Ltd., London.

Maier, C. T., C. R. Lemmon, J. M. Fengler, D. F. Schweitzer, and R. C. Reardon. 2004. *Caterpillars on the Foliage of Conifers in the Northeastern United States.* USFS Technology Transfer Bulletin, FHTET-02-06.

Martin, G. 2003. *Macrophotography: Learning from a Master.* Harry N. Abrams, Inc., New York.

McCabe, T. 1990 [1991]. *Atlas of Adirondack Caterpillars.* Museum Bulletin 470. State Education Department/New York State Museum, Albany, New York.

McFarland, N. 1964. Notes on collecting, rearing, and preserving larvae of Macrolepidoptera. *Journal of the Lepidopterists' Society*, **18**: 201–210.

McFarland, N. 1988. *Portraits of South Australian Geometrid Moths.* (available from author in Sierra Vista, Arizona).

McGuffin, W. C. 1958. *Larvae of the Nearctic Larentiinae (Lepidoptera: Geometridae).* Canadian Entomologist, Supplement 8.

McGuffin, W. C. 1967. *Guide to the Geometridae of Canada (Lepidoptera). I. Subfamily Sterrhinae.* Memoirs of the Entomological Society of Canada, No. 50.

McGuffin, W. C. 1977. *Guide to the Geometridae of Canada (Lepidoptera). II. Subfamily Ennominae, 2.* Memoirs of the Entomological Society of Canada, No. 101.

McGuffin, W. C. 1987. *Guide to the Geometridae of Canada (Lepidoptera). II. Subfamily Ennominae, 4.* Memoirs of the Entomological Society of Canada No. 138.

Miller, J. C. and P. C. Hammond. 2003 [2004]. *Lepidoptera of the Pacific Northwest: Caterpillars and Adults.* USFS Technology Transfer Bulletin, FHTET-2003-03.

Minno, M. C. and T. C. Emmel. 1993. *Butterflies of the Florida Keys.* Scientific Publishers, Gainesville, Florida.

Minno, M. C., J. F. Butler, and D. W. Hall. 2005. *Florida Butterfly Caterpillars and Their Host Plants.* University Press of Florida, Gainesville, Florida.

Mitter, C., J. W. Neal, Jr., K. M. Gott, and E. Silverfine. 1987. A geographic comparison of pseudogamous populations of the fall cankerworm (*Alsophila pometaria*). *Entomologia Experimentalis et Applicata*, **43**: 133–143.

Neck, R. W. 1996. *A Field Guide to the Butterflies of Texas.* Gulf Publishing Co., Houston, Texas.

Neil, K. A. 1981. The occurrence of *Noctua pronuba* (L.) (Noctuidae) in Nova Scotia: a new North American record. *Journal of the Lepidopterists' Society*, **35**: 248.

Opler, P. A. and G. O. Krizek. 1984. *Butterflies East of the Great Plains.* Johns Hopkins University Press, Baltimore, Maryland.

Opler, P.A. 1992. *A Field Guide to the Butterflies.* Houghton Mifflin, Boston, Massachusetts.

Opler, P.A., R. S. Peigler, M. Pogue, J. A. Powell, and M. J. Smith. 1999. Moths of North America. Jamestown, North Dakota: Northern Prairie Wildlife Research Center HomePage. http://www.npwrc.usgs.gov/resource/distr/lepid/moths/mothsusa.htm (Version 12DEC2003).

Pavulaan, H. and D. M. Wright. 2000. The biology, life history, and taxonomy of *Celastrina neglectamajor* (Lycaenidae: Polyommatinae). *The Taxonomic Report*, **2**: 1–19.

Poole, R. W. (ed.). 1996. *Nomina Insecta Nearctica. Volume 3. Diptera, Lepidoptera, Siphonaptera.* Entomological Information Services, Rockville, Maryland.

Porter, J. 1997. *The Colour Identification Guide to Caterpillars of the British Isles.* Viking Press, London.

Poulton, E. B. 1892. Further experiments upon the colour relation between certain lepidopterous larvae, pupae, cocoons, and imagines, and their surroundings. *Transactions of the Entomological Society of London, 1892*: 293–487.

Prentice, R. M. (compiler). 1962. *Forest Lepidoptera of Canada Recorded by the Forest Insect Survey. Vol. 2, Nycteolidae, Notodontidae, Noctuidae, Liparidae*. Publication 128. Canada Department of Forestry, Ottawa, Ontario.

Prentice, R. M. (compiler). 1963. *Forest Lepidoptera of Canada Recorded by the Forest Insect Survey. Vol. 3, Lasiocampidae, Drepanidae, Thyatiridae, Geometridae*. Publication 1013. Canada Department of Forestry, Ottawa, Ontario.

Pyle, R. M. 1981. *The Audubon Society Field Guide to North American Butterflies*. Chanticleer Press, New York.

Riley, A. M. and G. Prior. 2003. *British and Irish Pug Moths (Lepidoptera: Geometridae, Larentiinae, Eupitheciini). A Guide to Their Identification and Biology*. Harley Books, Essex.

Rings, R. W., E. H. Metzler, F. J. Arnold, and D. H. Harris. 1992. *The Owlet Moths of Ohio (Order Lepidoptera: Family Noctuidae)*. Ohio Biological Survey Bulletin. New Series, Vol. 9. College of Biological Sciences, Ohio State University, Columbus, Ohio.

Robinson, G. S., P. R. Ackery, I. J. Kitching, G. W. Beccaloni, and L. M. Hernández. 2002. *Hostplants of the Moth and Butterfly Caterpillars of America North of Mexico*. Memoirs of the American Entomological Institute, 69: 1–824.

Rockburne, E. W. and J. D. Lafontaine. 1976. *The Cutworm Moths of Ontario and Quebec*. Canada Department of Agricultural Research Branch Publication 1593.

Sargent, T. D. 1976. *Legion of Night: The Underwing Moths*. University of Massachusetts, Amherst, Massachusetts.

Schaefer, P. W., R. W. Fuester, R. J. Chianese, L. D. Rhoads, and R. B. Tichenor, Jr. 1989. Introduction and North American establishment of *Coccygomimus disparis* (Hymenoptera: Ichneumonidae), a polyphagous pupal parasite of Lepidoptera, including gypsy moth. *Environmental Entomology*, **18**: 1117–1125.

Schweitzer, D. F. 1979. A revision of the genus *Metaxaglaea* (Lepidoptera: Noctuidae, Cuculliinae) with descriptions of two new species. Postilla. No. 178. Peabody Museum of Natural History, New Haven, Connecticut.

Scott, J. A. 1986. *The Butterflies of North America*. Stanford University Press, Stanford, California.

Scudder, S. H. 1889. *The Butterflies of the Eastern United States and Canada, with Special Reference to New England*. Cambridge, Massachusetts.

Shaw, J. 1984. *The Nature Photographer's Complete Guide to Professional Field Techniques*. Amphoto, New York.

Shaw, J. 1987. *Closeups in Nature*. Amphoto, New York.

Shields, O. 1984. A review of migration in Libytheidae. *Tokurana*, **12**: 1–14.

Stehr, F. W. (ed.). 1987. *Immature Insects. Volume 1*. Kendall/Hunt Publ. Co., Dubuque, Iowa.

Sugi, S. (ed.). 1987. *Larvae of the Larger Moths of Japan*. Toppan Printing Co. Ltd., Tokyo, Japan.

Tietz, H. M. 1972. *An Index to the Described Life Histories, Early Stages and Hosts of the Macrolepidoptera of the Continental United States and Canada* (2 volumes). Allyn Museum of Entomology, Sarasota, Florida.

Toliver, M. E. 1987. Pieridae (Papilionoidea). pp. 441–443. *In* Stehr, F. *Immature Insects.* Kendall/Hunt Publ. Co., Dubuque, Iowa.

Tuskes, P. M., J. P. Tuttle, and M. M. Collins. 1996. *The Wild Silk Moths of the United States and Canada.* Cornell University Press, Ithaca, New York.

Tuttle, J. 2006. *The Hawk Moths of North America* (in preparation).

Tveten, J. and G. Tveten. 1996. *Butterflies of Houston and Southeast Texas.* University of Texas Press, Austin, Texas.

Wagner, D. L., V. Giles, R. C. Reardon, and M. L. McManus. 1998. *Caterpillars of Eastern Forests.* USFS Technology Transfer Bulletin, FHTET-96-34.

Wagner, D. L., D. C. Ferguson, T. L. McCabe, and R. C. Reardon. 2001 [2002]. *Geometroid Caterpillars of Northeastern and Appalachian Forests.* USFS Technology Transfer Bulletin, FHTET-2001-10.

Weiss, M. R. 2003. Good housekeeping: why do shelter-dwelling caterpillars fling their frass? *Ecology Letters,* **6**: 361–370.

West, L. and J. Ridl. 1994. *How to Photograph Insects and Spiders.* Stackpole Books, Mechanicsburg, Pennsylvania.

Winter, W. D. 2000. *Basic Techniques for Observing and Studying Moths and Butterflies.* Memoirs of the Lepidopterists' Society, No. 5. Natural History Museum, Los Angeles, California.

Wright, A. B. 1993. *Caterpillars: A Simplified Field Guide to the Caterpillars of Common Butterflies and Moths of North America.* Peterson First Guides. Houghton Mufflin, Boston.

Wright, D. M. and H. Pavulaan. 1999. *Celastrina idella* (Lycaenidae: Polyommatinae): A new butterfly from the Atlantic Coastal Plain. *The Taxonomic Report,* **1**: 1–11.

FOODPLANT INDEX

501

TAXONOMIC AND SUBJECT INDEX